MU00779469

Kraków,
the Jewish Community and Women

Five Centuries of Change

by **Geoffrey M. Weisgard**

מרכז עולמי לגנאלוגיה יהודית
The Global Home for Jewish Genealogy

A Publication of JewishGen
Edmond J. Safra Plaza, 36 Battery Place, New York, NY 10280
646.494.2972 | info@JewishGen.org | www.jewishgen.org

JewishGen is the Genealogical Research Division of the
Museum of Jewish Heritage – A Living Memorial to the Holocaust

MUSEUM OF
JEWISH HERITAGE
A LIVING MEMORIAL
TO THE HOLOCAUST

**Kraków, the Jewish Community and Women
Five Centuries of Change**

Copyright © 2024 by Geoffrey M. Weisgard. All rights reserved.
Published by JewishGen
First Printing: September 2024, Elul I 5784

Author: Geoffrey M. Weisgard

Cover Design: Rachel Kolokoff Hopper

This book may not be reproduced, in whole or in part, including illustrations in any form (beyond that copying permitted by Sections 107 and 108 of the U.S. Copyright Law and except by reviewers for public press), without written permission from the copyright holder.

JewishGen is not responsible for inaccuracies or omissions in the original work and makes no representations regarding its accuracy.

Library of Congress Control Number (LCCN): 2024945286

ISBN: 978-1-962054-07-2 (Paperback: 246 pages, alk. paper)

About JewishGen.org

JewishGen, is a Genealogical Research Division of the Museum of Jewish Heritage - A Living Memorial to the Holocaust, serves as the global home for Jewish genealogy.

Featuring unparalleled access to 30+ million records, it offers unique search tools, along with opportunities for researchers to connect with others who share similar interests. Award winning resources such as the Family Finder, Discussion Groups, and ViewMate, are relied upon by thousands each day.

In addition, JewishGen's extensive informational, educational and historical offerings, such as the Jewish Communities Database, Yizkor Book translations, InfoFiles, Family Tree of the Jewish People, and KehilaLinks, provide critical insights, first-hand accounts, and context about Jewish communal and familial life throughout the world.

Offered as a free resource, JewishGen.org has facilitated thousands of family connections and success stories, and is currently engaged in an intensive expansion effort that will bring many more records, tools, and resources to its collections.

Please visit https://www.jewishgen.org/ to learn more.

Vice President for JewishGen: Avraham Groll

About JewishGen Press

JewishGen Press (formerly the Yizkor Books-in-Print Project) is the publishing division of JewishGen.org, and provides a venue for the publication of non-fiction books pertaining to Jewish genealogy, history, culture, and heritage.

In addition to the Yizkor Book category, publications in the Other Non-Fiction category include Shoah memoirs and research, genealogical research, collections of genealogical and historical materials, biographies, diaries and letters, studies of Jewish experience and cultural life in the past, academic theses, and other books of interest to the Jewish community.

Please visit https://www.jewishgen.org/Yizkor/ybip.html to learn more.

Director of JewishGen Press: Joel Alpert
Managing Editor - Jessica Feinstein
Publications Manager - Susan Rosin

Cover Design

Cover designed by Rachel Kolokoff Hopper

Front Cover Photo: *Members of the Weiskerz Family,* page 3
Photo courtesy of Geoffrey M. Weisgard

Cover Background Color and Texture: Rachel Kolokoff Hopper

Front and Back Cover Background Photo: *Dried Grass*, Rachel
Kolokoff Hopper

Map of Poland, showing the location of **Kraków**

Geo Political Information

Kraków, Poland is located at 50°05' N 19°55' E and 157 miles SSW of Warszawa

	Town	District	Province	Country
Before WWI (c. 1900):	Kraków	Kraków	Galicia	Austrian Empire
Between the wars (c. 1930):	Kraków	Kraków	Kraków	Poland
After WWII (c. 1950):	Kraków			Poland
Today (c. 2000):	Kraków			Poland

Alternate Names for the town:

Kraków [Pol], Krakau [Ger], Kroke [Yid], Cracow [Eng], Krakov [Rus, Cz, Slov], Krakiv [Ukr]

Kraków, the Jewish Community and Women
Five Centuries of Change

Geoffrey M. Weisgard

Dedication

This book is dedicated to my female ancestors who lived in Kraków, including Dwora, born 1750, wife of Szmul, Świcarz (Samuel, the candle maker), their daughter in law, Dwora, born 1778, wife of Izaak Weiskerz, their daughter in law, Rachel, born 1812, wife of Józef Weiskerz and their daughter in law, Hannah, born 1852, wife of my great grandfather, Beniamin Weiskerz/Benjamin Weisgard

By the same author

Kraków: Sources of Information for Jewish Genealogy and History
Published by JewishGen Inc, 2022

*Members of the Weiskerz family
photographed at the studio of Simon Balicer
Ulica Grodzka No 80, Krakow*

https://kehilalinks.jewishgen.org/Krakow/kra_balicer.htm
and
www.kehilalinks.jewishgen.org/Krakow/images/default.asp

Contents

	Page
Introduction	5
The Early Modern Period – Her price is far above rubies?	15
The 'Austrian' Period – The first small steps to emancipation	45
The Interwar Period – Uneven roads to gender equality	74
The Holocaust - A world turned upside down	115
The Communist Period – Return and exile – the final chapter?	182
The Post Communist Period – Resurrecting the Jew	202
Appendix – Female researchers of the post Communist period	217
Name Index	221

Introduction

The purpose of this book is to take the reader on a journey through time – through a period of some five centuries. Reflecting the history of Poland, this period includes times of turbulence and war as well as quieter times of social evolution. The journey starts in 1485 when 'poor Jewesses have the right to sell, on all days, head dresses and neck jewels made by their own hands and craft' right up to the present day when a woman leads the official orthodox community, the Gmina Wyznaniowa Żydowska.

Hopefully the following pages will give the reader an insight as to how our female ancestors lived their lives in Kraków, and describe the developing roles of women and their impact on Kraków's Jewish community. At the same time the text will illustrate the considerable diversity within that community.

Before the journey starts, this introductory chapter will describe different attitudes to the role of women in Jewish society and how researchers have written about the subject since the latter part of the 19th century. The introduction then concludes with a brief description of the subject matter of each following chapter.

The traditional view of the role of women in Jewish society

Visitors to cities such as Vienna, Prague and Budapest may well come across fine hotels which form part of the 'K and K' Group. Most, though will be unaware that 'K and K' refers to the twin monarchies which were created by the Austro Hungarian Compromise, the Ausgleich, of 1867. These monarchies were the Kaiserreich of Austria and the Königreich of Hungary.

Rather more disturbing was the 'K and K' promoted by the Nazi leadership in 1934 when it adapted the late nineteenth century phrase, 'Kinder, Küche und Kirche' (Children, Kitchen and Church). It was argued that the world of the German woman was her husband, her family, her children and her home. That is to say 'Kinder and Küche'.[1] Roughly translated, 'The woman's place is in the home.'

The historically low status of women in Jewish communities is summed up by Pawel Sládek in his article 'Sixteenth Century Jewish Makers of Printed Books and the Shaping of Late Renaissance Jewish Literacy'.[2] The author notes 'The voice of early modern Jewish society was still predominantly masculine, and men looked down on women. Yet the respective evaluation of both sexes started to change, even though slowly and imperfectly. While some scholars such as Maharal denied women full humanity, others accorded them only inferior intellect. Speaking of the halachic work 'Kol bo', David Conforte (c1618-c1685) rejected the opinion that a scholarly book could have been authored by a woman.

Quoting the historian Edward Fram, Professor Sládek notes 'The one example of a public anti-misogynist stand ... is a lament by the Kraków printer Yitshak Prostitz in the preface to his 1589 edition of a Yiddish translation of the Scroll of

---

[1] https://en.wikipedia.org/wiki/Kinder,_Kuche,_Kirche
[2] In Simon Bronner and Caspar Battegay (Eds), 'Connected Jews; Expressions of Community in Analogue and Digital Culture'; Littman, London, 2018.

Esther: it is the way of the world that women especially are considered nothing at all and are regarded as good for nothing…'

The view that women play only a subsidiary role to men is reflected in the writings of early historians who wrote about the Jewish community of Poland in general, and Kraków in particular. Such historians include Feivel Hirsch Wetstein (1858-1924) and Bernhard (Chaim Dov) Friedberg (1876-1961). The research of these authors is considered by Professor Majer Bałaban (1877-1942) who wrote wide ranging historical accounts of the history of the Jewish communities of Kraków, and more generally, the province of Galicia. However, the names index in Professor Bałaban's work 'Dzieze Żydów w Krakowie i na Kazimierzu (1304-1868)'[3] (A History of the Jews of Kraków and Kazimierz) shows that the vast majority of people mentioned in the book are men. Where women are listed in the index, their names are often followed by the word 'córka' or 'zona', indicating that they are being mentioned only or mainly as the daughter of their father, or as a wife. It has to be admitted that the dedication at the beginning of this book suffers from the same defect.

As Sara Ajzenstein (b. 1912) notes at the beginning of her work 'Kobieta Żydowska w Polsce w XVI i XVII wieku' (Jewish Women in Poland during the 16th and 17th Centuries), women had been habitually 'omitted from history. A woman must be at least a queen or a national hero in order to draw attention to herself'.[4]

Gershon Bacon gives a further example in his article on Poland in the interwar period which can be found on the website of the Jewish Women's Archive.[5] He notes that Raphael Mahler's classic work 'The Jews of Poland between the Two World Wars' which was published in 1968 'makes not a single reference to women'.

Three 21st century publications may be taken to illustrate the emphasis, or possibly the perceived dominance, of males in the Kraków Jewish community. The first is a book about prominent Jews in Kraków from the 14th to the 20th century.[6] The second is about the cemetery at Miodowa Street in Kraków,[7] and the third is a book of biographies of graduates of the Jagiellonian University.[8] The first book describes about 60 leaders of the community, only three of whom are women. The second book includes biographies of some 50 people who are buried at the cemetery but only four relate to women, and the third work gives 29 biographies, but again only four relate to women.

---

[3] Published in Kraków in 1912. This work was revised in 1935 and 1936 when it was republished in two volumes as 'Historja Żydow w Krakowie i na Kazimierzu, 1304-1868'. The work has since been translated into modern Hebrew as 'Toldot ha'Yehudim b'Krakov u've Kazimierz, 1304-1868'.
[4] Quoted by Natalia Aleksiun in, 'Female, Jewish, Educated and Writing Polish Jewish History' in 'Polin' vol 29, 2017, page 210
[5] https://jwa.org/encyclopedia/article/poland-interwar
[6] Agnieszka Kutylak (Ed), 'Krakowianie wybitni Żydzi Krakowscy XIV-XX w'; Muzeum Historyczne Miasta Krakowa, Kraków, 2006
[7] Eugeniusz Duda and others (Eds), 'Powiększenie; Nowy cmentarz Żydowskie w Krakowie, Kraków, 2006
[8] Wiesław Kozub-Ciembroniewicz (Ed), 'Academics of Jewish Heritage in the Modern History of the Jagiellonian University'; Jagiellonian University Press, Kraków, 2014

A more modern view

The main purpose of the chapters which follow in this book is to illustrate that, contrary to the 'traditional' view, women have had, and continue to have, a significant impact on the Jewish community in Kraków. This impact has extended well beyond the sphere of the home, and the primary education of children, important though those spheres were, and continue to be. For centuries, Jewish women have been largely responsible for the maintenance of religious life and practices. The fact that those responsibilities have been different from those of their husbands makes them no less important. Furthermore, women have long been involved in economic activity. In earlier times this was largely in the nature of local trade. Often this activity was in support of their husbands, but sometimes women carried on trade, and even owned property, independently. From the end of the 19th century, the range of women's economic activity was opened up by their being able to access university education, and enter into a number of professional occupations. During the First World War, the male population of Kraków was depleted, as in very many other locations. This change gave not only new opportunities for women to extend their influence in society, but also a need for them to do so. Likewise, the horrors of the Holocaust resulted in an increased range of roles for women, and in some cases an exchange of roles with men. In the Communist and post Communist periods, women, many of them not Jewish, have continued to take active and developing, leadership roles in Kraków's Jewish society. It is these themes that will be explored in the following pages.

Opposition to the 'traditional' view of the role of women was expressed in Poland over a century ago. A particularly early reference is made in a biography of Ludwik Gumplowicz who, in 1863, married Franciszka Goldman. She is described as being 'in a sense his intellectual and spiritual partner; she was very well read and even quite possibly published books anonymously, ones containing early feminist ideas.'[9]

A book 'Głos kobiet w kwestyi kobiecej' (Female Voice in Female Issues) was published in Kraków in 1903 and this was followed four years later by 'Kobieta i Socyalism'.[10] Reference should also be made to the work of Puah Rakovsky (1865-1955). She spent much of her life in Warsaw where she opened a Hebrew language school for girls. Her memoir has been published as 'My Life as a Radical Jewish Woman; Memoirs of a Zionist Feminist in Poland'.[11] As Rachel Manekin notes, 'In the late nineteenth century, Kraków became a center of feminist activities'.[12]

---

[9] Wiesław Kozub-Ciembroniewicz (Ed), 'Academics of Jewish Heritage in the Modern History of the Jagiellonian University', page 127

[10] August Bebel, 'Kobieta i Socyalizm'; Nakładem Towarzysta Wydawnictwo Ludowych, Kraków, 1907. For other references to early Polish feminist works, see Archiwum Historii Kobiet (The Women's Historical Archive) website at www.herstorie.pl , and a 2011 discussion in Polish, 'Does Kraków Need a Women's Museum' at https://en.mocak.pl/does-krakow-need-a-women-s-museum/

[11] Indiana University Press, 2002, previously published in Yiddish

[12] Rachel Manekin, 'The Rebellion of the Daughters; Jewish Women Runaways in Habsburg Galicia'; Princeton University Press, Princeton, NJ, 2020, page 30. See also page 141

Arguably, some nineteenth and early twentieth century novels may indicate the role of women in the Jewish community. An example would be 'Żydówka' (The Jewess), a novel based in Kraków, which was written in about 1870 by the liberal author, Michał Bałucki. The author's mother was Jewish and the novel may contain autobiographical elements.[13]

Challenges to the traditional view of the role of Jewish women have been building over the last half century. The issue was identified by the modern feminist movement which became established in America during the 1970's. It is reflected in a book by Emily Taitz and Sondra Henry called 'Written out of History; Our Jewish Foremothers'.[14]

Bernard Weinryb's book, 'The Jews of Poland' was first published in 1972. The second edition runs to over four hundred pages but the word 'women' does not appear in the index, and the subject of women's status is limited to little more than one page. However, the author does note that 'in practice, women shared the burden of making a living and in some cases were the main bearers of this burden. Individual women were lauded for outstanding learning, charitableness or piety. They were also officially regarded as partners in property ownership'.[15]

By 1990, the traditional view of the role of Jewish women was being challenged in the United Kingdom as well as in the United States. For example, at the beginning of her paper 'Jewish Women and the Household Economy in Manchester, c1890-1920', Rickie Burman refers plainly to 'a persuasive andro-centric view which sees women as peripheral to the main thrust of history; women are defined in relation to men and are not perceived as active agents.'[16]

The Jewish Women's Archive was founded in 1995. The website at www.jwa.org states that the mission of the Archive is to document Jewish women's stories, elevate their voices, and inspire them to be agents of change. The site includes links to many articles and papers, including one by Professor Moshe Rosman of Bar Ilan University entitled, 'Poland Early Modern (1500-1795)'. This is available at https://jwa.org/encyclopedia/article/poland-early-modern-1500-1795. The author

---

[13] Maria Klańska (Ed), 'Jüdisches Städtebilt Krakau'; Jüdischer Verlag, Frankfurt am Main, 1994, pages 90-98

[14] Emily Tait and Sondra Henry, 'Written out of History; Our Jewish Foremothers'; Bloch Publishing, New York, NY, 1978. See also, for example, Susannah Heschel (Ed), 'On Being a Jewish Feminist'; Schoken Books, New York, NY, 1983

[15] Bernard A Weinryb, 'The Jews of Poland; A Social and Economic History of the Jewish Community in Poland from 1100-1800'; The Jewish Publication Society of America, Philadelphia, PA, second edition, 1976, pages 98 and 99

[16] In David Cesarani (Ed), 'The Making of Modern Anglo-Jewry'; Basil Blackwell, Oxford, 1990. See also Rickie Burman, 'The Jewish Woman as Breadwinner; The Changing Value of Women's Work in the Manchester Immigrant Community' (1982) at www.jstor.org/stable/40178716 For further reading see Rainer Leidtke, 'Jewish Welfare in Hamburg and Manchester c1850-1914'; Clarendon Press, Oxford, 1998, Chapter 7, 'Female Spheres and Recognition; The Welfare Involvement of Jewish Women'. For the legal status of women in England see Katherine O'Donovan, 'The Male Appendage – Legal Definitions of Women' in Sandra Burman (Ed), 'Fit Work for Women'; Croom Helm, London, 1979. Additionally see Frances Guy, 'Women of Worth; Jewish Women in Britain'; Manchester Jewish Museum, 1992.

starts by referring to the argument that little has been said about the role of women because there is a lack of source material. He then points out that this reasoning is not sound. On the contrary, there are at least three groups of sources. These are Yiddish books, archival sources, and literature. The author then challenges the traditional view that the role of women was wholly subsidiary to, and separate from, the role of men.

A further article by Moshe Rosman appears in volume 18 of 'Polin'. In this paper, entitled 'The History of Jewish Women in Early Modern Poland; An Assessment', the author includes a description of different methodologies adopted by researchers of the roles of Jewish women.[17] Reference can also be made here to Professor Rosman's book 'Categorically Jewish, Distinctly Polish', published by Littman Press in 2022, which includes two chapters on the history of Jewish women in the Polish-Lithuanian Commonwealth. As the professor noted at a launch of his book, the cultural role of Jewish women transformed over the centuries from observer to participant. This transformation is illustrated by a table in the book which is headed 'Male and Female Cultural Spheres in Jewish Eastern Europe'. Some of the content of that table is included in my own table which is shown at the end of this introduction.

Professor Rosman also writes, 'within overall Jewish culture controlled primarily by men, women were assigned two basic roles by the male hegemony: to be *observers* and *facilitators* of male economic, social and – especially – religious and cultural performance. … Over time the observer role was gradually transformed to allow for more female performance, but the underlying motivation for this was to enhance women's facilitator role.[18]

Whilst Professor Rosman is correct to point out the range of historical sources relating to Jewish women in the early modern period, it has to be recognised that the women who are described in these sources are exceptional. They are not the stereotypical or traditional quiet obedient wives who comply with the traditional view which has been described. As the American historian, Professor Laurel Thatcher Ulrich has stated, 'Well behaved women seldom make history'.

Gershon Bacon is another eminent researcher who has contributed an article to the Jewish Women's Archive. His paper 'Poland; Interwar' is at https://jwa.org/encyclopedia/article/Poland-interwar. The author notes that during the period between the two world wars, in terms of economic activity and education,

---

[17] Chaeran Freeze and others (Eds), 'Polin' vol 18, 'Jewish Women in Eastern Europe'; Littman, Oxford, 2005. See also Agatha Schwartz, 'Shifting Voices; Feminist Thought and Women's Writing in Fin de Siècle Austria and Hungary'; McGill-Queens University Press, Montreal, 2008

[18] Moshe Rosman, 'Categorically Jewish Distinctly Polish'; Littman, London, 2022, page 275, summarising chapter 13 of the book. Professor Rosman's central argument as stated in the preface to the book is 'The Jews' 'Marriage of Convenience' with the early modern Polish-Lithuanian Commonwealth was a dynamic relationship that developed into a saga of overall achievement and relative stability, punctuated by crisis and persecution.'

the role of Jewish women changed in different ways from community to community. He does, however, highlight a growing political and Zionist involvement.[19]

The traditional overlooking, or neglect, of women's achievements continues to be the subject of writings in the twenty first century. For example, it is reflected in the title of a chapter in the book 'Women in the Holocaust' which was published in 2012. The title is 'The Missing 52 per cent; Research on Jewish Women in Interwar Poland and its Implications for Holocaust Studies.'[20] Indeed, this century has seen an increased recognition of women's achievements generally and, for example, their role in Kraków has been identified in the 'Krakowski Szlak Kobiet' (Kraków Women's Trail) project. This includes a series of routes through the city, as well as a number of guide books entitled 'Krakowski Szlak Kobiet; Przewodniczka po Krakowie Emancypantek'.

Summary of this book

This book is organised in two ways. Firstly, the chapters are set out in chronological order. Secondly, each chapter is divided into sections, each dealing with a separate topic. It is therefore possible to read the book working from the start through to the end. Alternatively, some readers may wish to move from chapter to chapter, concentrating on just one or two subjects, such as trade and commerce, or religious observance. The chapters include numerous reference notes and links to web pages which will enable readers to carry out further research if they so wish.

The book results from a review of some academic source documents, and a wide range of publications which were written in the form of academic works, memoirs, and testimonies. It supports the commonly held view that, in the period up to the end of the twentieth century, little was written about the role of women in the Jewish community of Kraków in the early centuries of the community's development. The following additional broad conclusions can be reached.

In connection with periods prior to the First World War, the majority of authors, even in recent years, have given little attention to the activities and achievements of women compared with those of men. Arguably, this is because authors have not used, or even recognised, the range of sources which are available.

The 1595 Kraków Statute had a significant impact on society in Kraków for about two centuries, and it therefore features significantly in the chapter which relates to the early modern period. In relation to Poland, that is the period from around 1500 up to 1795, the date of the third and final partition of the country. Generally, the Statute restricted the roles of women rather than supporting them. Historically, the property rights of women were limited, for example to those assets which were acquired prior to marriage or upon a husband's death. Women trading on their own account, as opposed to jointly with their husbands or on their behalf, were the exception rather than the rule, and their trade was mainly on a local and

---

[19] See also Ityna Levchuk, 'Women in Ethnosocial Structure in the Second Polish Republic'; Intellectual Archive, vol 6, no 5, September/October, 2017

[20] In Dahlia Ofer (Ed), 'Women in the Holocaust'; Yale University Press, New Haven, CT, 2012. See also Joanna Michlic, 'Gender Perspectives on the Rescue of Jews in Poland; Preliminary Observations' in Eliyana Adler and Antony Polansky (Eds), Polin, no 30, 2018, and available on line

small scale. Little evidence of women in trade can be obtained from sources such as census returns, even in the first half of the nineteenth century. Women were active in religious life and observance, though in the early modern period, their religious roles were mainly separate from those of their male relatives.

The chapter on the 'Austrian' period describes the changes in women's roles which took place in the period between the third partition of Poland and the end of the First World War. This includes the period from 1815 to 1846 when, in theory at least, Kraków was a 'Free City' or 'Republic'. It is not until the 'Austrian' period, and more specifically the second half of the nineteenth century, that we see an expansion of the roles undertaken by women in both religious and secular life. These changes were driven largely by the Polonisation of a numerically small proportion of the Jewish population in Kraków who were generally members of the Progressive or Reform movement.

Women's involvement in the community did increase further around the time of the First World War, initially in the range of their occupations. However, in areas such as politics and sport their involvement developed very slowly, and largely not until the period between the two World Wars. That period saw the growth of a small number of women's cultural and social groups, including the WIZO Zionist group, and an increasing number of women who were active in journalism and more general literature, the arts, education, the professions, and trade as well as politics, sport and Zionism which have already been mentioned. Reflecting these changes, the chapter on the interwar period is the first which includes the names of a large number of individual females. Since some women were active over several decades, they are mentioned in more than one chapter. In this respect the chapters can be contrasted with earlier chapters which refer more generally to the roles of women but do not mention many by name.

As already indicated, historiography has not treated different periods of history equally. More seems to have been written about the Holocaust than about any other period – before or since. It is therefore, perhaps, inevitable that the chapter relating to the six years of the Holocaust is more than twice as long as that relating to the early modern period of more than two hundred years. Despite this, due to my extremely limited knowledge of the Polish language, the chapter does not adequately reflect some important works which are available only in that language – for example Martyna Grądzka-Rejak's book, 'Kobieta żydowska w okupowanym Krakowie (1939-1945)' (The Jewish Woman in Occupied Kraków (1939-1945)), which was published by Wysoki Zamek, Kraków in 2016. On the other hand, one aspect which is apparent from the sources mentioned in the chapter is how women took over roles previously undertaken by men, and how young women and girls often became the breadwinners, in a literal sense, as a result of their general survival skills. The chapter also highlights the bravery of women in the protection of fugitives from the Nazi regime. Many of these women were not Jewish and it is largely for this reason that the book is titled as it is rather than, for example, 'Women in the Jewish Community of Kraków'. The chapter on the Holocaust also includes short biographical notes on some ninety survivors, in order to demonstrate that not everybody was obliterated by the Nazi occupation.

During the 1980's, visitors to Kraków and local researchers wrote of the Jewish community as being in terminal decline – ageing, poor and with a reducing pool of religious knowledge and resources. Whilst many Jews had come to Kraków after the end of the war, few remained for very long. Antisemitism in its various forms resulted in waves of emigration. Yet during the Communist period, the Jewish community was able to maintain a number of communal institutions, and in the chapter relating to this period, particular reference is made to Róża Jakubowicz, 'the mother of the community'. Furthermore, the chapter describes how a number of Jewish women managed to adapt to Communism and were able to make their way in academia, literature or the arts.

The final chapter relates to the rebirth or 'resurrection' of Jewish life in Kraków since the fall of Communism, and the large number of individuals who have chosen to identify with Judaism in one way or another. Reference is made to a number of cultural, largely secular, institutions and to the fact that they are largely supported and maintained by non Jewish women. Reference is also made to a range of religious facilities which are wide and varied and which also rely to a significant extent on women.

Additionally, tribute is paid to the large number of academic researchers, in the main not Jewish, who during the post Communist period have written about the Jewish community of Kraków. In the spirit of this work, many of the female researchers, and their specialist subjects, are listed in the appendix to this book, which could not have been written without the works of those researchers, and their ability to translate source material into English from Polish, Yiddish, Hebrew and other languages. In common with trends in other areas of endeavour, the proportion of authors who are female is much greater now than in previous generations.

The chapters which follow do not, in general, provide new information. However, hopefully by summarising the information that is already available, they are of some use in understanding the role and impact of women on the Jewish community of Kraków over a period of some five centuries.

Acknowledgements

Many readers may not be aware that there is a lot more to producing a book that just writing it. I should therefore like to thank all at JewishGen who have worked towards the publication of this, my second book on the Jewish community of Kraków. In particular I wish to thank Joel Alpert and Susan Rosin of JewishGen Press, and Jessica Feinstein who tirelessly works in many roles, including that of Managing Editor of the Editorial Board of JewishGen Press.

I should also like to thank my many friends for their support and, most importantly, my long-suffering wife of some 53 years, Linda, for her patience. She clearly didn't know what she was letting herself in for when we married all those years ago.

Geoffrey M. Weisgard
Manchester, United Kingdom, 2024

Female Cultural Spheres in Kraków over Five Centuries

	The Early Modern Period	The Austrian Period	The Interwar Period
Economy	Women regarded as agents of their husbands. Mainly small-scale trade	Some increase in trading opportunities but no professional roles	Increased trading and participation in the professions
Education	Informal schooling in Yiddish with the objectives to be a faithful wife and observe 'women's rituals'	Slow expansion of secular education in private and state schools, particularly amongst the Reform (Progressive) community	Continuing secularisation and a growth of education in state and private non-Jewish academic and vocational schools and at the University but also at Bais Ya'akov
Leisure activities and the arts	No opportunities for leisure	Leisure opportunities for the wealthy, including travel to spa towns. Some theatre	Increased travel and participation in art, music, sport and the theatre
Literature	Restricted, mainly in Yiddish, written by men for a female readership. Religious rather than secular	Expansion of the range of material to include some Polish literature. Introduction of reading rooms	Growth of female participation in literature and journalism
Political and communal work	Giving charity was a religious obligation. No political role for women	Growing network of charities including support for widows and orphans	Increased range of organisations including support for the arts and Zionism. Limited political role
Property	Very limited rights. Assets generally regarded as belonging to a woman's husband	Little growth in property ownership among women	Increase in property ownership
Religion	Limited attendance at synagogue but more private and folkloric practices	Gradual increase in attendance at synagogue and in female participation in the Progressive community	Increased variations ranging from pious Chassidic to modern progressive

	The Holocaust	The Communist Period	The Post Communist period
Economy	Women became breadwinners, smugglers and black-market traders	Activity largely controlled by the state but some black-market trading	Women have the same economic rights and roles as men
Education	Largely prohibited by the Nazis but some religious and secular education in secret	Jewish school operated following the liberation, but many Jewish girls attended non-Jewish schools and some attended the University	Resurgence of Jewish education in the small but growing community
Leisure activities and the arts	Very limited opportunities but attempts to maintain social and romantic relationships	Some social groups established for an aging and diminishing population. Some artists settled briefly in Kraków	Groups cater for a wide range of social and artistic interests
Literature	Some underground press, and diaries	Considerable amount of Holocaust testimony published	Very large amount of material written by survivors and academics
Political and communal work	Communal work largely for orphans and the Resistance	State-sponsored and other groups supported orphans and the elderly. Róża Jakubowicz was particularly active	Wide range of groups supported mainly by Catholic women
Property	No property rights	Limited property ownership due to poverty and Communist policy	Opportunities for private ownership of property
Religion	Some observance in the Ghetto and at Płaszów	Religious observance limited by Communist policy. A decline in religious knowledge	Wide range of communities including the female-led Progressive community

THE EARLY MODERN PERIOD
Her price is far above rubies?

Introduction

'The Early Modern Period' can be defined in relation to Poland broadly as the period from around 1500 up to 1795, the date of the third and final partition of the country. It is a period which included the glorious 'Golden Age' of Kraków Jewry – an age of immense commercial and spiritual growth during which the Jewish district of Kazimierz became a major centre of learning. The fifteenth and sixteenth centuries saw the building of several fine synagogues and the works of towering Rabbinical leaders, including Rabbi Moshe Isserles, who was known as the REMU.

The glory of the age was enjoyed almost entirely by men – and not all of them. For example, women did not take part in the leadership of the community. Names of householders which are available from the eighteenth century are nearly all those of men. The National Archive in Kraków, the Jewish Historical Institute in Warsaw, and the Central Archives for the History of Jewish People in Jerusalem all hold large quantities of communal and State records, but they relate almost exclusively to men. Scholars such as Majer Bałaban and, before him, Feivel Hirsch Wetstein and Bernhard Friedberg, have recorded the results of their research – which again relates almost entirely to men.

What then constituted the 'ideal' woman at the beginning of the early modern period? Since social values were based on religious principles it may be appropriate to look at a Biblical source, Proverbs, chapter XXXI.

'Who can find a virtuous woman? For her price is far above rubies. The heart of her husband doth safely trust in her, so that he shall have no need of spoil. She will do him good and not evil all the days of her life. She seeketh wool and flax and worketh willingly with her hands. She is like the merchants' ships. She bringeth her food from afar. She riseth also while it is yet night and giveth meat to her household....'

On this basis, a woman is not to aim to have a life which is in any way independent of her husband. On the contrary, her role is to support him, and to see to his needs and those of the household.

Nevertheless, the eminent historian Moshe Rosman does identify some areas in which the roles of women changed and expanded. In his article 'Poland: Early Modern (1500-1795)' on the website of the Jewish Women's Archive[21], he writes by way of introduction 'Jewish women in Poland were integral to the cultural framework of society but were often segregated from men in religious practices … Strict gender roles dictated women should be modest, clever, pious, of scholarly pedigree, and submissive to their husbands. At times these boundaries were crossed, as the world grew slightly more progressive, women were allowed to read more

---

[21] https://jwa.org/encyclopedia/article/poland-early-modern-1500-1795

scripture and study with their husbands. In addition, women were sometimes expected to work outside the home to subsidize the husband's income'.

Professor Rosman explores gender more fully in part IV of his book, 'Categorically Jewish, Distinctly Polish'. He includes a table, 'male and female cultural spheres in Jewish Eastern Europe' which incorporates some conclusions which have been reached by three eminent researchers, Shaul Stampfer, Chava Weissler and Iris Parush.[22]

It is these themes which, in relation to Kraków, will be explored in the following pages.

Kraków Statute of 1595

Although the sections in this book are generally set out in alphabetic order of subject matter, it is firstly appropriate to consider the legal and social framework in which Jewish women lived out their lives in early modern Kraków. This framework was provided by the Statute of 1595.

It is well documented that local Jewish communities in Poland were largely self governing until the rule of King Poniatowski in the eighteenth century.[23] The Kraków community was governed by its Statute of 1595, and a number of supplements or amendments to that statute.[24] Extracts from the Statute are available in English largely thanks to the work of Shmuel Cygielman, author of 'Jewish Autonomy in Poland and Lithuania until 1648 (5408)' which was published in Jerusalem in 1997.

The Statute governs a wide range of subjects, some purely religious and others which today would be regarded as secular, whether matters of civil law or criminal law. For example, the Statute governs the conduct of communal elections. As might be expected from the standards of the time, the individuals who were entitled to vote were 'taxpayers and those entitled to call themselves 'chaver' (brother) or 'morenu' (our teacher),[25] terms which excluded women.

On the other hand, some protection was given to brides. For example, in the case of a marriage to a person from out of town it was the duty of the communal leaders to ensure that no betrothal be permitted in which the father gives his daughter less than 150 gulden. There were also provisions to protect the bride if a man broke off the marriage after the betrothal.[26] The importance of not causing embarrassment to

---

[22] Moshe Rosman, 'Categorically Jewish, Distinctly Polish'; Littman, London, 2022, page 283

[23] See generally, 'Polin', vol 34, 'Jewish Self Government in Eastern Europe'; Liverpool University Press, 2022

[24] Anna Jakimyszyn, 'Statut Krakowskiej gminy Żydowskiej z roku 1595 i jego uzupełnienia'; (The Statute of the Jewish Community of Kraków in the year 1595 and its Amendments); Księgarnia Akademicka, Kraków, 2005. This work, which is based partly on a translation by Professor Bałaban, includes the statute in Polish and Yiddish. See also articles in English by Anna Jakimyszyn in 'Scripta Judaica Cracoviensia', vols 3 and 4 (2005 and 2006)

[25] Shmuel Cygielman, page 54, footnote

[26] Shmuel Cygielman, pages 67 and 89

a poor bride is illustrated by the case where the famous Kraków Rabbi, Moshe Isserles ('the Remu') (1520-1572) authorised the performance of a marriage ceremony after the beginning of the Sabbath.[27] As already noted, the Remu was a highly influential authority, and several of his decisions are mentioned in the section of this chapter headed 'Religious observance'.

The Kraków Statute provides for the appointment of different levels or ranks of judges. One provision states that lower level judges are 'competent, should they perceive some deceit, to judge as they see fit on the testimony of a single witness – and in women's matters, even a single woman [is a competent witness]'.[28] However, women are not considered competent witnesses other than 'in women's matters' or other than 'in matters within their particular knowledge'.[29] From these principles, there was some question as to whether generally a husband should attend court to give evidence on behalf of his wife. This matter is considered in a following section of this chapter.

Sources relating to the 1595 Statute do not comment to any significant extent on the question of divorce. It appears that the communal authorities had the power to imprison husbands who did not co-operate in the divorce procedure, and that they even had the power to ban them from the community. However, as in current times, there appears to have been no provision which enabled the Courts to grant a divorce ('Get') to a wife against the express wishes of the husband. In order to illustrate this point, Dr Edward Fram refers to a teacher from Kraków who left his wife for more than twelve years and continually ignored the coaxing of the communal leaders to give her a bill of divorce.[30]

Two further examples of wives being deserted by their husbands are given by the Kraków preacher, David Darshan, in his book 'Shir Hama'alot l'David' which was published in 1571. In one case the husband was Rabbi Mordecai, the alchemist, who had abandoned his wife and four unmarried daughters, and in the other the husband was Dan bar Tuvia 'a teacher of young boys'. In the first of these cases, remedies available to the authorities included 'gentle persuasion and failing that … compulsion, sparing him no expense'. In the second case, the authorities signed a ban of excommunication 'until he satisfies the claim of this woman [his wife].[31]

In his book, 'Jewish Autonomy in Poland and Lithuania', Shmuel Cygielman quotes evidence given by various witnesses concerning three Jewish men from Lwów who were killed whilst on a journey 'to the land of Ishmael'. However, the

---

[27] Shmuel Cygielman, pages 350-351. See also Henryk Halkowski, 'The Legends from the Jewish Town in Kazimierz near Cracow'; Mercury, Kraków, 1998, pages 18-21
[28] Shmuel Cygielman, page 70
[29] https://www.jewishvirtuallibrary.org/witness
[30] Edward Fram, 'Personal Piety' in 'Ideals Face Reality; Jewish Law and Life in Poland, 1550-1655'; Hebrew Union College Press, Cincinnati, OH, 1997, page 59, note 49.
[31] David Darshan, 'Shir Hama'alot l'David' (Song of the Steps of David) translated by Hayim Goren Perelmuter; Hebrew Union College Press, Cincinnati, OH, 1984, pages 100 and 107

author does not state whether the evidence was strong enough to release the wives so that they could remarry.[32]

Daniel Tollet refers to other aspects of the 1595 Statute in his paper, 'The Private Life of Polish Jews in the Vasa Period', i.e. during parts of the 16th and 17th centuries.[33] He points out that generally, the Statute prevented women from having access to synagogues. In terms of business, the Statute provided that a merchant's wife was allowed to help her husband, or to take his place in his absence, but she could not make any decisions. He quotes a Kraków based case where a wife was able to demonstrate that she had entered into a trading transaction in accordance with an instruction from her husband. However, a rich woman was judged to be so dangerous and provocative that the Statute placed restrictions on her dress code. In the same spirit of modesty, the Statute forbade women who were supervising expectant mothers to play cards and dice.

In his work, 'Ideals Face Reality', Edward Fram points out that in practice Jewish women did engage in business and that in this aspect of life, as in others, the Rabbis were forced to accept the customs and practices of the community, even though they did not strictly comply with Jewish law (halacha).[34] The acceptance of customs and practices in relation to women's ownership of property, and attendance at synagogue are considered in following sections of this chapter.

Childbirth and children

In modern times it is difficult to appreciate how dangerous childbirth was for both mother and child. Mortality rates were high, and the high frequency of pregnancies amongst Jewish women often left them in a weakened state. The risks were particularly high in view of the limited knowledge of midwifery, even in large centres of Jewish population and it has argued that these circumstances resulted in men outnumbering women in the over thirty age group. For example, the 1791 census shows that in Kazimierz, the Jewish district of Kraków (and a separate town at the time), there were 65 men aged 50 to 54 as opposed to only 42 women.[35]

Birkat Hagomel is a prayer which is said in gratitude for having survived a dangerous experience and, as noted in a following section of this chapter, in earlier centuries it was said by a husband on his wife's safe delivery of a child.

In her book 'Voices of the Matriarchs', Professor Chava Weissler mentions the practice of biting off the stalk of a citrus fruit (the pitam of an esrog) on the festival of Hashanah Rabba, the seventh day of Succos. This custom is designed to dissociate the woman from Eve's sin in the Garden of Eden, in order to ensure an easier

---

[32] Shmuel Cygielman, pages 375 – 377. During part of the first half of the 19th century it was possible for Jews in 'Poland' to obtain secular divorce decrees in the civil courts. See Piotr Zbigniew Pomianowski, 'The Number of Divorces Adjudicated on Polish Soil under the Napoleonic Code'; Czasopismo prawno-historyczne, LXXII, 2020

[33] Antony Polonsky and others (Eds), 'The Jews in Old Poland, 1000-1795'; I B Tauris, London, 1993, pages 53-56

[34] Edward Fram, 'Dealing with women in the Market Place' in 'Ideas Face Reality', pages 76-81

[35] Jacob Goldberg, 'Jewish Marriage in Eighteenth Century Poland' in 'Polin' vol 10, 1997, page 22 and table 3 on page 33

childbirth, since 'had Eve not eaten from the Tree of Knowledge, each woman would give birth as easily as a hen lays an egg, without pain'.[36] A connected, and possibly more current, remedy or protection (segula) is the eating of the esrog itself, or esrog jam, in order to ensure an easier childbirth.[37] S Y Agnon describes the benefits of eating etrog jam in his novel 'The Bridal Canopy'.[38]

David Darshan was born in about 1527 and was also known as David ben Menaseh. He was a student of Rabbi Moshe Isserles, and a popular preacher in Kraków. His sermons attracted large audiences of men and women. He earned his living largely by writing amulets, many of which were intended to protect women in childbirth, and also to protect their babies. In particular protection was required against Lillith, the first wife of Adam. One of Rabbi Darshan's essays includes a consideration of the circumstances in which it is permissible to wear such an amulet on the Sabbath.[39]

In his short story 'The Last Demon', Isaac Bashevis Singer mentions another folk custom which is designed to ward off an evil spirit, though it is not specifically for the protection of mothers and children. The main character of the story notes that 'The women don't pour out water any longer on the night of the winter solstice'. This refers to the custom of 'Tefukah' which arises out of the belief or superstition that water becomes contaminated at the time of the solstice. The custom seems to have been known in Kraków, since Rabbi Moshe Isserles ruled that the contamination could be avoided or eliminated by putting a piece of iron into the water.[40]

In his article 'The Role of Women at Rituals of their Infant Children',[41] Lawrence Hoffman describes how at one time mothers took an active part in the circumcisions of their sons, and the redemption of their firstborn sons. He notes, however, that Rabbi Moshe Isserles excluded women from the circumcision ritual stating, 'A woman may not serve as a sandek (person holding the baby during the ceremony), because that would constitute brazenness, although she may help her husband take the boy to the synagogue, where the man takes him from her and becomes the sandek.'

---

[36] Chava Weissler, 'Voices of the Matriarchs; Listening to the Prayers of Early Modern Jewish Women'; Beacon Press, Boston, MA, 1998, page 73
[37] Chana Weisberg, 'Expecting Miracles; Finding Meaning and Spirituality in Pregnancy through Judaism'; Urim Publications, 2005, page 134
[38] S Y Agnon, 'The Bridal Canopy'; Schocken Books, New York, NY, 1968, page 31
[39] 'Shir ha'Maalot l'David' translated by Hayim Goren Perelmuter; Hebrew Union College Press, Cincinnati, OH, 1984, pages 82-91 and 117. See also Rev Myer S Lew, 'The Jews of Poland; Their Political, Economic, Social and Communal Life in the Sixteenth Century as reflected in the Works of Rabbi Moses Isserles'; Edward Goldston, London, 1944, pages 164, 165
[40] Wikipedia and the Jewish Encyclopaedia entry for 'Tekufah'
[41] In Lawrence Fine (Ed), 'Judaism in Practice from the Middle Ages through the Early Modern Period'; Princeton University Press, Princeton, NJ, 2001, page 114

The exclusion of mothers from their sons' circumcisions was noted by Omi Morgenstern Leissner in an article which commented generally on the exclusion of mothers and daughters from rites relating to the giving of names.[42]

Maurycy Horn writes, 'The birth of a child and circumcision were celebrated in Jewish families in a special way. The bed of the mother was decorated and guests were served sweetmeats and wine. On the night before the ceremony of circumcision of a new born baby, women kept watch in the room of the mother. The purpose was not so much looking after her as, according to the convictions prevailing in the era of the spreading Kabbalah, the guarding of the baby against witches and evil spirits.'[43]

In her book 'The Bagel', Maria Balinska refers to a regulation issued by the Jewish Council of Kraków in 1610 concerning 'the vigil traditionally held by women the night before a circumcision, to protect the child and mother from the wiles of the demon Lilith, Adam's first wife, who was believed to snatch the newborn'. Earlier in the text, the author links bagels with childbirth and the giving of bagels to midwives.[44]

The exclusion of mothers from the circumcision ceremony might be explained, or justified, on the grounds that the ceremony would be very distressing to the mothers. However, this explanation or justification cannot be extended to the more benign ceremony of the redemption of first born sons. Even in modern times, 'The mother is not obligated to redeem her son; and if the father has died the Beis Din (Jewish Court) redeems him'.[45]

The need to protect babies is illustrated by the case of a woman who is widowed whilst still nursing, i.e breast feeding, her baby within twenty four months of its birth. According to halacha, such a woman may not marry within the twenty four months. Israel Ta-Shma notes that this prohibition was established 'for fear that she might neglect her baby' and that 'Ashkenazi Jewry took this prohibition very seriously throughout the centuries'.[46] This theme is one of several taken up by Zvi Eckstein and Anat Vaturi in their paper, 'Newborn Care and Survival among Jews in Early Modern Poland'. The authors describe a range of customs and beliefs concerning the care of young babies. Amongst these is a widespread belief that mothers should breast feed their babies themselves, although there are occasions when it may be appropriate or even necessary to employ wet nurses. The authors also refer to various authorities such as Rabbi Moshe Isserles, and two of the books which are mentioned in the section set out below headed 'reading habits'. There are

---

[42] Omi Morgenstern Leissner, 'Jewish Women's Naming Rights and the Rights of Jewish Women' on academia.edu and at https://www.jstor.org/stable/40326538 and in 'Nashim; A Journal of Jewish Women's Studies and Gender Issues'; No 4, Indiana University Press, 2001, page 147

[43] Maurycy Horn, 'Jewish Culture in Poland until the End of the 18th Century' in 'The Polish Jewry, History and Culture'; Interpress, Warsaw, 1982, pages 30, 31

[44] Maria Balinska, 'The Bagel; The Surprising History of a Modest Bread'; Yale University Press, New Haven. CT, 2008, pages 44-47

[45] Rabbi Avraham Davis (translator), 'Kitzur Shulchan Aruch'; Metsudah Publications, New York, NY, 1996, vol II, page 1083

[46] Israel M Ta-Shma writing about Rabbi Jacob Svara of Kraków in Gershon Hundert (Ed), 'Polin' vol 10 'Jews in Early Modern Poland'; Littman, London, 1997, page 294

'Brantspigl' and Rivka bat Meir's 'Meneket Rivkah'.[47] For example, 'Meneket Rivkah' advises mothers as follows'

'As soon as the child is born, she must watch over the child, and be careful not to give the child to anyone else for nursing …. Some are so undutiful that … they let the child be nursed by another woman. In the meantime, her milk goes bad and becomes bitter. A woman who does this will never nurse well'.[48]

Clothing and fashion

Mention has already been made in passing that the Kraków Statute of 1595 placed restrictions on the dress code of women, and it must also be said, of men. Put another way, 'It has been ordained concerning what is forbidden to women in respect of jewellery and clothing…..Whosoever shall violate even one of the above things shall pay a fine …. The parnas of the month must proclaim [the offenders' names] in the synagogue, declaring them recalcitrant.'[49]

As Maria Balinska notes, 'These so called 'sumptuary laws' were formulated with two things in mind; to avoid causing the envy of gentile neighbours and, in true paternalistic fashion, to make sure that poorer Jews were not living beyond their means. Only pregnant women, for example, were allowed to wear a ring with diamonds 'because of [the diamonds'] curative powers.'[50]

A little information is available about the costumes of wealthy Jewish women in the Polish early modern period. Stefan Gąsiorowski of the Jagiellonian University writes about Esterka in his contribution to the book 'Nie tylko Kroke; Historia Żydów krakowskich' (Not Just Kraków; The History of the Jews of Kraków).[51] Esterka is referred to again in the following section of this chapter relating to property. Stefan Gąsiorowski's account of her includes a portrait. At the risk of stating the obvious, only wealthy men could afford to pay for their wives to be the subject of portraits, and there are therefore few images of Jewish women which date back to the early modern period of Poland. One other example appears on the front cover of Gershon Hundert's book 'Jews in Poland-Lithuania in the Eighteenth Century'.[52] The cover of that book shows Krzystof Radzillowski's 'Portrait of Chajka ca 1781'. Although Esterka and Chajka lived some four centuries apart, their costumes are similar in at least two respects. Firstly, each one is wearing a close fitting cap which completely covers the top of her head and her ears. Esterka's but not Chajka's appears to be decorated with pearls. Secondly, both are wearing large

---

[47] Zvi Eckstein and Anat Vaturi, 'Newborn Care and Survival among Jews in Early Modern Poland' in Natalia Aleksiun (Ed), 'Polin', vol 36, Littman, Liverpool, 2024

[48] Frauke von Rohden, 'Meneket Rivkah' (Rebecca's Nurse); The Jewish Publication Agency, Philadelphia, PA, 209, pages 154, 155

[49] Shmuel Cygielman, 'Jewish Autonomy in Poland and Lithuania until 1648 (5408)' Jerusalem, 1997, page 95

[50] Maria Balinska, 'The Bagel; The Surprising History of a Modest Bread'; Yale University Press, New Haven, CT, 2008 page 46

[51] Edyta Gawron and Michał Galas (Eds), 'Nie tylko Kroke; Historia Żydów krakowskich' (Not only Kroke [the Yiddish word for Kraków]; The History of the Jews of Kraków); Wydawnictwo Literackie, Kraków, 2022

[52] Gershon Hundert, 'Jews in Poland-Lithuania in the Eighteenth Century; A Genealogy of Modernity'; University of California Press, Berkeley, CA, 2004

medallions hung from long chains around their necks – probably just the kind of expensive and ostentatious adornment which was strongly opposed by the Jewish religious authorities, and prohibited by the Kraków Statute.

At the other end of the social scale, female market traders were accustomed to wearing male garments, a practice which Rabbi Joel Sirkis (1561-1640) held to be permissible, despite the general prohibition of cross dressing.[53]

Łukasz Sroka touches on the topic of clothing and fashion in his paper 'The Jewish Community of Kraków in Autonomous Galicia'. This is included as a chapter in volume 23 of 'Polin' published by Littman in 2011. Quoting Klemens Grąbowski as a source, he notes

'In 1797, nobody saw a Jewish woman dressed differently than wearing a white bedsheet, starting at the head, fastened under the chin, and flowing all the way down to the ground. Their heads were covered with pearl headbands.'

Education

Education has been built into Judaism since Biblical times. The Shema is an important daily prayer which includes extracts from Deuteronomy, chapter IV. It includes a verse which requires parents to 'teach children diligently'. It is therefore perhaps unsurprising that by the 16th century the Kraków Jewish community had established systems of education, through 'privately funded 'cheders' and the publicly funded Talmud Torah which was established by a statute of 1551.[54] Having said that, the provision of education was directed almost exclusively to boys and young men. Paul Kriwaczek notes that obligatory universal schooling 'for Jewish boys' raised the Yiddish speakers' cultural level far above that of their gentile contemporaries.[55] Similarly, when referring to Kraków's educational ordinances of 1551, Edward Fram notes that 'almost every Jewish boy' in the town was taught to read.[56] Boys are mentioned, but not girls.

Another historian, Shmuel Cygielman, refers, in the main, to the education of 'children' and 'pupils' without mentioning their gender. However, he does note that girls learned to read and write in Yiddish and that they were also taught to do book-keeping and accounting and to handle family correspondence. They were also encouraged to read material which was judged to be of a high moral standard, as described below in the section headed 'reading habits'. The author further notes that 'on rare occasions' very talented girls would have a Talmudic education. [57]

---

[53] Moshe Rosman, 'Categorically Jewish, Distinctly Polish', page 323
[54] See, for example, Daniel Tollet, 'The Private Life of Polish Jews in the Vasa Period' in Antony Polonsky (Ed), 'The Jews of Old Poland, 1000-1795'; I B Taurus, London, 1993, page 51
[55] Paul Kriwaczek, 'Yiddish Civilisation; The Rise and Fall of a Forgotten Nation'; Phoenix, London, 2005, page 134
[56] Edward Fram, 'My Dear Daughter'; Hebrew Union College Press, Cincinnati, OH, 2007, page 18
[57] Shmuel A Arthur Cygielman, 'Problems of Organization and Curricula in the Educational System of the Kraków Jewish Community around the end of the 16th and beginning of the 17th Centuries,' in 'Jewish Autonomy in Poland and Lithuania until 1648 (5408)';

Marriage

'Jewish Marriage in Eighteenth Century Poland' is the title of Jacob Goldberg's paper which is included in volume 10 of 'Polin', published by Littman in 1997. The author notes that it was usual for couples to marry whilst still young, at an age when they and their children often had to be financially supported by other family members. Sexual infidelity was rare, though a few exceptions have been identified. At the end of his paper, Professor Goldberg shows a number of tables which summarise information taken from a census carried out in 1791. Some of the information relates purely to Kraków's Jewish district of Kazimierz. Table 8, as explained on page 23, shows that in that district 73.6% of women were married under the age of 20. Table 17 shows that nearly 20% of Jewish couples in Kazimierz lived with the parents of one of the spouses, whilst the percentage was much higher when the husband was under the age of 30. Perhaps surprisingly, table 18 shows that very few households included three or more children. However, the author notes that this may result from a deliberate understatement by householders who will have been suspicious of the census process.

Table 3 shows that in the age groups above 30 years, there were more men than women, and, as noted above, the author suggests that to a significant extent this was as a result of high female mortality in and shortly after childbirth. Such mortality is reflected in the recital of the Birkat Hagomel prayer following a safe delivery, and the use of talismans or amulets which likewise have already been mentioned. The table showing an analysis of the 1791 census for Kazimierz by age and gender is available at https://www.ics.uci.edu/~dan/genealogy/Krakow/other/population.htm This is part of Dan Hirschberg's extensive genealogical site.

Property (realty), other assets and bankruptcy

In terms of pure halacha, there is a general provision that a married Jewish woman cannot own property independently of her husband. This view is reflected in some modern works. For example, when considering a prozbul (an avoidance of the release of a debt) for wage earning women, Rabbi Yisroel ha'Levi Belsky writes, 'a married woman may also be in a position where she controls a certain amount of asset with the permission of her husband. The basic rule is that all her income belongs to her husband.'[58] However, the general halachic bar on a married Jewish woman owning property is subject to the rule that a woman retains ownership of property she owned before her marriage. By contrast, a right acquired after her marriage for a woman to occupy a seat in a synagogue is an asset in her husband's

---

Jerusalem, 1997, pages 484, 485. See also Majer Bałaban, 'Historja Żydów w Krakowie i na Kazimierzu, 1304-1868', (The History of the Jews of Kraków and Kazimierz), vol 1, chapter 25, 'Skolnictwo Żydowskie w Krakowie w XVI i XVII w'; (Jewish Education in Kraków in the 16th and 17th Centuries) Kraków, 1931

[58] Rabbi Yisroel ha'Levi Belsky, 'Shulchan ha'Levi'; Simchas ha'Torah, Kiryet Sefer, Israel, page 237. In modern Anglo Jewry, even very orthodox authorities take a different view. For example, a notice issued in September, 2022 by the Manchester, UK, Beis Din included the comment, 'A woman, married or otherwise, who has debts in her own right should sign her own Pruzbul authorisation form.'

bankruptcy which is available to his creditors even if the seat is registered in her name.[59]

The restriction on the ownership of property by Jewish women is illustrated by a 16th century dispute considered by David Darshan of Kraków. This concerns a case where Reuben sued the wife of Simeon. Simeon argued that he should appear in Court rather than his wife, because 'for whatever she deals with from our household is mine, for she has no possessions of her own ... Therefore, should she lose the litigation, the payment would have to be made from my resources'. David Darshan's responsum is not entirely conclusive to a lay reader, but it does appear to leave open the possibility that the litigation could be heard without the attendance of Simeon's wife.[60]

The general rule that a Jewish wife does not have an independent financial status seems to be consistent with various provisions of the 1595 Statute which are based on the assumption that a person who owes money, a debtor, is a married man. For example, 'Regulations against Bankrupts of the Year 5395 and 1603 [1594/5 and 1603/4]' provide 'there shall be no distinction between him and his wife – for she is considered a debtor – he and his wife must pay'. In summary, the wife's assets, subject to limited exemptions, must be sold to pay the husband's debts.[61]

In reality, a few Jewish women in Kraków did own property independently of their husbands. In modern times, in his two volume work 'Money in Halacha', Rabbi Yitzchock Silver notes that 'if a married woman engages in financial matters independently [of her husband] with money given to her for her personal use and she borrows money for this purpose, her husband is not obligated to pay her debts. If, however, her dealings are with household funds, her husband does carry responsibility for whatever she borrows.'[62]

The story is told of King Kazimierz the Great and his Jewish mistress, Esterka.[63] Out of devotion to her, the King is said to have built many manor houses for her. Whilst some writers treat Esterka as a purely legendary character, others write of her more in historical terms.

---

[59] Shmuel Cygielman, 'Jewish Autonomy in Poland and Lithuania until 1648 (5408)'; Jerusalem, 1997. Page 97. Note that in any event, general restrictions in the 1595 Statute limited women's access to synagogues. For wider reading see 'Jewish Bankruptcy Law, including References to the Jewish Community of Kraków in the 14th to 18th Centuries', available on academia.edu

[60] David Darshan, 'Shir hama'alot l'David'; Kraków, 1571, translated by Hayim Goren Perelmuter; Hebrew Union College Press, Cincinnati, OH, 1984, pages 95-98.

[61] Shmuel Cygielman, page 97

[62] R. Yitzchok Silver, 'Money in Halacha'; Center for Jewish Values, Jerusalem, 2013. Vol 1, page 277

[63] For example, see Artur Kiela, 'Legends of Jewish Kraków'; Wydawnictwo Bona, Kraków, 2012, and Ewa Basiura, 'The Jews of Poland in Tale and Legend'; Storyteller, Kraków, 1997. See also Chone Shmeruk, 'The Esterke Story in Yiddish and Polish Literature; A Case Study in the Mutual Relations of Two Cultural Traditions'; Zalman Shazar Center, Jerusalem, 1985, and for an extract see Maria Klańska (Ed), 'Jüdisches Städtebild Krakau'(The Jewish Cityscape of Kraków); Jüdischer Verlag, Frankfurt am Main, 1994, pages 47-56

Whether or not the story of Esterka has much, or even any, historical validity it may be taken to indicate that a few Jewish women had independent property rights from the earliest days of Jewish settlement in Poland. For example, Rachel Fiszel, the mother in law of Rabbi Jakob Pollak, who is mentioned below in the section headed 'trade and commerce', was the only Jewish person to receive the right to own a house in Kraków after the general expulsion of the Jews in 1495.[64] Another record from the fifteenth century shows that at one time a house in St. Anne Street was owned by Sara, the widow of 'a Jew named Smerl'.[65] On the other hand, a partial list of property owners in Kazimierz dating from 1653 does not include any women.[66]

Another example of property being owned by a Jewish woman independently of her husband is given in a work by Feivel Hirsch Wetstein. The author quotes extracts from the record book of the Kraków Jewish community from the mid seventeenth century.[67] One extract dated 1646 records that the community is asked to protect Eidel, the wife of Zundel the bookseller, and her half of a house from her husband's creditors. Another extract records a man promising to allow his sister to continue living in one third of the family home, thereby giving her rights as a tenant.

Rabbi Moshe Isserles ruled that a creditor cannot take the clothes of a debtor's wife, apparently including the clothes that the husband gave to his wife after their marriage.[68] In accordance with the general rules which define assets which cannot be seized by creditors this provision applies only to ordinary clothing and not to luxury goods.

The law and practice relating to the rights of Jewish women to inherit property are complicated. In Bbiblical times, daughters did not inherit from their fathers if there were surviving sons. However, following the ruling in Numbers/Bamidbar, XXVII, when the father left no sons then the daughters could inherit.

The right of Jewish women to inherit during the sixteenth and seventeenth centuries is considered in some detail by Edward Fram in his paper, 'Expanding the Rights of Daughters to Familial Wealth'.[69] The author describes ways in which, even where there were surviving sons, daughters inherited from their fathers who would use 'half a male's portion' contracts, and other legal devices. He also describes how

---

[64] Bernard A Weinryb, 'The Jews in Poland'; The Jewish Publication Society of America, Philadelphia, PA, 1976, page 99. As to whether the expulsion was complete, see Bożena Wyrozumska, 'Did Jan Olbracht Banish the Jews from Cracow?' in Andrzej Paluch (Ed), 'The Jews in Poland', vol 1, Jagiellonian University Press, Kraków, 1992
[65] Dariusz Niemiec, 'Jewish Properties in Medieval Kraków; in 'Cracovia Iudaeorum 3D'; Muzeum Historyczne Miasta Krakowa, Kraków, 2013, page 49
[66] Bogusław Krasnowolski and Marek Łukacz, 'Residential Architecture of the Jewish Town in Kazimierz before the mid Seventeenth Century' in 'Cracovia Iudaeorum 3D', pages 151 and 153
[67] Feivel Hirsch Wetstein, 'Mi'Pinkasi ha'Kahal b'Kruke' (From the Record Book of the Community of Kraków); Breslau, 1901, particularly pages V-VII
[68] R. Eliyahu Touger, 'Mishneh Torah, Sefer Mishpatim, Hilchot Malveh v'Loveh', chapter 1, para 5
[69] In Edward Fram, 'Ideals Face Reality; Jewish Law and Life in Poland, 1550-1655'; Hebrew Union College Press, Cincinnati, 1997, pages 81-95

and why leading Rabbis including Moshe Isserles of Kraków, were obliged to accept the validity of these devices, even though they did not comply with strict halacha.

As a general rule, then, a daughter did not inherit from her father in the absence of a contract or other legal device which made specific provision for her to receive an inheritance. On the other hand, if a woman became widowed and no bankruptcy was involved, she inherited from her husband. It appears that this inheritance remained part of the woman's property even if she remarried, since it was acquired before the second marriage. The catalogue of the Jewish Historical Institute in Warsaw includes a reference to a document dated 1774 which refers to the entitlement of a widow to a pension following the death of her husband.[70]

In the rare case of separation or divorce, the husband had to pay his wife compensation as repayment of her dowry.[71]

Householders' lists from the beginning of the nineteenth century show a few females, but no women's names are readily apparent on a list dated 1783 at the National Archive in Kraków.[72]

Reading habits

Reference has been made in the introduction to this book to both the traditional and a more modern view of the role of women in Jewish society. One of the leading researchers into these topics is Professor Moshe Rosman of Bar Ilan University, Ramat Gan, Israel. The professor has written various papers which appear, for example, on the website of the Jewish Women's Archive,[73] and in volume 18 of 'Polin' which is devoted to the subject of Jewish women in Eastern Europe.[74] The professor's more recent work is his book 'Categorically Jewish, Distinctly Polish' which was published by Littman, in 2022. This book includes two chapters on the history of Jewish women in the Polish-Lithuanian Commonwealth. The second of these chapters includes a short section entitled 'A literature accessible to women'. The professor concludes that defining male and female spheres of activity is of limited value since gender boundaries were continually crossed. He notes, for example, that men needed the Yiddish language as much as women.

Rabbi Moshe Rosman, and other scholars, nevertheless point out that during the fifteenth to seventeenth centuries Jewish women read a wide range of books, most, but not all, of which were produced in Yiddish. These books became more readily available following the invention and development of printing. This theme, and various publications which were aimed at a female readership, are considered in the paper 'The Jewish Book Trade in Kraków during the 16th and 17th Centuries' which is available at www.academia.edu/63761025. Amongst the literature which was designed to be read by women were translations and re-workings of the Bible, based

---

[70] Emanuel Ringelblum Collection, Gmina Kraków, 1774

[71] Daniel Tollet, 'The Private Life of Polish Jews in the Vasa Period' in Antony Polonsky and others (Eds), 'The Jews in Old Poland, 1000-1795'; I B Taurus, London, 1993, page 55

[72] Sygnatura (file group) 29/34/0/1.5.4/358

[73] https://jwa.org/encyclopedia/article/poland-early-modern-1500-1795

[74] Chaeran Freeze (and others, editors), 'Polin', vol 18, 'Jewish Women in Eastern Europe'; Littman, Oxford, 2007, including Moshe Rosman, 'The History of Jewish Women in the Early Modern Period; An Assessment'

on Rabbinic interpretation. These works often formed the basis by which mothers gave religious education to their daughters prior to the formalisation of education for orthodox girls.

In her article in the Jewish Women's Archive, 'Old Yiddish Language and Literature' at https://jwa.org/encyclopedia/article/old-yiddish-language-and-literature Chava Turniansky notes that two categories of works were expressed explicitly to females. These are 'Frauenbüchlein' and 'Tkhines'. The author describes the first of these as focusing on women's three specific obligations referred to as 'Mitzves Noshim', whilst the 'Tkhines' are supplicatory prayers. The topic of 'Tkhines' is explored more fully in Chava Weissler's book, 'Voices of the Matriarchs'.[75]

The three specific obligations which have been mentioned refer to the laws of niddah (menstruation), challah (bread making) and the lighting of candles. These are mentioned again in the next section of this chapter headed, 'religious observance'. As Magda Teter and Edward Fram note, 'For women who lived outside large towns [such as in one of the many hamlets or villages in the area around Kraków][76] and had no local Rabbi to whom they could ask halachic questions, this [a book of instruction or Frauenbuch] was a potential godsend if they or a family member or friend were literate'.[77]

Reference can also be made to a paper by Alicia Ramos-González entitled 'Daughters of Tradition; Women in Yiddish Culture in the 16th-18th Centuries'[78] where in the abstract the author refers to Yiddish as 'the language of the home and kitchen … of female spaces'. The author, along with other researchers such as Chava Turniansky, also points out that a few women were involved in the production of books, and did not merely read them. This topic is explored in the following section of this chapter headed 'trade and commerce'.

Maurycy Horn notes that one aim of Jewish religious writing was to spread a knowledge of the Bible among women who knew little Hebrew, or none at all. The first book with this aim was written by Rabbi Anschel of Kraków and was published in the city in 1534. This was 'Mirkeveth ha'Mishna', an alphabetic 'concordance' (index) and glossary of the Bible.[79] The year of publication was the year in which the Halicz brothers established their printing house in Kraków.[80]

---

[75] Chava Weissler, 'Voices of the Matriarchs; Listening to the Prayers of Early Modern Jewish Women'; Beacon Press, Boston, MA, 1998
[76] See Geoffrey Weisgard, 'Kraków; Sources of Information for Jewish Genealogy and History'; JewishGen Press, 2022, Part 3, 'Jewish Communities and Places of Jewish Interest around Kraków'
[77] Magda Teter and Edward Fram, 'Apostacy, Fraud and the Beginnings of Hebrew Printing in Cracow', page 33
[78] European Journal of Women's Studies, Sage Publications, 2005, 12(2)
[79] Maurycy Horn, 'Jewish Culture in Poland until the end of the 18th Century' in 'Polish Jewry; History and Culture'; Interpress Publishers, Warsaw, 182, page 20 and internet search for 'Anshel of Cracow'. See also, for example, Miriam Borden, 'Di Waybershe Bibel; The Myth and Mythopoetics of The Women's Bible', available on academia.edu
[80] Geoffrey Weisgard, 'The Jewish Book Trade in Kraków during the 16th and 17th Centuries' available on academia.edu at www.academia.edu/63761025

Other works included 'Azhores Noshim' (1535) which has been described as a book of Jewish laws for women, 'Seder Noshim' (1541) which set out seven tractates covering subjects such as betrothals, marriage contracts and divorces, and Ester Buch (1589).

Whilst some men were anxious to spread knowledge amongst women during the sixteenth and later centuries, some male leaders of the Jewish community in Kraków clearly felt that women had limited mental capacity. In his book 'Shir ha'ma'alot l'David', published in 1571, David Darshan (the preacher) of Kraków was proud to state that he gave his sermons 'with plain language and clear speech, so that even women and children would understand'. This is consistent with the ruling by Moses ben Maimon (Maimonides) that 'Instruction to the masses must be by allegory and parables, so that even women, youths and children might comprehend..'[81]

David Darshan clearly felt that females were inferior to males, declaring, 'woe is me that, because of my sins, I have nothing but daughters [and no sons]', and that he would have to 'collect enough zlotys and coins for dowry and ornament, and marry them off'.[82]

Some books which were directed primarily to a female readership did not relate directly to the Bible, but were nevertheless works of religious and ethical instruction. The earliest of these which was produced in Kraków was Rabbi Benjamin Slonik's work 'Seder Mitzvot ha'Nashim' which was first published in 1577. This book is considered in the following section of this chapter which is headed 'religious observance'.

A further example is Rabbi Moshe Altschul's book 'Brantshpigl' (Burning Mirror) which was first published in Kraków in 1596. This was a comprehensive ethical work which became very popular, to the extent that it was called 'the encyclopaedia of the Jewish woman'.[83] The work includes a collection of about 50 Kabbalistic passages from the Zohar. In her article 'Old Yiddish Language and Literature' which has already been mentioned Chava Turniansky notes that the work provided 'practical and spiritual guidance on multiple aspects of daily life' and was therefore 'constantly recommended to women by rabbis and teachers'. 'Brantshpigl' is one of several works considered by Chava Weissler in her book, 'Voices of the Matriarchs',[84] and it is mentioned again in the following section which is headed 'Religious observance'.

Although Moshe Altschul wrote his book for the benefit of women, he can hardly be regarded as a feminist. He advised against teaching one's daughter Torah, based

---

[81] David Darshan, 'Shir ha'ma'alot l'David' (Song of the Steps of David), translated by Hayim Perelmuter'; Hebrew Union College Press, Cincinnati, OH, 1984, pages 5 and 116.
[82] David Darshan, 'Shir ha'ma'lot l'David', page 117
[83] https://yivoencyclopedia.org/printarticle.aspx?id=55 See also Max Erik, 'The Brantshpigl, Di Entsiklopedye fun der Yidisher Froy in 17tn Yohrhundert' (The Brantshpigl; The Encyclopaedia of the Jewish Woman in the 17th Century) in Tsayshrift, 1926
[84] Chava Weissler, 'Voices of the Matriarchs; Listening to the Prayers of Early Modern Jewish Women'; Beacon Press, Boston, MA, 1998

on a fear that it would lead her to idolatry, 'for they [i.e. women] have no understanding (sekel) to differentiate between things'.[85]

Jean Baumgarten considers ethical works, including 'Brantshpigl', in his paper 'Listening, Reading and Understanding; How Jewish Women read Yiddish Ethical Literature (seventeenth to eighteenth century)'.[86] The author considers the ways in which various works were read and studied by reference to prefaces, introductions and the texts themselves. The examples he gives include several references to 'Seder Mitzves ha'Nashim', Rabbi Slonik's work which has already been mentioned.

The works which have been mentioned were, at the risk of stating the obvious, written by men and as such they reflected a male understanding of the role of women in society. By contrast, 'Meneket Rivkah' (Rebecca's Nursemaid) was written by a woman, for the benefit of women. The author was Rivkah bat Meir Tiktiner, and her work was first published posthumously in Prague in 1609. However, a second edition was published by Josef bar Mordechai Grozmark in Kraków in 1618. The book comprises 36 pages, divided into seven short chapters which deal with domestic relationships in the life of a married woman, for example with her husband, parents and parents in law.[87] The text of the book is set out in English and Yiddish, and is considered in detail by Frauke von Rohden in her book 'Meneket Rivkah; A Manual of Wisdom and Piety for Jewish Women'.[88] A much earlier analysis of 'Meneket Rivkah' was carried out by Sondra Henry and Emily Taitz in their 1978 work, 'Written Out of History'.[89]

Frauke von Rohden's book has been reviewed by Rivka Chaya Schiller, of YIVO, amongst others. Ms Schiller notes that, in contrast to male authors, who for example view the pain of childbirth as punishment for Eve's sin of having eaten from the forbidden fruit, Rivka bat Meir Tiktiner 'distances herself from such a misogynistic approach instead attributing these physiological functions to 'women's natural character''. She continues, 'For this reason, Von Rohden states that we might even consider Tiktiner's book an outright feminization of exegesis'.[90]

Despite what has been stated, it must not be assumed that Jewish women read only books of a religious or ethical nature. It is true that in his paper 'The Private Life of Polish Jews in the Vasa Period', Daniel Tollet, quoting Majer Bałaban, states, 'It should be added that men spent Saturday mornings in the synagogue and read the Talmud after meals, while women studied the bible for women.' But he also adds 'In the sixteenth and seventeenth centuries women read German romances about

---

[85] Quoted by Edward Fram in 'My Dear Daughter', page 45
[86] Journal of Modern Jewish Studies, vol 16, no 2; Routledge, 2017 and at
https://doi.org/10.1080/14725886.2016.1246700
[87] https://www.jewishvirtuallibrary.org/Rebecca-bat-meir-tiktiner and
https://yivoencyclopedia.org/article.aspx/Rivke_bas_meir_of_Tikotin
[88] Frauke von Rohden, 'Meneket Rivkah'; Jewish Publication Society, Philadelphia, PA, 2008
[89] Sondra Henry and Emily Taitz, 'Written Out of History; A Hidden Legacy of Jewish Women Revealed Through their Writings and Letters'; Bloch Publishing, New York, NY, 1978, pages 92-101
[90] Rivka Chaya Schiller, 'Tiktiner (bat Meir), Rivka. 'Meneket Rivka: A Manual of Wisdom and Piety for Jewish Women'. Review available on academia.edu

Theodoric from Verona or the knight Hildebrandt, translated and published in Kraków' commenting that this latter practice was opposed by the Rabbis.[91]

This theme is taken up by Professor Fram who notes 'By the mid sixteenth century, medieval epic tales had captured the imaginations of contemporary Yiddish readers and listeners and forged their literary tastes. Yiddish writers took note of this trend and sought to merge traditional Jewish culture and medieval western literature in their works'. He then mentions Shmuel Buch and Melochim Buch as early examples. These works were loosely based on the Biblical books of Samuel and Kings and were published in the 1540's. [92]

A further important work which was published towards the end of the eighteenth century was 'Tkhine Imohos', a short work written by Leah Horowitz of Bolechów, to the south of Lwów. This work was written by a woman for the benefit of women and is described in some detail by Professor Moshe Rosman in his article, 'Leah Horowitz's 'Tkhine Imohos'; A Proto-Feminist Demand to Increase Jewish Women's Religious Capital'. As the author explains, the work is only an eight page booklet, but nevertheless it had a wide readership and considerable influence. It is divided into three parts – a Hebrew introduction, an Aramaic liturgical poem, and a Yiddish supplicatory prayer.[93]

Religious observance

Introduction

Nearly all the historical comment on religious observance concentrates heavily on the roles undertaken by men. There is therefore a good range of material concerning the teachings of Rabbis and, for example, researchers have access to synagogue membership lists, and to lists of synagogue officers, all of whom until very recently have been male.

In his book 'Categorically Jewish; Distinctly Polish', Professor Rosman notes that the main mission of Jewish women was to facilitate the achievements of their husbands and sons. He also observes that the feminine ideal was considered to be 'modest, quiet, obedient, chaste and pious'.[94] In his conclusion to chapter 14, however, he points out that women had active religious roles. Some of these were, and continue to be, separate from male roles, and not merely in support of them. This theme is explored not only by Professor Rosman in the book which has been mentioned, but also in his paper on the website of the Jewish Women's Archive at https://jwa.org/encyclopedia/article/poland-early-modern-1500-1795. At the most personal level, women observed the laws of personal hygiene and sexual separation

---

[91] In Antony Polonsky (and others, editors), 'The Jews in Old Poland, 1000-1795', I B Taurus, London, 1993, page 50

[92] Edward Fram, 'My Dear Daughter', pages 87 and 88, quoting Jean Baumgarten, 'Introduction to Old Yiddish Literature'.

[93] Moshe Rosman, 'Leah Horowitz's 'Tkhine Imohos' in 'Polin' vol 33, Jewish Religious Life in Poland since 1750'; Littman, 2021 and in 'Categorically Jewish, Distinctly Polish'; Littman, 2022. See also Chava Weissler, 'Voices of the Matriarchs'; Beacon Press, Boston, MA, 1998, Chapter 7

[94] Moshe Rosman, 'Categorically Jewish; Distinctly Polish', page 325

(hilchos niddah), and attended the ritual baths (mikvah) on a regular basis. This topic is considered below in a separate sub section in this chapter.

There is at least one book which explains fully and clearly some of the religious observances of Jewish women in Poland during the sixteenth century. That is Professor Edward Fram's work, 'My Dear Daughter; Benjamin Slonik and the Education of Jewish Women in Sixteenth Century Poland', This was published by Hebrew Union College Press, of Cincinnati, OH, in 2007. The main purpose of the book is to describe, and comment on, Rabbi Slonik's book of religious instruction to women, 'Seder Mitzvot ha'Nashim' (The Order of Women's Commandments). Rabbi Slonik had been a student of Rabbi Moshe Isserles, and his book was first published in Yiddish, in Kraków in 1577. The book proved so popular that it was republished in 1585, and again in 1595. Seder Mitzvot ha'Nashim gives detailed instructions regarding hilchos niddah, and also hilchos challah (the laws concerning the separation of dough when making bread) and hilchos neros (lighting candles for Sabbath and festivals). Chapter 3 of Professor Fram's book sets out the cultural context of Rabbi Slonik's work, and is entitled 'Glimpse into the Lives of the Main Audience (Mainly through the eyes of men)'.

Rabbi Moshe Rosman's review of Professor Fram's book is available on academia.edu, whilst there is an entry for 'Seder Mitzvot Nashim' on the website of the Jewish Women's Archive. Additionally, Rabbi Slonik's book has been considered by some other researchers, including Chava Weissler[95] and Paris based historian, Jean Baumgarten.[96]

Cemetery attendance

There is some photographic evidence that Jewish women visited cemeteries from time to time. One occasion for such a visit was the minor festival of Lag B'Omer. Rabbi Moshe Isserles, the Remu, died on Lag B'Omer in 1572 and it became a custom of women, as well as men, to visit his grave on that festival.[97] However, it was not the widespread custom for women to attend funerals, particularly when pregnant, and indeed this is still not the custom in some orthodox communities. As Rabbi David Weinberger and Rabbi Jacob Shacter note in 'The Funeral and Cemetery Handbook'; Art Scroll/Mesorah, Brooklyn, NY, 2003 on page 96, 'It is accepted custom that pregnant women do not attend the grave site funeral service or visit the cemetery. Nonetheless, where there is a strong desire to do so … they are

---

[95] See also Chava Weissler, 'Voices of the Matriarchs; Listening to the Prayers of Early Modern Jewish Women'; Beacon Press, Boston, MA, 1998, pages 69 and 70.

[96] Jean Baumgarten, 'Listening, Reading and Understanding; how Jewish Women read the Yiddish Ethical Literature (seventeenth century)' at https://doi.org/10.1080/14725886.2016.1246700

[97] Teresa Leśniak (Ed), 'A World Before Catastrophe'; International Cultural Center, Kraków, 2007, pages 96, 97

permitted to go.'[98] Edward Fram notes that when women did attend funerals, they 'walked to the cemetery behind the men, ostensibly for reasons of modesty'.[99]

In her book 'Voices of the Matriarchs' and also in volume 10 of 'Polin', Professor Chava Weissler describes the custom of 'Kneytlach legn'. This is a folk ritual in which women lay candle wicks around, or in, a cemetery in the period between Rosh Hashanah and Yom Kippur. The wicks are then used in the making of candles 'for the living' and 'for the dead'. The author notes that Zechariah Mendel ben Arieh Loeb of Kraków (c1640-1706) states '…and from this custom has spread to measure the cemetery's circumference with wicks that are afterwards made into wax candles and given to the Synagogue, and this is a good custom'.[100]

The same author provides a further explanation, and the text of devotional prayers which are to be recited by women in her later article, 'Measuring Graves and Laying Wicks' which is included in a book 'Judaism in Practice'.[101] It is still the custom in some communities to light two candles on the day before Yom Kippur, one for the light of the Torah and the other for the deceased.[102]

Charity

The giving of charity is an important part of Judaism, as well as other religions, and Jewish women were active in charitable work during the sixteenth and seventeenth centuries. In his book, 'My Dear Daughter' Edward Fram notes that in Kraków women were encouraged to collect money for the poor. Indeed, the Statute of 1595 ordered the male collectors of taxes and donations to gather 'proper and dear women and send them around the town to collect money for the poor four times a week.' Women who, without reasonable excuse, refused to serve as charity collectors were subject to a fine.

The extent of women's involvement in charitable work varied over the years. By the 1630's, female collectors in Kraków were involved in the distribution of the money they had collected – but subject to restrictions set out by the male community leaders who accused women of improprieties.[103]

---

[98] See also, for example, Rabbi Chaim Goldberg, 'Mourning in Halacha'; Art Scroll/Mesorah, Brooklyn, NY, 1991, paragraph 10-10

[99] Edward Fram, 'My Dear Daughter; Rabbi Benjamin Slonik and the Education of Jewish Women in Sixteenth Century Poland'; Hebrew Union College Press, Cincinnati, OH, 2007, page 45

[100] Chava Weissler, 'Voices of the Matriarchs; Listening to the Prayers of Early Modern Jewish Women'; Beacon Press, Boston, MA, 1998, pages 133-146. See also, by the same author, 'For the Human Soul is the Lamp of the Lord; The Tkhine for Laying Wicks by Sarah bas Tovim' in 'Polin', vol 10; Littman, London, 1997, page 52

[101] Lawrence Fine (Ed), 'Judaism in Practice from the Middle Ages through the Early Modern Period'; Princeton University Press, NJ, 2001

[102] See, for example, Rabbi Avrohom Davis, 'Kitzur Shulchan Aruch', chapter 131, paragraph 7; Metsudah Publications, New York, NY, 1996

[103] Edward Fram, 'My Dear Daughter'; Hebrew Union College Press, Cincinnati, OH, pages 78 and 79

Conversions to Christianity

Whilst this section is devoted primarily to women's adherence to the laws and traditions of Judaism, it would be wrong to believe that all the Jewish women of Kraków were pious or religiously observant. Even in pre-modern Poland, well before the periods of Enlightenment (Haskalah) and secular Zionism, a few women were drawn away from traditional Judaism to such an extent that they converted to Christianity.

Rabbi David Darshan has been mentioned in a previous section as a well known preacher in Kraków. In 1557 he wrote a responsum regarding the religious status of a man whose grandparents had converted to Christianity and whose parents both lived as assimilated Christians. The man lived as a Christian but 'determined to return to his ancestral heritage'. He met a young woman who was in the same circumstances, and the two of them married following the Jewish ritual. Rabbi Darshan was asked whether this marriage was valid according to Jewish law. His resposum is long and, to a layperson, inconclusive.[104]

Adam Kazimierczyk's paper, 'Converted Jews in Kraków, 1650-1763' appears in Tel Aviv University's journal, 'Gal-Ed', volume 21, which was published in 2007. It is also available on line. In the article, the author draws from several sources including the National Archives, the Archives of St Mary Basilica (the Mariacka), and the Archives of the Metropolitan Curia. He notes that some Jews converted, not so much out of religious conviction, but in order to promote their trades or to avoid or reduce criminal penalties. Another motive was to reduce the impact of bankruptcy and to hasten a financial rehabilitation, such as in the case of the Halicz brothers who ran a printing business in Kraków. The author also refers to cases where coverts to Christianity returned to Judaism.

Adam Kazimierczyk continues, 'In the first half of the eighteenth century the number of baptised women rose visibly until it reached about thirty three percent of all converts. Married Jewish women would abandon not only Judaism but also their husbands and sometimes even children when those remained with their original faith.' The author's paper includes several appendices which give separate numbers of male and female converts, year by year.

Adam Kazimierczyk is also the author of 'Kazimierz Woliński and his Assistance Foundation for Converts at St Mary's Church in Kraków'. This foundation was established in 1731. In that paper, Adam Kazimierczyk refers to Father Turczynowicz, 'whose main aim was the evangelisation of Jewish women'.

In her paper, 'The Catholic Church and the Jews in Cracow and Kazimierz in Pre-partition Poland', Dr Judith Kalik refers to a case in 1759 in which a convert, with church assistance, fought for the custody of her children against her husband who remained Jewish.[105] Additionally, Przemysław Zarubin includes a chapter

---

[104] David Darshan, 'Shir ha'ma'alot l'David' translated by Hayim Goren Perelmuter; Hebrew Union College Press, Cincinnati, OH, 1984, pages 70-82

[105] Judith Kalik, 'ha'Knesiyah ha'Katolit v ha'Yehudim b'Krakuv uve Kazimierz ad ha'Lukot Polin' (The Catholic Church and the Jews in Cracow and Kazimierz in Pre-partition Poland) in Elchanan Reiner (Ed), 'Kroke-Kazimierz-Cracow'; The Center for the History of Polish Jewry, Tel Aviv, 2001, page 81

entitled 'Problem Konwersji' in his book relating to the Jews of Kraków and the surrounding area during the reign of King August Poniatowski. Referring to the second half of the eighteenth century, the author notes that the ages of converts varied from 60 years down to six months. He adds that as many as thirty percent of baptisms were given to women, nine of them in the parish of św. Krzyża (The Holy Cross).[106]

Dietary laws (kashrut)

It may be argued that ultimately 'the Master' of the house had overall responsibility for ensuring that religious law (halacha) and custom (minchag) were observed within his home. However, in practice this objective could not be achieved without the active participation of his wife. On a day to day basis, the laws and customs were implemented largely by the women of each household. For example, it was the women who ensured compliance with the dietary laws (kashrut). They would ensure that only kosher food was consumed by the family and that milk was not mixed with meat. The question of kosher food in the home is considered by Professor Fram in his work 'Maintaining Personal and Communal Probity', in which he discusses Rabbi Isserles' response to a problem which arose out of some Jews drinking wine which was not kosher.[107]

The fact that such an eminent Rabbi had to concern himself with such a matter illustrates that the laws of kashrut were probably not as strictly or universally observed as might be assumed in current times. Another example is given by resolutions which were passed at the fair in Lublin in 1607. These included a provision that 'the women shall take care to soak and salt the meat themselves, or by a Jewish maidservant – never by a gentile maidservant.' In a further attempt to reduce wilful or accidental breaches of kashrut the legislators also provided that 'no person may manufacture cheese or butter in the countryside for the purpose of selling it to Jews unless he first presents himself to the President of the Rabbinical Court in his location.'[108]

Prayers

Reference has been made in the previous section to the book, 'Brantshpigl' which was published in Kraków in 1596. Morris Faierstein's paper, 'The Brantshpigl (1596) and the Popularization of Kabbalah'[109] describes a chapter of 'Brantshpigl' which relates to the practices of 'Tiqqun Chasot' and 'Ma'amadot'. These are the practices under which men rise before dawn in order to recite prayers of lamentation over the destruction of the Temples in Jerusalem, and then recite a selection of Psalms before moving on to Shacharis, the morning service. The chapter begins with

---

[106] Przemysław Zarubin, 'Żydzi w aglomeracji Krakowa w czasach Stanisławowskich' (Jews in the Kraków Region in the time of Stanisław [King Stanisław August Poniatowski]); Księgarnia Akademicka, Kraków, 2012, page 265

[107] In 'Ideals Face Reality'; Hebrew Union College Press, Cincinnati, OH, 1997, pages 95-105. For a video of a discussion concerning Rabbi Moshe Isserles' responsum on this topic see http://jewishdrinking.com/rema124

[108] Shmuel Cygielman, 'Jewish Autonomy in Poland and Lithuania until 1648 (5408)'; Jerusalem, 1997, pages 274-276

[109] https://www.academia.edu/1522102/ The paper includes, as an appendix, an English translation of chapter 39 of Brantshigl

advice to wives that they should not allow their husbands to sleep late, but should wake them before dawn so that they should not miss the pre-dawn prayers. This is consistent with the quotation from the Book of Proverbs set out in the introduction to this chapter, which states that a woman should rise whilst it is still night

Rabbi Moshe Altschul, the author of 'Brantshpigl' also advises that women should recite their own techinnot (supplementary prayers) whist their husbands are engaged in their prayers. In this way, women would contribute to the redemption of the Jewish people. This advice is consistent with women having a power and purpose, through prayer, in their own right, and not merely as enablers of their husbands.

It is worth mentioning at this stage that books of techinot were produced in Kraków in later centuries. For example, Rozalia Saulson's work 'Techynoth: Modlitiwy dla polek wyznania mojżeszowego' (Prayers for Women of the Jewish Faith) was published in 1861.[110]

Ritual bath (Mikveh) attendance

Anna Jakimyszyn is the author of two works which describe the Jewish ritual bath, or mikveh, in Kazimierz. The first is a book, 'Mykwa; Dzieje Żydowskie łaźni rytualnej ul. Szerokiej w Krakowie' (Mikveh; The History of the Jewish Ritual Bath on Szeroka Street in Kraków) which was published by Austeria in 2012. Extracts from the book are set out by the same author in an article 'The Mikveh in Kazimierz until the Middle of the Seventeenth Century; A Few Remarks on the History and Appearance of the Building'.[111] Dr Jakimyszyn notes that a 'balneum Iudaeorum' (Jewish bathhouse) was mentioned in documents dating from 1485. The term refers to a pool of rainwater in which women are required to immerse themselves after every menstrual cycle, prior to marriage, after childbirth, and for the last time in their lives, after they ceased to menstruate. As indicated above, the procedures to be followed before, during and after immersion are described in considerable detail by Rabbi Benjamin Slonik in his book, 'Seder Mitzvot ha'Nashim'.[112]

Anna Jakimyszyn mentions a wide range of sources relating the Kazimierz mikveh in the early modern period. These include one which refers to an accident in 1567 in which ten women drowned after a wooden platform collapsed.

A brief account of the mikveh and two photographs are included in a Catalogue published by the Art Institute of the Polish Academy of Sciences in 1995.[113]

---

[110] Wikipedia wolna encyklopedia entry for Rozalia Saulson
[111] In 'Cracovia Iudaeorum 3D'; Muzeum Historyczne Miasta Krakowa, Kraków, 2013, pages 141-145
[112] The detailed regulations are set out in Edward Fram, 'My Dear Daughter', pages 181-204
[113] Izabella Rejduch-Samkowa and Jan Samek (Eds), 'Katalog Zabytków Sztuki w Polsce, (A Catalogue of Art Monuments),Tom IV, Miasto Kraków, Częśc VI, Kazimierz i Stradom'; Instytut Sztuki Polskiej Akademii Nauk, Warszawa, 1995, pages 37 and 38 and photographs 77 and 78

Synagogue attendance

It is largely true that in medieval times, even observant orthodox women did not attend synagogue anything like as often as their male counterparts. Indeed, separate galleries for women, or 'matronea', did not become widespread in the synagogues of Kraków until the seventeenth century.[114]

The topic of women's attendance at synagogue is discussed by Professor Edward Fram who notes that an area in a synagogue which was reserved for women was known as a 'beyt keneset shel nashim'. This translates as a 'women's synagogue'. He makes it clear that female attendance at synagogue was an exception to the rule that the place of the Jewish women was in the home – an exception justified by the view that communal prayer was 'more efficacious than private prayer'.[115] The topic of 'women in the synagogue' is also taken up by Professor Rosman in chapter 14 of his book 'Categorically Jewish; Distinctly Polish'.

The 'Hilkhot Nashim' series of Halachic source guides is published jointly by Maggid Books and the Jewish Orthodox Feminist Alliance. Volume 1 of the series is concerned with women and some of the rituals connected to the synagogue. The authors draw on rulings of various authorities over the centuries, including Rabbi Moshe Isserles (1530-1572) and Rabbi Joel Sirkis (1560-1640) who in 1619 was appointed head of the Kraków religious court (Beth Din) and the Rabbinical College (Yeshiva). Rabbi Sirkis is the author of the major work 'Bayit Chadash' which was first published in 1630. These two authorities are noted as stating as follows:-

(Rabbi Isserles) – Mourners kaddish can be made for a deceased mother as well as for a deceased father, but in either case the prayer is to be said by a son; not by a daughter.

(Rabbi Sirkis) – The prayer, birkat hagomel, is to be said after surviving a dangerous experience. Childbirth is such an experience. It is therefore appropriate for a husband to recite the prayer on behalf of his wife 'who is considered to be an extension of his own body and flesh'.

(Rabbi Isserles) – A woman is obliged to hear the reading of the book of Esther on the festival of Purim. She may read the book herself but is not obliged to do so.[116]

In her article, 'Women and Ritual Immersion in Medieval Ashkenaz', Judith Baskin notes that in some communities, women who were in a state of niddah, (i.e.

---

[114] Bogusław Krasnowolski, 'The Synagogues and Cemeteries of the Jewish Town of Kazimierz' in Michał Niezabitowski (and others, editors), 'Cracovia Iudaeorum 3D'; Muzeum Historyczne Miasta Krakowa, Kraków, 2013, pages 113-120. More generally, see Geoffrey Wigoder, 'The Story of the Synagogue'; Wiedenfeld and Nicolson, London, 1986, for example pages 38 and 39. See also Dr Alan Unterman, 'Encyclopedia tradycji i legend Żydowskich' (The Encylopaedia of Jewish Tradition and Legend); Książka i wiedza, Warsaw, 1994, pages 146 and 147, 'Kobieta' (Women), previously published in English as 'Dictionary of Jewish Law and Legend'; London, 1991

[115] Edward Fram, 'My Dear Daughter; Rabbi Benjamin Slonik and the Education of Jewish Women in Sixteenth Century Poland'

[116] Rahel Berkovitz (Ed), 'Hichot Nashim', vol 1, 'Kaddish, Birkat Hagomel, Megillah'; JOFA and Maggid Books, New Milford, CT, 2018, pages 16, 17, 19, 162 and 367. Volume 2, dealing with rituals connected to the Sabbath was published in 2022.

who were ritually 'unclean') would not attend synagogues. In Kraków, however, Rabbi Moshe Isserles notes that on 'white' days they were admitted even in the strictest places. The Rabbi seems to suggest that on High Holidays a woman could enter the synagogue even when in niddah 'otherwise it would cause her great sorrow to remain outside while everyone congregates in the synagogue.'[117]

The interest that some Jewish women had in religious matters may be illustrated by another of Rabbi Isserles' rulings which is mentioned by Rabbi Rosman in his paper. That is a ruling to the effect that in strict legal (halachic) terms, it is permissible for women to wear prayer shawls but in practice they should not do so as that would show arrogance (yo'harah) on their part.

Sarah bas Tovim lived in Podolia rather than in the Kraków region. Nevertheless, she was known beyond Podolia largely because of her authorship of prayers connected with the 'laying of wicks'. This custom has been mentioned above in the sub section headed 'cemetery attendance'. In her separate work 'The Tkhine of the Three Gates', Sarah bas Tovim warns strongly against the sin of talking in synagogue and coming to synagogue 'all dressed up in jewellery'.[118]

Wives and daughters of Rabbis and other communal leaders

Information about the wives and daughters of various Rabbis is available as a result of research into the cemetery which adjoins the Remu Synagogue on Szeroka Street in the Kazimierz district of Kraków. This cemetery was in general use up to the end of the eighteenth century. Possibly the first historian to record this type of information was Bernhard (Chaim Dov) Friedberg (1876-1961) who wrote 'Luchot Sikoron' in 1897.[119] His works were followed by those of authorities such as Feivel Hirsch Wetstein, Majer Bałaban, Eugeniusz Duda and Leszek Hońdo. A description of the cemetery, and the writings of Majer Bałaban are summarised in 'Jewish Genealogy and History for Kraków in the 18th Century; Sources of Information' which is available at www.academia.edu/81620461

Particular reference can be made to Dr Hońdo's book, 'Stary Żydowski cmentarz w Krakowie' which includes a lengthy bibliography. The work also includes a short section, 'Tytulatura kobiet' which explains the wording on the graves of women, including the use of the word 'Rabbanit' to describe the wife of a Rabbi.[120]

---

[117] Judith R Baskin, 'Women and Ritual Immersion in Medieval Ashkenaz'; The Sexual Politics of Piety' in Lawrence Fine (Ed), 'Judaism in Practice from the Middle Ages through the Early Modern Period'; Princeton University Press, Princeton, NJ, 2001, page 134 and Moshe Rosman, 'Categorically Jewish, Distinctly Polish', page 317

[118] Chava Weissler, 'For the Human Soul is the Lamp of the Lord; The Tkhine for Laying Wicks by Sarah bas Tovim' in 'Polin', vol 10, Littman, London, 1997, pages 46-49

[119] Bernhard Friedberg, 'Lichot Sikoron; Epitaphen von Grabsteinen des Israelitischen Friedhofes zu Krakau' (Stones of Memory; Epitaphs on the Gravestones of the Israelite Cemetery in Kraków) (Hebrew); A H Żupnik, Drohobycz, 1897. A second edition was published in Frankfurt am Main in 1904

[120] Leszek Hońdo, 'Stary Żydowskie cmentarz w Krakowie' (The Old Cemetery in Kraków); Wydawnictwo Uniwersytetu Jagiellońskiego, Kraków, 1999, pages 142, 143

A website at https://kehilalinks.jewishgen.org/krakow/kra_eminent.htm lists the following women who were buried in the Remu cemetery up to the end of the eighteenth century.

Grave number	Date of death	Name
195	1552	Golda, daughter of Szalom Szachny, and first wife of Mojzes Isserles
196	1552	Gitel, daughter of Mojzesz Auerbach and grandmother of M Isserles
197	1617	Miriam Bella, sister of Mojzesz Isserles
204	1650	Braindel, wife of Izaak Jakubowicz
222	1642	Debora, daughter of Natan Spira
224	1642	Róża, daughter of Mojzesz Jakubowicz, and wife of Natan Spira
237	1615	Maita, daughter of Jozef Antolabnet (?)
257	?	Sara, daughter of Mojzesz
259	1560	Drezel, daughter of Mojzesz Isserles and wife of Symche Meisels
260	1552	Malka, mother of Mojzesz Isserles
270	1593	Rachela, wife of Eliezer Aszkenaze
390	1576	Kaila, daughter of Azriela
432	1608	Chawa, daughter of Aszer Altszul, and wife of Leib Chalpnisa
503	1612	Rebeka daughter of Szalom, and
640	1629	Chaja, daughter of Nachman, and wife of Mojzesz Izaak, a banker

Information about wives and daughters of Rabbis has also survived in the form of extracts from old community record books, or 'Pinkasim'. For example, Feivel Hirsch Wetstein notes that Rabbi Nathan Nata Spira (1585-1633) had a daughter, Chavaleh Frieda, who married three times. In another extract from the communal record book reference is made to a document dated 1646 by which Gitl, the wife of Yakov Lezer Tribitscher, agrees to raise the baby Batsheva, daughter of Benjamin Zev Wolf Sirkes Horowicz who was a religious judge (Dayan) in Kraków.[121]

Trade and commerce

Introduction

A reference to some of the earliest Jewish women in the Kraków work place is given by Mark Wischnitzer in his book about Jewish crafts and guilds. He notes that in 1485 the Jewish community concluded an agreement with Christian merchants providing that 'Jews and Jewesses are permitted daily to sell garments and collars made by them'. The author then explains that the articles were not made to order for individuals, but were manufactured for sale on the market. He adds that the tailors and furriers were poor, and did not own their materials. These were supplied by the

---

[121] Feivel Hirsch Wetstein, 'M'Pinkasi ha'Kahal b'Krokuv'; Breslau, 1901, pages III to VI

entrepreneurs for whom they worked, under a system which came to be known in later centuries as 'cut, make and trim' in the English textile trade.[122]

Another researcher translates the 1485 agreement as 'Poor Jewesses have the right to sell on all days headdresses and neck jewels made by their own hands and craft'.[123]

Mark Wischnitzer also refers to female apprentices, noting that, unlike boys, they probably continued to live with their parents during the period of their apprenticeships. In one case, the father of a girl apprenticed to an embroiderer in Kraków supplied the coloured yarn needed for the first three months of her training.[124] He also notes that, Jewish silversmiths in Kraków were required to 'undertake on oath not to receive anything from boys or women…'[125]

Another reference to early female trading – at the opposite end of the economic scale - is to Rachel, sometimes known as Raśka Fiszel. This is the same person who was allowed to retain a house in the city of Kraków after the end of the fifteenth century when nearly all the Jewish community moved to what was then the separate town of Kazimierz on the south side of the Vistula River. Rachel was active as a money lender to the Royal Court.'[126] In particular, as Hanna Zaremska notes, she was 'a creditor to Kings Casimir Jagiellon, John Albert and Alexander Jagiellon. She represented a family which for almost a century had a decisive say in the Kraków kahal – herself being mother of the famous convert Stefan Fiszel and the mother in law of Rabbi Jacob Polak, the Talmudist.'[127]

George Alexander devotes a whole chapter to Rachel Fiszel in his book 'Generations'.[128] He notes that not only did she supply finance to royalty but she 'provided advice not only in matters of costumes, palace décor and purchase of

---

[122] Mark Wischnitzer, 'A History of Jewish Crafts and Guilds'; Jonathan David Publishers, New York, NY, 1965, page 211
[123] Anat Vaturi, 'From Contested Space to Sacred Topography; Jews, Protestants and Catholics in Reformation Cracow'
[124] Mark Wischnitzer, 'A History of Jewish Crafts and Guilds', page 269 and see Bernard D Weinryb, 'The Jews of Poland; A Social and Economic History of the Jewish Community in Poland from 1100-1800'; The Jewish Publication of America, Philadelphia, PA, 1976, page 67. See also an article which describes a book published in 1505 which shows women working alongside men in Kraków guilds which is available at
https://blog.lostartpress.com/2016/04/14/women-in-the-workshop/
[125] Rev Myer S Lew, 'The Jews of Poland; Their Political, Economic Social and Communal Life in the Sixteenth Century as Reflected in the Works of Rabbi Moses Isserls'; Edward Goldston, London, 1944, page 100
[126] Majer Bałaban, 'Historja Żydów w Krakowie i na Kazimierzu, 1304-1868', vol I, Kraków, 1931, pages 106-112
[127] Summary to Hanna Zaremska, 'Żydzi w Średniowiecznej Polsce, Gmina Krakowska' (Jews in Mediaeval Poland, The Kraków Community), part II chapter 4, 'Postacie: Lewko i Rachela Fiszel'; Instytut Historii PAN, Warszawa, 2011. The same author also wrote 'Rachel Fishel; Jewish Widow in Mediaeval Kraków' which was published in 2003. See also, for example, the names index in Moshe Rosman, 'Caregorically Jewish, Distinctly Polish'
[128] George J Alexander, 'Generations; A millennium of Jewish history in Poland from the earliest times to the Holocaust told by a survivor from an old Kraków family'; Congress for Jewish Culture, New York, NY, 2008, chapter 7

jewellery and art, but also in matters of domestic policy and back door intrigues at the court. She was surprisingly active in royal foreign policy, mainly offering suggestions for advancing the dynastic interests of the royal family through advantageous marriages of royal children.'

Rachel Fiszel is the subject of research by several historians other than Hanna Zaremska and George Alexander. These include Sara Ajzenstejn in her work 'Kobieta Żydowska w Polsce w XVI i XVII wieku' (Jewish Women in Poland in the 16th and 17th Centuries)[129] and Stefan Gąsiorowski in his paper, 'W Średnionowiecznym Krakowie' (Kraków in the Middle Ages).[130] However, it should be recognised that Rachel Fiszel was just one member of a large and powerful family, and apparently the only female in the family to achieve prominence.[131] Indeed those who have written about her indicate that no other Jewish woman, with the possible exception of the legendary or historical Esterka, wife or mistress of King Kazimierz the Great, achieved such power amongst the Polish royalty and nobility.

Professor Moshe Rosman's paper, 'Poland: Early Modern (1500-1795)' can be found on the website of the Jewish Women's Archive at https://jwa.org/encyclopedia/article/poland-early-modern-1500-1795/ . The author refers to Raśka Fiszel, and also to 'the perennial controversy over rules intended to limit the activities of women peddlers and requiring that they be chaperoned'. In his paper 'The Chronology and Distribution of Jewish Craft Guilds in Old Poland, 1613-1795',[132] Maurycy Horn notes that a Jewish peddlers' guild was established in Kazimierz in 1620. However, he does not state whether the guild was open to women as well as men.

Additionally, Professor Rosman identifies documents from the fifteenth century which gave trading concessions to both men and women. He also mentions Gitl Kożuchowska, the widow of David Todros, as being prominent in business in Kraków during the seventeenth century. Several female members of the Kożuchowska family are listed in the names index to Majer Bałaban's classic work, 'Historja Żydów w Krakowie i na Kazimierzu, 1304-1868' which was published in 1936.

Professor Rosman also considers the economic status of Jewish women in his book, 'Categorically Jewish; Distinctly Polish'. At the end of chapter 14 of the book, he concludes that women were partners, all be it junior partners, in their husbands' economic endeavours, rather than mere spectators.

This conclusion differs a little from that expressed by Anat Vaturi. She notes that the trading restrictions on Jews introduced in the latter part of the 15th century 'forced

---

[129] See Natalia Aleksiun, 'Female, Jewish, Educated and Writing Polish Jewish History'; Polin, vol 29, 2017, page 212
[130] Stefan Gąsiorowski, 'W Średniowiecznym Krakowie' (In Mediaeval Kraków) in Edyta Gawron and Michał Galas (Eds),; 'Nie tylko Kroke; Historia Żydów krakowskich'; Wydawnictwo Literackie, Kraków, 2022
[131] Jüregn Heyde, 'The Economic Elite and Community Leadership; The Fischel Family of Kraków'; in 'Polin', vol 34, Liverpool University Press, 2022, pages 61-64
[132] In Antony Polonsky and others (Eds), 'The Jews in Old Poland, 1000-1795'; I B Tauris, London, 1993. See also Majer Bałaban, 'Dzieze Żydów w Krakowie i na Kazimierzu (1304-1868)', Kraków, 1912, pages 318 and 319

Jewish merchants to develop marketing methods that would overcome the urban mercantile cartel, such as … the enrolment of family members and especially women as free help to increase the sales of handicraft products.'[133]

Book trades

Reference has already been made to the range of reading material which was available to Jewish women in Kraków. A few women were involved in the production of books, and did not merely read them, for example, Reyzl bas Yosef ha'Levi, also known as Reyzl reb Fishls. When visiting Hannover Reyzl found the manuscript of the Yiddish rhymed 'Tehilim Bukh' (Book of Psalms) by R Moshe Stendal. She copied it, brought it to Kraków and promoted its first publication there in 1586. In her introduction, Reyzl reb Fishls notes 'for the women and young girls, I copied it entirely and I thought it could be good to have it printed.'[134] This Rejzl is not to be confused with Raśka Fiszel, the money lender who lived some hundred years earlier and has already been mentioned in this section.

Alicia Ramos-Gonzáles refers to Reyzl reb Fishls' work in her paper 'Daughters of Tradition'. She notes that Reyzl added an extensive preface of her own to her transcription. Alicia Ramos-Gonzáles notes additionally that Reyzl reb Fishls published some books she composed herself, using the Shmuel Bukh as a model.[135]

Tsherna (Czerna) Meisels was another female engaged in the production of books. She worked in her family's printing business which was prominent in Kraków between 1631 and 1670. Mention can also be made of 'Hannah Ashkenazi of Cracow (1593) who was a writer on moral subjects'[136] and to Leah Horowitz's eight page booklet 'Tkhine Imohos'. Although this was published in Lemberg it was read by women over a wide geographical area.[137]

On the other hand, a list of Jews engaged in the Kraków book trade in the first half of the seventeenth century which has been prepared by Renata Żurkowa does

---

[133] Anat Vaturi, 'From Contested Space to Sacred Topography; Jews. Protestants and Catholics in Reformation Cracow'

[134] Jean Baumgarten, 'Listening, Reading and Understanding; How Jewish Women Read the Yiddish Ethical Literature (17th and 18th Century)'; Journal of Modern Jewish Studies, 2007. See also Chava Turniansky's article on the website of the Jewish Women's Archive, 'Old Yiddish Language and Literature' at https://jwa.org/encyclopedia/article/old-yiddish-language-and-literature

[135] Alicia Ramos-Gonzáles, 'Daughters of Tradition; Women in Yiddish Culture in the 16th-18th Centuries'; European Journal of Women's Studies, Sage Publications, 2005

[136] Sondra Henry and Emily Taitz, 'Written out of History; A Hidden Legacy of Jewish Women Revealed Through their Writings and Letters'; Bloch Publishing, New York, NY, 1978, page 90

[137] Moshe Rosman, 'Leah Horwitz's 'Tkhine Imohos'; A Proto-Feminist Demand to Increase Jewish Women's Religious Capital' in 'Polin' vol 33, Littman, London, 2021 and in 'Categorically Jewish, Distinctly Polish'; Littman, 2022, and Chava Weissler, 'Voices of the Matriarchs'; Beacon Press, Boston, MA, 1998, Chapter 7.

not include the names of any women. This list appears to relate to the buying and selling of books rather than printing and publishing.[138]

Customs registers

There have been a number of detailed studies into the customs registers, and other trade records, for Kraków for the several centuries up to the end of the eighteenth century. This topic has received the attention of historians who have included F W Carter, Szymon Kasuzek, Jan M Małecki and Bożena Wyrozumska,[139] However, these studies are largely concerned with international rather than local trade. Some of the books resulting from research do include indexes of the names of traders, but there are very few Jewish female names.[140]

Marriage brokers (shadchans)

One occupation in which women were likely to have been at least as active as men was that of marriage broker or matchmaker (shadchan), though many authors do not explicitly recognise this.[141] It is difficult to find references to this occupation in Kraków. However, the famous Kraków Rabbi Moshe Isserles ruled that a matchmaker was entitled to payment for his or her services, and could sue for his or her fee just as any other provider of a service. As usually seems to be the case in halacha, there are exceptions to this rule. For example, the rabbi ruled that the shadchan cannot make a charge if he or she had originally intended to provide his or her service free of charge. Neither can he or she charge more than one sixth above the going rate, unless exceptional skill or effort is required.[142]

Rivkah bat Meir makes reference to arranged marriages in her work, 'Meneket Rivkah'. She advises mothers to speak to their sons as follows;- 'if you study

[138] Renata Żurkowa, 'Handel książka żydów krakowskich w pierwszej połowie XVII w' (The Jewish Book Trade in Kraków in the first half of the 17th Century) in 'Rocznik biblioteki Polskiej akademii nauk w Krakowie, rok XXXV, 1990
[139] F W Carter, 'Trade and Urban Development in Poland; An Economic Geography of Cracow from its Origins to 1795'; Cambridge University Press, Cambridge, UK, 1994. Szymon Kasuzek, 'Żydzi w handlu Krakowa w połowie XVII wieku' (Jews in Kraków Trade in the mid 17th Century); Towarzystwo Naukowe Societas Vistulana, Kraków, 2005. Jan M Małecki, 'Jewish Trade in Cracow at the end of the XVI Century and in the XVII; Selected Records from Cracow Customs Registers, 1593-1683'; Polska Akademia Umiejętności, Kraków, 1995 and his earlier paper 'Jewish Trade at the End of the Sixteenth Century and in the first half of the Seventeenth Century' in Antony Polonsky (Ed) 'The Jews in Old Poland, 1000-1795'; I B Taurus, London, 1993 and Bożena Wyrozumska, 'The Jews in Mediaeval Cracow; Selected Records from Cracow Municipal Books'; Polska Akademia Umiejętności, Kraków, 1995
[140] See also, Szymon Kazusek, 'The municipal elite of Cracow and its role in the economic life of the city in the seventeenth century' in Cristian Luca (and others) (eds), 'Social and Political Elites in Eastern and Central Europe (15th – 18th Centuries); University College, London, 2015. The author names several Jewish merchants but they are all male
[141] See, for example, Rev Myer S Lew, 'The Jews of Poland'; Edward Goldston, London, 1944, page 119
[142] Rabbi Tzvi Spitz, 'Cases in Monetary Halacha'; Mesorah Publications, Brooklyn, NY, pages 198-202

enthusiastically, you will, God willing, be a well respected young scholar, and you will be given to the daughter of a Torah scholar with a lot of money'.[143]

Money lenders

Reference has already been made to Rachel (Raśka) Fiszel as a money lender to the Royal Court. However, Moshe Rosman notes that money lending on a much smaller scale was a common trade amongst the Jews of early modern Poland, and that 'pawnbroking was usually a sideline and often became the responsibility of the woman of the family'. He adds, 'Women's money lending …. was an inseparable part of the family enterprise – and widows played an especially important role'.[144]

Peddlers and market traders

Writing his PhD thesis in 1944, Rev Myer S Lew appears ahead of his time in that he includes a section specifically dealing with 'the position of women' in sixteenth century Kraków'.[145] Quoting from Rabbinic and other sources, he refers to women being charitable and having a high standard of religious life, but also carrying on trade, sometimes with their husbands and sometimes independently. He mentions a case of a young man liquidating his own business to join in a trading partnership with his betrothed. When the engagement was cancelled, he claimed compensation from her for the loss which he had sustained.

Rev Lew and others also refer to the dangers encountered by women who travelled between towns, or even from house to house, as part of their business ventures. The dangers arise out of the likelihood that female traders might come into unchaperoned contact with men, thereby entering into a halachically forbidden situation of 'yihud'.

This topic is taken up by Edward Fram in a section of one of his books headed 'Dealing with Women in the Marketplace'. He notes 'When they went to market to buy food and other daily necessities, businessman had to look at women, and deal with women; it was practically unavoidable'. In line with the general theme of the book he then describes how the Rabbis had to deal 'with the incongruity between contemporary practice and the halakhah'.[146] In the early eighteenth century, therefore, there was concern at 'the unseemly participation of women in commerce, and especially in peddling'. In general, the leaders of the community (the kahal) strongly discouraged such activity by women and imposed severe penalties on them.

[143] Frauke von Rohden, 'Meneket Rivkah'; Jewish Publication Agency, Philadelphia, PA, 2008, page 173
[144] Moshe Rosman, 'Categorically Jewish, Distinctly Polish', pages 18 and 326
[145] Rev Meyer S Lew, 'The Jews of Poland; The Political, Economic, Social and Communal Life in the Sixteenth Century as reflected in the Works of Rabbi Moses Isserls'; Edward Goldston, London, 1944, pages 102 and 121-124
[146] Edward Fram, 'Women in the Marketplace' in 'Ideals Face Reality; Jewish Law and Life in Poland, 1550-1655'; Hebrew Union College Press, Cincinnati, 1997, pages 76-81. See also Edward Fram, 'My Dear Daughter; Rabbi Benjamin Slonik and the Education of Jewish Women in Sixteenth Century Poland'; Hebrew Union College Press, 2007, pages 54-56. Additionally see Debra Kaplan, 'Because our Wives Trade and Do Business with our Goods'; Gender, Work and Jewish-Christian Relations' in Elisheva Carlebach and Jacob J Shacter (Eds), 'New Perspectives on Jewish-Christian Relations'; Brill, Leiden, 2012

However, there is a record of a submission to the Kraków municipal authorities, as opposed to the kahal, by a group, possibly a guild, of Jewish women peddlers who sought permission to continue their commercial activities, 'because we do not belong to the elders of the community of Kazimierz, but only to the treasury of the city of Kraków'.[147]

Although, in some respects, Rev Lew appears ahead of his time, he also writes, 'As in all ages, the women of our period showed a fondness for expensive clothes and costly jewellery, and the community of Cracow found it necessary to pass a regulation against ostentatious dress and precious ornaments.'

In his paper, 'Women's Labour Migration and Serfdom in the Polish-Lithuanian Commonwealth, (Sixteenth to Eighteenth Centuries)'[148] Mateusz Wyżga notes that many inhabitants of villages, including some Jewish women, would sell their agricultural wares in Kraków and other market towns.

In his paper on the Jewish Women's Archive, 'Poland Early Modern (1500-1795)[149] Professor Moshe Rosman of Bar Ilan University quotes Professor Weinryb as identifying further evidence that Jewish wives often worked outside their homes in the eighteenth century. He refers to a document in the 1720's where a husband makes it clear that he did not insist that his wife 'go to the Cracow market to deal in a livelihood to make a living for them and their family *as is customary for men and women* who always look for a way to make a living.'

Despite what has been stated, the fact remains that there is rather limited information about the role of Jewish women in trade and commerce in eighteenth century Kraków. This can be illustrated by Przemysław Zarubin's detailed book, 'Żydzi w aglomeracji Krakowa w czasach Stanisławowskich' which was published by Księgarnia Akademicka of Kraków in 2012. The whole of the second part of the book is devoted to economic issues and the work includes an extensive index of names – very few of which are those of women.

Furthermore, little information about the economic roles of women is given by the censuses that were carried out in the years 1790 to 1792 and again in 1795. Whilst these censuses list individuals by name, they do not generally disclose the occupations of married women. In this regard, Professor Hundert notes that most female participation in the economy was a form of collaboration with their husbands. He then adds, 'It is thus difficult to compute the degree of female commercial and artisanal activity, which was accounted as part of their husbands' businesses.'[150]

---

[147] Gershon David Hundert, 'Jews in Poland-Lithuania in the Eighteenth Century; A Genealogy of Modernity'; University of California Press, Berkeley, CA, 2004, pages 52 and 53

[148] Available at https://doi.org/10.1007/978-3-030-99554-6_6

[149] At https://jwa.org/encyclopedia/article/poland-early-modern-1500-1795

[150] Gershon Hundert, 'Jews in Poland-Lithuania in the Eighteenth Century'; A Genealogy of Modernity'; University of California Press, Berkeley, CA, 2004, page 53

THE 'AUSTRIAN' PERIOD
The first small steps to emancipation

Introduction

Throughout the nineteenth century and up to 1918, the area we now know as Poland was occupied by three imperial powers. That is to say, Prussia, Russia and Austria. The Austrian sector, known as Galicia, extended across the southern part of Poland to include Kraków in the west and Lemberg or Lwów (now Lviv, Ukraine) in the east. This 'Austrian' period saw major changes in the lives of Jewish women which were impacted by factors such as several changes in political administration, access to further education, a growing feminist movement, and the upheavals caused by the First World War.

The term 'the Austrian period' is not entirely consistent with history. It is used, however, as a matter of convenience. The first partition of Poland in 1772 brought Kazimierz, the Jewish district of Kraków, under Austrian control. However, the area to the north of the old branch of the River Vistula, including the central part of Kraków, was not incorporated into Austria until the third partition in 1795. In 1809, the whole of Kraków including Kazimierz was incorporated into the Napoleonic but sovereign state of the Duchy of Warsaw. This state was brought to an end by the Congress of Vienna in 1815. At that point, the three occupying powers were unable to agree which one was to control Kraków and therefore the city, and a surrounding area of some 1,165 square kilometres, with about 140,000 inhabitants, became the Free City of Kraków, also known as the Kraków Republic. During the period from 1815 to 1846 the Free City enjoyed, in theory a period of autonomy and neutrality. However, the 'freedom' was largely illusory. Between 1836 and 1841 the area was largely controlled by Austria and, following an uprising in 1846, the 'Free City' was annexed by Austria in November of that year. As a result of nationalist pressure, constitutional changes were introduced in 1867. It is hardly surprising, therefore, that the lives of Jewish women, as well as men, underwent significant change during the 'Austrian' period.

The final months of the period covered by this chapter were marred by an increased level of antisemitism, and an anti Jewish riot broke out in Krakow in April 1918 - as in 1945 following the end of the Second World War. In both cases the Jews were targeted as the 'cause' of failings by the State, and in 1918, particularly food shortages.[151]

Censuses

Lidia Zyblikiewicz of the Jagiellonian University has written several papers in which she analyses and comments on nineteenth century census returns for Kraków. One of these is 'Kobieta w Krakowie w 1880r. w świetle ankiet powszechnego spisu ludności. Studium demograficzne' (Women in Kraków in 1880 in the Light of the Census. A Demographic Study). A review of this work by Cezary Kuklo has been

---

[151] Ana Cichopek-Gajraj, 'Pogroms in Kraków in 1918 and 1945; Historical Analysis' and 'Today in World War I; Pogrom in Cracow' at https://today-in-wwi.tumblr.com/post/172995172568/pogrom-in-cracow

published in English and refers to the following conclusions which cast significant light on the lifestyle of Jewish women.[152]

Jews accounted for 33% of the total population of the city.

There were more widows among Catholic women (12%) than Jewish women (7.5%)

The percentage of women aged under 25 was higher amongst Jewish women than Catholics. Lidia Zyblikiewicz attributes this more to the lower death rate of Jewish children rather than a higher fertility of Jewish women.

82% of Jewish women had been born in Kraków – a much higher proportion than for Catholic women.

Jewish women were more strongly linked with their family than Catholics. 70 to 90% of Jewish women in all age brackets lived with their family – a much higher percentage than for Catholic women.

'Women of the Judaic faith usually ran their households without the help of servants. They often worked in the shop or workshop of their husband or father without being formally employed or receiving a fixed payment for their work.'

From the middle of the nineteenth century the Municipal Office of Statistics has prepared and published extensive summaries which have been drawn mainly from census returns and occupational surveys. A publication dated 1887, and based largely on the 1881 census (referred to above as the 1880 census) includes as table XXI an analysis of the population by district and gender. This shows that in the predominantly Jewish district of Kazimierz (district VIII), females accounted for 55% of the population. This was a higher proportion than for any of several other cities for which overall percentages are given. Analyses by age and gender for each district are also given.[153]

A further analysis shows that for district VIII, there were 903 widows, as opposed to only 170 widowers and 80 divorced women as opposed to only 11 divorced men.[154]

Yet another analysis shows occupations. This shows that out of 10,477 females in district VIII, 6,440 or were 'osoby należące do rodziny' (family members).[155] Although this description might be taken to indicate no occupation outside the home it is likely that some women in this category worked with their husbands in their family businesses, at least on a part time basis. That interpretation would seem to be supported by statistics based on later census returns as will now be described, and it is consistent with the view expressed by Lidia Zyblikiewicz.

---

[152] www.rcin.org.pl/dlibra/publication/26659/edition/14424/
[153] Statystyka Miasta Krakowa, (Statistics for the City of Kraków) zeszyt I; Biuro Statystyczne Miejskie, Kraków, 1887, pages 53, 62 and 65. Table XXXIII on page 85 shows that in district VIII approximately 83% of the population were Jewish
[154] Statystyka Miasta Krakowa, zeszyt I, 1887, page 67
[155] Statystyka Miasta Krakowa, zeszyt I, 1887, page 98

A further publication is based largely on the census of 1901. This shows that in district VIII Jewish females accounted for 51.5% of the total Jewish population,[156] and that a much higher proportion of women in district VIII were working outside the home than twenty years previously, some 3,400 working as 'handel towarami' (trading in goods).[157]

A summary by occupation has been prepared for the year 1891 on a slightly different basis by Łukasz Sroka. This shows that for the whole of Kraków, rather than just district VIII, a total of 4,417 women were engaged in 'handel toworami' and that the majority of these, 3,401 were 'członkowie rodzin'. This translates as 'family members' and implies they were working in family businesses.[158]

Charities

At a particularly solemn part of the Synagogue service on Yom Kippur (The Day of Atonement) the congregation proclaims 'But Penitence, Prayer and Charity turn away the severe decree', reflecting that the giving of charity is a central theme of Judaism as it is of other religions. It is therefore not surprising that from the earliest days of the Jewish community in Kraków, charities were established to support the needs of the poor, including widows and orphans.

In her paper, 'Support Your Own', Hanna Kozińska-Witt describes how the municipal authorities gave financial support to Jewish charities, and she identifies three such charities which were run in 1867 by or for the benefit of women and girls. These are:

- A society of women providing aid to the poor, directed by Rebbetzin (Rabbi's wife) Schreiber
- The Hachnasat Kalah, providing clothing to poor girls, and
- 'The Society of Welfare for Women in Childbed'[159]

The Progressive (Reform) movement in Kraków was particularly active in charitable work. This aspect is described by Alicja Maślak-Maciejewska in her book 'Modlili sie w Templu' (They Prayed in the Temple). Charities which were established under the guidance of Rabbi Dankowicz included at least one which supported widows, the Krakowskiego Stowarzyszenia Kobiet dla Wsparcia Wdów (The Kraków Women's Association for the Support of Widows), which was founded in 1874.[160]

---

[156] Statystyka Miasta Krakowa, zeszyt IX, część II, Biuro Statystyczne Miejskie, Kraków, 1907, page 18

[157] Statystyka Miasta Krakowa, zeszyt IX, cześć, II, 1907, pages 111 and 113-119

[158] Łukasz Tomasz Sroka, 'Żydzi w Krakowie; studium o elicie miasta, 1850-1918',(Jews in Kraków; a Study of the City's Elite); Wydawnictwo Naukowe Akademii Pedagogicznej, Kraków, 2008, page 28

[159] Hanna Kozińska-Witt, 'Support Your Own, On Your Own; Local Government Subsidies for Jewish Institutions during the Period of Galician Autonomy, 1866-1914'; Scripta Judaica Cracoviensia, vol 15 (2017)

[160] Alicja Maślak-Maciejewska 'Modlili się w Templu' (They Prayed in the Temple); Wydawnictwo Uniwersytetu Jagiellońskiego, Kraków, 2018, pages 204-206, which include the names of several women who were active in the Association

The Baruch family was particularly wealthy and influential. Their interests included a brickyard and extensive involvement in the grain trade. Members of the family lived in Podgórze from the end of the eighteenth century and throughout the nineteenth. In her paper 'Wzloty i upadki pzemysłowców z okolic Krakowa – Maurycy Baruch i jego potomkowie' (Ups and Downs of Industrialists from Kraków – Maurycy Baruch and his Descendants), Hanna Kozińska-Witt describes how various women in the family were engaged in charitable works. These included supplying hot meals to poor children, and supporting the construction of a Poor Shelter in Podgórze.[161]

Hanna Kozińska-Witt is also the author of 'Wzloty i upadki przemysłowców zokolic Krakowa – Maurycy Baruch i jego potomkowie' (The Rise and Fall of Industrialists in the Kraków area – Maurycy Baruch and his Descendants).[162]

The Jewish Orphanage is described below in a separate section of this chapter.

Education

Introduction

A useful summary of Jewish education in Kraków during the first half of the nineteenth century is to be found in Krystyna Samsonowska's work which forms the first section of a book 'This was the Hebrew School of Kraków'.[163] Additionally, the largely unsuccessful attempts of the authorities to introduce secular education to the Jewish community are described by Anna Jakimyszyn in her article 'Jewish Primary and Secondary Education in the Free City of Kraków, 1815-1846'. In the second of these articles, the author notes that most teachers of Jewish children were Christian and male. However, the teaching staff did include two Christian females, Anna Sieradzka and Anna Bobrowska-Bendziszewska.[164]

It is clear from these sources that during the early 1800's education within the Jewish community was almost entirely religious rather than secular – and directed to boys rather than girls. However, largely under the influence of the Progressive (Reform) section of the community, there was a gradual expansion of secular and vocational education to girls, and later to young women. Thus, in 1835, the Jewish Junior High School was attended by 146 boys and 36 girls. The girls studied languages, history, geography, arithmetic – and domestic activities.[165] A few years later, the Jewish Junior High School merged with the Elementary School for

---

[161] See also Barbara Zbroja, 'The History of the Jewish Community of Podgórze' in 'Polin' vol 23, page 113

[162] In Alicja Maślak-Maciejewska (Ed), 'Żydzi krakowscy; Nowe kierunki badań'; (Kraków Jews; New Research Directions); Austeria, Kraków, 2021. See also, by the same author, 'Pioneers of Industrialisation in Western Galicia; The Baruch Family in the Nineteenth Century' and 'Od Barucha do Libana. Działalność gospodarcza Żydów Podgórskich' (From Baruch to Liban; Economic Activity of the Jews of Podgórze)

[163] Kamil Jurewicz (Ed), 'This was the Hebrew School of Kraków; The Hebrew Secondary School 1918-1939'; Muzeum Historyczne Miasta Krakowa, Kraków, 2011. See also, for example, 'A History of Jewish Education in Kraków' at www.academia.edu/33768075

[164] In Michał Galas and Antony Polonsky (Eds), 'Polin' vol 23, Littman, Oxford, 2011, page 58

[165] 'Polin' vol 23, page 57

Children and Adolescents of the Jewish Faith to form a new institution, The School of Trade and Industry. This catered for both boys and girls.

The range of topics taught to Jewish girls expanded further after the constitutional changes of the 1860's, as the following examples demonstrate.[166] In the academic year 1871/72, 551 girls were registered at schools in Kazimierz, as opposed to only 286 boys.[167]

Education is one of the many topics covered by Anna Jakimyszyn-Gadocha and Alicja Maślak-Maciejewska in their summary of the history of Kraków Jewry in the nineteenth century. They note:

'Secondary education was intended for boys from the age of ten. It ended after eight years with passing the matriculation examinations. The possibility of taking the secondary school leaving examination in extra mural mode resulted in [the fact that] since the [18]90's women have joined the candidates. Nevertheless, even by the end of the 19th century some communal leaders were reluctant to give young women the level of education which was available to young men.[168]

The first Jewish [female] extra mural student in 1899 was the Helena Donhajser. Among the others we find future graduates of the Jagiellonian University – Gizela Gutmann, Helena Rosenzweig-Hecker, Frania Herbstów, Maria Horowitz and Dora Immerglück.'[169] Further information regarding Jewish students at the Jagiellonian University is set out in the next section of this chapter.

The Jewish School

The web page at https://kehilalinks.jewishgen.org/krakow/kra_1866sch.htm shows that in 1866 what is described as the 'Jewish school' was attended by the children of just over a hundred families – which represents only a small proportion of the total Jewish population of Kraków. The page shows the names of the 140 pupils, of whom 89 were girls.

A list of students who passed their examinations at the Kraków Jewish School in 1870/71 is available at https://kehilalinks.jewishgen.org/Krakow/kra_school.htm

---

[166] See also, for example, 'Szkolnictwo i życie kulturalne' (Education and Cultural Life), a chapter in Andrzej Żbikowski, 'Żydzi Krakowscy i ich gmina w latach 1869-1919' (Kraków Jews and their Community); Wydawnictwo DiG, Warszawa, 1994

[167] Eugenia Prokop-Janiec, 'Mapping Modern Jewish Kraków' in Halina Goldberg (Ed), 'Polish Jewish Culture beyond the Capital'; Rutgers University Press, New Brunswick, NJ, 2023, page 191, quoting Andrzej Żbikowski, 'Żydzi krakowscy'

[168] Rachel Manekin, 'The Lost Generation; Education and Female Conversion in Fin-de-Siècle Kraków'. See also by the same author, 'Orthodox Jewry in Kraków at the turn of the Twentieth Century'; Polin, vol 23, Oxford, 2011, pages 189-192 'The Education of Women' and her book 'The Rebellion of the Daughters'; Princeton University Press, Princeton, NJ, 2020

[169] Anna Jakimyszyn-Gadocha and Alicja Maślak-Maciejewska, 'XIX Stulecie' (19th Century) in Edyta Gawron and Michał Galas (Eds), 'Nie tylko Kroke; Historia Żydów krakowskich' (Not Just Kroke [Yiddish for Kraków]; The History of the Jews of Kraków); Wydawnictwo Literackie, Kraków, 2022, page 216

This page lists girls and boys distinguishing between prize winners, those receiving an honourable mention, and those achieving grade A. Other students are not listed.

Eugenia Prokop-Janiec notes that during the latter half or the 19th century 'separate classes for girls were already created in the first modern school for Jewish children, the so-called Casimir the Great School (Szkoła Kazimierzowska)'. This came to be located in the town hall in Kazimierz, though lessons for girls were originally taught in rented private rooms.[170]

Króla Jana III Sobiesko Gimnazjum

In her book 'Never Tell Anyone You're Jewish'[171] Maria Chamberlain refers to the records of the Liceum Ogólnokszłałcące im Króla Jana Sobieskiego, which translates as King Jan Sobieski's General High School. This appears to be the same establishment as the Gimnazyum im. Króla Jana III Sobieskiego mentioned by Alicja Maślak-Maciejewska in her book about the Progressive community in Kraków.[172] Maria Chamberlain notes that lists of students who attended the school from 1883 onwards are available at http://www.sobieski.krakow.pl/historia/absolwenci-1883-1939 The main list indicates the school was for boys only but there is a second list, showing the names of women who passed their matura exams at the school. These include Ela Wajsman (1912), Gittel Rosenzweig (1913) and Julia Weiss (1913).

Podgorze

Podgórze lies to the south of the river Vistula. Until 1915 it was a township outside the city of Kraków and by then it had become increasingly popular amongst Jewish families who wished to move away from the old Jewish quarter of Kazimierz. These included the family of Julia Glasner who is mentioned below in relation to the Jagiellonian University.

The Central Archive for the History of Jewish People which is based in Jerusalem holds copies of reports and correspondence relating to the reorganisation of elementary schools attended by Jews, including a list of girls dated 1878.

Marilyn Robinson's website 'Jewishgem' (http://yourjewishgem.blogspot.com) includes a list of Jewish students who attended the Podgórze School in 1901, but all the names on the list are male.

Public schools

It is well established that by the period between the two world wars, the majority of Jewish girls in Kraków did not attend Orthodox Jewish schools.[173] However, even

---

[170] Eugenia Prokop-Janiec, 'Mapping Modern Jewish Kraków' in Halina Goldberg (Ed), 'Polish Jewish Culture Beyond the Capital'; Rutgers University Press, New Brunswick, NJ, 2023, page 193
[171] Maria Chamberlain, 'Never Tell Anyone You're Jewish'; Vallentine Mitchell, London, 2022, page 115
[172] Alicja Maślak-Maciejewska, 'Modlili się w Templu'; Wydawnictwo Uniwersytetu Jagiellońskiego, Kraków, 2018. See bibliography at pages 426, 427
[173] See for example Sean Martin 'Jewish Life in Cracow, 1918-1939'; Vallentine Mitchell, London, 2004 chapter 4

in the nineteenth century a number of Jewish boys and girls were educated in public, or State, schools. In her book concerning Jewish life during the time of the Krakow Republic (1815-1846), Anna Jakimyszyn describes the education system in some detail. Unfortunately, information relating specifically to girls and young women seems to be limited – at least to a reader who understands very little Polish – but the author does include a table which shows that between 1838 and 1845 more Jewish girls than boys attended public schools to study for an initial degree.[174]

The św. Scholastyki and other schools

Rachel Manekin notes that in the latter part of the 19th century the św. Scholastyki School was the most prestigious public middle school for girls in Kraków. It was established in the 1870's and developed to offer a wide range of courses. It attracted girls from Hassidic homes. Michalina Araten attended the school of Gertha Rehefeld, 'a private eight grade girls' school for daughters of upper class Polish families' before she converted to Christianity. This school advertised itself as 'an English school for young ladies' and was located on ul. Poselslka. Additionally, Rachel Manekin records that Anna Kluger attended the school of Ludmila Tschapek, a school which was founded in 1881 and which taught Polish, German, French and English, as well as music and other subjects.[175]

Eugenia Prokop-Janiec mentions that Jewish girls attended not only the św. Scholastyki School, but also a school at 7 Bernardyńska Street and a Private Gymnasium for Girls which operated initially at św. Jan Street. She also mentions how Jewish young women were able to undertake training to become teachers.[176]

Wieliczka

The education of Jewish girls in Wieliczka, a town some 10 miles (15 km) south east of Kraków, is considered in the final section of this chapter.

Jagiellonian University

Even by the end of the nineteenth century, higher education for women throughout the Habsburg Empire was very limited. As Rachel Manekin states in her book 'The Rebellion of the Daughters', 'It should be noted that the general atmosphere in the Habsburg Empire, including that of the government authorities, was not particularly supportive of higher education for women at the same level as their male counterparts.'. The author then notes that 'As a result only private gymnasia initially prepared their female students for the matriculation exams... A private female gymnasium was established in Kraków in 1896'. However, a teachers' seminary for women had been established in the city in 1871.

---

[174] Anna Jakimyszyn, 'Żydzi krakowscy w dobie Rzeczypospolitej Krakowskiej' (Kraków Jews at the time of the Kraków Republic); Austeria, Kraków, 2008, page 240
[175] Rachel Manekin, 'Rebellion of the Daughters; Jewish Women Runaways in Habsburg Galicia'; Princeton University Press, Princeton, NJ, 2020, pages 26, 58-60 and 136
[176] Eugenia Prokop-Janiec, 'Mapping Modern Jewish Kraków'

One chapter in Rachel Manekin's book describes the struggle of Anna Kluger for higher education. Anna was born in Podgórze in 1890. She ran away from home and converted to Catholicism in her pursuit of her educational aims.[177]

Anna Jakimyszyn-Gadocha and Alicja Maślak-Maciejewska make the following observations regarding the Jagiellonian University:-

'It should be noted that data from the nineteenth century refers only to men. Women were allowed to study at the Faculty of Philosophy only from 1897, and in Medicine from 1900. Finally, only in 1918 they obtained the right to study law. The first [female] student at the Jagiellonian University of Jewish pedigree was Julia Glasner, born in 1873 in Podgórze, who started [to study] science in the academic year 1897/8.'

The authors then note that by 1917 in the Faculty of Medicine, some 56% of all female students were Jewish, and that women most often chose medicine or pharmacy for prestige and financial reasons.[178]

Julia Glasner is mentioned by Mariusz Kulczykowski in his paper 'Młodzież Żydowska z Podgórza na studiach na Uniwersytecie Jagiellońskim w latach 1866/67 – 1917/18' (Jewish Youth from Podgórze at the Jagiellonian University). The paper includes two tables. The first sets out the ages of students and their numbers. The total number in the column headed 'kobiety' (women) is 182 as opposed to only 49 'mężczyźni' (men). Unfortunately, in the second table the numbers are reversed – 182 men and 49 women. The second table shows that of the 49 women, 18 studied medicine and 31 studied philosophy. In view of the late admission of women into the University, it appears that the headings in the first table have been reversed in error.

Because of the severe restrictions on University education for females, some women attended the Baraneum. This college 'did not grant academic or other degrees, but it provided access to knowledge on a high level'. Subjects, including topics in evening courses, covered by the college included literature, science and the arts.[179]

The difficulties facing young women are illustrated by the case of Helene Bauer (née Gumplowicz) (1871-1942), who was born into a well known Kraków Jewish family, the daughter of a book seller, Felix Gumplwicz. Helene completed her teacher training in the city but was unable to pursue a doctorate there. Like other

---

[177] Rachel Manekin, 'Rebellion of the Daughters' particularly chapter 4, 'Intellectual Passion; Ann Kluger and her Struggle for Higher Education'

[178] Anna Jakimyszyn-Gadocha and Alicja Maślak-Maciejewska, 'XIX Stulecie' in Edyta Gawron and Michał Galas (Eds), 'Nie tylko Kroke; Historia Żydów krakowskich'; Wydawnictwo Literackie, Kraków, 2022, page 219. See also Eugenia Prokop-Janiec, 'Mapping Modern Jewish Kraków', page 197

[179] Rachel Manekin, 'The Rebellion of the Daughters'; Princeton University Press, Princeton, NJ, 2020, pages 30, 31, and Eugenia Prokop-Janiec, 'Mapping Modern Jewish Kraków', page 198

Jewish women in Galicia, she therefore studied for her doctorate in Switzerland. She later became active in the Social Democratic Workers' Party of Austria.[180]

A further example, is Anna (Chaja) Kluger who was born into a Chassidic family and fled home in 1909 in her determination to obtain a higher secular education. She eventually earned a PhD at the University of Vienna. A detailed account of these events is given by Professor Rachel Manekin in her book 'The Rebellion of the Daughters', which has already been mentioned.

'Academics of Jewish Heritage in the Modern History of the Jagiellonian University is the leading work of its subject which has been published in English. The main part of the book comprises biographical information concerning a large number of individuals who taught or studied at the University. However, only four of these are female. Two of these, Zofia Ameisen and Laura Kaufman began their studies before the end of the first world war.

Laura Kaufman (1889-1972) was born in Kraków. In 1902 she attended the Private High School for Girls on ul. Wolska and five years later she took her school leaving certificate examinations as an extramural student at the St Anna Boys' Secondary School. She then enrolled at the Jagiellonian University choosing a degree in natural sciences. In 1911 she began her doctoral research and successfully defended her doctorate in 1916. Laura Kaufman continued her career as a biologist and geneticist.[181]

Zofia Ameisen (1897-1967) came from Nowy Sącz and commenced her studies at the Jagiellonian University in 1915. Her main subjects were art history and archaeology. She obtained her doctorate at the University and became a renowned art historian specialising in illuminated manuscripts.[182]

Eugenia Prokop-Janiec refers to a number of other Jewish women who obtained their doctorates at the Jagiellonian University in the first two decades of the 20th century. These include Franciszka Schiffmann, Sara Hollander and two art historians, Henryka Fromowicz-Stillerowa and Stefania Zahorska, nèe Lesser.[183]

One exception to the bar on women attending the University during the nineteenth century might have been in the field of midwifery. The All Galicia Database which is operated by the genealogical group Gesher Galicia includes data relating to Jewish midwifery students who attended the University between 1802 and 1850.[184] It might be assumed that most of these students were women.

---

[180] Wikipedia and Aneta Bołdyrew, 'Merited, (Un)appreciated, (Un)remembered Women in Educational and Social Policy Sciences as a Scholarly Discipline in Poland, 1900-1939'; Acta Poloniae Historica, 117, 2018

[181] Wiesław Kozub-Ciembroniewicz (Ed), 'Academics of Jewish Heritage in the Modern History of the Jagiellonian University'; Jagiellonian University Press, Kraków, 2014, pages 133, 134

[182] Wiesław Kozub-Ciembroniewicz (Ed), 'Academics of Jewish Heritage in the Modern History of the Jagiellonian University', pages 69, 70. See also Agnieszka Kutylak (Ed), 'Krakowianie; wybitni Żydzi krakowscy XIV-XX w' (Krakovians; Outstanding Kraków Jews); Muzeum Historyczne Miasta Krakowa, Kraków, 2006, pages 133-135

[183] Eugenia Prokop-Janiec, 'Mapping Modern Jewish Kraków', pages 197, 198

[184] Gesher Galicia digest, March 21, 2018 and the GG members' portal, 'record inventories'

Literature

Little seems to have been written about female Jewish authors who wrote in Kraków during the nineteenth century, and possibly there were few such authors. One exception, however, was the poet, writer and translator, Rozalia Saulson (1807-1896). She wrote mostly on religious subjects. For example, in 1861 she wrote 'Techynoth. Modlitwy dla polek wyznania mojżeszowego' (Prayers for Polish Women of the Jewish Faith) and four years later she wrote 'Osienaście kantyków z rytualowych modlitw Izraelitów' (Eighteen Canticles from the Israelite Prayer Ritual). Further information is set out by Agata Rybińska in her work 'Krakowskie lata Rozalii Saulson – Mikrohistoria niedokończona' (The Kraków Years of Rozalia Saulson – an Unfinished Microhistory).[185]

Aniela Korngut (1868-1942) was a Jewish feminist writer who wrote under the pen name Aniela Kallas. In 1913 she wrote a novel 'Córki marnotrawne' (Prodigal Daughters) based on the true story of Anna Kluger and her yearning for an academic education, contrary to the more traditional wishes of her parents. Korngut was, herself, among the first generation of Jewish women educated at Polish schools in Galicia. She was a non degree student at the Jagiellonian University before working as a teacher and writer. Some of her plays were performed at the Teatr Ludowy, on the outskirts of Kraków.[186]

Aniela Korngut/Kallas was one of several Jewish women who wrote for the weekly integrationist 'Tygodnik' and other local newspapers in the early part of the 19th century. During this period Helena Hecker wrote for the Zionist monthly, 'Ha'atid' (The Future).[187]

Eugenia Prokop-Janiec notes that Regina Pniowerówna (1863-?) wrote several short stories and dramas for children. She worked at the elementary school for girls and published her works in the Polish-Jewish and Polish press. Professor Prokop-Janiec also mentions three reading rooms which were frequented by young Jewish women at the end of the 19th century. The first of these was the Zionist orientated Ruth Reading Room which was founded in about 1898 by a group which included Antonina Silberfeld, Salomea Bester and Franciszka Glassheit. The second was the Juliusz Słowacki Reading Room for Women. The founders of this second room included Jewish women from assimilationist circles, such as Malwina Garfeinowa-Garska (1870-1932). The third reading room mentioned by Eugenia Prokop-Janiec is Czytelnia Towarzyska (the Social Reading Room) which was established in 1912. Additionally, the author describes the involvement of Jewish women such as Maria Feldman (nèe Kleinman) in the progressive and feminist journal, 'Krytyka'.[188]

---

[185] Agata Rybińska, 'Krakowskie lata Rozalii Saulson; Mikrohistoria niedokończona' (Kraków at the Time of Rozali Saulson) in Alicja Maślak-Maciejewska (Ed), 'Żydzi krakowscy; nowe kierunki badań'; Austeria 2021 and see Wikipedia wolna encyklopedia entry
[186] Eugenia Prokop-Janiec, 'Mapping Modern Jewish Kraków', pages 195-197. See also Rachel Manekin, 'The Rebellion of the Daughters', pages 176-181
[187] Eugenia Prokop-Janiec, 'Mapping Modern Jewish Kraków', pages 195-197
[188] Eugenia Prokop-Janiec, 'Mapping Modern Jewish Kraków', pages 194 and 198

Marriage and divorce

The interaction between the religious and civil aspects of marriage and divorce are described by Rachel Manekin in her article 'The Laws of Moses and the Laws of the Emperor'.[189] A main theme of the author is that well into the nineteenth century, Jews did not comply with the secular law relating to the registration of marriages. Often, the children of unregistered marriages carried their mother's last name and were considered illegitimate under Austrian law. At this time marriages arranged by parents, sometimes with the aid of marriage brokers, were still common.

Marek Minakowski and Anna Lebet-Minakowska have considered delays in registering marriages with the civil authorities in relation to the Jewish community of Kraków in particular.[190] They conclude that in some cases, marriages were registered several years after children were born, and in other cases marriages were not registered with the secular authorities at all. The complete failure to register in some cases may seem surprising in view of the extensive nature of marriage records which are available to genealogists and other researchers.

Dan Hirschberg is another researcher into nineteenth century marriage records for the Jewish community of Kraków. He has considered 4,208 marriages in the period 1798 to 1888 for which both partners' ages have been extracted, summarised at https://www.ics.uci.edu/~dan/genealogy/Krakow/analysis.html

Piotr Zbigniew Pomianowski notes that in Kraków the civil authorities kept divorce records separately for Christians and Jews from 1810. He notes, however, that the Jewish records have not been organised yet. In any event, Jewish couples who were late in registering their marriages, or who did not register them at all with the secular authorities were unlikely to have registered their divorces.[191]

The failure or delay in registering Jewish marriages with the civil authorities is discussed by Zdzisław Zarzycki. Additionally, he notes that under the General Austrian Civil Code of Law of 1811 (which remained in force until 1945), divorce in Jewish marriage could be initiated in two ways – by the voluntary uncontested request of both spouses, or by way of divorce application filed by the husband. Both procedures involved the husband presenting the wife with a bill of divorce.[192] The civil procedures therefore mirrored the religious procedure in that a woman could not obtain a divorce without her husband's consent or 'release'.

---

[189] Rachel Manekin, 'The Laws of Moses and the Laws of the Emperor; Austrian Marriage Legislation and the Jews of Galicia' in 'Polin', vol 33, Littman, 2017, pages 248-251
[190] Marek Jerzy Minakowski and Anna Lebet-Minakowska, 'Jewish Birth and Marriage Registrations in 19th Century Cracow and What They Reveal about the Dynamics of Ritual Marriage' in 'Poland's Demographic Past', vol 40, 2018
[191] Piotr Zbigniew Pomianowski, 'The number of divorces adjudicated on Polish soil under the Napoleonic Code'; Czasopismo Prawno Historyczne, Tom LXXII, 2020
[192] Zdzisław Zarzycki, 'Post Austrian Divorce Law in Małopolska from 1918 to 1945. Selected Issues'; Krakowskie Studia z Historii Państwa i Prawa, 2019.

Orphanages

A Jewish orphanage, Beth Megadle Jesomim, which was established in Kraków during the nineteenth century is described in some detail by Martyna Grądzka in her bilingual (Polish and English) book 'A Broken Childhood'.[193] Although the book is devoted primarily to the Holocaust period, the first chapter describes the formation and early development of the orphanage, and demonstrates the leading role taken by women. For example, the author notes that in the mid nineteenth century the Women's Society for the Protection of Israelite Orphans – Der Krakauer Israelitischer Frauen-Verein der Israelitischen Waisen – was formed by the wives of influential and wealthy Jews living in Kazimierz. Cerka Goldgart was one of the early leaders, being in charge for over a decade. The orphanage occupied premises on Bawół Square and then Ester Street, before moving to 64 Dietla Street in the early 1870's. The orphanage was led in that decade and the following one by Maria Schreiber (1822-1892), the wife of the Kraków Rabbi, Simon Schreiber.[194] Shortly after the turn of the century Debora (Dora) Fränkel was in charge of it.[195]

Ognisko Pracy (literally 'work focus') was established in 1916 to alleviate the plight of Jewish orphaned girls. The founders included Helena Berggrün, a child welfare activist in Chrzanów as well as Kraków, and her daughter Eliza Fraenkel (Fränkel). Others who took leading roles in the institution included Gustawa Lindenbaum and Jadwiga Falter. The group organised courses in sewing and dressmaking for war orphans in 1917.[196]

Political activities

The fact that female participation in politics was, at best, severely restricted in Austrian Poland may be obvious to some but may need to be emphasised to others. This is because at first sight some modern historians appear to give the contrary impression. For example, in his book 'The Jews of Eastern Europe, 1772-1881' Israel Bartal describes the effects of the Austro-Hungarian Compromise of 1867 (the Ausgleich) stating, 'The participation of all of the inhabitants of the state in the general elections was an unheard-of innovation in Eastern Europe. The equal rights of the Jews of Galicia within the overall reform of the Austrian kingdom gave them a new type of political power in the elections to the parliament'.[197]

Israel Bartal is a learned professor at the Hebrew University in Jerusalem. Nevertheless, by referring to 'all the inhabitants of the state' and 'the Jews of Galicia' he seems to be considering only the men. The Ausgleich did not introduce votes for women, as is made clear in three sources which are mentioned by way of example. The first is Dobrochna Kałwa's paper 'Uneven Roads to Gender Equality; The

---

[193] Martyna Grądzka, 'A Broken Childhhood; The Fate of the Children from the Jewish Orphanage at 64 Dietla Street in Cracow during the German Occupation'; Wydawnictwo Wysoki Zamek, Kraków, 2012, see particularly chapter 1
[194] Sean Martin, 'Future Generations; Associations for Jewish Children in Kraków' in 'Polin' vol 23, Littman, Oxford, 2011, page 295
[195] Martyna Grądzka, 'A Broken Childhood', page 267
[196] Sean Martin, 'Future Generations; Associations for Jewish Children in Kraków' in Michał Galas and Antony Polonsky (Eds), 'Polin', vol 23; Littman, Oxford, 2011, page 307
[197] Israel Bartal, 'The Jews of Eastern Europe, 1772-1881'; University of Pennsylvania Press, Philadelphia, PA, 2005, page 130

Situation of Women in the Second Polish Republic',[198] the second is 'Women's Suffrage in Austria; An Overview' by Hannes Richter,[199] and the third is Maureen Healey's 'Becoming Austrian; Women, the State and Citizenship in World War One' which is available at https://www.jstor.org/stable/4547145 These three sources make it clear that women's suffrage was not introduced into Austria until after the First World War, by which time Kraków was part of the Second Polish Republic. In the interests of balance, it should also be stated that according to Hannes Richter, universal suffrage for men was not achieved in Austria until 1907.

In fairness to Professor Bartal, he is not the only modern author who appears to have apparently ignored women in considering the impact of the Ausgleich. In her short book 'The Architects of Modern Kraków', Anna Jodłowiec-Dziedzic writes about the 1867 Constitution saying 'For Jews this meant, amongst others, a free choice of the place of residence, full right of ownership, unconstrained activities in the fields of economy, politics, education and science, as well as in the public domain, and access to numerous professions'.[200] It is true that the book includes a photograph of a woman 'in a voting room', but the photo was taken in 1938 and all the officials who appear in the photo are men, and the book as a whole is dominated by men.

The Jewish Social Democratic Party (Żydowska Partia Socjalno-Demokratyczna) operated in Galicia from 1905 until 1920. It was established as a result of a split from the Polish Social Democratic Party of Galicia, and it held inaugural May Day rallies in Kraków and other cities. The party, along with Poale Zion was active in Kraków and 'for two decades prior to the outbreak of the First World War, Cracow was the principal center of the Jewish Labor Movement in Poland'. However, women seem to have been conspicuous by their absence from the movement's leadership in the city.[201]

For many Jewish men, the benefits of the Ausgleich were probably more theoretical than practical; for Jewish women many were not available even in theory until the early part of the twentieth century. Indeed, Anna Jodłowiec-Dziedzic recognises this because later on in her work, when describing the Municipal Government of Kraków she states 'the active voting right belonged to men of a specified property qualification'. She then names a number of Jewish councillors, and Jewish leaders in the Kraków Chamber of Commerce and Industry, and the Municipal Savings Bank in the period leading up to the Second World War. They

---

[198] In Michał Niezabitowski and others (Eds), 'Is War Men's Business? Fates of Women in Occupied Kraków in Twelve Scenes'; Muzeum Historyczne Miasta Krakowa, Kraków, 2011
[199] www.austria.org and search for 'women'.
[200] Anna Jodłowiec-Dziedzic, 'The Architects of Modern Kraków; Jews in the Municipal, Economic, and Finance Authorities in the City, 1866-1939'; Muzeum Historyczne Miasta Krakowa, Kraków, 2014, pages 15 and 16
[201] Arye Gelbard, 'Cracow and the beginning of the Jewish Labour Movement in Poland' in Elchanan Reiner (Ed) 'Kroke-Kazimierz-Cracow; Studies in the History of Cracow Jewry', Tel Aviv University, 2001. See also
https://yivoencyclopedia.org/article.aspx/Zydowska_Partia_Socjalno-Demokratyczna and Wikipedia entries for 'Jewish Social Democratic Party' and 'Poale Zion'

were all men. One of the Jewish councillors, though, Adolf Gross (1862-1936) was an advocate of women's emancipation.[202]

Jewish participation on the Kraków Municipal Council during the nineteenth century and the early twentieth century is the subject of a detailed book 'Politycy czy klakierzy?' (a title which does not translate readily into English) written by Hanna Kozińska-Witt. The book includes a list of Jewish councillors who served in the period 1866 to 1914. They are all men.[203] A chapter on substantially the same subject and by the same author appears in English in volume 34 of 'Polin', published in 2022.

Again, in the interest of balance, it should also be stated that before the Second World War women were largely excluded from politics in Jewish and non Jewish communities well beyond Kraków.

Despite what has been said, Anna Jodłowiec-Dziedzic does identify one area of life in which Jewish women in Kraków had voting rights before the end of the nineteenth century. She points out that, under the 1897 constitution of the Kraków Jewish community, women were granted active voting rights, although they had to cast their votes by proxy. Surprisingly, women's suffrage was removed from communal elections by changes introduced in 1926.[204]

Female membership of the Progressive Congregation in Kraków is mentioned in the following section headed 'Religious observance'. It appears female members of that congregation had voting rights which were the same as those of the male majority.

Professional lives

In the earlier section relating to the Jagiellonian University, it has already been noted that further education was generally closed to women in the 'Austrian' period, subject to the possible exception of midwifery. It is therefore difficult to find references to women who were engaged in those professions such as the law and medicine which required a university education. For example, Bartosz Heskel's detailed book about Jewish lawyers in Kraków[205] does not list any females who were in practice before the First World War. This is unsurprising since, as noted above, women could not study law at the Jagiellonian University until 1918.

The following words are taken from Aleksander Skotnicki and Władysław Klimczak (Ed), 'Jewish Society in Poland; Many Faces of Cracovian Jewry' which was published in 2009 in which gives a description of the Jewish Hospital

---

[202] Andrzej Nowakowski (Ed), 'Blow Up; The New Jewish Cemetery in Kraków'; Universitas, Kraków, 2006, page 182. See also Agnieszka Kutylak (Ed), 'Krakowianie; Wybitni Żydzi krakowscy XIV-XX w'; Muzeum Historyczne Miasta Krakowa, Kraków, 2006, pages 42-44

[203] Hanna Kozińska-Witt, 'Politycy czy klakierzy? Żydzi w krakowskiej radzie miejskiej w XIX wieku'; (Jews on the Kraków City Council); Wydawnictwo Uniwersytetu Jagiellońskiego, Kraków, 2019, pages 97 and 98

[204] Anna Jodłowiec-Dzidzic, 'The Architects of Modern Kraków', page 17

[205] Bartosz Heskel, 'Żydowscy adwokaci w przedwojennym Krakowie' (Jewish Lawyers in Pre-war Kraków); EMG, Kraków, 2020

'In 1900 there were four independent wards [one of which was gynaecological] … There was from seven to nine doctors employed. Many acknowledged doctors worked for the hospital including … the only woman, Dr Irena Korngold'.

No further information is given about Dr Korngold and it appears that the comments regarding the doctors, as opposed to the wards, relate to a period after 1900, particularly since the information is given in a chapter headed 'Jewish Society in Kraków during the Interwar Years.'

In her paper about the professional lives of women in Kraków during the second half of the 19th century, Lidia Zyblikiewicz has extracted information from the censuses of 1869, 1880 and 1890. The paper includes a section headed 'The Professional Activity of Women according to Religion' and one of the author's conclusions is that 'only' a quarter of professionally active women were Jewish. Despite the use of the word 'only' this seems a high proportion taking into account the restrictions on female further education in the Jewish community, created by the university as well as by religious tradition.[206]

Property (realty) and other assets

Reference has been made in an earlier chapter to an eighteenth century document recording the right of a widow to a pension. A further example is the case of Scheindla, widow of Szachna Markusfeld. For many years during the nineteenth century Szachna was a member of the Jewish committee of Kazimierz district. After his death, in 1845 his widow received a lump sum of 300 złoty as an 'honorary wage'.[207]

Arguably, the extent to which women owned land and buildings (realty) in Kraków at the beginning of the nineteenth century can be established by a list of householders that was prepared in 1807 and 1808.[208] The list includes about 200 properties in the Jewish Town (Miasto Żydowskie or Judenstadt) together with the names of householders. Out of the registered owners, it appears that only the following four are female. Ester Goldgürtel (house number 73), Adel Elster, a widow (house 104), Perla Brechsler (176) and Freidle Rosin (178). A quick review of the entries for one of the non Jewish areas, Piasek, shows that women were very much in the minority of householders, but that they accounted for a higher proportion of property ownership than in the Jewish town.

Volume 35 of 'Krzystofory' was published by Muzeum Historyczne Miasta Krakowa in 2017 to mark the 60th anniversary of the opening of a branch of the museum in the Old Synagogue. The work includes, on pages 53-55, an 'Index of People Residing on ul. Szeroka from the End of the 18th Century to the middle of

---

[206] Lidia Zyblikiewicz, 'Aktywność zawodowa kobiet w Krakowie w II połowie XIX wieku' (the Professional Activity of Women in Kraków in the Second Half of the 19th Century'. See https://doaj.org/article/920f008fe59848debb5074ecdd9c20ff

[207] Pawel Jasnowolski, 'A Case Study of Radical Assimilation in Poland; The Markusfeld Family'; Scripta Judaica Cracoviensia, vol 14 (2016), page 118, quoting Majer Bałaban, 'Historja Żydów w Krakowie i na Kazimierzu, 1304-1868', vol II, page 737

[208] Published with Ignace Enderle, 'Plan miasta Krakowa Senacki', sometimes known as the Senate Plan' Muzeum Historyczne Miasta Krakowa, 1959. The list is headed 'Wykaz realnośći'(List of realty) and 'Grundbuch' (Land register)

the 19th'. This lengthy list has been drawn up from sources which include specifications of houses at the end of the 18th century, the list of householders for 1807 and 1808, and mortgage documents for the period of the Free City of Kraków, 1815-1846. Female names are very much in the minority, but include Chana Bünen, Baza Gernreichowa, Ester Goldgürtel, Chaja Herszlowiczowa, Ickowa (wdowa, a widow), Resel Kranikowa, Chana Ledicerowa, Bluma Lewkower, Petra Lichtingowa, Szaba Magerowa, and Hanna Zonnenfeldowa.

House numbers were changed at different times during the nineteenth century and, reflecting one such change, a new address book was published in 1858.[209] This too showed very few female householders in the Jewish district of Kazimierz. It can be mentioned in passing however, that there are separate entries on Izaak Platz/Plac Izaka for the women's and men's sections of the Izaak Synagogue, Izaak Bethaus für Frauen being at building number 167, and für Männer at number 168.

It was only toward the latter part of the nineteenth century that we can identify women as less rarely owners of property and other assets. For example, by reference to a list dated 1887 which can be viewed at http://minakowski.pl/wlasciciele-domow-na-Kazimierzu-1861-i-1887/ . By that time some women owned not only land and buildings but also trading stock (inventories) and other assets which they used in the course of trade. Some indication of this is given by a list of the Jewish community of Kraków dated 1883. The list, on Marek Minakowski's website at http://www.sejm-wielki.pl/najbogatsi_zydzi_krakowa.php, contains the names of over five hundred Jewish individuals, both men and women, who paid a wealth tax of 5 złoty or more. The following four women are listed as paying 15 or 20 złoty:

- Amalia Flinter, dress maker, 20 zł
- Gittel Goldblum, property owner, 15 zł
- Sara Kolländer, house owner, 15 zł
- Rachel Rapaport, property owner, 15 zł

Not only did women form a minority of property owners, they were also in the minority of principal tenants. Thus, at the beginning of the twentieth century there were only 627 Jewish female tenants in Kraków, as opposed to 4,385 Jewish male tenants.

Prostitution

Aleksandra Jakubczak seems to be one of very few historians who have researched the question of Jewish involvement in prostitution and the sex trade. Her book 'Polacy, Żydzi i mit handlu kobietami' (Poles, Jews and the Myth of Trafficking in Women) was published by Warsaw University Press in 2020.[210] It was

---

[209] Uebersicht der Neuen Eintheilung und Gebäude-Nummerirung der Landes Hauptadt Krakau/ Przegląd nowego podziału i oliczbowania domów w główném mieśce krajowem Krakowie, 1858 (An overview of the new Division and Numbering of Houses in the Regional Capital City of Kraków, 1858)

[210] For wider reading, see Agata Dziuban, 'Threats, Victims and Unimaginable Subjects of Rights; A Genealogy of Sex Worker Governance in Poland'; Studies in Social Justice, vol 18, 2024, particularly pages 250, 251 where references are made to Alexandra Jakubczak's work

reviewed by Joanna Sliwa and her review can be found at https://www.h-net.org/reviews/showrev.php?id=56732

Specific references to Kraków are made in Ms Jakubczak's dissertation 'Protecting the Jewish Daughters; Mass Migration, Trafficking, and the Crisis of Traditional Jewish Society, 1880's-1914'. The author notes that at the end of the nineteenth century Jewish women accounted for 29% of the sex workers in Kraków. That is almost exactly the proportion of the Jewish population to the total population of the city as shown by the 1901 census.[211] By the time of the First World War, Jewish organisations fighting trafficking had been established in several Polish cities, including Kraków.

In 1903 an assembly of secular Jewish leaders and European Rabbis was held in Lemberg (Lwów). Like others before and after them, they considered that poor education for girls and the acculturation of young women were two of the causes of widespread immorality. These were themes which were also considered by a Rabbinical conference which was held in Kraków in August, 1903. In due course the issues were to be taken up by Sarah Schenirer, the founder of the Beis Yaakov movement for girls' secondary education. However, according to Aleksandra Jakubczak, the 1903 Rabbinical conference avoided serious discussion of the connection between Jewish prostitution and the faulty education of girls.

Aleksandra Jakubczak is also the author of 'Prostitution in Jewish Galicia; History in a Police Registry'. This is included in the December, 2023 issue of 'The Galitzianer', which is published by the genealogical group, Gesher Galica. The author describes registers maintained by the police in Kraków between 1891 and 1926. An early entry relates to Betti Kiesler, who registered herself as a prostitute around 1899. The author notes that Ms Kiesler was one of about 250 Jewish women who appear in the registers, and that most of the women had come to Kraków in order to work their trade away from their home towns.

Religious observance

It has been noted earlier that in the eighteenth and previous centuries, women had observed their Jewish religious obligations somewhat differently and separately from men. To some extent, this reflected the different roles of men and women, and the fact that women were less well educated than their male counterparts. The nineteenth century saw a significant movement away from this state of affairs as will now be illustrated. This movement was particularly marked in the Reform or Progressive section of the community, which is the subject of a separate sub section in this chapter.

In earlier centuries, the general rule was that Jewish women in Kraków used Yiddish as their day to day language. However, the incorporation of the city into the Austrian province of Galicia saw an increasing use of German, particularly amongst the Progressive and educated population. The second half of the nineteenth century saw an increase in Polish nationalism and the Polonisation of language. At the same time Jewish women became more likely to attend synagogue, and more familiar with

---

[211] Statystyka Miasta Krakowa; Biuro Statystyczne Miejskie, Zeszyt IX, Część II, Table VI, Kraków, 1907 shows the Jewish population accounted for 28.07% of the total

Hebrew, so that by the end of the century books of prayer and devotion in that language, and designed primarily for women, had become well established. One such book was published in Breslau but was used by women in other parts of Poland. It included prayers for Sabbath and the festivals, in the home and at the cemetery. Substantially the whole of the book was published in German, with only a short section in German and Hebrew.[212] Such manuals of private devotion came to be known as 'techinnot'.[213]

Chassidism

There is a Chassidic story that shortly after the Spanish Inquisition a Spanish Jew named Joseph Jospa arrived in Kraków. He was a great scholar and was known as the Spanish Tzaddik. However, he was unmarried at the age of fifty. Thirty years went by until a young businessman from Kraków was killed whilst on a business trip to Prague, leaving a widow with no children. Her husband's brother performed a chalitza ceremony in order to release the widow from the obligation of marrying him in accordance with Deuteronomy (Devorim) Chapter 25. Shortly afterwards the widow married the Spanish Tzaddik and gave birth to a baby who would become Rabbi Elijah Baal Shem, an ancestor of the Baal Shem Tov.[214]

Some centuries later, the Chassidic movement reached Kraków from the east, but little has so far been written about how it impacted upon women in that city. A popular conception may well be that the movement was primarily for men, and it has been stated that 'there is no indication in Chassidic literature that women had any role or importance as actors in this new spiritual path'.[215] This view is supported by Marcin Wodzinski, author of 'Women and Hasidim; A 'Non-Sectarian' Perspective'. Quoting the testimony of Dora Moszkowska, who was born in Kraków in 1901, the author notes 'Women were excluded from services not only when the male Hasidim gathered for prayer in their shtibl but also during domestic celebrations when women were not allowed in the big room while the men were praying and singing'.[216]

It is well recorded that, following the end of the First World War, the educational reformer Sarah Schenirer sought the advice of the Belzer Rebbe before establishing the Bais Ya'akov movement. She was in the room when the Rebbe approved her plans for female education, but the note to the Rebbe (kvitl) was written by her brother rather than Sarah, herself.[217] This is entirely consistent with Marcin Wodzinski's observations as follows:-

---

[212] Jakob Freund, 'Gebet und Andachtsbuch für Israelitische Frauen und Mädchen' (Book of Prayer and Devotion for Jewish Women and Girls); Breslau, first published in 1867, with later editions

[213] See, for example, Norman Tarnor, 'A Book of Jewish Women's Prayers; Translations from the Yiddish'; Jason Aronson, Inc, Northvale NJ, 1995

[214] Various website searches for 'Joseph Jospa Krakow'

[215] Gershon Hundert, 'Jews in Poland Lithuania in the Eighteenth Century'; University of California Press, Los Angeles, CA, 2006, page 203, quoting Ada Rapoport-Albert, 'On Women in Chassidism'.

[216] Marcin Wodzinski, 'Women and Hasidism; A 'Non-Sectarian' Perspective'; Jewish History, 2013, page 411

[217] Pearl Benisch, 'Carry Me in your Heart'; Feldheim Publishers, Jerusalem, 1991, page 28

'At many ... hasidic courts women were entitled to come before the tsadik and even to listen to his personal counsel and receive his blessing, but this does not mean that they participated equally in the experience of pilgrimage to the court.....Only men could fully participate in the pilgrimage and submit their petition to the tsadik. The women on whose behalf they were pleading could take part only when accompanied by male relatives.'[218]

As Ada Rapaport-Albert states in the article which is mentioned below, 'It is clear from all the available evidence that even if they were granted a private audience with the Rebbe the women were never admitted to the all-important sessions at his 'table' where he would deliver his Hasidic teaching to an exclusively male audience'.

The historian Gershon Hundert refers to Chassidic women seeking advice as to how to obtain a husband's release in divorce (agunah), and regarding barrenness. He also refers to anti Chassidic literature which describes 'the Rebbes as shameless exploiters of the naïve'.[219]

A somewhat negative interpretation of Chassidism can be found on the website of the Jewish Women's Archive. In a lengthy article on that site, Ada Rapaport-Albert notes that Chassidism 'has sometimes been depicted as nothing less than a feminist revolution in early modern Judaism', and that it has been claimed, for example, that 'the connection between the Rebbe and the community created an equalizing force between husband and wife'. She argues that the opposite is true, saying that Chassidism has undermined the institution of marriage, for example by 'drawing young men in their early years of marriage away from their wives and children for periods ranging from several weeks to several months or more'.[220]

One of the few favourable accounts of Chassidism given by a woman is the testimony of Sara Rosen in her book 'My Lost World; A Survivor's Tale'. In that work the author writes 'Our family was typical of well established Hassidic families in Galicia. Closely knit, relying on one another for advice, moral and material support...'[221]

Conversions to Christianity

It has been noted in earlier chapters that Jewish conversions to Christianity are by no means only a modern occurrence. The topic was the subject of Rabbinic comment in Kraków in the sixteenth century, and possibly earlier. By the late nineteenth century, significant numbers of Jewish women and girls were being drawn away from traditional orthodox Judaism, not only by the Progressive movement but by such influences as the Enlightenment (Haskalah), secular Zionism and Socialism.

---

[218] Marcin Wodzinski, 'Women and Hasidism: A 'Non-Sectarian' Perspective'; Jewish History, 2013, pages 414 and 415

[219] Gershon Hundert, 'Jews in Poland Lithuania in the Eighteenth Century', page 203

[220] https://jwa.org/encyclopedia/article/hasidism

[221] Sara Rosen, 'My Lost World; A Survivor's Tale'; Vallentine Mitchell, London, 1993, part 1

By 1902, the newspaper Kol Machazikei Hadat, and other elements of the Jewish press in Kraków and elsewhere carried comments and correspondence which described how the secular education of young women was leading them away from religious observance, and even to conversion. Kol Machazikei Hadat went so far as to compare the situation in Galicia to that which had prevailed in Germany a century earlier. Comment related largely to the case of a young Hassidic woman from Kraków, Michalina Araten, who fled from her parents' house to a local convent with the intention of converting and marrying her lover, an army doctor.[222]

The topic of female conversion is the subject of Rachel Manekin's paper, 'The Lost Generation; Education and Female Conversion in *Fin-de-Siècle* Kraków' which is included in volume 18 of 'Polin', 'Jewish Women in Eastern Europe' published by Littman in 2005. In August 2005 an article 'Conversion of Jewish Women in the Convent of Felician Sisters in Cracow from 1873 to 1914' appeared in 'The Galitzianer', the journal of the genealogical group, Gesher Galicia.

Rachel Manekin covers the subject matter in more detail in her book 'The Rebellion of the Daughters'. Professor Manekin notes that in one fifteen year period beginning in 1887 over 300 Jewish women converted in Kraków alone, almost all of them at the convent of the Felician Sisters. Most, but by no means all, of the converts came from small villages around Kraków and the author describes the detailed papers which relate to the conversion of Deborah Lewkowicz, a teenager from the village of Rzeszotary, some nine miles (fourteen kilometres) south of the city. Deborah returned to Judaism shortly after her conversion, but such a return seems to have been an exception.[223] The introduction to the book provides a useful overview of the educational and other influences which led to the conversion of young Jewish women, many of whom came from religious families, in the Kraków area.

The author notes that the National Archive holds detailed files on conversions under the heading 'Pełamocnik do spraw metryk Izraelickich w Krakowie'.

Another source is Justyna Kutrzeba's article 'Jewish Converts in Kraków at the Turn of the 19th and 20th Centuries'. This is included, in Polish, in 'Krzystofory', number 35, published by Muzeum Historyczne Miasta Krakowa in 2017. An English summary states that the author draws information from ecclesiastical and municipal records for the period 1871 to 1911, and that the majority of converts were young unmarried women under 30 years of age. Most, but not all, chose Roman Catholicism as their adopted religion. Like Rachel Manekin, Justyna Kutrzeba refers to the emancipation of women and access to secular education as factors leading to conversion.

The conversion of several members of the Feintuch family is considered by Jacek Purchla in his article 'The Polonization of Jews; Some Examples from Kraków'. This is included in volume 23 of 'Polin'. The Feintuchs, like other families who

---

[222] Rachel Manekin, 'Orthodox Jewry in Kraków at the Turn of the Twentieth Century' in Michał Galas and Antony Polonsky (Eds), 'Polin', vol 23, pages 189, 190. For a more detailed analysis, see Rachel Manekin, 'The Rebellion of the Daughters; Jewish Women Runaways in Habsburg Galicia'; Princeton University Press, Princeton, NJ, 2020, chapter 2
[223] Rachel Manekin, 'The Rebellion of the Daughters', chapter 3

converted such as the Markusfelds and the Blumenstocks, appear to have been drawn away from Judaism not so much out of religious conviction but as a means of social and economic progression. In this way the conversions differed from that of, say Michalina Araten who was motivated by romance. It is also notable that the Feintuch conversions took place in 1848, half a century before those considered by Rachel Manekin. Finally, it can be noted that the Feintuch conversions were to Lutheranism rather than Catholicism. The article by Jacek Purchla includes portraits of three female members of the Feintuch family, all in western or 'modern' clothing. These are Helena (née Ciechanowska), Salomea (née Dattelbaum) and Józefa (née Rosenzweig).[224]

Progressive Judaism

Whereas the Chassidic movement reached Kraków from the east, Progressive Judaism arrived from the opposite direction. In the first two decades of the nineteenth century the Progressive movement introduced confirmation ceremonies for girls, as well as boys, 'in emulation of parallel Christian initiation rites'. As early as 1846, the Breslau Conference of Progressive Rabbis announced that women must enjoy identical obligations and prerogatives in worship and communal affairs as men, although 'this decision had virtually no effect in practice'.[225]

Since the last quarter of the nineteenth century, Progressive Judaism has demonstrated an increased, or at least changed, role for women. One detailed work on the Kraków Progressive community is by Alicja Maślak-Maciejewska. This is a book which includes a whole chapter on the role of women, including their participation in religious life, their prayers, and religious education for girls. As mentioned above in the section headed 'Charities', the book also gives information about the Krakowskiego Stowarzyszenia Kobiet dla Wsparcia Wdów, an association which was established to support widows.[226]

A further feature of Alicja Maślak-Maciejewska's book is that it includes lists of members of the Progressive community for 1885 and the years 1898 to 1912. Furthermore, the names of female members are printed in bold font. The first list includes the names of nine women representing four per cent of the total membership of 218. They are Karolina Fogelstrauch, Goldblum [no first name or initial given], R Judkiewicz, F Kolberg, A Rapaport, Karolina Rapaport, H Tramer, S Wachtel and Weisslitz [no name or initial given].

By contrast, the list for the years 1898 to 1912 includes the names of 63 females, representing nearly ten percent of the total membership. Having said that, perhaps unsurprisingly, a list on the JewishGen website at https://kehilalinks.jewishgen.org/Krakow/kra_jewish_reform.htm reveals that in the early 1870's the Progressive Synagogue did not have any female committee members.

---

[224] Jacek Purchla, 'The Polonization of Jews; Some Examples in Kraków' in Michał Galas and Antony Polonsky (Eds), 'Polin', vol 23; Littman, Oxford, 2011, pages 202-211
[225] Wikipedia entry for 'Reform Judaism'
[226] Alicja Maślak-Maciejewska, 'Modlili się w Templu; Krakowscy Żydzi postępowi w XIX wieku'; Wydawnictwo Uniwersytetu Jagiellońskiego, , Kraków, 2019, Chapter VIII

The Progressive community promoted not only a modern form of Judaism, but also a strong sense of patriotism. For example, in 1911 a memorial in memory of King Kazimierz the Great was installed in the old town hall in Kazimierz. This was funded largely by the progressive Jewish committee, including a women's committee. Members of the committee included the author Aniel Korngut, as well as panie Eibenschütz, Cohn, Rossenberg, Epstein and Propper.[227]

Austeria, based in Kraków and Budapest, publishes a wide range of books relating to Jewish matters. In 2012 it published a book, edited by Michał Galas, entitled 'Synagoga Tempel i środowisko krakowskich Żydów postępowych' (The Tempel Synagogue and the Progressive Jewish Community of Kraków). In one chapter, Sławomir Pastuszka describes the Synagogue's building, and lists information about several stained glass windows in the ladies' gallery and stairwells which were donated in 1894-1895 (and some others donated in 1925). A number of these include inscriptions of the names of women.

Ritual bath (Mikveh) attendance

Several sources relating to the ritual bath on ul. Szeroka have been given in the paper relating to women in Kraków in the early modern period. Particular mention can be made again of Anna Jakimyszyn's book 'Mykwa; Djieje Żydowskie łażni rytualney ul. Szerokiej w Krakowie' which was published by Austeria in 2012.

In relation to the period of the Kraków Republic, the same author describes the mikveh briefly in her book, 'Żydzi krakowscy w dobie Rzeczypospolitej Krakowskiej' (Kraków Jews at the time of the Kraków Republic), also published by Austeria.[228]

Rubenstein, Helena

Helena Rubenstein (1872-1965) made her fortune in cosmetics after she left Kraków at the age of 18. It is worth noting, however, that she was born with the name Chaja to Naftali Hirsz and Gittel Rubenstein. Many commentators note that Chaja was born in a house on Szeroka Street in Kazimierz, but in a lecture given at the Galicia Jewish Museum in 2023, Dr Edyta Gawron showed a birth registration document showing that she was actually born in Podgórze. Having said that, the family moved to Szeroka Street, and other addresses in Kazimierz, shortly after her birth. Chaja's father was a general merchant, selling naphtha and then eggs.[229]

---

[227] Alicja Maślak-Maciejewska, 'Pamięci Kazimierza Wielkiego Żydzi-Polacy – o zapomnianym projekcie budowy pomnika królewskiego na krakowskim Kazimierzu' (In Memory of Casimir the Great) with an abstract in English. See also, by the same author, 'The Layered Meanings of an Unbuilt Monument' in Halina Goldberg (Ed), 'Polish Jewish Culture Beyond the Capital'; Rutgers University Press, New Brunswick, NJ, 2023, chapter 9

[228] Anna Jakimyszyn, 'Żydzi krakowscy w dobie Rzeczypospolitej Krakowskiej'; Austeria, Kraków, 2008, pages 181, 182

[229] Ewa Dąbrowska and Anna Kielczewska (Eds), 'Residents of Jewish Kraków', vol IV, Women, EMG, Kraków, 2021, page 40 and Henryk Halkowski, 'Żydowski Kraków: Legendy i ludzie' (Jewish Kraków. Legends and People); Austeria, Kraków, 2009, pages 307, 308

Dr Gawron notes that the young Ms Rubenstein went to Vienna before emigrating to Australia, and there is some suggestion that she may have left Kraków in order to avoid an arranged marriage.

The life of Helena Rubinstein is the subject of an article in the March, 2023 issue of 'The Galitzianer' which is published by the genealogical group, Gesher Galicia. The author, Kinga Banasik, a curator at the Galicia Jewish Museum, notes 'Rubenstein's story is about the breaking down of social and cultural barriers, about the assimilation of Jews and the emancipation of women, and about the achievement of success through determination and hard work.'

Spa resorts

The diversity of the Jewish community of Kraków in the latter part of the 19th century is illustrated by the fact that, whilst many women were living in religious poverty, others were spending time in fashionable spa towns. Possibly the best known spa town in the Kraków area is Rabka Zdrój some 40 miles (65 km) south of the city but there were and continue to be other spa towns such as Krynicy Zdrój which lies 80 miles (130 km) south east of Kraków.

In accordance with standards of the time, visitors to spa towns were announced in local newspapers. By way of example the following ladies from Kraków were amongst those staying in Krynicy Zdrój during the period from 29 July to 4 August, 1886:

- Rebeka Dreizner, a merchant, with her daughter, Anna, and a servant
- Ludwika Hochstein, a merchant's daughter
- Golde Birnbaum, wife of an industrialist, with three daughters and two servants
- Karolina Fogelstrauch, who is listed above as a member of the progressive synagogue, a merchant's wife with her daughter and governess
- Julia Liban, a person of private means ('prywatna')
- Teresa Geisler, prywatna
- Ryfka Auerbach, a merchant's wife

It seems that kosher food was available at the resort since the guest list also includes Rachel Horowitz, a Rabbi's wife from 'Mielca' (possibly Mielec)[230]

Theatre

Several sources show the extent to which women participated in Yiddish theatre. One such source is 'Teatr Żydowski w Krakowie' which was published by the Jagiellonian University in 1995. The book includes a lengthy names index, and also images of programmes relating to performances in 1887. These show female characters and actors in performances of plays such as 'Der Kartenspieler (The Card Player) and The Dybbuk.

---

[230] www.jbc.bj.uj.edu.pl/Content/99521/PDF/NDIGCZAS002207_1886_013.pdf

A short history of the Yiddish Theatre can be found at
https://sztetl.org.pl/en/towns/k/512-krakow/102-education-and-culture/25493-
jewish-theatre-krakow-prior-1939 This states that in the early days some
performances were directed by Anna Bruch-Mezler, though her name does not
appear in the names index at the back of the book mentioned above. The web page
indicates that Jewish theatrical events in Kraków were irregular during the 19th
century, and that the development of Jewish theatre in the city was inhibited mainly
by the lack of an adequate place to host performances.

Trade and commerce

Reference has been made in earlier chapters to the place of Jewish women in
trade and commerce, particularly as peddlers and market traders. Jewish peddlers
were to be seen in the Kraków area over the course of several centuries, despite the
concerns of the religious authorities at women travelling from village to village, and
door to door, often on their own. Speaking of the nineteenth century, Arnon Rubin
states, 'Amongst Jews [living in Kraków or more precisely Kazimierz] were many
itinerant peddlers buying in the villages from peasants, eggs, skins, horses and pigs
bristles, and selling them cheap clothes, tools [and] haberdashery'.[231]

Nevertheless, the point has been made that little material is available which
describes female economic activity in Kraków compared with the volume of
material that describes roles of men in trade and commerce. As illustrated in the next
section of this chapter, the position is slightly different regarding female occupations
in the town of Wieliczka, but this seems to be due the research of just one author –
who happens to be a woman.

In her book which describes the life of Sarah Schenirer, the Kraków born founder
of the Bais Ya'akov Schools, Leah Zussman relates, 'In Tammuz 5646 [1886],
Golda, the spice merchant and Rivkah, the greengrocer sat at the entrance to their
shops'.[232] It may well be that Golda and Rivkah are fictional characters. However,
they do illustrate that in the Chassidic community at the very least women were
engaged in trade. It is well established that by the latter part of the nineteenth century,
Sarah Schenirer herself worked as a dress maker in order to supplement the family
budget.

Arguably, more information relating to Jewish women should be obtainable from
three types of sources which became available during 'the Austrian period'. These
are;

- Address and trade directories
- Censuses, and
- Registrations of births, marriages and deaths.[233]

---

[231] Eng Arnon Rubin, 'The Rise and Fall of the Jewish Communities in Poland and their
Relics Today', vol 3, District Kraków, Tel Aviv University Press, Tell Aviv, 2009, page 62
[232] Leah Esther Zussman, 'Sara Schenirer; Life Story'; C H Publishing, Jerusalem, 2011,
pages 15 and 16
[233] Further information about these sources can be found in the author's book 'Kraków;
Sources of Information for Jewish Genealogy and History'; JewishGen Press, 2022

During the nineteenth century, there were several changes to the numbering of houses in the Jewish district of Kazimierz. Two such changes took place in 1858 and 1892, and on each occasion, directories were published in order to record these changes.[234] These directories include the names of many women, but they give no information relating to their (or to men's) occupations. A large number of other directories can be viewed at http://genealogyindexer.org and many of those, particularly from the nineteenth century, do give information about trades and occupations. However, these directories do not seem to have been examined yet in any consideration of the role of Jewish women.

The second group of sources which has been mentioned relates to census returns. Censuses were carried out in Poland well before the commencement of 'the Austrian period' and, for example, general statistical information is available from one which was carried out in 1765.[235] However, this has not yet been considered in relation to women's occupations. In any event, as Gershon D Hundert has noted, the census would represent no more than a picture at a particular time, since during the eighteenth century, 'people tended not to engage consistently in one precise category of livelihood'.[236] Furthermore, the detailed returns for Kraków and the surrounding area, which are believed to have been held in Warsaw, are generally understood to have been destroyed during the Second World War.

By contrast some detailed information has survived for censuses which were carried out in and around Kraków from 1790 onwards. Again, no research has been conducted on these early censuses from the perspective of women's occupations, but the following examples may indicate what information is generally available, and what is not available. The examples relate to the Weiskerz family – an ordinary 'working class' family; one which was a long way from being part of the communal elite.

The 1790 census, house number 96, shows the head of the household as Szmul, swicarz (candle maker). However, his wife, Dwora, is shown only as 'żona' (wife) without any occupation, despite her children being adults. Similarly, in the 1795 census, Szmul's son Izaak is shown as a producer of candles and soap but Izaak's wife, Ester, is shown without an occupation, though as the mother of two young children. This is consistent with information about late eighteenth century censuses given by George J Alexander in his book 'Generations' which also shows that occupations were not shown for married women.[237]

---

[234] Przegląd nowego podziału i oliczbowania domów w głowném mieście krajowem Krakowie, 1858 r and Wykaz ulic, placów I właścicieli domów w mieście Krakowie, 1892 (A list of streets, squares and house owners, 1892)

[235] Majer Bałaban, 'Historja Żydów w Krakowie i na Kazimierzu, 1304-1868', Kraków, 1936, chapter 25. See also Shaul Stampfer, 'The 1764 Census of Polish Jewry' in the Annual of Bar Ilan University, Studies in Judaica and Humanities, vol XXIV-XXV, Ramat Gan, 1989

[236] Gershon D Hundert, 'Jews in Poland-Lithuania in the Eighteenth Century'; University of California Press, Los Angeles, CA, 2006, page 53

[237] George J Alexander, 'Generations; A Millennium of Jewish History in Poland from the Earliest Times to the Holocaust told by a Survivor from an Old Kraków Family'; Congress for Jewish Culture, New York, NY, 2008, chapter 13

Likewise, many census returns around the middle of the nineteenth century show the occupation of men, but not of women. By way of example, a return dated 31 December, 1869 shows Rachel Weiskerz, born 1820, as head of her household but with no occupation. Her elder son, Benjamin, born 1847, is shown as a 'mydlarz' (soap maker), but no occupation is shown for the younger son, or the daughters.

On the other hand, there is an entry for 31 December, 1849 which shows Dwojra Weiskerz, born 1781, and listed as a 'przekupka' (market trader) living with her son, Dawid.

One may conclude that the majority of married women did not have occupations outside the home, or that they did not wish to disclose their occupations to the census enumerators. A more accurate conclusion is likely to be that the recording of occupations of women, particularly married women, was not considered important by the enumerators, or was not required by the authorities. Although further research is probably required, it does appear that the census returns do not provide a reliable basis for evaluating women's roles in the economy in the late eighteenth or the early to mid nineteenth century. It can also be noted in passing that at the time of the English census of 1851, the employment of Jewish women in cities such as Liverpool, Manchester and Birmingham, was also under-recorded.[238]

To quote Professor Gershon Hundert again, 'Of course, most participation by women in the economy was not a form of resistance but collaboration with their husbands. It is thus difficult to compute the degree of female commercial and artisanal activities which were accounted as part of their husbands' businesses'.[239] Although this comment was made in relation to the eighteenth century, it would appear to be equally applicable to most of the nineteenth.

A review of early birth, marriage and death registrations leads to the same unhelpful conclusion. For example, in 1813 Izaak son of Szmul married for the second time. The entry states that the groom was Izaak Weiskerz, mydlarz (soap maker) and widower aged 45, the son of Szmul (who was himself the son of Mark/Mordechai) and Dwora (daughter of Izaak). The entry further states that the bride was Dwora aged 28 the widow of Jakob, a blacksmith and merchant. However, no mention is made of the bride's trade or occupation. It can be mentioned in passing that until very recently the situation in the United Kingdom was only a little better from a feminist point of view. A UK marriage certificate did show the 'rank or profession' of both the bride and groom, but additionally it showed that information only for the fathers of the bride and groom, and not their mothers.

Nineteenth century marriage records for the Jewish community of Kraków may be incomplete or unreliable for a second reason. That is because, as described in the earlier section of this chapter headed 'marriage and divorce', couples sometimes delayed registering their religious or 'ritual' marriages with the civil authorities, or failed to do so altogether. As previously noted, this topic is discussed by Marek Jerzy Minakowski and Anna Lebet-Minakowska in their paper 'Jewish Birth and Marriage

---

[238] Alysa Levene, 'Jews in Nineteenth Century Britain; Charity, Community and Religion, 1830-1880'; Bloomsbury, London, 2020, pages 90-93
[239] Gershon D Hundert, 'Jews in Poland-Lithuania in the Eighteenth Century', page 53

Registrations in 19ᵗʰ Century Cracow and What they Reveal about the Dynamics of Ritual Marriage' which is available on line.

Information relating to the occupations of women became significantly more available from the latter part of the nineteenth century. This was due largely to the work of the Kraków municipal office as indicated in the section headed 'Censuses'. For example, the office's publication for 1907, based on the 1901 census, shows the following figures.[240]

	Self employed Independent (samoistni)	Others active in occupations (zawodowo Czynni)	Passive (inni zawodowo bierni)	Totals
Men	3,764	3,339	5,535	12,638
Women	1,211	888	10,933	13,032

The totals include 4,200 men who are described as trading in goods (handel towarami), including 1,2249 self employed, and 4,519 women in the same occupation of whom only 232 were self employed.

Some evidence of female traders in the late nineteenth century and the early twentieth is available from photographic collections. For example, Stanisław Markowski's book 'Krakowski Kazimierz; Dzielnica Żydowska, 1870-1988' shows a number of female market and street vendors.[241] It has to be said, however, that most photographs of the period which have survived are of buildings and street scenes, or of men rather than women.

Wieliczka

The town of Wieliczka is about 10 miles (15 km) to the south east of Kraków. As a tourist destination it is best known for its salt mines. Jewish settlement in Wieliczka was prohibited until the late 1860's but previously there was a Jewish presence in the nearly districts of Klasno and Siercza.[242]

The sources which describe Jewish life in Klasno, Siercza and Wieliczka in the period leading up to the 1860's include very little information about Jewish women. However, Małgorzata Międzobrodzka's excellent book, 'Żydzi w Wieliczce' shows an image of a passport permitting Maria Landsberger of Klasno to travel to Podgórze via Kraków. This document is dated April, 1850 but it is not clear whether the

---

[240] Statystyka miasta Krakowa, Zeszyt IX, Część II', Nakładem gminy miasta Krakowa, 1907, pages 114, 115.
[241] Stanisław Markowski, 'Krakowski Kazimierz; Dzielnica Żydowska, 1870-1988' (Kraków's Kazimierz; The Jewish District); Wydawnictwo Arka, Kraków, 1992, pages 59, 62 and 63. See also Roman Vishniac, 'Polish Jews; A Pictorial Record'; Schocken Books, New York, NY, 1965, photo no 11.
[242] For sources of information relating to Klasno, Siercza and Wieliczka see Geoffrey Weisgard, 'Kraków; Sources of Information for Jewish Genealogy and History'; JewishGen Press, 2022, pages 151, 152, 178 and 187-192

permitted journey was for pleasure, for example to visit family members, or for the purpose of trade.[243]

Małgorzata Międzobrodzka's book also includes a list of Jews in Klasno 'according to an electoral list dated 1870'. Nearly all the names are of men but the list does include a few women. Examples are Baila Herschberger, a trader, and Channe Jentel Brenner, a grain merchant. The author also names other women who were engaged in business in Wieliczka such as Jetta Attermann and Marya Rosenblatt, who were engaged in the alcohol trade, and Blima Königsberger and Golda Perlberger who ran butchers' shops. Shop and market traders in Wieliczka included Malka Bergmann, Anna Armer, Blima Goldschmidt and Fanny Bergmann, whilst Scheindl Glassscheib of Klasno was a supplier of agricultural products.[244]

The education of girls in Wieliczka during the period of Austrian rule is considered in some detail by Małgorzata Międzobrodzka. For example, she lists the names of several Jewish girls who attended the state primary school in 1903/4. These include:

In the second class - Feitsche Goldschmidt, Reisla Grossman, Gusta Grübner, Sara Güttel and Tauba Manne, Ryeka Wachsman, Jentl Weinberger, Joehebet Weinberger, Rachel Weiss, and Lea Wolf.

And in the fourth class – Lea Dembitzer, Chaja Frank, Loria Goldberger, Hana Goldlust, Frimet Grossmann, Deborah Knobloch, Hinda and Beila Kwalwasser, Lea Licht, Sara Seidenfrau, Sala Templer, Feigel Wasserheardt and Marian and Lewsza Weinberger.[245]

After the First World War, Jewish schools were established in Wieliczka by the Tarbut, Tachkimoni and Yavneh movements.[246] However, Rachel Manekin notes that 'most orthodox [parents] sent their daughters to the government schools'.[247] The same author explores this theme in more detail in her book, 'The Rebellion of the Daughters'. In that work, she considers the case of Deborah Lewkowicz who attended the girls' state school in Wieliczka during the 1880's and 1890's before converting to Catholicism, and later returning to Judaism.[248]

Information about Wieliczka in the period prior to the First World War is to be found in a Yizkor (Memorial) Book which was published in Tel Aviv in 1980. One

---

[243] Małgorzata Międzobrodzka, 'Żydzi w Wieliczce'; Wydawnictwo Żyznowski, Siercza, 2022, page 57

[244] Małgorzata Międzobrodzka, 'Żydzi w Wieliczce', pages 224, 225, 227 and 442-444,

[245] Małgorzata Międzobrodzka, 'Żydzi w Wieliczce', pages 192 and 193. Also listed are the fathers' or mothers' names, occupations and addresses

[246] Arnon Rubin, 'The Rise and Fall of the Jewish Communities in Poland and their Reics Today', vol 3, District Kraków, Tel Aviv University Press, Tel Aviv, 2009, page 344.

[247] Rachel Manekin, The Lost Generations: Education and Female Conversion in Fin-de-Siecle Kraków' in 'Polin' vol 18, Oxford, 2005, page 197, note 28. See also Moshe Yahrblum, 'Wieliczka – The Salt City' which forms part of the English section of Shmuel Meiri (Ed), 'Kehilat Wieliczka; Sefer Zikaron'. Tel Aviv, 1980, available at
https://www.jewishgen.org/Yizkor/Wieliczka/Wieliczka.html

[248] Rachel Manekin, 'The Rebellion of the Daughters; Jewish Women Runaways in Habsburg Galicia'; Princeton University Press, Princeton, NJ, 2020, pages 106-108

of the authors notes that in 1905 the town hosted a meeting of the women's charitable group, 'Miriam' at which members heard a lecture on 'Zion versus Uganda'.[249]

[249] Yehoshua Ofer, 'Zionism in Our City in the Second and Third Decade of this Century' in the English section of Shmuel Meiri (Ed), 'Kehilat Wieliczka; Sefer Zikaron', Tel Aviv, 1980, which is available at https://www.jewishgen.org/Yizkor/Wieliczka/Wieliczka.html

THE INTERWAR PERIOD
Uneven roads to gender equality

Introduction

'Uneven Roads to Gender Equality; The Situation of Women in the Second Polish Republic' is the title of a chapter written by Dobrochna Kałwa which is included in a book 'Is War Men's Business?'.[250] Despite the theoretical constitutional changes that took place in the 1860's and the admission of women into the Jagiellonian University at the turn of the twentieth century, the author notes that 'the modern woman came into existence in the years of the First World War'. Following the mass conscription of men, it was the women who became the heads of their families and their roles were changed for ever. As a result of this turning point the position of women 'changed in almost every sphere of life, from the acquisition of political rights, through their presence in the public space and new vocational opportunities to the new fashion which made them throw away the corset, put on a short skirt, and cut their hair short.'

Hopefully, the following sections of this chapter will illustrate how these changes impacted on Jewish women in Kraków.

Art and photography

The independence of the Polish State coincided with a growing independence of Jewish artists and, as noted below in the section headed 'literature', Jewish writers. Both groups, including many women, expressed themselves in the interwar years on a wide range of Jewish and secular topics. From the early part of the 20th century, Jewish women attended art schools in Kraków, including the Free School of Drawing and Painting which was established in 1918.[251]

In 2008 the Kraków City Museum published an exhibition catalogue 'Jewish Artists in Kraków, 1873-1939'.[252] This includes a chapter written by the specialist researcher Natasza Styrna and gives information about a large number of artists who worked or studied in the city. Nearly all of them are men. However, the following three female artists are noted.

Dorota Berlinerblau-Seydenmann (1898-1942), was born in Vienna[253] or Warsaw[254] but studied at the Academy of Fine Arts in Kraków from 1920 until 1924,

---

[250] Dobrochna Kałwa, 'Uneven Roads to Gender Equality; The Situation of Women in the Second Polish Republic' in 'Is War Men's Business? Fates of Women in Occupied Kraków in Twelve Scenes'; Muzeum Historyczne Miasta Krakowa, 2011
[251] Eugenia Prokop-Janiec, 'Mapping Modern Jewish Kraków' in Halina Goldberg (Ed), 'Polish Jewish Culture Beyond the Capital'; Rutgers University Press, New Brunswick, NJ, 2023, page 198
[252] Natasza Styrna, 'Jewish Artists in Kraków'; Muzeum Historyczne Miasta Krakowa, 2008. More generally see Halina Nelken, 'Images of a Lost World; Jewish Motifs in Polish Painting 1770-1945'; I B Tauris, London, 1991
[253] Natasza Styrna, 'Jewish Artists in Kraków', page 212
[254] Ewa Dąbrowska (Ed), 'Jewish Residents of Kraków, vol II, Art and Culture'; EMG, Kraków, 2020, pages 80-85

being one of the first female students there. She then spent some time in Paris. Her works include scenes from Kraków and other landscapes.

Berta (Blima) Grünberg (1912-1993) studied at the Academy of Fine Arts in Kraków from 1931 to 1934 and then also spent some time in Paris. Her works include oil paintings and watercolours, landscapes and still lifes.[255]

Alicja Halicka (1894-1975) was a painter, illustrator and stage designer. She was born in Kraków and studied at the private School of Fine Arts for Women run in the city by Maria Niedzielska. She also spent time in Paris where she died in 1975. Her works included cityscapes showing the Kazimierz district of Kraków.[256]

2009 saw the publication of Natasza Styrna's book, 'Zrzeszenie Żydowskich artystów malarzy i rzeźbiarzy w Krakowie (1931-1939).'[257] This work describes the activities of the Kraków Association of Jewish Artists, Painters and Sculptors. The Association was not the first artists' group to be established in the Jewish community of Kraków but it seems to have been the most successful. Its activities were frequently reported in the Jewish press, particularly Nowy Dziennik, and the Association also published its own periodical, 'Szuka i życie spółczesne' (Art and Modern Life). Natasza Styrna's book gives biographical information about a large number of artists, most of whom are men. However, the following female artists are also included.

Helena Grabschrift (Grabschrift-Taffet) (1896-1992) was born in Tuchów, not far from Tarnów. Her works include 'Podwórko' a yard, apparently in Kazimierz. Natasza Styrna observes, 'She started her artistic education at the end of the 1920's at the Kraków Academy of Fine Arts, and her progress was rated highly. Having finished her studies in the late 1930's she became involved in the city's vibrant Jewish art community, and was one of the most active members of Kraków's Association of Jewish Artists, Painters and Sculptors. Not only did she participate in the Association's exhibitions, presenting her works which aroused much interest, but she also co-organised them. It seems that it was mostly thanks to her effort that the community functioned efficiently until as late as the last months before the war.'[258]

Jadwiga Sperling (Jadwiga Sperling-Cetic) (1906-1978), whose works include 'Portret' (1931) and 'Hucułki' (1935), both of which were reproduced in the journal 'Głos Plastyków'(The Voice of Visual Artists). During her time in Kraków, Jadwiga Sperling belonged to the Association of Visual Arts, 'Zwornik' (Keystone) and her works were exhibited in several cities in Poland.[259]

---

[255] Natasza Styrna, 'Jewish Artists in Kraków', page 221
[256] Natasza Styrna, 'Jewish Artists in Kraków', pages 221, 222
[257] Natasza Styrna, 'Zrzeszenie Żydowskich Artystów Malarzy i Rzeźbiarzy w Krakowie (1931-1939); Wydawnictwo Neriton, Warszawa, 2009
[258] Natasza Styrna, 'Helena Grabschrift-Taffet, a Kraków Artist born in Tuchów'; Folia Historica Cracoviensia, Pontifical University of John Paul II, Kraków, see https://orcid.org/0000-0002-8368-5863 and Natasza Styrna, 'Zrzeszenie Żydowskich Artystów', page 257
[259] Natasza Styrna, 'Zrzeszenie Żydowskich Artystów', page 288 and Wikipedia

Erna Zollmanówna (b. 1906), who pointed portraits and landscapes.[260]

Both of the books which have been mentioned include copies of works created by Jewish artists in the interwar period.

Elsewhere, Natasza Styrna refers to Henryka Kerner, who was educated in Vienna but was one of eleven women who belonged to Kraków's Association of Jewish Artists, being described as 'one of the most interesting artistic personalities in the group'. She exhibited several of her works in the city during the 1930's.[261]

Maria Zentara notes that Erna Rosenstein was born in 1913 in Lwów. She studied in Vienna between 1932 and 1934, and then Academy of Fine Arts in Kraków under the direction of Wojciech Weiss. She was associated with the surrealist movement, and more particularly with the leftist First Kraków Group. In 1937 she took a short trip to Paris. She survived the Holocaust, hiding under various aliases and, post war, she co-founded the Second Kraków Group of artists. She is one of three artists whose works are described in a book 'Holocaust Survivors; Jonah Stern, Erna Rosenstein and Artur Nacht-Samborski'.[262]

The fourth volume in the 'Residents of Jewish Kraków' series[263] is devoted to women. Reference is made in that work to the following, in addition to Alicja Halicka and Berta (Blima) Grünberg:-

Elza Sare (1882-1957), daughter of Celina and Józef, the architect, a collector and lover of art and a great benefactress of the National Museum in Kraków.

Maria Fromowicz (1897-1974) who in the academic year 1919/1920 was one of the first female students to study painting at the Academy of Fine Arts in Kraków. She was an artist whose works were exhibited in Kraków and internationally in the interwar period, and who made puppets which were used in performances at the Yiddish Theatre in Kraków.[264]

Henryka Fromowicz-Stiller (1894-1942), an art historian and journalist, as well as being an advocate of votes for women. She was art critic for the Nowy Dziennik newspaper – the only Jewish daily in Kraków – and for Głos Kobiety Żydowskiej' (Jewish Women's Voice). Between 1937 and 1939 she worked as publisher and editor of a bi-weekly paper for children and youth called 'Okienko na świat' (Window to the World). Her significant involvement in the Jewish press in the

[260] Natasza Styrna, 'Zrzeszenie Żydowskich Artystów', page 295
[261] Wikipedia and Natasza Styrna, 'Malarki, rzeźbiarki i graficzki z krakowskiego Zrzeszenia Żydowskich Artystów (1931-1939)/ Women Painters, Sculptors and Graphic Artists from the Kraków Association of Jewish Artists (1931- 1939)
[262] Maria Zentara, 'Holocaust Survivors: Jonasz Stern, Erna Rosenstein, Artur Nacht-Samborski'; Muzeum Historyczne Miasta Krakowa, Kraków, 2012. See also Wikipedia and Natasza Styrna, 'Jewish Artists in Kraków, 1873-1939' pages 29 and 30, and Natasza Stern, 'Zrzeszenie Żydowskich Artystów Malarzy i Rzeźbiarzy w Krakowie', page 135, note 337 as well as https://culture.pl/en/artist/erna-rosenstein
[263] Ewa Dąbrowska and Anna Kielczewska (Eds), 'Residents of Jewish Kraków, vol IV, Women': Wydawca EMG, Kraków, 2021
[264] Jan Michalik and Eugenia Prokop-Janiec (Eds), 'Teatr Żydowski w Krakowie'; Uniwersytet Jagielloński, Kraków, 1995, page 113. See also Czesław Brzoza, 'Żydzi Krakowa międzywojennego; kalendarium'; Historia Iagellonica, Kraków, 2018, page 66

interwar period is reflected in Czesław Broza's lengthy book, 'Żydzi Krakowa międzywojennego; Kalendarium' (The Jews of Interwar Kraków; Calendar) which reproduces extracts from Nowy Dziennik and several other interwar newspapers.[265] Further information about Henryka Fromowicz-Stiller is given in the section which follows under the heading 'literature'.

The website at https://kehilalinks.jewishgen.org/krakow/kra_notables.htm lists Fryda Fenich and Mala Schmarcek as 'painters and sculptors', whilst other sources mention the following:-

Margaret Michaelis-Sachs (1902-1985), a Jewish photographer who was born in Bielsko and who studied photography in Vienna. She is noted for her images of the Jewish quarter in Kraków in the 1930's, including scenes from the Jewish market.[266]

Helena Lustgarten-Ogrodzka (1876-1958), a painter, ethnographer and collector of folk art. In the interwar period she donated many of her pieces to the Ethnographic Museum in Kraków and she worked there as a curator in the early 1950's.[267] Salomea Eibenschutz (née Oppenheim) and Helena Lauer (née Eibenschutz) were further examples of female collectors who supported art exhibitions in Kraków in the interwar period.

In the following section headed 'Trade and commerce' reference is made to women in the Aleksandrowicz family who ran a successful business selling art supplies.

Charitable and social organisations

As noted in a previous chapter, charity is a central feature of Judaism, as it is of other religions. Sean Martin notes that by the interwar period a large number of charitable organisations had been established in Kraków and each of these was registered with the police. Some charities were engaged in the running of orphanages, which are the subject of a separate section in this chapter, whilst nine registered charities were exclusively women's organisations. Of these, four were purely charitable, a further two were devoted to the support of working women and three were specifically nationalist in orientation. The author points out that these numbers were very small compared with the total number of Jewish charities and other associations in Kraków in the period between the wars.[268]

Czesław Brzoza includes a section on 'Wspomożenie kobiet i dzieci' (Aid for women and children) in his account of the Kraków Jewish community during the interwar period. He refers to groups such as 'Tomchej Kala' and Stowarzyszenie

---

[265] Czesław Brzoza, 'Żydzi Krakowa międzywojennego; kalendarium'; Historia Iagellonica, Kraków, 2018 see names index
[266] Wikipedia
[267] Ewa Dąbrowska (Ed), 'Residents of Jewish Kraków', vol I, EMG Publishers, Kraków, 2019, page 32 and vol V, 2022, page 100
[268] Sean Martin, 'Jewish Life in Cracow, 1918-1939'; Vallentine Mitchell, London, 2004, page 197

Kobiet Żydowskich (The Association of Jewish Women), as well as the work of Rebbetzin (Rabbi's wife) Breindel Blanka Kornitzer.[269]

A list of Jewish Associations in Kraków in 1939 is given by Aniela Kielbicka in her paper 'The Liquidation of the Jewish Associations in Cracow during the Nazi Occupation' published by Yad Vashem in 1986. The list includes 'The Late Karolina Horowitz Society for the Supply of Clothes and Shoes to Needy Pupils' and 'Maria Frenkel's Convalescent Home for Children in Rabka'.

The theme of women's charities is considered by Bogusław Czaecka in his paper, 'The Activities of Jewish Women's Associations (Professional, Educational and Charitable) in Cracow in the Years 1869-1939'.[270]

February, 1927 saw the establishment of 'Tymczasowy Zarząd Związku Kobiet Żydowskich' (The Provisional Council of the Union of Jewish Women) at the 'Tel Awiw' club in Kraków. The officers and members of the Council were Regina Zimmermann, Laura Tigner, Nella Rost, Mala Süsskind, Golda (Gusta) Lindenbaum, Sara Berkelhammer, Selmanowicz, Dora Gross, Paulina Buchweitz, Nina Szmulewicz, Malwina Kleinberżank, and Maria Fink.[271]

The Menachem Avelim Gemilat Chassidim Synagogue at ul. Stroma, 9 was one of several places of worship in the Podgórze district. In 1936 a plaque was unveiled there in memory of Amelia (Malka) Wassserberger (1869-1936). She was a well known philanthropist who donated a house at ul. Krakusa, 8 for use by the Jewish Orphans' Home Association.[272]

A few lists of charity donors are available on the JewishGen kehilalinks website. For example, donors in 1924 to the 'Beth Lechem' charity, established to support Jews in Palestine, are listed at

www.kehilalinks.jewishgen.org/krakow/kra_betlech1924.htm and

www.kehilalinks.jewishgen.org/krakow/kra_betlechdonor1924.htm

The vast majority of the donors were men, but a significant number of women are listed. For example, Bracia Wachs is shown as donating the relatively large sum of 30 zloty.

Education – schools

The following paragraphs relate to schools, the majority of which provided education only to girls and young women, It should be borne in mind, however, that many females attended co-educational establishments. Many of these are described

---

[269] Edyta Gawron and Michał Galas (Eds), 'Nie tylko Kroke; Historia Żydów krakowskich'; Wydawnictwo Literackie, Kraków, 2022, pages 287 and 288

[270] In Krzystof Pilarczyk (Ed), 'Jews and Judaism in Contemporary Polish Research', Kraków, 1997

[271] Czesław Brzoza, 'Żydzi Krakowa międzywojennego; kalendarium'; Historia Iagellonica, Kraków, 2018, page 240

[272] Teresa Leśniak (Ed), 'Świat przed katastrofą/ A World Before a Catastrophe'; International Cultural Centre Kraków, 2007, page 119

in 'A History of Jewish Education in Kraków' which is available at www.academia.edu/33768075

Bais Ya'akov

Arguably, more has been written about Sarah Schenirer (1883-1935) than any other female Jewish resident of Kraków. As Wikipedia puts it, 'she was a pioneer of Jewish education for girls and began a change in the way women were perceived in Orthodox Judaism. In 1917 she founded the Bais Ya'akov school network....' Some information about her immediate family is given below in a separate section of this chapter.

The young Sarah attended a secular state school even though she was born into an orthodox Chassidic family. This was by no means exceptional. On the contrary, by 1885 the majority of Jewish children in Kraków were attending schools in the state (public) sector.[273]

The issue of orthodox girls attending secular schools is considered by Rachel Manekin in her article 'Orthodox Jewry in Kraków at the Turn of the Twentieth Century'.[274] Such attendance was strongly opposed by local Rabbis who noted that the religious education of young women was being sacrificed. There were some recorded instances of women marrying out of Judaism or even entering prostitution. Nevertheless, many orthodox parents considered Catholic secondary schools to be suitably conservative institutions where attendance was a status symbol. Professor Manekin considers these matters in more detail in her book 'The Rebellion of the Daughters'.[275] The response of Sarah Schenirer to these issues and the development of the Bais Ya'akov movement are described in chapter 6 of the book, 'Bringing the Daughters Back; A New Model of Female Orthodox Jewish Education'.[276]

Various sources relate in greater or lesser detail that as she grew older, Sarah Schenirer became increasingly concerned that a lack of formalised religious education for girls was a major factor in their becoming less observant. Many orthodox authorities of the time were opposed to formal instruction for girls and young women. Yet, despite this opposition, Sarah persuaded the Belzer Rebbe, a senior leader in the Chassidic movement, and members of the orthodox Agudas Yisroel movement to support the establishment of a religious girls' school in Kraków. Additionally, she had the support of Rebbetzin Chaya Fradel Halberstam, a granddaughter of the founder of the Sandz Chassidic dynasty.[277] The school, and the associated teachers' seminary in Kraków ultimately formed the basis of the Bais

---

[273] Sean Martin, 'Jewish Life in Cracow, 1918-1939'; page 159 quoting Andrzej Żbikowski, 'Żydzi Krakowscy i ich gmina w latach 1869-1919'; Żydowski Instytut Historyczne w Polsce, Warsaw, 1994, page 249
[274] 'Polin' vol 23, Littman, Oxford, 2011, pages 189-192, 'The Education of Women'. Regarding the Polonisation of Hasidic girls and young women see also Gershon Bacon, 'Poland; Interwar' on the website of the Jewish Women's Alliance at https://jwa.org/encyclopedia/article/poland-interwar
[275] Rachel Manekin, 'The Rebellion of the Daughters; Jewish Women Runaways in Habsburg Galicia'; Princeton University Press, Princeton, NJ, 2020
[276] For a brief description of the Bais Ya'akov schools, see Sean Martin, Jewish Life in Cracow, 1919-1939'; pages 179-182
[277] Rachel Manekin, 'The Rebellion of the Daughters', page 200

Ya'akov network of schools which is now spread throughout the orthodox Jewish world.

It appears that, as a woman, Sarah did not have direct access to the Belzer Rebbe. On the contrary, it was her brother who wrote the 'kvitl' (request or note) to the Rebbe and had the audience with him. It seems that Sarah was only an observer in the room at the time of the audience.[278]

Hinda and Devorah Birenbaum were amongst the first pupils of Sarah Schenirer. Devorah's report card shows grades in the following subjects;- ethics, diligence, religion, blessings, prayer, translating, Yiddish and German readings, and Jewish history. Devorah emigrated to Palestine in 1934. Her older sister, Hinda, married in 1925. Her husband eventually became Av Beis Din (Head of the Religious Court) in Tel Aviv.[279]

Reizel Nechama Dym was another student of Sarah Schenirer. She was born in Kraków in 1917 into a Chassidic family. Her father, Yehuda Dym, gave over the first floor of his house to be used as the Beltzer shtiebel (small prayer room), and during the Holocaust the Belzer Rebbe stayed with the family. Reizel married Chaim Shmuel Wohlhendler in 1940. Both Reizel and Chaim survived the war and emigrated to New York. Reizel died in April, 2022 at the age of 104.[280]

Most articles regarding Sarah Schenirer and the Bais Ya'akov movement are based on 'internal sources' such as promotional literature and the movement's journal. By contrast, Rachel Manekin's piece, 'The Cracow Bais Ya'akov Teachers' Seminary and Sarah Schenirer; A View from a Seminarian's Diary'[281] is based largely on a diary which was written by Bracha Levin. Ms Levin was a Polish Lithuanian student who attended the Kraków seminary in 1929 and 1930. Ester Goldstoff and Chana Grossfeld were amongst the teachers at the seminary.[282]

Many other articles and books have been written about Sarah Schenirer and her legacy, but just some examples will be given here. The first source is the website of the Jewish Women's Archive, a group which according to its website at www.jwa.org has a mission which 'documents Jewish women's stories, elevates their voices and inspires them to be agents of change'. The site includes at least four relevant articles. One of these is written by Dr. Deborah Weissman, who is an eminent specialist in the history of the education of Jewish girls and young Jewish women. Her article, which is at https://jwa.org/encyclopedia/article/schenirer-sarah summarises Sarah Shenirer's life, the establishment and development of Bais Ya'akov, and her legacy. These themes are developed in a second paper by Deborah Weissman and Lauren Granite at https://jwa.org/encyclopedia/article/bais-yaakov-schools A third article on a related topic, written by Gershon Bacon, which is at https://jwa.org/encyclopedia/article/agudat-israel-interwar-poland describes the role

---

[278] Pearl Benisch, 'Carry Me in Your Heart; The Life and Legacy of Sarah Schenirer'; Feldheim, Jerusalem, pages 27, 28 and Rachel Manekin, 'The Rebellion of the Daughters', page 199

[279] Pearl Benisch, Carry Me in Your Heart', pages 33-39, and Rachel Manekin, 'The Rebellion of the Daughters', pages 200 and 201

[280] https://vinnews.com/2022/04/28/sara-schenirers-last-known-living-student-dies-at-104/

[281] Jewish Quarterly Review, vol 112, no 2; University of Pennsylvania Press, 2022

[282] https://kehilalinks.jewishgen.org/krakow/kra_notables.htm

of Agudat Israel (Agudas Yisroel) in the development of Bais Ya'akov. A fourth article on the JWA website is by Elie Klibaner-Schill and is available at https://jwa.org/blog/risingvoices/tracing-roots-jewish-womens-education.

One of Dr Weissman's works which is not on the site of the Jewish Women's Archive is her paper 'Bais Ya'akov; A Historical Model for Jewish Feminists'.[283] In this paper the author argues that the motivation for orthodox girls to attend secular schools was mainly economic, to enable girls to obtain vocational training, and learn skills that 'would help them in business dealings with non-Jews'.

Reference can be made to the same author's doctoral thesis, 'Bais Ya'akov; A Woman's Educational Movement in the Polish Jewish Community; A Case Study in Tradition and Modernity' which was published by New York University in 1984. Yet another work by Dr Weissman is 'Bais Ya'akov as an Innovation in Jewish Women's Education; A Contribution to the Study of Education and Social Change'.[284] Finally, in relation to Dr Weissman, a further reference can be made to https://jwa.org/encyclopedia/author/weissman-deborah which is another article on the website of the Jewish Women's Archive.

Readers can also refer to the website of the Jewish Orthodox Feminist Alliance at https://www.jofa.org where there are two articles about Sarah Schenirer and the Bais Ya'akov schools. According to the site, the Alliance 'advocates for expanding women's rights and opportunities within the framework of halacha to build a vibrant and equitable Orthodox community'.

Naomi Seidman is another researcher who has written extensively about Sarah Schenirer and the Bais Ya'akov movement. Two of her articles are on the website of the Jewish Women's Archive at https://jwa.org/encyclopedia/author/seidman-naomi. Another of her works which has been posted on to the academia.edu site (reference 138209330) and various other sites is entitled 'Legitimising the Revolution; Sarah Schenirer and the Rhetoric of Torah Study for Girls'. Professor Seidman is also the author of a book 'Sarah Schenirer and the Bais Ya'akov Movement; A Revolution in the Name of Tradition', which was published by Littman in 2019. The book, which was reviewed by three authors in the Shofar Journal,[285] and no doubt elsewhere, explores the Bais Ya'akov movement through the tensions that characterised it, including the impact of socialism, feminism, Zionism and Polish electoral politics. The book includes selections from Sarah Schenirer's writings which have not previously been published in English.

A further, shorter work by Professor Seidman is 'A Revolution in the Name of Tradition; Orthodoxy and Torah Study for Girls'. This appears as a chapter in volume 30 of 'Polin' which was published by Littman in 2018 and is devoted to Jewish Education in Eastern Europe.

Whilst references have already been made to the Jewish Feminist Alliance, mention should also be made of another organisation which supports Orthodox

---

[283] In Elizabeth Koltun (Ed), 'The Jewish Woman; New Perspectives'; Schoken Books, New York, NY, 1976
[284] In Studies in Jewish Education, 7 (1995), as listed in 'Polin' vol 18, pages 302 and 303
[285] Shofar Journal, vol 38.1; Purdue University Press, West Lafayette, IN, 2020

Jewish feminists. That is Kolech, which is based in Jerusalem and operates a website at www.kolech.org.il/en/

Volume 23 of 'Polin', published in 2011, is devoted to 'Jews in Kraków'. It includes two articles relating to Sarah Schenirer. They are 'Sarah Schenirer; Founder of the Beit Ya'akov Movement; Her Vision and Legacy' by Caroline Scharfer, and 'The Beit Ya'akov School in Kraków as an Encounter between East and West' by Agnieszka Oleszak.

Volume 33 of 'Polin', published in 2021, includes an article by Iris Brown (Hoizman), 'At the Centre of Two Revolutions; Beit Ya'akov in Poland between Neo-Orthodoxy and Ultra-Orthodoxy'. The author explores, amongst other aspects, the role of Dr Judith Grunfeld, née Rosenbaum (1902-1998) in the development of the Bais Ya'akov movement. For five years from 1924 Dr Rosenbaum was engaged in in the Kraków teachers' seminary and in raising funds for the movement.[286] She is the author of a chapter about Sarah Schenirer which is included in a book 'Jewish Leaders, 1750-1940'.[287]

Amongst the books which have been written on the subject, in addition to that written by Naomi Seidman, two more can be mentioned. The first is Leah Esther Zussman's work, 'Sarah Schenirer Life Story'. Although this is not a long book, it does include a reference to Dr Grunfeld.[288] The second book, of some 470 pages, is Pearl Benisch's 'Carry Me in Your Heart'.[289] This work, like others, draws on Sarah Schenirer's autobiographical essays, 'Gezamelte Schrifn' (Collected Writings).[290] Mrs Benisch's book describes in some detail the establishment of Bais Ya'akov and its development in Poland and beyond. Unfortunately, however, it does not include an index of names or geographical locations.

Other sources of information relating to Sarah Schenirer include:-

- Leo Deutschlander, 'Bajs Jakob. Sein Wesen und Werden' (Bais Ya'akov. Its Character and Development); Verlag der Keren Hatorah-Zentrale, Vienna, 1928
- Moshe Prager and Arye Bauminger (Eds), 'Sefer Kraka, Ir v'Am b'Yisrael' (Memorial Book of Kraków, A Mother City in Israel); Rav Kuk Institute and the Association of Cracovians in Israel, Jerusalem, 1959, pages 369-376
- Agnieszka Kutylak (Ed), 'Krakowianie wybitni Żydzi Krakowscy XIV-XX w' (Krakowians; Outstanding Kraków Jews); Muzeum Historyczne Miasta Krakowa Kraków 2006, pages 73-75
- Henryk Halkowski, 'Żydowski Kraków; Legendy i ludzie' (Jews in Kraków; Legends and People); Austeria, Kraków, 2009, pages 289-291, and

---

[286] See also Wikipedia entry for 'Judith Grunfeld'
[287] Leo W Jung (Ed), 'Jewish Leaders, 1750-1940'; New York, NY, 1964
[288] Leah Esther Zussman, 'Sarah Schenirer Life Story'; C H Publishing, Jerusalem, page 148
[289] Pearl Benisch, 'Carry Me in Your Heart; The Life and Legacy of Sarah Schenirer, Founder and Visionary of the Beis Ya'akov Movement'; Feldheim, Jerusalem, 2003
[290] See 'Polin', vol 18, Littman, 2005, page 286

- Aleksander Skotnicki and Paulina Najbar, 'Rodziny Żydowskie przedwojennego Krakowa/Jewish Families of Pre-war Kraków'; Stradomskie Centrum Dialogu w Krakowie, Kraków, 2015, pages 28-37.

Sarah Schenirer had much in common with the orthodox Jewish feminist reformer, Bertha Pappenheim (1859-1936) who spent a week at the Bais Ya'akov school in Kraków in 1935. The relationship between the two women is described by Hanna Kozińska-Witt in her article 'Bertha Pappenheim and Jewish Women from Eastern Europe', which is available on academia.edu.[291]

Hebrew Secondary School

The very large amount of material which has been written about the Bais Ya'akov movement must not be allowed to hide the fact that in interwar Kraków the vast majority of Jewish girls and young women, like Sarah Schenirer, did not attend strictly orthodox schools.

The Hebrew Secondary School or Gymnazium was a significant co-educational establishment in Kraków during the interwar years. It was broadly 'modern Zionist' in outlook rather than 'traditional orthodox'. One of several books which describe the school was published by the Kraków City Museum in 2011, and more than one chapter of that book describes the teaching staff. Although the majority of senior teachers there appear to have been men, the following female teachers are listed;-

Anna Bross (PhD, history and geography), Regina Fallman (physical education), Fryderyka Feldman-Sternberg (MA philology and German), Rachel Goldwasser (natural sciences and geography), Regina Hausman-Juer (MA practical classes), Etla Horn (mathematics), Ada Nadel-Hecht (MA practical classes), Zofia Leinkram, Ilza Perlberg-Schinaglow (MA physical education), Sara Perlmutter (geography and natural sciences), Helena Rozenzweig-Hecker (PhD Polish), Nella Rost (PhD Polish and French), Laura Rympl (natural sciences), Hudes Steinberger (Latin) and Róża Vogel (MA English). Additionally, Maria Pechner is listed as the school medic, and Wacława Zastocka as commandant of the women's army cadet unit.[292] A further list on the Kehilalinks website shows Anna Bross, Rifka Haber, Gustawa Johannes, Malwina Kleinberżank , Ada Nadel Hecht, and Etta Taffet.[293] The sources do not state that all those named were Jewish, but the length of the list, taken with the names of various female teaching trainees, demonstrates that women played a major role in what was probably the most important Jewish school in Kraków during the period between the wars.

Both the book which was published by the Kraków City Museum, and an earlier book published by the Association of Cracovians in Israel show photographs of female students engaged in a wide range of activities including Purim plays,

[291] Previously published in German in Scripta Judaica Cracoviensia, vol 9, 2011
[292] Michał Niezabitowski and others (Eds), 'This Was the Hebrew Secondary School of Kraków; The Hebrew Secondary School, 1918-1939'; Muzeum Historyczne Miasta Krakowa, Kraków, 2011, pages 70 (photograph) and 182-184, quoting Natan Gross (Ed), 'To była Hebrajska Szkoła w Krakowie; Historia i wspomnienia';
[293] https://kehilalinks.jewishgen.org/krakow/kra_notables.htm See also Eugenia Prokop-Janiec, 'Mapping Modern Jewish Kraków' in Halina Goldberg, 'Polish Jewish Culture beyond the Capital'; Rutgers University Press, New Brunswick, NJ, 2023, page 199

Hanukah presentations, and a trip to the Wawel Hill in 1939. Other photographs show girls in groups such as the 'Ha-Cofeh' choir and a movement based on Scouts and Guides (Girl Scouts).

Several genealogical websites incorporate databases which include the names and other details of boys and girls who attended the Gymnazium. Some sites can be searched only by individual names. However, the website of the Association of Cracovians in Israel, at http://www.cracow.org.il, incorporates lists of students who attended the school between 1928 and 1939.

Merkaz ha'Avoda

The Merkaz ha'Avoda (Centre of Work) was established in 1916 as a 'professional' or trade school for girls. Initially pupils learned cutting and sewing but in 1923 the school was enlarged and courses were introduced for knitting, embroidery and household maintenance. By contrast, trade schools for boys taught the skills of locksmiths and mechanics. In 1930 there were 200 girls at the Merkaz ha'Avoda school.[294]

Ognisko Pracy

Ognisko Pracy also translates as the Centre of Work (or Work Focus). This opens up the possibility that Merkaz ha'Avoda and Ognisko Pracy were the same school. Having said that, Sean Martin states that Ognisko Pracy, unlike Merkaz ha'Avoda, opened in 1923 thanks to funds from the American Joint and the Fränkel family. It offered courses in dressmaking and tailoring, linen manufacturing, embroidery, knitting and home economics. In 1935, the Ognisko Pracy school moved into purpose built premises in Kazimierz.[295] It was managed for some thirty years by Eliza Fränkel (1882-1957).[296] Judging from the names of the establishments, and on the assumption that they were two separate schools, Merkaz was the more Zionist of the two. The location of the Ognisko Pracy building, and the locations of many other former communal buildings are identified by Eugeniusz Duda in his modern guide book 'Jewish Cracow; A Guide to the Historical Buildings and Places of Remembrance'.[297]

Nasza Szkola

In 1937, Bronia Infeld founded the Nasza Szkola (Our School) girls' school near the main market square in Kraków. This operated as a secular school for Jewish girls and was likely a response to both the increased antisemitism of the late 1930's and the need for a different type of Jewish education not found in other schools. In particular, Nasza Szkola was established as a progressive alternative to the Hebrew gymnasium. Education at Nasza Szkola was provided in Polish, and the philosophy

---

[294] Arnon Rubin, 'The Rise and Fall of the Jewish Communities in Poland and their Relics Today', vol 3, District Kraków, Tel Aviv University Press, 2009. Page 74
[295] Sean Martin, 'Jewish Life in Cracow, 1918-1939', pages 186, 187
[296] Andrzej Nowakowski, 'Powiększenie/ Blowup (Enlargement); The New Jewish Cemetery in Kraków': Universitas, Kraków, page 184 and Leszek Hondo (Ed), '200 lat nowego cmentarza Żydowskiego w Krakowie'; Księgarnia Akademicka, Kraków, 2010, page 77
[297] Published by Vis-à-vis Etudia, Kraków, 2014, pages 28, 29

of the school was less Zionist that that of the gymnasium.[298] Possibly because of its wide curriculum, the school attracted daughters of wealthy Polonised Jews, such as Nella Thon, the daughter of the communal leader Ozjasz.[299]

The need for private Jewish schools in the 1930's was highlighted by several Jewish educators in Kraków. These included Henryka Fromowicz Stiller who in June 1936 described the problems Jewish children encountered in public schools. The issue of antisemitism in public schools is also described by several Holocaust survivors, including Halina Nelken in her memoir and diary, 'And Yet I Am Here'[300]

Private and state schools

It has already been noted that the majority of girls did not attend Orthodox Jewish schools in Kraków during the interwar period, but the truth is that very many did not attend schools which were Jewish in any sense. They attended institutions which were run by the state, or private schools which were funded by fees paid by parents or other benefactors. In relation to families engaged in the bakery trade it has been stated 'These were Hassidic families whose daughters went to Polish State schools, learned the romantic Polish poets by heart, and spoke Polish with their siblings at home. In the afternoons they had private religious instruction.'[301]

As Eugenia Prokop-Janiec states, 'Women were reportedly the most Polonized group among the Jews in Kraków, which stemmed from their attending Polish schools, common even among Orthodox families'. The author then focuses on the various forms of Jewish women's cultural activity that was practiced by learning and using Polish, as opposed to Yiddish or Hebrew.[302]

Sean Martin refers to the Queen Jadwiga Private Gymnazium for Girls. He points out that in 1937, 28 per cent of the girls attending that school were Jewish, and that similar proportions applied during the 1920's and most of the 1930's. The school had an exceptionally good reputation and offered extra-curricular classes in diction, singing, drawing, stenography and foreign languages. The school even presented a theatrical performance in the Słowacki Theatre.[303]

Sean Martin also refers to the public (state) school Klementyna z Tańskich Hoffmaowa School Nr 15 which was attended by Jewish as well as non Jewish girls. A large scrapbook produced by pupils between 1933 and 1939 has survived and is held at the Jewish Historical Institute in Warsaw. The scrapbook 'includes original student writings, newspaper clippings and drawings illustrating the events that happened at the school'. These events include national commemorations such as

---

[298] Sean Martin, 'Jewish Life in Cracow, 1918-1939'; pages 182-184
[299] Sean Martin, 'Jewish Life in Cracow, 1918-1939', pages 142, 143
[300] Sean Martin, 'Jewish Life in Cracow, 1918-1939', pages 151 and 152 and notes on page 190. See also Halina Nelken, 'And Yet I am Here'; University of Massachusetts Press, Amherst, MA, 1999
[301] Maria Balinska, 'The Bagel; The Surprising History of a Modest Bread'; Yale University Press, New Haven, CT, 2008, page 76
[302] Eugenia Prokop-Janiec, 'Mapping Modern Jewish Kraków; Women – Cultural Production – Space' in Halina Goldberg (Ed), 'Polish Jewish Culture Beyond the Capital'; page 188
[303] Sean Martin, 'Jewish Life in Cracow, 1918-1939', pages 142, 143

those relating to Marshal Piłsudski, and the 3 May Constitution Day.[304] In 2006 the scrapbook was reproduced by Austeria publishers as 'Kronika uczennic Żydowskich z lat 1933-1939' (A Chronicle of Jewish Schoolgirls). The publication clearly shows the names of the girls who contributed to the scrapbook and, at the back, there is a list of 'schoolgirls in Class 7 at the Klementyna Tańskich-Hoffmanowa Municipal Public School in Kraków at ul. Miodowa, 36'. Extracts from the book in English are included in a book 'Jewish Society in Poland'.[305]

Irena Bronner attended the Klementyna z Tańskich Hoffmanowa School, describing it as 'a warm and clean elementary school. The parquet floors sparkled brightly. After entering, we took off our boots and put on felt slippers. The walls were very prettily decorated. I remember that on the landing General Dąbrowski smiled down at me from his portrait.'[306]

The number two Middle School in Kraków, also known as the Adam Mickiewicz School, was another establishment which was attended by Jewish pupils. In 2017, the school commemorated the lives of 87 Jewish girls who attended in the 1930's but who subsequently disappeared. The event was attended by Rabbi Avi Baumol who records the commemoration in his book 'In My Grandfather's Steps'. His article includes a table showing not only the names of the girls but also, for each of them, their birth date and place of birth, and the names of their mother and father, and the school grade (class) they attended.[307] Rabbi Baumol's article can also be found on line at https://shavei.org/jestem-a-school-in-poland-does-teshuvah by searching for 'school does teshuvah'. 'Jestem' – I am [here or present] possibly recalls the response of the girls when the school register was called.

Halina Nelken attended the Dąbrowki Elementary School and then a State Gymnazium. In Halina's class at that school there were 48 students of whom only six were Jewish. Five of the six came from families which were fully assimilated into Polish society, families of the 'working intelligentsia'. Following an antisemitic incident there, in 1938 Halina transferred to the private Kollataj Gymazium. This was attended by both girls and boys, but in her class the two genders sat in separate parts of the room. She comments, 'Here the professors are so friendly that no one is nervous. Every lesson is fun and we learn without even realising it. Even the building itself, close to the Planty, is much jollier than the old sullen edifice of the state gymnazium'. Halina Nelken also describes how, in 1937, she attended a summer school in Harbutowice, some 20 miles (32 km) south of Kraków.[308]

Miriam Akavia refers to the Scholastica and Teofil Lenartowicz schools, noting that the girls attending the former looked down on the girls attending the latter. Some

---

[304] Sean Martin, 'Jewish Life in Cracow, 1918-1939', pages 132, 133

[305] Aleksander Skotnicki and Władysław Klimczak, 'Jewish Society in Poland; Many Faces of Cracovian Jewry'; Wydnawnictwo AA, Kraków, 2009, pages 128-134

[306] Sean Martin, 'Jewish Life in Cracow, 1918-1939' page 121 quoting Irena Bronner, 'Cykady nad Wisła i Jordanem'. See also pages 132-135

[307] 'Jestem; A School in Poland does Teshuva' in Rabbi Avi Baumol, 'In My Grandfather's Footsteps'; Austeria, Kraków, 2019. See also www.ynetnews.com/articles/0,7340,L-4966490,00.html

[308] Halina Nelken, 'And Yet, I am Here'; University of Massachusetts Press, Amherst, MA, 1986, pages 28 and 38-43

classes were held on Saturdays but 'Israelite girls' (a term considered to be more polite than 'Jewish girls') did not attend; instead they copied up their lessons from non Jewish girls on Sundays.[309] The author does not have favourable memories of the special classes the Jewish girls attended for the purposes of religious education. She states:

'A pale and bored teacher would teach a very mixed class, made up of girls from different schools. He told them about [various Bible stores] all in Polish and in a very monotonous voice. His lesson was held during the girls' free time. No wonder then … that their interest was minimal.'[310]

Shosana Adler attended the Maria Konopnicka School on Sebastian Street. This 'was a school for Polish girls, but I remember that most of its students or even all of them were Jewish'.[311]

Emilia Leibel 'went to a Polish elementary school in Podgórze. It wasn't called an elementary school but the Queen Kinga Common School on Józefinska Street'. She remembers three teachers, Mrs Tarnowska (her class teacher), Mrs Jarosz (maths) and Miss Swierzowna (Polish or history). She continues, 'all the Jewish girls in Podgórze had religious instruction together. I don't remember which school in Podgórze it was in, but not ours.'[312]

Vocational schools

Jewish vocational education, as opposed to academic education, is described by Sean Martin in his work on the interwar years.[313] He refers to courses which were held at the Middle School for Trade which was for young women over the age of seventeen. He notes that 'the school's curriculum aimed to provide a traditional education in the humanities with an emphasis on practical skills and trade courses'. The author then refers to the Ogniski Pracy school which is described above.

Reference can also be made to two Jewish schools which were opened in 1933. One of these was the School of Handicraft. Originally, this was situated on ul. Brzozowa, but just before World War II it moved to new premises on ul. Podbrzezie, and at the same time achieved the status of a secondary technical school. The other school was the Secondary Commercial School on ul. Stradom. This was established with support from the Association of Jewish Merchants, and it eventually had 400 students, most of them girls.[314]

---

[309] A similar observation is made by Emilia Leibel. See
https://www.centropa.org/en/biography/emilia-leibel
[310] Miriam Akavia, 'My Own Vineyard; A Jewish Family in Kraków Between the Wars'; The Library of Holocaust Testimonies, Vallentine Mitchell, London, 2006, pages 256, 257
[311] Aleksander Skotnicki and Władysław Klimczak (Eds), 'Jewish Society in Poland; Many Faces of Cracovian Jewry'; Wydawnictwo AA, Kraków, 2006 page 136, quoting 'Ich miasto; wspomnienia Izraelczyków' (Their City; The Memoirs of Israelis); The Association of Cracovians in Israel, 2004
[312] https://www.centropa.org/en/biography/emilia-leibel
[313] Sean Martin, 'Jewish Life in Cracow, 1918-1939', pages 184-186
[314] Eugeniusz Duda, 'The Jews of Cracow'; Wydawnictwo Hagada, Kraków, 1999, pages 49, 50

Wieliczka

The development of the Jewish community in Wieliczka, to the south east of Kraków, following the constitutional changes of the 1860's, has been described in the chapter of this book relating to the 'Austrian' period. In her book, 'Żydzi w Wieliczce' (Jews in Wieliczka), Małgorzata Międzobrodzka refers to the education of girls in that period more than in the interwar period. However, the topic is mentioned by Moshe Yahrblum in his paper 'Wieliczka – The Salt City'. Dr Yahrblum, like other commentators such as Rachel Manekin, notes 'Most Orthodox sent their daughters to governmental schools and their everyday language was Polish'. He also refers to the Bais Ya'akov School but this is probably the school in Kraków which had good rail links with Wieliczka.

Dr Yahrblum also describes the sorry state of affairs suffered by the wife of the typical cheder/heder (religious primary school) teacher. He states 'The melamdim (heder teachers) lived in poverty. Teaching was generally conducted in his one room flat. The melamed's wife cooked meals and brought forth her children in that same room, when only a thin partition divided between her and the heder'.[315]

Jagiellonian University

As noted in the last chapter, it was not until the end of the nineteenth century that women were admitted for degrees at the Jagiellonian University, and that two of the earliest female graduates were Laura Kaufman (1889-1972) and Zofia Ameisen (1897-1967).

Laura Kaufman became a prominent biologist and geneticist in the interwar period. By 1930 she had thirty publications to her credit. She specialised in research into animals, including birds and some of her work resulted in increased productivity on poultry farms. Having worked for several years at the State Scientific Institute for Rural Economy, she returned to a teaching role at the Jagiellonian University as well as carrying out further work on the breeding of poultry.[316]

Zofia Ameisen started her studies at the University in 1915 and then wrote her PhD thesis on Medieval Murals in Kraków. In 1920 she started to work at the University Library where she wrote catalogues for several exhibitions. She later worked as an art historian, specialising in illuminated manuscripts. She was considered a great expert of European miniature painting and a remarkable figure in the field of human sciences.[317]

---

[315] Moshe Yahrblum, 'Wieliczka – The Salt City' in the English section of Shmuel Meiri (Ed), 'Kehilat Wieliczka; Sefer Zikaron'; Tel Aviv, 1980, available at
https://www.jewishgen.org/Yizkor/Wieliczka/Wieliczka.html
[316] Wiesław Kozub-Ciembroniewicz (Ed), 'Academics of Jewish Heritage in the Modern History of the Jagiellonian University'; Jagiellonian University Press, Kraków, 2014, pages 134-137
[317] Wiesław Kozub-Ciembroniewicz (Ed), 'Academics of Jewish Heritage in the Modern History of the Jagiellonian University', pages 69-73. See also Agnieszka Kutylak (Ed), 'Krakowianie; Wybitni Żydzi krakowscy XIV-XX w'; Muzeum Historyczne Miasta Krakowa, Kraków, 2006, pages 133-135 and Andrzej Nowakowski, 'Blow Up: The New Jewish Cemetery in Kraków'; Dział Hanlowy Universitas, Kraków, 2006, page 183

Mention can also be made of another female Jewish graduate of the University, Maria Einhorn-Susułowska (1915-1998). Having graduated from the University, she obtained her teaching diploma at the University in 1938. Unable to find a job as a teacher in her home town of Gorlice, she remained in Kraków giving private lessons. She spent much of the Holocaust in Lwów before returning to Kraków and spent the whole of her academic life there.[318]

Gizela Reicher-Thon (1904-Holocaust) studied Polish and English philology, linguistics and philosophy at the Jagiellonian University in the 1920's. Her doctoral thesis concerned the Irony of Juliusz Słowacki, a 19th century romantic poet, and in 1933 it was published by the Polish Academy of Learning. During the Holocaust she was secretary of CENTOS, a charity which cared for orphans.[319]

Teofila Mahler (1912-?) grew up in Kraków where she attended secondary school. However, she moved to Warsaw to enrol at the university there, possibly in order to concentrate on Jewish history. In 1934 she defended her PhD thesis which was concerned with the struggle between the Orthodox and Progressive communities in Kraków. This has since been published as 'Walka między ortodoksją a postępowcami w Krakowie w latach 1843-1868'.[320]

Eugenia Prokop-Janiec refers to the Jagiellonian University as 'a center of both public and private space', and by way of example notes how Mala Mandelbaum, a teacher at Polish and Jewish schools, valued her time there. However, the author also notes that during the late 1930's the number of Jewish women who studied at the University decreased considerably.[321]

In 'Jewish Student Organisations at the Jagiellonian University during the Second Polish Republic' Julian Kwiek mentions by name the officers of several associations and fraternities. The vast majority are male but female student leaders include Amalia Mandelbaum who was treasurer of The University Association of Jewish Academic Youth, otherwise known as Arlosorowia.[322] It may be assumed that this is the same person as Mala Mandelbaum mentioned by Eugenia Prokop-Janiec.

Further information about female graduates of Jewish origin is available from two papers written by Jadwiga Suchmiel. These are 'Kariery Naukowe Żydówek na Uniwersytecie Jagiellońskim do czasów Drugiej Rzeczpospolitej' (The Academic Careers of Jewish Women at the Jagiellonian University up to the Time of the Second

---

[318] Wiesław Kozub-Ciembroniewicz (Ed), 'Academics of Jewish Heritage in the Modern History of the Jagiellonian University', pages 103-108. See also Ewa Dąbrowska and Anna Kielczewska (Eds), 'Residents of Jewish Kraków, vol 4, Women'; Wydawca EMG, Kraków, 2021, page 160

[319] Ewa Dąbrowska and Anna Kielczewska (Eds), 'Residents of Jewish Kraków; Women', page 72

[320] Natalia Aleksiun, 'Female, Jewish, Educated and Writing Polish Jewish History' in 'Polin, vol 29 and 'Walka między ortodoksją a postępowcami w Krakowie w latch 1843-1868'; Austeria, Kraków, 2017

[321] Eugenia Prokop-Janiec, 'Mapping Modern Jewish Kraków' in Halina Goldberg (Ed), 'Polish Jewish Culture Beyond the Capital', page 201

[322] Julian Kwiek, 'Jewish Student Organisations at the Jagiellonian University during the Second Polish Republic' in Wiesław Kozub-Ciembroniewicz (Ed), 'Academics of Jewish Heritage in the modern History of the Jagiellonian University', page 30

Republic)[323] and 'Żydowski ze stopniem doktora wszech nauk lekarskich oraz doctora filozofi w Uniwesytecie Jagiellońskim do czasów Drugiej Rzeczypospolitej' (Jewish Women with the Degree of Doctor of Medicine as well as Doctor of Philosophy at the Jagiellonian University up to the time of the Second Republic).[324] Both of these works are included in an extensive bibliography concerning Jewish Women in Eastern Europe which is included in volume 18 of 'Polin'.[325]

The limitations, and then prohibition on Jewish students attending the University in the late 1930's are well recorded in personal testimonies and by historical researchers.[326] One female student, Malvina Graf, refers to increasing difficulties she encountered, due largely to the anti-Semitic Endek party. She also describes how, shortly after their invasion, the Nazi appeared to reopen the University – but only as a means of gathering the professors in one place so that they could be deported.[327]

Natalia Aleksiun is an example of a female researcher who has written about increasing difficulties faced by Jewish students, and the steps they took to manage those difficulties. In her paper, 'Together but Apart' the author describes the financial challenges facing students as well as the restrictions on numbers of Jewish students, physical violence against them, and the introduction of separate seating, known as 'ghetto benches'.[328]

Literature

Reading newspapers, magazines and books, was a popular pastime of women in different sections of the Jewish community of Kraków as the amount and range of material increased. In the late nineteenth century Kraków became a centre of feminist activities, and a women's reading room (Czytelnia dla kobiet) was established in the city at the end of the century. In the early years, it was attended by Jewish feminists, though after 1910 its direction became more conservative.[329]

Eugenia Prokop-Janiec's book, 'Polish-Jewish Literature in the Interwar Years', illustrates the amount and variety of works written by Jewish authors, ranging across a range of Jewish and Polish aspects. The index includes the names of many female authors, such as Irma (Irena) Kanfer, who wrote 'Dwa akordy' (Two Chords) in 1936 and 'W mleczną drogę' (Into the Milky Way) the following year. She also wrote for

---

[323] In Aleksandra Bilewicz and Stefania Walasek (Eds), 'Rola mniejszości narodowych w kulturze i oświacie Polskiej w latach 1700-1939'; Wocław University Press, 1998
[324] Published by Wydawnictwo WSP, Częstochowa, 1997
[325] Chaeran Freeze (and others) (Eds), 'Polin', vol 18, Jewish Women in Eastern Europe, Littman, Oxford, 2005, page 300
[326] See, for example, those mentioned in the article at www.academia.edu/33768075
[327] Malvina Graf, 'The Kraków Ghetto and the Płaszów Camp Remembered'; Florida State University Press, Tallahassee, FL, 1989, pages 4, 5, 17 and 18
[328] Natalia Aleksiun, 'Together but Apart; University Experience of Jewish Students in the Second Polish Republic'; Acta Poloniae Historica, 2014. See also, for example, Zofia Trębacz, 'Ghetto Benches at Polish Universities; Ideology and Practice' in Regina Fritz (Ed), 'Alma Mater Antisemitica; Akademisches Milieu, Juden und Antisemitismus an den Universitäten Europas zwichen 1918 und 1939'; New Academic Press, Vienna, 2016
[329] Rachel Manekin, 'The Rebellion of the Daughters'; Princeton University Press, Princeton, NJ, 2020, page 30

the Nasz przegląd (Our Review) journal and featured in press reports of the interwar period.[330]

Additionally, the appendix to Eugenia Prokop-Janiec's book lists the following five female authors who had connections with Kraków:

- Anda Eker who wrote for the Jewish press, including 'Nowy Dziennik' (The New Daily) and 'Okienko na świat' (The Little Window on the World), publications which are mentioned below,
- Riwka (Regina) Gurfein who studied at the Jagiellonian University and wrote for the press, including 'Nowy Dziennik',
- Maria Hochberżanka (Hochberg-Mariańska) who also wrote for the press in Kraków, as described below,
- Runa Reitman (Próchnik) who from 1928 to 1933 was editor of 'Dzienniczek', a supplement of 'Nowy Dziennik', and
- Minka Silberman, another contributor to the Jewish press in Kraków.

However, the book and a paper entitled 'Jewish Literature in Kraków, 1918-1948' which can be found at www.academia.edu/34140767 indicate that the vast majority of authors in the period prior to 1939 were men.[331] The paper describes the wide range of newspapers which were in circulation in Kraków during the interwar period. These include the only Jewish daily, Nowy Dziennik. The wide appeal of this publication is reflected by the range of supplements which the paper published. These covered topics such as home and school. There was also a supplement 'Głos Kobiety Żydowskiej' (The Jewish Women's Voice).[332] During the 1920's Nella Rost, daughter of the Zionist leader Ozjasz Thon, was one of the contributors to this publication.[333]

The role of female journalists is considered in another paper which is available on www.academia.edu. That is Monika Szabłowska Zaremba's paper, 'Dziennikarki międzywojennej prasy polsko-żydowskiej (wstępne rozpoznaie)' (Journalists of the interwar Polish-Jewish Press (preliminary research)). The author refers to several Kraków based writers including Zuzanna Ginczanka (pen name, Zuzanna Polina Gincburg) (1917-1944) who was a poet and who also wrote a book 'O centaurach' (On Centaurs) in 1936.[334] The author also refers to the Jewish feminist weekly which was published between 1928 and 1933, under the editorship of Paulina Appenszlak.

---

[330] Eugenia Prokop-Janiec, 'Polish-Jewish Literature in the Interwar Years'; Syracuse University Press, Syracuse, NY, 2003, pages 12 and 22 and see also pages 64, 139 and 247 and Czesław Brzoza, 'Żydzi Krakowa międzywojennego; kalendarium'; Historia Iagellonica, Kraków, 2018 , names index.

[331] For wider reading see, for example, Volume 28 of 'Polin', Jewish Writing in Poland, including Zuzanna Kołodziejska's paper, 'Czesława Rosenblattowa's Works as an Example of Women's Integrationist Literature'.

[332] 'A World Before Catastrophe'; International Cultural Centre, Kraków, 2007, page 59. See also Eugenia Prokop-Janiec, 'Mapping Modern Jewish Kraków' in Halina Goldberg (Ed), 'Polish Jewish Culture Beyond the Capital'; Rutgers University Press, New Brunswick, NJ, 2023, page 201

[333] https://link.springer.com/chapter/10.1007/978-3-030-55532-0_2 note 11

[334] See also, for example, https://ukrainianjewishencounter.org/en/zuzanna-ginczanka-1917-1945/

Although the magazine was produced in Warsaw, it was read in Jewish communities well beyond that city.

The Jewish politician Róża Pomeranc-Melcer (1880-1934) was a correspondent for Nowy Dziennik. She is mentioned briefly in the following section headed 'Political activities'.

Maria Hochberg Mariańska (1913-1996) and Miriam Peleg-Mariańska appear to be the same person. She was born on a farm belonging to her parents, not far from Kraków, where she spent her early youth. She attended the Helena Kaplińska Private secondary School for Girls in Kraków, but there seems to be conflicting information as to whether she studied at the Jagiellonian University. Researchers agree, however, that Maria/Miriam had undoubted literary talent, that she made her working debut as author and editor of the children's supplement to Nowy Dziennik in 1937, and that she published many stories and poems. During the Holocaust, she survived on Aryan papers and worked as editor of 'Wolność' (Freedom), the journal of the PPS (Polish Socialists Party) underground movement.[335]

Felicja Infeld-Stendig (1895-1945) graduated from the Hebrew Gymnazium in Kraków, and went to business school before becoming an essayist, journalist and literary critic. Able to speak eight languages, she wrote for various publications, including Nowy Dziennik and Przegląd Społeczny (Social Review). She was a supporter of the Women's International Zionist Organisation, feminist causes, and children's welfare, including Ognisko Pracy, which was formed to alleviate the plight of orphaned girls.[336] Her sister, Bronia, founded the New School in Kraków.[337] Copies of documents, photos and articles by Felicja Infeld-Stending are held at the Central Archives for the History of Jewish People in Jerusalem. Felicia had a daughter, Gustawa (1926-2008) who left Poland very soon after the liberation and became a pioneer in research on magnesium in medicine and biology. Between 1941 and 1943, in the Kraków Ghetto, Gustawa wrote many poems. During this period, she was with her mother who taught her English.[338]

Henryka Fromowicz-Stillerowa (1894-1947) has been mentioned in the earlier section headed 'art and photography'. She was a member of the 'Social Reading Room' and wrote for Nowy Dziennik in the 1920's. She also wrote for Nasza Opinja (Our Opinion), and was active in the Zionist WIZO movement. Additionally, she is the author of 'Emalje Malarskie z Limoges w Muzeum KS Czartoryskich w Krakowie' (Painted Enamels from Limoges in the Czartory Museum in Kraków) which was published in that city in 1922. Between 1937 and 1939 Henryka

---

[335] Anna Biedrzycka (Ed), 'Is War Men's Business?'; Museum Historyczne Miasta Krakowa, Kraków, 2011, pages 54-57. See also Martyna Grądzka-Rejak, 'Kobieta Żydowska w okupowanym Krakowie (1939-1945); Wysoki Zamek, Kraków, 2016, entries in names index and Miriam Peleg-Mariańska and Mordecai Peleg, 'Witness; Life in Occupied Krakow' Routledge, London, 1991, page ix

[336] See, for example, Sean Martin, 'Future Generations: Associations for Jewish Children in Kraków' in 'Polin' vol 23, Littman, Oxford, 2011, page 312. Presumably, the organisation was linked with the vocational school which had the same name.

[337] The Virtual Shtetl website, www.sztetl.org.pl/en and Ewa Dąbrowska and Anna Kielczewska (Eds), 'Residents of Jewish Kraków, vol IV, Women'; EMG, Kraków, 2021, page 48

[338] www.profmagnesium.org/Biography.htm

published a magazine for Jewish children, 'Okienko na świat'.[339] This magazine is described by Monika Szablowska-Zaremba in her paper, 'Okienko na Świat. Pismo dzieci i młodzieży, 1937-1939' (Little Window on the World. Children's and Youth Magazine).[340] Henryka had a sister, Maria (Fromowicz-Nassau/Fromowicz-Simeoni). After studying at the Jagiellonian University, Maria attended the Kraków Academy of Fine Arts before moving to Italy, where she survived the war.[341] An account of Henryka's relative, Irena Fromowicz-Pisek, and her, and her family's, escape to Jerusalem via Tehran can be read on the iranwire.com website under the title 'From Krakow to Tehran to Jerusalem; One Jewish Family's Story'.[342]

Marta Hirschprung (1903-?1942) was a translator and journalist. She also edited 'Okienko na świat' under the direction of Henryka Fromowicz-Stillerowa. Additionally, she contributed to children's supplements during the war years, up to 1942.[343]

Jadwiga Migowa, née Gancwohl (1891-1942) was a successful journalist and novelist. In the interwar period she published several magazines including 'Ilustrowany Kurier Codzienny' (The Illustrated Daily Courier) and 'Nowości Ilustrowane' (The Illustrated News). She also published popular novels under the pen name Kamil Norden. Jadwiga Migowa died in Ravensbrück in 1942.[344]

Reference can also be made to the poet Stella Feldhorn, née Landau. She together with her husband Julius were killed at Wieliczka during the Holocaust.[345] Additionally Eugenia Prokop-Janiec mentions Anna Bross (1890-1942), who wrote about the history of Italy, France and Poland, Gizela Reicher-Thon, who published pioneering studies on literature, and the poet Wanda Kragen (1893-1982).[346]

Teofila Mahler was born in Kraków in 1912 and has already been mentioned in the section of this chapter relating to the Jagiellonian University. Following her primary and secondary education in Kraków, Ms Mahler went to Warsaw where she completed her PhD thesis. This has since been published as 'Walka między ortodoksją a postępowcami w Krakowie w latch 1843-1868' (The Struggle between the Orthodox and the Progressives in Kraków in the Period 1843-1868).[347]

---

[339] Sean Martin, 'Jewish Life in Cracow, 1918-1939', page 214
[340] Available on request at https://www.academia.edu/96965278/
[341] For information about both sisters, Henryka and Maria see Agnieszka Janczyk, 'Fromowiczowie – portret rodziny' (A Portrait of the Fromowicz Family) in 'Krzysztofory', vol 35; Muzeum Historyczne Miasta Krakowa, Kraków, 2017, pages 475-494
[342] https://iranwire.com/en/society/61783/
[343] Monika Szabłowska Zaremba, 'Marta Hirschprung: A Forgotten Journalist and Author from Cracow'; Rocznik Historii Prasy Polskiej, vol XXII, 2019
[344] Ewa Dąbrowska (Ed),'Residents of Jewish Cracow, vol II, Art and Culture': EMG, Kraków, 2020, pages 64, 65
[345] 'Legacy of the Feldhorn family', papers held at the Jewish Historical Institute in Warsaw and at the United States Holocaust Memorial Museum, Washington DC
[346] Eugenia Prokop-Janiec, 'Mapping Modern Jewish Kraków' in Halina Goldberg (Ed), 'Polish Jewish Culture Beyond the Capital' page 201
[347] Teofila Mahler, 'Walka między ortodoksją a postępowcami w Krakowie w latach 1843-1868'; Wydawnictwo Austeria, Kraków, 2017

Reference has been made in the section headed 'Education' to the Bais Ya'akov School for orthodox Jewish girls. From 1933 the Bais Ya'akov movement published its own periodical for women and their daughters. Originally this appeared in Polish and Yiddish, including a section in Yiddish, 'Kinder-gortn', for young children and a Polish section, 'Echo Szkolne' (The School Echo), for older children. Later the journal was published only in Yiddish. It 'became an important publication in the homes of observant Jews throughout Europe for sixteen years'.[348] Bais Ya'akov also operated a small library during the interwar period.[349]

Marriage, divorce and family life

Rafael Scharf (1914-2003) was brought up in Kraków in what today might be called a modern orthodox family. He attended the Hebrew Secondary School and was familiar with Polish as well as Jewish culture. Yet when he refers to Jewish marriage, he writes as follows.

'Young women of marriageable age were divided between those of whom it was known that they had a dowry and those who had none. It was understood that the dowry should be in inverse ratio to the beauty of the bride.' He continues to explain that when his parents got married the match was 'of course' brokered before adding 'marriage broking in that society was an indispensable institution.[350]

It is true that the author's parents married shortly before the outbreak of the First World War. However, his observations suggest that very traditional standards relating to marriage and married life were still maintained within parts of the Kraków Jewish community throughout most of the interwar period. Having described the workings of the marriage broker, he adds, 'The husband was the one who, above all, was to earn a living and provide for the family; the wife was to look after the home, prepare meals, bear children and bring them up', though he does note that 'not all that infrequently the burden of earning a living would fall on the wife'. In this chapter, several women are identified who were active, or even prominent, in the professions or in trade or commerce, but, on the evidence of Rafael Scharf, it does seem that such women were exceptions rather than the rule.

Gershon Bacon refers to marriage in his paper on Poland during the interwar period. This is to be found on the website of the Jewish Women's Archive at https://jwa.org/encyclopedia/article/poland-interwar The author notes in particular the progressive rise in marriage age of both Jewish men and Jewish women and the erosion in the practice of early marriage common in traditional Jewish society. He further notes that according to the 1921 Polish census, there were almost no married Jewish males or females under the age of seventeen.

Several Holocaust survivors describe their interwar family lives as part of their memoirs. One example is Sara Rosen, author of 'My Lost World'. Part one of her

---

[348] Deborah Weissman, 'Bais Ya'akov; A Historical Model for Jewish Feminists' in Elizabeth Koltun, 'The Jewish Woman; New Perspectives'; Schocken Books, New York, NY, 1976, , page 142. See more generally Adina Bar-el, 'Jewish Children's Periodicals in Poland between the Two World Wars – in Three Languages'
[349] Deborah Weissman, 'Bais Ya'akov; A Historical Model for Jewish Feminists', page 141
[350] Rafael Scharf, 'Poland, What Have I To Do With Thee'; Vallentine Mitchell, London, 1998, pages 18, 19

book is devoted to 'The Family'. It describes members of the Landerer and Weinberg branches of her family, and their observances of the Sabbath and the various religious festivals.[351] A second example is George Alexander's book, 'Generations', which describes several female relatives.[352]

Other books written in memory of Jewish communities also focus on families, and just two examples will be give here.

The first example is bilingual and entitled 'Rodziny Żydowskie przedwojennego Krakowa/Jewish Families of the Pre-war Cracow'. The book contains a large number of photographs showing girls and women in various family settings, whether they be religious or educational. For example, one photo shows members of the Lauterbach family during the Seder dinner of Pesach (Passover) in March, 1937, another is a commemorative picture from the Camp of the Hebrew High School at Szczyrk in 1936, whilst a third shows Lola Taube and Irena and Nitta Schorr on holiday in Rabka in the same year.[353]

The second example is a substantial book about the town of Wieliczka which is about 10 miles (15 km) south east of Kraków. Photographs show female members of several families including the Kleinberger, Klinghofer, Licht, Perlberger, Szmulewicz, Weiss and Wimmer families. The book also includes a photo of market day on the Rynek Górny, the Upper Market. Substantially all the people in the picture are girls and women. Many of the women are wearing scarves, shawls and long skirts.[354]

As noted in the previous chapter, the General Austrian Code of Law relating to marriage and divorce remained in force until 1945. In his article on the subject, Zdzisław Zarzycki notes that by the interwar period the practice of Jews failing to register their 'ritual' marriages with the civil authorities had reduced significantly. Having described the manner in which the failure could be rectified, he notes that it is estimated that the issue affected only 3.4% of the Jewish population in 1931.[355]

Music

Some, but not many, Jewish women were musicians in Kraków during the interwar period. Parts of the work 'Jewish Music in Poland between the World Wars' by Issacher Fater are available on the JewishGen website at www.jewishgen.org/yizkor/musicians/Musicians.html. References are made there to

---

[351] Sara Rosen, 'My Lost World; A Survivor's Tale'; Vallentine Mitchell, London, 1993
[352] George J Alexander, 'Generations: A Millenium of Jewish History in Poland from the earliest times to the Holocaust told by a survivor from an old Krakow family'; Congress for Jewish Culture, New York, NY, 2008
[353] Aleksander B Skotnicki and Paulina Najbar, 'Rodziny Żydowskie przedwojennego Krakowa/Jewish Families of the Pre-war Cracow'; Stradomskie Centrum Dialogu w Krakowie, Kraków, 2015, pages 91, 97 and 122
[354] Małgorzata Międzobrodzka, 'Żydzi w Wieliczce'; Wydawnictwo Żyznowski, Siercza (Wieliczka), 2022, pages 254, 260, 261, 313, 328 329 and 365
[355] Zdzisław Zarzycki, 'Post-Austrian Divorce Law in Małopolska from 1918 to 1945, Selected Issues' in Krakowskie Studia z Historii Państwa i Prawa, 2019

the following Kraków based female pianists:- Jutta Flaster, Izabella Freiman, Helena Landau, Pauline Sznajder[356] and Natalia Weissman-Hubler.

Natalia Weissman-Hubler, later Natalia Karp (Karpf) (1911-2007) was born in Kraków and began learning to play the piano at the age of only four. Having spent time in Germany, she returned to Kraków where she married Julius Hubler, a lawyer. On the liquidation of the Kraków Ghetto, she was taken to Płaszów and was forced to play for the camp commandant Amon Göth on his birthday. Göth was so impressed by her performance that he spared her life and the life of her sister. Natalia's biography is given in a book by her daughter, Anne Karpf, 'The War After; Living with the Holocaust'. This was published by Minerva in 1996.

Natalia Weissman is one of several musicians mentioned by Sylwia Jakubczyk-Ślęczka in her paper 'Activité de la Loge Cracovienne 'Solidarność' dans la Domaine de la Culture Musicale Juive dans L'entre-deux-guerres' (The Activity of the 'Solidarność' Kraków [B'nei B'rith] Lodge in the Field of Jewish Musical Culture during the Interwar Period) which appears in Scripta Judaica Cracoviensia vol 10 (2012). The paper is divided into three sections in addition to an introduction. These are music in the context of Jewish culture, Jewish musical institutions and Jewish music broadcast by Kraków Radio. The author notes that in May, 1933 Ms Weissman performed in a concert which included works by Tartini, Mendelssohn, Debussy and other composers. Sylwia Jakubczyk-Ślęczka also refers to a concert by the pianist Maria Zimmerman in May, 1934.

The same author also wrote 'La Musique Juive à Cracovie de L'entre-deux-guerres salon les Informations du Journal Nowy Dziennik' (Jewish Music in Kraków in the Interwar Period according to Information in the Nowy Dziennik Newspaper) which was published in Scripta Judaica Cracoviensia, vol 9 (2011). This article includes a section about the 'Chir' Association of Singers in which mention is made of Helena Immergluck and Helena Brünn. The article also includes a section regarding Jewish music broadcast by Kraków Radio. In this context Marie Salz-Zimmerman (Maria Zimmerman), Stéphane Schleichkorn and Stella Dortheimer are amongst the names which are mentioned.

In her paper, 'Musical Life of the Jewish Community in Interwar Galicia', Sylwia Jakubczyk-Ślęczka mentions 'singer Brün' in relation to Yiddish folk songs which were performed on the stage of Kraków's 'Arbetheym'.[357]

Sylwia Jakubczyk-Ślęczka is also the author of 'Za kulisami sceny koncertowej – polityka kulturalna Żydowskiego Towarzystwa Muzycznego w Krakowie' (Behind the Scenes of the Concert Stage – The Cultural Policy of the Jewish Music Society

[356] Brief information relating to Helena Landau and Paulina Sznajder is available on www.sztetl.org.pl For further information about Jewish music in Poland see www.zchor.org/fater/musicians.htm

[357] Sylwia Jakubczyk-Ślęczka, 'Musical Life of the Jewish Community in Interwar Galicia; The Problems of Identity of Jewish Musicians' in 'Kwartalnik młodych muzykologów UJ, nr 34 (3/2017), page 146. See also the same author's work 'Jewish Music Organizations in Interwar Galicia'

in Kraków) [358] The author includes as an appendix a list of concerts performed by the Society as well as other groups. This list shows several female performers, including the singer Helena Immergluck and the musicians, Maria Salz-Zimmerman and Natalia Weissman-Hubler.

Róża Arnold-Hersztajn was born in Rzeszów in 1896 but she was educated in Kraków where she performed as a pianist in the interwar period. Additionally, she ran a music school on Jasna Street in the Prądnik Biały district of the city.[359] It appears that Ester Dym was another music teacher in interwar Kraków. She directed a music programme in connection with a music school operated by Żydowskie Towarzystwo Muzyczne, The Jewish Music Society, in 1935.[360]

One of the most musical Jewish families in Kraków before and during the Holocaust was the Rosner family. Members included Marysia, a pianist, and Mela who played the piano accordion. Mela and her young son were murdered, but other members of the family survived thanks to their musical skills, and Oskar Schindler.[361]

The website at https://kehilalinks.jewishgen.org/Krakow/kra_notables.htm lists the following female musicians in addition to Maria Zimmerman who has already been mentioned:- Dola Hoffman, Stella Margulies and Hannah Zimmerman. Additionally, a lexicon which is included in Issachar Fater's 'Jewish Music in Poland between the World Wars' is available at www.zchor.org/fater/lexicon.htm and lists the Kraków based music patron Helena Landau as well as the pianists Roza Arnold-Herstein, Juta Flaster, Isabella Freiman-Sosnowska and Natalia Weissman-Hubler.

There appears to have been a significant enthusiasm for jazz amongst Kraków's Jewish community in the 1930's, but little or nothing has been written about Jewish female jazz performers.[362] Similarly, a band at the Hebrew Secondary School appears to have been all male.[363] On the other hand, a music school founded by the Jewish Music Society was directed by a woman, Róża Arnold.[364]

---

[358] In Alicja Maślak-Maciejewska (Ed), 'Żydzi krakowscy; kierunki badań'; Austeria, Kraków, 2021. See also, by the same author, Sylwia Jakubczyk- Ślęczka, 'Jewish Music Organizations in Interwar Galicia' in vol. 32 of 'Polin', 2020

[359] Virtual shtetl website and Czesław Brzoza, 'Żydzi Krakowa międzywojennego; kalendarium'; Historia Iagellonica, Kraków, 2018, see names index for several references

[360] Czesław Brzoza, 'Żydzi Krakowa międzywojennego', page 559

[361] Anna Rosner Blay, 'Leo Rosner; A Man of Note' at www.hybridpublishers.com.au and search for 'Rosner'. See also various books concerning Oskar Schindler, for example Elinor J Brecher, 'Schindler' Legacy; True Stories of the List Survivors'; Plume/Penguin, New York, NY, 1994, pages 1-38

[362] See, for example, Ewa Dąbrowska and Anna Kielczewska (Eds), 'Residents of Jewish Kraków', vol IV, Women'; EMG, Kraków, 2021, pages 76-84, and vol V 'Places and People', 2022, page 240

[363] 'This was the Hebrew School of Kraków'; Muzeum Historyczne Miasta Krakowa, Kraków, 2011, photograph on page 204 and also 'To była Hebrajska Szkoła w Krakowie'; Wydawnictwo Ekked, Tel Aviv, 1989

[364] Sean Martin, 'Jewish Life in Cracow, 1918-1939', page 187

Orphanages

By the end of the First World War, the Jewish Orphanage at 64 Dietla Street had become well established, and was under the leadership of its President, Róza Rock (1871-1926). Whilst it seems that little has been written about previous heads of the orphanage, rather more has been written about Mrs Rock, 'mother of Jewish orphans' and a social activist who had graduated from a university in Germany where she studied modern rules for running orphanages. She was head of the Kraków Jewish Orphanage only from 1918, eight years before her death, but the changes she introduced made the orphanage 'one of the best functioning foster institutions in Poland'. During her presidency the orphanage expanded the range of education to include secular and vocational subjects and in 1924 the premises were considerably expanded.[365] Her activities were frequently reported in the press.[366]

Mention can also be made of Matylda Schenker who founded and led the Bursa Żydowskich Sierot Rękodzielników – The Jewish Orphan Craftsmen Dormitory - at 53 Krakowska Street. This reflected an expansion of the role of the orphanage to include practical skills training to some of its residents. Matylda Schenker continued to aid children during the Holocaust.[367]

There was also a Jewish orphanage in the district of Podgórze, over the river from Kazimierz. Amalia (Małka) Wasserberger (1869-1936) was a well known philanthropist. An example of her generosity is that she donated a house at 8 Krakusa Street, Podgórze to the Jewish Orphans' Home Association. In 1936 a plaque in her memory was unveiled by the Menachem Awejlim Association in Podgórze to recognise her charitable work[368]

A list of Jewish charities and other organisations in Kraków in 1939 is provided by Aniela Kielbicka in her article 'The Liquidation of the Jewish Associations in Cracow during the Nazi Occupation'; Yad Vashem, 1986. The list includes:

- The Shomer Emunim orphanage, 53, Krakowska Street
- The Eksternat shelter for needy children, 51 Dajwór Street
- The shelter for very poor children, 2 Mostowa Street
- The Beyt Megadley Yetomim orphanage at 64 Dietla Street and

---

[365] Martyna Grądzka, 'A Broken Childhood; The Fate of the Children from the Jewish Orphanage at 64 Dietla Street in Cracow during the German Occupation'; Wydawnictwo Wysoki Zamek, Kraków, 2012, page 274. See also Agnieszka Kutylak (Ed), 'Krakowianie; Wybitni Żydzi krakowscy XIV-XX w'; Muzeum Historyczne Miasta Krakowa, Kraków, 2006, pages 71 and Andrzej Nowakowski (Ed), 'Blowup; The New Jewish Cemetery in Kraków, 2006, page 172. For a further source, see Edyta Gawron and Michał Galas (Eds), 'Nie tylko Kroke; Historia Żydów krakowskich'; Wydawnictwo Literackie, Kraków, 2022 , pages 283-285, 'Pomoc dla sierot i starców'
[366] Czesław Brzoza, 'Żydzi Krakowa międzywojennego; kalendarium'; Historia Iagellonica, Kraków, 2018, see the names index
[367] Martyna Grądzka, 'A Broken Childhood'; Wydawnictwo Wysoki Zamek, Kraków, 2012, page 287 and Sean Martin, 'Future Generations' in 'Polin', vol 23, page 507
[368] Teresa Leśniak (Ed), 'Świat przed katastrofą/ A World Before a Catastrophe'' The International Cultural Centre, Kraków, 2007, page 119. See also
https://pl.m.wikipedia.org/wiki/Amalia_Wasserberger

- The Educational Institute for Orphans at Izydor House in memory of Józefina Judt

Rabka was, and continues to be, a popular spa town to the south of Kraków. After the Holocaust, Lena Kuchler Silberman established an orphanage there. What is less known is that before the war a healing centre for Jewish children was situated in the town under the direction of Maria Fraenkel, née Liban.[369]

Political activities

As noted in a previous chapter, women were generally excluded from political activities until shortly after the first world war. As a result, for example, no Jewish women served on the Kraków Municipal Council. However, as in other countries, the interwar period in the newly independent Poland saw the introduction and expansion of women's suffrage. A photograph of a woman casting her vote, apparently alongside her husband, is included in a short book about Jewish participation in municipal affairs which was published by the Kraków City Museum in 2014. On the other hand, women do not otherwise feature in the book, which shows on its front cover a photograph of over thirty leaders of the Jewish community – all men.[370]

A paper, 'Cracow's Jews and the Parliamentary Elections, 1919-1939' names a number of Parliamentary candidates, the vast majority of whom were men. However, two female candidates are mentioned, both candidates of the Zionist Organisation of Western Galicia. These are Dr Berta Schwartzbart, a physician who stood in 1918 and Laura Tenger who was a candidate ten years later. The author also notes that in January, 1919, the leading candidate, Ojasz Thon, had a meeting with Jewish women.[371]

Further information about political Zionism in Kraków is given by Ignacy Schwartzbart in his book 'Tzvishn beide Welt Milchomos' (Between Both World Wars).[372]

Maria Balsiger (née Lipszyc) (c1870-1944) was a feminist sociologist who settled in Kraków in 1908. She was active in various movements, including the Women's Organisation of the Polish Social Democratic Party, and she continued her

---

[369] Andrzej Nowakowski (ed), 'Blowup [Enlargement] The New Jewish Cemetery in Kraków'; Universitas and Księgarnia Internetowa, Kraków, 2006, page 184. See also the chapter 'The Secrets of Rabka Zdroj' in Anna-Ray Jones and Roman Ferber, 'Journey of Ashes; A Boyhood in the Holocaust'; Artists Rights Society, New York, NY, 2014. Additionally see Arnon Rubin, 'The Rise and Fall of the Jewish Communities in Poland and their Relics Today', vol 3, District Kraków, Tel Aviv University Press, 209, pages 274-277
[370] Anna Jodłowiec-Dziedzic, 'The Architects of Modern Kraków'; Muzeum Historyczne Miasta Krakowa, Kraków, 2014, page 21
[371] Czesław Brzoza, 'Cracow's Jews and the Parliamentary Elections, 1919-1939' in Sławomir Kapralski (Ed), 'The Jews of Poland, vol II'; Jagiellonian University Press, Kraków, 1999 pages 165 and 174
[372] Yitzchak (Ignacy) Schwartzbart, 'Tzwishn beide Welt Milchomos; Zichronos vegn den Yidishn Lebn in Kroke in der Tkufeh 1919-1935'; The Association of Polish Jews in Argentina, Buenos Aires, 1958

socialist work in Warsaw after Poland gained its independence.[373] Several other Jewish women were active in left wing politics in Kraków. For example, the site at https://kehilalinks.jewishgen.org/Krakow/kra_notables.htm lists the following female members of The Bund – Luśka Aleksandrowicz, Moniek Glaser, Gusta Joffe, Moniek Nadler, Moniek Ostry, Bronia Pomeranc, Helena Spilling, Mania Silberstein, Cyla Wolfgang and finally (Doctor) Pola (Paulina) Wasserberg who is mentioned in the following section of this book. Additionally, Irena Blatt and Halina Steinhaus are listed as members of the Polish Communist Party.

Mention can also be made of Róża Pomeranc-Melcer (1873-1934), a strong supporter of Zionism who was elected to both the lower and upper houses of Parliament in the 1920's. Although she was based in Lwów, as noted above she was a contributor to the Kraków newspaper, Nowy Dziennik.[374]

The page at www.kehilalinks.jewishgen.org/krakow/kra_1935_voters.htm shows a partial list of voters in the Jewish communal elections (as opposed to municipal council elections) in 1935. Although the list is lengthy, no females are included in it. Similarly, a note on the kehilalinks JewishGen website refers to 'a list of almost 7,000 male Jews' in Kazimierz who were eligible to vote in the 1929 Polish general election.

Professional lives

Introduction

Reference has already been made to the roles of Jewish women in education and childcare. In this section, consideration will be given to their roles in other professions.

In writing about the establishment of the Warsaw School of Nursing in 1923, Daniel Kupfert Heller wrote, 'Whether orthodox or secular, rich or poor, Bundist or Zionist, many claimed that women's supposedly delicate nervous system, inferior intellectual capacity, and periodically erratic behaviour determined by their reproductive systems rendered them biologically unfit to wield professional power'.[375]

Whilst these opinions might have been common in times gone by, more recently there has been mounting evidence of the wide range of roles undertaken by Jewish women in the professional life of Kraków in the twentieth century. By way of example, reference can be made to a book 'Residents of Jewish Kraków: Women'.[376] Mentioning the fact that the bilingual (Polish and English) book is one of a series,

---

[373] Ewa Dąbrowska and Anna Kielczewska (Eds), 'Residents of Jewish Kraków, vol IV, Women'; EMG, Kraków, 2021, page 124

[374] Entry on websites of the Jewish Women's Archive and the YIVO Institute. See also Czesław Brzoza, 'Żydzi Krakowa Międzywojennego: kalendarium'; Wydawnictwo 'Historia Iagellonica'; Kraków, 2018

[375] Daniel K Heller, 'The Gendered Politics of Public Health; Jewish Nurses and the American joint Distribution Committee in Interwar Poland' in Jewish History (2018) 31: 319-352 available at https://doi.org/10.1007/s10835-018-9301-9

[376] Ewa Dąbrowska and Anna Kiecizewska (Eds), 'Residents of Jewish Kraków; Women; Wydawca EMG, Kraków, 2021

the editors note, 'This fourth volume is entirely devoted to women, although there is also some room for men here – as supporting characters, in the background of the main stories evoked by the characters of women'. The book includes a detailed bibliography which, for example, gives a link to the website of Archiwum Historii Kobiet at http://www.herstorie.pl/kobiety

Architects

Barbara Zbroja has written extensively about architecture in Kraków and the role of Jewish architects in the development of the city. One of her articles in English is 'Jewish Architects in Cracow 1868-1939' which is included in volume 4 of Scripta Judaica Cracoviensia. She notes that Jews were able to qualify as architects well before the end of the nineteenth century but she illustrates that at that time the profession was dominated by men. It was only in the 1930's when a new generation included three women, Irena Bertig (born in Łódz, 1905), Diana Reiter (born in Drohobycz, 1902), and Rela Schmeidler (born in Kraków, 1905), 'the first women to practice the profession of an architect in the area of Cracow'.[377]

Of the three female architects, most has been written about Diana Reiter (1902-1943). Barbara Zbroja notes that her designs were innovative and related to styles promoted by the Bauhaus School.[378] Ms Reiter survived the Kraków Ghetto, but was shot in the head at Płaszów after insisting that the camp commandant permit the reconstruction of an improperly built barrack building.[379]

The life and works of Diana Reiter are considered by Kamila Twardowska in her paper 'Identity and Gender as Obstacles? A Comparison of Two Biographies of Jewish Architects from Kraków'.[380]

Rela Schmeidler (1905-1988) attended the Faculty of Architecture of the Academy of Fine Arts in Kraków from 1924 to 1929. After a short period in Warsaw, she returned to Kraków where she was secretary of the Association of Architects between 1931 and 1934. In 1939 she prepared a project for a dormitory of the Private Secondary Vocational School for Jewish Girls but the project ceased with the outbreak of war.[381]

---

[377] Barbara Zbroja, 'Jewish Architects in Cracow 1868-1939'; Scripta Judaica Cracoviensia, vol 4, 2006, pages 36, 42 and 43. The author's most recent book is 'Leksykon architektów i budowniczych pochodzenia żydowskiego w Krakowie w latach 1868-1939'; Wydawnictwo Wysoki Zamek Iwona Tokarska, Kraków, 2023 – a lexicon of architects and builders of Jewish origin
[378] 'Jewish Architects in Cracow', page 39
[379] Elinor J Brecher, 'Schindler's Legacy; True Stories of the List Survivors'; Plume/Penguin, New York, NY, pages 101 and 185. Also Joseph Bau, 'Dear God, Have You Ever Gone Hungry'?'; Arcade Publishing, New York, NY, 1998, page 120 and see various references in Thomas Keneally, 'Schindler's Ark/List'. Additionally, see Ewa Dąbrowska (Ed), 'Residents of Jewish Kraków; Notebook for Reading', vol 1: EMG Publishers, Kraków, 2019, pages 44 and 45 and the names index in Ryszard Kotarba, 'Żydzi Krakowa w dobie zagłady (ZAL/KL Płaszów)' Instytut Pamięci Narodowej, Kraków, 2022
[380] In Elana Shapira (Ed), 'Designing Transformation; Jews and Cultural Identity in Central European Modernism'; Bloomsbury, London, 2021
[381] Wikipedia

Little seems to have been written about Irena Bertig, but brief biographical information relating to her is recorded on a site, 'Pamięci architektów Polskich', at https://www.archimemory.pl/pokaz/irena_bertig,1273167

Doctors and nurses

Following the constitutional changes of the 1860's, the faculty of medicine was one of the two most popular faculties at the Jagiellonian University amongst Jewish students, and the twentieth century saw an increasing number of female Jewish graduates. That was until admission into the faculty was severely, and then totally, restricted in the 1930's.[382] Address books and professional directories, which can be viewed at www.genealogyindexer.org , show that in that decade a large number of doctors were Jewish, and many of them were women.

For example, lists of doctors, dentists and chemists, and information concerning the Jewish hospital, are included in the Kraków address book for 1932 at https://mtg-malopolska.org.pl/images/skany/ksiegaadresowa1932djvu/ksiegaadresowa1932.pdf (images 169–184; pp. 52–67 of part III).

An extensive list of Jewish doctors is included on pages 195 and 196 of 'W 3cia rocznincę zagłady ghetta w Krakowie' (On the Third Anniversary of the Destruction of the Ghetto in Kraków). This was published by Centralny Komitet Żydów Polskich (The Central Committee of Polish Jews) in 1946. The list, which can be viewed at https://kehilalinks.jewishgen.org/krakow/kra_notables.htm includes the following women – Felicja Blamkstein, Rozalia Blau, Helena Czapnicka, Fryderyka Distler, Hanna Fleischman, Amalia Goldman, Gizella Guttman, Dora Haber, Erna Hollander, Maria Hirschtal, Gustawa Joffe, Czesława Jurowicz, Gruna Spira Lewinger, Deborah Lazer, Eugenia Mirowska, Manesse Zucker, Ela Natel, Maria Pechner, Gustawa Praetzel, Dora Rubenstein, Bronisława Schenkel, Berta Silberberg, Stefania Silberberg, Regina Thur, Lila Wandstein and Wanda Zaks.

Volume 5 of the series, 'Residents of Jewish Kraków' includes information about the city's Jewish Hospital and its staff,[383] and this work refers specifically to the high number of medically qualified women who were employed at the hospital. The author then continues, 'Those days it was frowned upon to employ women as hospital staff and they often found it difficult to make a living because of patients' negative attitude towards them. The fact that they worked where they worked resulted from their great engagement and it was nearly a miracle: numerus clausus at the Medical Faculty of the Jagiellonian University included women – there could be only 5% of them among the students. The Council of the Faculty explained … in 1923 … that women were neither diligent nor did they progress in academic achievements and they should not be given any place at university.'

---

[382] Wiesław Kozub-Ciembroniewicz (Ed), 'Academics of Jewish Heritage in the Modern History of the Jagiellonian University'; Jagiellonian University Press, Kraków, 2014
[383] Ewa Dąbrowska (Ed), 'Residents of Jewish Kraków', vol V, Places and People, EMG Publishers, Kraków, 2022, pages 116-129. See also Arieh Bauminger (Ed), 'Sefer Kroke; Ir v'Am b'Yisrael'; Rav Kuk Publishers, Jerusalem, 1959, pages 324, 325 and Aleksander Skotnicki, 'Szpital gminy wyznaniowej Żydowskiej w Krakowie, 1866-1941'; Sradomskie Centrum Dialogu; Wydawnictwo AA, Kraków, 2013.

A list of doctors employed at the Jewish Hospital in Kraków in 1935 is available at   https://kehilalinks.jewishgen.org/Krakow/kra_Jewish_hospital.htm   The   list includes the following women:

- Dr Marja Leinkram (née Goldberger), physician in the internal medicine department
- Dr Dora Wasserberg, head of dentistry
- Dr Wanda Lachs (née Bluhbaum), head of bacteriology and biochemistry, and
- Dr Stephania Hochman, Dr Dora Lazer and Dr Marja Schonberg, other doctors working at the hospital.

Paulina Wasserberg (1882-1943) and her sister Dorota (Dora) (1885-1943) were doctors in Kraków during the interwar period. Paulina passed her school leaving exams at St Anna's Gymnazium and then studied at the Jagiellonan University. Her work included a period at the military garrison hospital in Kraków, and other periods when she worked as a general practitioner. As indicated in the list which has been mentioned, Dorota spent some time as a senior registrar of the dental ward in the Jewish Hospital.[384]

Henryka Gottlieb (1883-1959) was another doctor practising in Kraków, and also in Zakopane. She specialised in Gynaecology and 'nervous and women's diseases'.[385] Amalia Jurkowicz (1892-1942) also practiced as a doctor in Kraków. In 1941 she was amongst a group of intelligentsia who fled the city and travelled to Wieliczka. However, the following year she died at Bełżec.[386]

Until recently, nursing was considered to be mainly a female occupation. However, in the context of Kraków very little has been written about Jewish nurses. The work of nurses during the Holocaust has been mentioned in general terms, but not in detail. It is known, however, that 'The Joint' was active in promoting healthcare in the interwar period. Dr Zofia Syrkin-Binstejn (1898-1942) was instrumental in setting up training schools for Jewish nurses in various cities, though the school she proposed for Kraków never materialised.[387]

On the other hand, Perel Singer (1881-1955) who was born in the village of Bronowice near Kraków worked as a nurse during the First World War, and later established a nursing and physiotherapy practice in Kraków.[388] Reference should

---

[384] Ewa Dąbrowska and Anna Kielczewska (Eds), 'Residents of Jewish Kraków, vol IV, Women', pages 128-133

[385] Ewa Dąbrowska and Anna Kielczewska (Eds), 'Residents of Jewish Kraków, vol IV, Women', page 168

[386] Małgorzata Międzobrodzka, 'Żydzi w Wieliczce'; Wydawnictwo Żyznowski, Siercza, 2022, page 381 and the Geni genealogical website

[387] Daniel K Heller, The Gendered Politics of Public Health; Jewish Nurses and the American Joint Distribution Committee in Interwar Poland' in Jewish History (2018) 31: 319-352 available at https://doi.org/10.1007/s10835-018-9301-9

[388] Ewa Dąbrowska (Ed), 'Residents of Jewish Kraków, vol II, Art and Culture, EMG Publishers, Kraków, 2020, page 48

also be made to the high number of medically qualified women who worked at the Jewish Hospital on Skawińska Street.[389]

Lawyers

It is worth repeating that women were not able to obtain degrees at the Jagiellonian University before the last decade of the nineteenth century. Whilst women took up degrees in medicine and philosophy, fewer took law degrees, and women could not study law at all at the University in the period up to 1918.[390] The absence of female lawyers before the First World War is illustrated by the Kraków Address and Business Directory for 1907 and a Directory of the Kraków Bar Association dated 1912 – Wykaz adwokatów do Krakowskiej izby adwokackiej należących - which is available on the Jagiellonian Digital library. It is further demonstrated by Bartosz Heksel in his book about Jewish lawyers in Kraków.[391]

A lengthy list of lawyers is available in the Kraków address book for 1932 at https://mtg-malopolska.org.pl/images/skany/ksiegaadresowa1932djvu/ksiegaadresowa1932.pdf (images 165 to 167). It includes virtually no women, one exception being Aniela Steinberg (1886-1988) who is listed at ul. Sławkowska, 9. She graduated in law from Warsaw University in 1920 and she passed her bar exams two years later. Working with her husband, Emil, in 1923 she became the first woman to practice in a Court of Law. In 1930 she became the first female lawyer in the whole of Galicia.[392]

Some 35 lawyers are included in a partial list of voters for the Kraków Jewish community in 1935: https://kehilalinks.jewishgen.org/krakow/kra_1935_voters.htm. This list, too, shows an absence of female lawyers. However, at least one authority notes that in 1936, ten female lawyers were registered in Kraków.[393]

It is clear that by 1939 several women were practising as lawyers. Bartosz Heksel lists the following members of the Kraków Bar, with brief biographical details:-

Olga Bannet, Hanna (Halina) Brauman, Cecylia Dallet, Anna Drach, Irena Folkman, Maria Gottlieb, Bronisława Horowitz, Rachela Kneller, Emilia Lamensdorf, Róża Leinkram, Flora Lillienthal, Ela Pleszowska, Ewa Scheidlinger, Paulina Spira, Aniela Steinberg and Lola Weindling.

---

[389] Ewa Dąbrowska (Ed), 'Residents of Jewish Kraków, vol V, Places and People'; EMG, Kraków, 2022, page 120

[390] Marek Minakowski, 'Family Network of an Emerging Jewish Intelligentsia (Cracow, 1850-1918)'; Journal of Historical Network Research 2 (2018), 53-75, table 2 and page 67

[391] Bartosz Heksel, 'Żydowscy adwokaci w przedwojennym Krakowie'; EMG, Kraków, 2020. See in particular chapter 1 and the lists from 1909 and 1913 inside the front and back covers

[392] Bartosz Heskel, 'Żydowscy advokaci w przedwojennym Krakowie', page 209 and Ewa Dąbrowska (Ed), 'Residents of Jewish Kraków', vol I, EMG, Kraków, 2019, pages 40, 41

[393] Ewa Dąbrowska and Anna Kielczewska (Eds), 'Residents of Jewish Kraków, vol IV, Women'; EMG, Kraków, 2021, page 188

It is perhaps notable that none of these is mentioned by Dr Zygmunt Fenichel in his paper 'Jewish Legal Practice in Kraków', which is included in the Yizkor book, 'Sefer Kroke; Ir v'Am b'Yisroel', published in Jerusalem in 1959.

Erna Eibenschütz (1906-Holocaust), who is not included in Bartosz Heksel's book was another early Jewish female lawyer in Kraków. She studied at the Jagiellonian Law Faculty between 1924 and 1928, receiving a doctorate in law in 1931. Initially she helped her father run his legal practice in Jaworzno, some 30 miles (48 km) north west of Kraków, but she moved to Kraków at the beginning of the 1930's. Although registered as a lawyer in Kraków, from 1936 she also ran her own practice in Jaworzno.[394]

Religious observance

A photograph of women praying out of doors in Kraków in 1926 is one of many images at https://yivoencyclopedia.org/search.aspx?query=krakow+after+1795. The image was taken on the fast of Tisha b'Av, which commemorates the destruction of the first and second temples in Jerusalem.

The minor festival of Tu b'Av occurs six days after Tisha b'Av and is in direct contrast to it. Tu b'Av is in effect a Jewish Valentines Day – a holiday of love and an auspicious day for weddings. In the interwar years the festival was revived and celebrated by the Bais Ya'akov movement which is described in the section of this chapter headed 'education'. In 1932, the movement's founder Sarah Schenirer led such a celebration in the woods of Skawa, a village some thirty miles south of Kraków where seminary students were spending the last summer before they left for their assigned teaching posts.[395]

Orthodox Judaism

Accounts of orthodox Jewish life are given by several Holocaust survivors in their memoirs. For example, in her book 'My Lost World', Sara Rosen describes her upbringing in a Chassidic home. She emphasises the traditions associated with the Sabbath and each of the religious festivals. From her perspective, 'It was a world of women. Mothers, aunts, maids, and teachers, always close by. Houses full of familiar aromas and cooking and baking, an atmosphere of warmth and security'. Her testimony reflects the importance of women in Chassidic life, though in the interwar period the separation of roles between men and women was still being carried forward from earlier times.[396]

Progressive Judaism

The growing participation and membership of females in the Progressive community of Kraków which began in the nineteenth century continued into the

---

[394] Ewa Dąbrowka and Anna Kielczewska (Eds), 'Residents of Jewish Kraków, vol IV, Women'; EMG, Kraków, 2021, page 188

[395] Wikipedia entry for 'Tu b'Av' and National Library of Israel blog by Naomi Seidman, 'The Feminist Revival of Tu b'Av, the Jewish Festival of Love', 21 July, 2021 at https://blog.nli.org.il/en/bais-yaakov-tu-bav

[396] Sara Rosen, 'My Lost World; A Survivor's Tale'; The Library of Holocaust Testimonies, Vallentine Mitchell, London, 1993, page 52

twentieth. For example, in the interwar years, women sang in the choir at the Synagogue on Miodowa Street.[397]

Sarah Schenirer's family

Sarah Schenirer has already mentioned in the section of this chapter relating to education, and particularly the Bais Ya'akov movement. Sarah was born on 3 July, 1883, the third of nine children of Bezalel and Róża (Lack) Schenirer, a family of Belzer Hassidim. Sarah's sisters were:-

- Lea, (1875-1942), married to Kalman Mandelbaum. They had six children
- Helena/Chaya (1888-1942) who lived in Kraków and worked as a Hebrew teacher.
- Matylda/Mania (1892-1942) who worked as a secretary in a brick factory in Bonarka and apparently never married.

All the sisters died in Belzec.[398]

Sport

In his book on Jewish Life in Cracow in the interwar period,[399] Sean Martin devotes a whole chapter to voluntary associations covering areas such as sport, libraries and reading rooms, art and theatre. His observations, which relate largely to football and Maccabi, do not include any suggestion that females held positions of leadership in these associations – except in the case of one reading room, and those groups relating to a small number of sports.

More detailed information is given in the book 'The Maccabees of Sport; Jewish Sport in Kraków' which was published by the Kraków City Historical Museum in 2012. The book describes a wide range of sports and it is clear from this publication that some women were active in various sports such as skiing, gymnastics, tennis, athletics, swimming and water polo. For example, the book features a volley ball team from Maccabi in the 1920's and the water polo team of Jutrzenka Kraków with the Polish champion, Helena Schönfeld in about 1926. Also featured are female competitors at the Maccabi Winter Games at Zakopane in 1933, and female members of the Jutrzenka swimming team, including Olga Schreiber. [400]

Volume 4 of the series 'Residents of Jewish Kraków' gives a brief biography of Maryla Freiwald (1911-1962) who was an athlete and a member of Maccabi,

---

[397] Eugeniusz Duda, 'Jewish Cracow: A Guide to the Historical Buildings and Places of Remembrance'; Vis-à-vis Etudia, Kraków, 2014, page 86
[398] Naomi Seidman, 'Sarah Schenirer and the Bais Yaakov Movement'; Littman, Oxford, 2017, appendix B and https://thebaisyaakovproject.religion.utoronto.ca/person/sarah-schenirer-2/
[399] Sean Martin, 'Jewish Life in Cracow, 1918-1939'; Vallentine Mitchell, London, 2003, chapter 6, 'Voluntary Associations and the Varieties of Cultural Life'
[400] 'The Maccabees of Sport; Jewish Sport in Kraków'; Muzeum Historyczne Miasta Krakowa, Kraków, 2012, pages 31, 78, 169, 172 and 173

Kraków. She became Polish champion in hurdling and long jump and represented her country at several international events.[401]

Theatre

Several sources demonstrate the extent of female participation in the Yiddish theatre. One such source is a book 'Teatr żydowski w Krakowie; studia i materialy' (The Jewish Theatre in Kraków; Studies and Material) which was published by the Jagiellonian University in 1995 and which includes an extensive names index. Rachela (Róża, Rejzl, Rokhl) Holcer (Holzer) (1889-1998) is one of many female actors who are mentioned. She was born in Kraków where her father was a Bundist and chairman of the Kraków Yiddish Workers' Union. Rachela made her debut on the stage of the Union's theatre at the age of six. In 1925 she began performing in the Polish theatre 'Piekarski'. The following year she joined the Kraków Jewish Dramatic Theatre and the newly formed Krakauer Yidisch Kunst Teater (the Kraków Yiddish Art Theatre). By way of example, in May 1933 she presented works of Polish and Jewish poets at the Jewish Theatre. In 1938 she migrated to Australia.[402]

Sean Martin refers to Rachel Holcer in his book about Jewish life in Kraków between the Two World Wars. He notes that she felt the Yiddish Theatre, under the directorship of Mojżesz Kanfer, bridged a gap between Orthodox Jews who spoke Yiddish but were opposed the theatre, and more assimilated Jews who supported theatre but found the Yiddish language marginal to their cultural identity.[403]

Runa Wellner also features prominently in 'Teatr Żydowski w Krakowie'. Her performances were frequently reviewed in the Jewish press, as indicated by the names index in Czezław Brzoza's book 'Żydzi Krakowa międzywojennego; Kalendarium'.

Eugenia Prokop-Janiec describes how the theatre offered many opportunities for Jewish women to expand their cultural production before and during the interwar period. She mentions the Teatr Ludowy (The People's Theatre) on the outskirts of Kraków which staged plays by the Jewish writer Aniela Kallas (Korngut). The author also mentions the Jewish actress Julia Romowicz (Julia Monderer, b. 1889).[404]

Zofia Jasińska-Filipowska (1908-2003) is an example of a Jewish actress who performed mainly in non Jewish venues, particularly the Juliusz Słowacki Theatre. During the 1930's she performed in plays directed by Julisz Osterwa. She survived

---

[401] Ewa Dąbrowska and Anna Kielczewska (Eds), 'Residents of Jewish Kraków, vol IV, Women'; EMG, Kraków, 2021, page 56

[402] https://jwa.org/encyclopedia/article/holzer-rokhl See also the YIVO Institute, Archival Collections, Yidisher Artistn Fareyn membership book of Rachela Holcer and The Yiddish Melbourne website at http://www.monash.edu.au/ See also Czesław Brzoza, 'Żydzi Krakowa międzywojennego; kalendarium'; Historia Iagellonica, Kraków, 2018, names index and particularly page 471

[403] Sean Martin, 'Jewish Life in Cracow 1918-1939'; Vallentine Mitchell, London, 2003, page 222

[404] Eugenia Prokop-Janiec, 'Mapping Modern Jewish Kraków' in Halina Goldberg (Ed), 'Polish Jewish Culture Beyond the Capital'; Rutgers University Press, New Brunswick, NJ, 2023, page 195

the Holocaust and performed in the Siedem Kotów (Seven Cats) cabaret and the Kraków Operetta House before emigrating to Israel in 1956.[405]

Hanka Landau (Landau-Eiger) (1904-1999) was a member of Zrzeszenie Żydowskich Artystów Malarzy i Rzeźbiarzy w Krakowie (The Kraków Association of Jewish Artists, Painters and Sculpters), and also Zawodowy Związku Polskich Artystów Plastyków (The Professional Union of Polish Visual Arts). In 1935 she joined the cabaret cast of 'Bury Melonik' (The Grey Bowler Hat) and performed on the theatre stage 'Tam Tam'.[406]

Hanka Lewkowicz (1918-?) was a sculptor, painter and dancer. She was educated at the Hebrew Gymnasium in Kraków and participated in the activities of the city's Żydowski Towarzystwo Teatralne (Jewish Theatrical Society). Her activities were reported in Nowy Dziennik and other publications, as for example were the performances of Gusta Lindenbaum-Kohn.[407]

Amateur theatrical performances were staged by various schools during the interwar period. In her paper, 'The Theatrics of Bais Yaakov', Naomi Seidman describes the performances of the orthodox girls' school in various towns and cities, including Kraków.[408]

The theatre attracted many female actors from well beyond the Kraków area. These included Ida Kamińska (1899-1980) and Miriam Orleska (1900-1943), best known for her role as Leah in S Ansky's 'The Dybbuk', who were based in Warsaw in the interwar period.[409]

Further information is available from a second publication of the Jagiellonian University. That is Mirosława Bułat's book 'Krakowski teatr żydowski; między szundem a sztuką' (The Kraków Jewish Theatre; between Imagination and Art) which was published in 2006, and a short history of the theatre can be read at https://sztetl.org.pl/en/towns/k/512-krakow/102-education-and-culture/25493-jewish-theatre-krakow-prior-1939

Since 2008, the tradition of Jewish theatre in Kraków has been continued by the Midrash Theatre under the directorship of Tanya Segal. The theatre undertakes innovative educational projects and its website is at https://jewishtheatre.krakow.pl.

Trade and commerce

---

[405] Ewa Dąbrowska and Anna Kielczewska (Eds), 'Residents of Jewish Kraków, vol IV, Women'; EMG, Kraków, 2021, page 180

[406] Natasza Styrna, 'Zrzeszenie Żydowskich Artystów Malarzy i Rzeźbiarzy w Krakowie (1931-1939), ; Wydawnictwo Neriton, Warszawa, 2009, page 266

[407] Wikipedia and Natasza Styrna 'Zrzeszenie Żydowskich Artystów' page 267. For an example of a report in Nowy Dziennik see http://jbc.bj.uj.edu.pl/dlibra/plain-content?id=114616 page 5. See also references in Czesław Brzoza, 'Żydzi Krakowa międzywojennego; Kalendarium'

[408] Naomi Seidman, 'The Theatrics of Bais Yaakov', in Halina Goldberg, 'Polish Jewish Culture Beyond the Capital'; Rutgers University Press, New Brunswick, NJ, 2023, chapter 5

[409] See a large number of references in the names index to 'Teatr żydowski w Krakowie' and an English summary on page 108, as well as Wikipedia and Czesław Brzoza, 'Żydzi Krakowa międzywojennego; Kalendarium', names index

Art supplies

Iwona Kawalla-Lulewicz's book about shops and trades in interwar Kraków[410] illustrates the extent to which the Jewish population was engaged in trade and commerce. The detailed names index includes several Jewish women, including Regina Aleksandrowicz. The Aleksandrowicz family established a small stationery business in Kraków during the 1870's. Regina (1853-1940) was widowed at the age of 35 and she considerably expanded the company. Regina's daughter, Róża (1886-1973) ran a business selling painting accessories. In this way, mother and daughter served the needs of Kraków based artists before the first world war and in the period between the wars.[411] Róża 'created the best painting materials department in Cracow' and had many friends among painters. She sponsored the National Museum to which she donated 30 paintings in 1950. Róża died in Tel Aviv in 1973.[412]

Books

In his article 'Jewish Antiquarian Booksellers in Kraków'[413], Ryszard Löw explains how members of the Jewish community were active in the sale of second hand books over a period of many decades. He refers to the purchase and sale of books of historical and academic value rather than low grade items. The book shops were concentrated in streets to the north of the main market square, particularly on ul. Szpitalna. The author mentions several female members of the Taffett, Seiden and Himmelblau families who ran their own businesses independently of their male relatives.

Ryszard Löw quotes from Róża Nowotarska, a Catholic who was born in Kraków in 1920 and who emigrated to America and worked at the radio station of the Polish Section of the Voice of America. She wrote:-

'Szpitalna Street was full of antiquarian bookshops. Dark, with a smell of mould, they contained treasures. Three steps up, a long and dark hallway, the counter sagging under the weight of books. All around, from floor to ceiling, books, books, books.'[414]

The activities of Dina, Maria and Paulina Seiden receive particular attention in a brief article 'Antiquarians from Szpitalna Street'.[415] The author includes a photo of

---

[410] Iwona Kawalla-Lulewicz, 'Kupiectwo i handel w międzywojennym Krakowie (1918-1939); Biblioteka Krakowska nr 166, Księgarnia Akademicka Internetowa, Kraków, 2020
[411] George J Alexander, 'Generations: A Millennium of Jewish History in Poland from the Earliest Times to the Holocaust told by a Survivor from an Old Kraków Family'; Congress for Jewish Culture, New York, NY, 2008, pages 215, 216, 230 and 231, and Teresa Leśniak (Ed), 'A World Before a Catastrophe'; International Cultural Centre, Kraków, 2007, pages 89 and 112
[412] Ewa Dąbrowska (Ed), 'Residents of Jewish Cracow, vol II, Art and Culture'; EMG Publishers, Kraków, 2020, pages 36-41
[413] In 'Polin' vol 23, Littman, Oxford, 2011
[414] Ryszard Löw in 'Polin', vol 23, page 344, quoting Róża Nowotarska,'Moi krakowscy Żydzi'; Wiadomości, 1967. See also Wikipedia and obituaries
[415] Ewa Dąbrowska and Anna Kielczewska (Eds), 'Residents of Jewish Kraków, vol IV, Women'; EMG, Kraków, 2021, pages 100-117. See also Ryszard Löw, Jewish Antiquarian Booksellers in Kraków' in 'Polin' vol 23, page 342 and Marek Sroka, 'Migrating Volumes; Jewish Immigrants from Kraków and their Personal Book Collections, 1949-1950'

the Taffett family bookshop and also refers to an article by Ryszard Löw, 'Pod znakiem starych foliantów' (Under the Sign of the Old Volumes), published by Universitas in 1993.

Rafael Scharf describes how 'at the beginning of each school year that street provided a background to a veritable carnival – crowds of students of all ages milled around the pavements and shops, buying, selling and bartering old books, for new, having a great deal of fun on the way.'[416]

Other businesses

Formal announcements relating to changes in the status of businesses, legal matters and, for example insolvencies, are to be found in the State publication 'Gazetta Lwowska'.[417] In the interwar period these announcements often indicate the involvement of women. For example, the November, 1931 issue includes an announcement relating to the firm of Hirsch Rubinstein & Co, which ran a steam sawmill in the Kraków district of Czyzyny. The entry notes that the owners, who had died, were replaced by several individuals including Weronika Koplowitz Hirch, Fryda Margules Hirsch and Gitle Hirschowa. The same issue also records the bankruptcy of Reizli (Rozy) Rakower, a shopkeeper in Podgórze.[418]

Sara Gross (1891-1959) and her husband, Jakób, ran a very successful glass and china business from the main square in Kraków. They had a large and prestigious customer base. Photographs of the shop, and of additional premises which were opened in 1935, are shown in Iwona Kawalla-Lulewicz's book which has already been mentioned. Additionally, Sara's role in the running and development of the business is described in the book.[419]

Mina Pfefferberg (1890-1941 or 1942) ran a manufacturing company for artistic needlework, and sold a wide range of soft furnishings for home interiors. Additionally, she was a talented interior designer – to the extent that Oskar Schindler hired her to design his personal apartment on ul. Straszewskiego.[420]

Nathan and Amalia Krieger ran the photographic business of their father, Ignacy, after his death. Following Nathan's death in 1903, Amalia (1846-1928) continued to run the studio in Kraków until 1926, when she donated her collection of many thousand photographic plates to the city of Kraków.[421] 'While running the company, Amalia Krieger continued the work begun by her predecessors, providing a

---

[416] Rafael Scharf, 'Poland, What Have I To Do With Thee'; Vallentine Mitchell, London, 1998, page 66
[417] See, for example, http://jbc.bj.uj.edu.pl/dlibra/plain-content?id=26467 which shows an issue from 1904 and http://jbc.bj.uj.edu.pl/publication/17732
[418] https://yourjewishgem.blogspot.com/search/label/Podgorze
[419] Iwona Kawalla-Lulewicz, 'Kupiectwo i handel w międzywojennym Krakowie (1918-1939). See also Ewa Dąbrowska and Anna Kielczewska (Eds), 'Residents of Jewish Kraków, vol IV, Women', page 92
[420] Ewa Dąbrowska and Anna Kielczewska (Eds), 'Residents of Jewish Kraków, vol IV, Women, page 144
[421] Ewa Dąbrowska (Ed), 'Residents of Jewish Kraków, vol I'; EMG, Kraków, 2019, page12. See also Edyta Gawron and Michał Galas (Eds), 'Nie tylko Kroke; Historia żydów krakowskich'; Wydawnictwo Literackie, Kraków, 2022, pages 243 and 244

collection of plates for the needs of various publishers, publications and scientific magazines, and the illustrated press.'[422]

A lengthy article 'Jewish themes in photographs from the collection of the Historical Museum of the city of Kraków; Part I; Pre-1939 Photographs' is included in volume 35 of 'Krzysztofory'. It includes photos of several women, for example Anna Drobner, who is mentioned below, and the artist, Dorota Berlinerblau.[423] A further photographic collection, which features women, as well as men, is included in the book 'Jewish Families of the Pre-War Cracow' which was published in 2015. This work relates to the Allerhand, Schenirer, Akavia, Spira, Rakower and Anisfeld, Lauterbach, Mosberg and Taube families.[424]

Volume III in the series 'Residents of Jewish Cracow' is devoted to food and culture. Although several businesses are mentioned, all were run by men with the exception of two – and in both cases the women worked with their husbands. The first example is Anna Drobner who ran a café whilst the second is the appropriately named Rywka Beigel who ran a bakery.[425]

As noted in the previous chapter, in her book about the Jews of Wieliczka (a town about 10 miles or 15 km south east of Kraków), Małgorzata Międzobrodzka identifies several women who were engaged in trade during the period of the Austrian occupation. Her chapter about the interwar period focuses less on the economic activity of women but, for example, several female traders are noted to have been exempt from paying communal tax, or to have had their tax debts written off due to poverty or even insolvency in 1930 and 1931. The traders include Ryfka Baron, Rozalia Hönig, Debora Lewita, Beila Paliborska, Rozalia Tisch, Dowra Weinberger, Chaja Wimmer, and Anna and Helena Zuckermann.[426]

Zionism

A number of women's Zionist associations were established in Kraków at the turn of the nineteenth and twentieth centuries. These included B'not Zion (Daughters of Zion) (1899), Chevrat Rut (The Ruth Sisterhood) (1901) and the Socialist group 'Jehudit' (Judith).[427] Sarah Schenirer is said to have attended the Rut Association but it was not religious enough for her.[428]

---

[422] https://muzeumkrakowa.pl/nasze-wydawnictwa/amalia-krieger
[423] Ewa Gazcoł and Joanna Gellner, 'Wątki żydowskie w fotografii ze zbiorów Muzeum Historycznego Miasta Krakowa; Część 1' in Krzysztofory, tom 35, Muzeum Historyczne Miasta Krakowa, Kraków 2017, pages 285-364
[424] Aleksander Skotnicki and Paulina Najbar, 'Rodziny żydowskie przedwojennego Krakowa/Jewish Families of the Pre-War Cracow'; Stradomskie Centrum Dialogu w Krakowie, 2015
[425] Ewa Dąbrowska (Ed), 'Residents of Jewish Cracow, vol III, Food and Culture'; Wydawca EMG, Kraków, 2020, pages 60 and 140
[426] Małgorzata Międzobrodzka, 'Żydzi w Wieliczce'; Wydawnictwo Żyznowski, Siercza (Wieliczka), 2022, pages 288, 289
[427] Arnon Rubin, 'The Rise and Fall of the Jewish Communities in Poland and their Relics Today', vol 3, District Kraków; Tel Aviv University Press, 2009, page 66
[428] Rachel Manekin, 'The Rebellion of the Daughters'; Princeton University Press, Princeton, NJ, 2020, pages 31, 32. See also page 201

The 'Haszachar' Zionist group catered for religious youth. Sara Grossbart-Perlmutter and Nella Rost were amongst its female leaders and, for example, they represented the group at a World Conference of Jewish Women which was held in Basel in 1927.[429] Nella Rost was also active in the Zionist group 'Hitachdut'. She survived the Holocaust, following which she was active with the Jewish Historical Commission in recording the events of the Nazi occupation.[430]

Dora Birnbach was born in 1911 to a Chassidic family in Sokolów Podalski, not far from Warsaw. She rebelled against her religious upbringing and at the age of 16 she moved to Kraków where she joined the left wing Zionist movement, Hashomer Hatzair. She left for Palestine in 1933 and later served as a nurse in the International Brigade during the Spanish Civil War.[431]

A branch of the Women's International Zionist Organisation (WIZO) was established in Kraków during the 1930's.[432] Maria Apte was its president for several years.[433] Her activities were often reported in the press, for example her attendance at the World Congress of Jewish Organisations which was held in Geneva in 1936.[434]

Isaac Schwartzbart's work on Jewish life in Kraków between the World Wars[435] includes a chapter entitled 'Di Zionistische Freien-Bavegung' (The Zionist Women's Movement) which describes the WIZO, Young WIZO and Haddasah groups. Although the author praises the WIZO membership, he notes that the movement did not attract many members compared with non Zionist female groups.

Schwartzbart's discussion on this issue is considered by Gershon Bacon in his article about Jewish Women in Poland in the interwar period at https://jwa.org/encyclopedia/article/poland-interwar. Professor Bacon notes that according to Isaac Schwartzbart, 'The Jewish female student was for the most part in the camp of non-Zionist socialism and cosmopolitanism and participated in the general Polish socialist movement, and in the Bund, rather than among Zionists'.

Isaac Schwartbart's book also includes a chapter 'Di Yunge Frei in unser Renessance' (Young Jewish Women in our Renaissance).

---

[429] Czesław Brzoza, 'Żydzi Krakowa międzywojennego; kalendarium'; Historia Iagellonica, Kraków, 2018, page 251

[430] See for example, her article 'Społeczeństwo Żydowskie w Krakowie w okresie okupacji' in 'W 3cia rocznice zagłady ghetta w Krakowie'; Centralny Komitet Żydów Polkich. Kraków, 1946

[431] Raanan Rain and Susanne Zeff, 'Untold Stories of the Spanish Civil War'; Routledge, London and New York, 2023, page 48

[432] Catalogue of the Central Archives of the History of the Jewish People, Jerusalem at http://cahjp.nli.org.il The Archives hold minutes and correspondence relating to various Zionist organisations

[433] Edyta Gawron and Michał Galas (Eds), 'Nie tylko Kroke; Historia Żydów krakowskich'; Wydawnictwo Literackie, Kraków, 2022, page 320

[434] Czesław Brzoza, 'Żydzi Krakowa międzywojennego; Kalendarium'; Historia Iagellonica, Kraków, 2022, pages 600 and 603

[435] Isaac Schwartzbart, 'Tsvishn Beyde Velt Milchomes; Zikhroynes Vegn dem Yiddishn Leben in Kroke in der Tkufeh 1919-1936'; The Central Committee for Jews in Argentina, Buenos Aires, 1958

Isaac Schwartzbart refers in his book not only to Maria Apte but also to Elza Silberstein (1890-1942), a graduate of the Jagiellonian University, who was a Vice President of WIZO in Kraków. Henryka Stiller (née Fromowicz) (1900-1942) was another activist in WIZO. She, like her sister Maria, studied art in Kraków. Henryka was also associated with the Zionist leading daily newspaper, Nowy Dziennik.[436] This and other newspapers frequently published information relating to WIZO and women's affairs generally.[437]

Further information about WIZO in Poland can be found in Puah Rakovsky's book 'My Life as a Radical Jewish Woman; Memoirs of a Zionist Feminist in Poland': Indiana University Press, Bloomington, IN, 2002.[438]

A branch of WIZO was re-established in Kraków shortly after the Holocaust, and some paper relating to the years 1946-1948 are held at the United States Holocaust Memorial Museum.

Whilst married women may have been attracted mainly to single gender Zionist associations such as WIZO, the Zionist aims of single young women along with single young men were met by a range of other groups, ranging for the religious to the secular. This is one of the topics considered by Sean Martin in his paper 'Jewish Youth between Tradition and Assimilation; Exploring Polish Jewish Identity in Interwar Kraków. This can be read at http://www.jstor.org/stable/25779295

One further source is a book which was published in 1990 to commemorate the Silver Anniversary of the New Cracow Friendship Society. This includes an article by Emanuel Melzer entitled 'Zionism in Cracow – The Interwar period', in which the author mentions youth groups such as Akiva, Mizrachi, Poaelei Zion and Hashomer Hatzair.

A list of 'notable Jews in pre-war Kraków' can be found on the Kehilalinks website at https://kehilalinks.jewishgen.org/krakow/kra_notables.htm. The following women are listed as being members of general Zionist organisations –

Maria Apte, Hanka Bloss, Mina Brenner, Gustawa Dranger, Szelona Dranger, Matylda Karmel, Hanka Landwirth, Mina Liebeskind, Helena Schneide, Elza Silberstein,[439] Hanka Spritzer, and Maria Thon.

Additionally, the website lists the following members of Hitachdut and Gordonia – Rena Bauminger, B Bilha Berglas, Dora Blumenstock, Rega Brandsdorfer, Cecylia Freiman, Celina Galster, Salomea Glückstein, Regina Grün, Regina Kluger, Rozalia Metzger, Anna Metzger, Ryfka Oppenheim, Fryda Schmerlowitz, Erna Schmerlowitz, Helena Stiel, Flora Schwartzfeld, and Fela Schneider;

---

[436] Agnieszka Janczyk, 'Fromowiczowie – Portret Rodziny' in 'Krzystofory' nr 35, Museum Historyczne Miasta Krakowa, 2017, page 493

[437] Czesław Brzoza, 'Żydzi Krakowa międzywojennego; kalendarium; Historia Iagellonica, Kraków, 2018, see the index entries for 'Zjednoczenie Kobiet Żydowskich' (Jewish Women's Associations)

[438] Originally published in Yiddish in 1954. See also the website of the Jewish Women's Archive for entries relating to Puah Rakovsky, and an article by Ela Bauer, 'Zionism in Galicia and Poland, 1880-1939'

[439] See also names index in Czesław Brzoza, 'Żydzi Krakowa międzywojennego'.

and members of Poale Syjon – Rywka Fajer, Tosia Frydman, Rena Fuchs, Eda Ladau, Róża Lux, Hanka Poller, Helena Schonfeld, Bella Weissbardt, and Adela Zeif.

In 1920, Keren Hajesod was established in London to provide the Zionist movement with resources to establish a Jewish homeland in Palestine. In May of the following year the Jewish press in Kraków reported on a meeting in the city where no fewer than 73 women put their names to a declaration in support of this cause. The women are listed by name in Nowy Dziennik, 1921, nr 138.[440]

Yehoshua Ofer describes Zionism in the town of Wieliczka in the Yizkor (Memorial) Book 'Kehilat Wieliczka; Sefer Zikaron'. He refers briefly to WIZO and also notes that many households kept collection boxes so that families could make small but frequent donations to Zionist causes. He notes 'Every Sabbath and holiday eve, the housewife deposited pennies into the Baal Haness box and its white blue companion box'.[441] Małgorzata Międzobrodzka also describes Zionism in Wieliczka and refers to a talk given by a speaker from Kraków entitled 'The task of the Jewish woman at the present time'.[442]

At least one source records that there was a branch of WIZO at Krzeszowice, some 15 miles (25 km) to the north west of Kraków. Searching on the 'Virtual Shtetl' website of the POLIN Museum at www.sztetl.org.pl reveals that a 'temporary' committee of WIZO was established at the turn of 1928 and 1929. Additionally, during the 1930's a branch of WIZO was established in Wadowice, about 32 miles (50 km) south west of Kraków.[443]

---

[440] Wikipedia and Czesław Brzoza, 'Żydzi Krakowa międzywojennego' pages 99 and 100
[441] Yehoshua Ofer, 'Zionism in Our City in the Second and Third Decade of this Century' in the English section of Shmuel Meiri (Ed), 'Kehilat Wieliczka; Sefer Zikaron', Tel Aviv, 1980, which is available at https://www.jewishgen.org/Yizkor/Wieliczka/Wieliczka.html
[442] Małgorzata Międzobrodzka, 'Żydzi w Wieliczce'; Wydawnictwo Żyznowski, Siercza, 2022, pages 309 – 314, 'Wieliccy sjoniści'
[443] Arnon Rubin, 'The Rise and Fall of the Jewish Communities in Poland and their Relics Today'; vol 3, District Kraków, Tel Aviv University Press, 2009, page 338

THE HOLOCAUST
A world turned upside down

Introduction

On the one hand, it can hardly be necessary to state that the period of the Holocaust had an overwhelming impact on the lives of Jewish men, women and children; on the other hand, it may well be appropriate to point out that the enormity of the events of just six years has had a significant impact on our views on Polish Jewish relations which existed over a number of centuries. As Gershon Hundert writes, 'Our knowledge of where history leads acts as a distorting prism, impeding our vision of what became before'.[444]

Perhaps, it is also appropriate to keep in mind a further quote as we consider in detail the role of women in the Kraków area during the Holocaust. That is the opening paragraph of Joanna Tokarska-Bakir's paper 'The Unrighteous Righteous and the Righteous Unrighteous'. She notes

'It is said that both Polish and Jewish memories are clouded by two forms of denial. According to the self-exonerating version of their history, in which they present themselves as righteous, the Poles deny that any members of their nation murdered Jews during the period of German occupation. On the other hand, Jews, with their post-Holocaust anguish, reflexively deny that any Poles helped or saved Jews.'

In this context, it may be of interest to read the writings of an American writer, Edward Reid. He describes himself as a 'historian who specialises in Polish World War History as well as media' and a person 'who became frustrated with the narrative in the United States that basically leaves out the suffering of non-Jews'. He argues that the role of Poles in the Holocaust has been misrepresented to their detriment.[445]

The Centralna Żydowska Komisja Historyczna (Central Jewish Historical Commission) started to collect survivors' testimonies very shortly after the Holocaust came to an end, and during the first three years of its operation the Kraków branch of the CŻKH collected more than 1,300 testimonies. These form part of collection group 301 of the Żydowski Instytut Historyczny (Jewish Historical Institute) in Warsaw.[446]

The last four decades have seen a substantial flow in the amount of information which has been published in relation to the Holocaust. This flow, which is significantly greater than that of the previous three decades, arises partly out of the fall of the Iron Curtain in the late 1980's which has resulted in access to archives in the former Communist territories. A further factor is that survivors who had

---

[444] Gershon David Hundert, 'Jews in Poland-Lithuania in the Eighteenth Century'; University of California Press, Berkeley, CA, 2006, page 4
[445] See for example various articles on www.polishtruth.com
[446] Monika Price, 'What! Still Alive?!; Jewish Survivors in Poland and Israel Remember Homecoming'; Syracuse University Press, Syracuse, NY, 2017, page 61

previously kept their experiences relatively secret have chosen to give their testimonies, both oral and written, before the memory of the experiences passes away with the survivors themselves. Arguably, a third factor can be added – the establishment and development of Holocaust Museums around the world, not least of which are Yad Vashem in Jerusalem, the United States Holocaust Memorial Museum in Washington, DC, and the Polin Museum in Warsaw. These are mentioned briefly in the next section of this chapter. Additionally, there are less well known institutions such as the Shoah Foundation at the University of Southern California. What is stated in the following pages cannot possibly do justice to the quality and volume of publications and testimonies which are held there but hopefully it will give some indication of the sources which are available to researchers.

Yet another factor which has cast a light on the Jews of Kraków during the Holocaust has been Thomas Keneally's book, 'Schindler's Ark'. This work was originally published in 1982 and, as is well known, it was followed by a film 'Schindler's List'. The amount of material which has been written about the book and film is too great to be considered in this chapter. However, reference can be made here to an item on the JewishGen website entitled, 'The Schindler Women'. The author of this article describes how in the autumn of 1944 some 300 women who had been protected by Oskar Schindler in Kraków left the Płaszów concentration camp on route to Schindler's factory at Brünnlitz, only to be diverted to Auschwitz. They were eventually released and 'the Schindler women were the only known group of women, having been brought into the camp [Auschwitz] for labor or the gas chamber, who left the camp unmolested.' Amongst the women who are mentioned by name are Anna Hofstatter (née Laufer) and Helena Fortheimer.[447]

Just as the following words are wholly inadequate to describe the enormous barbarity of the Nazis, or the quality and volume of publications and testimonies, so too are they are wholly inadequate to do justice to the bravery and sacrifice of very many women, and indeed men, during the period of the Holocaust under the most appalling of conditions – a period when mere survival was an act of defiance. Whether as members of the Jewish underground or as smugglers of food or arms, or even as passive resisters of the occupation, these individuals put themselves in mortal danger on a daily basis. Furthermore, very few of us in Western democracies are in the unfortunate position of being able to imagine the sacrifices Jewish mothers took to feed and protect their children, in some cases surrendering them over to non Jewish families and highly uncertain futures.

In the pages which follow, topics are considered in alphabetic order of subject matter. As a result, the sections on Żegota, the interfaith support group, and Żydowska Organizacja Bojowa, The Jewish Fighters' Organisation, appear at the end. Possibly this is a fitting climax to the chapter; alternatively, the sections should appear at the very beginning as a tribute to the fighters' bravery and self sacrifice. In any event, it is hoped that these sections will counteract the largely held perception that all Jews went to their death without resistance or even a murmur. In a similar vein hopefully the sections which describe how non Jewish women saved Jewish

---

[447] https://www.jewishgen.org/yizkor/schindler/sch019.html

lives will counter the widely held generalisation that all Catholic Poles were enthusiastic anti Semites.

In any event, it should be noted that the section headings which are shown are only for general reference and guidance. The sections should not be regarded as watertight compartments. For example, it is perfectly possible for the same individual to have fulfilled different roles at different periods of her life.

Just as it is difficult to describe the catastrophic impact that the Holocaust had on the Jews of Poland, much of what follows serves to illustrate that a small but significant number of Jews survived. Several estimates have put the survival rate at about ten percent.[448] The Jewish population of Kraków just before the Holocaust is widely put at about 60,000.[449] A survival rate of 10 per cent would result in 6,000 survivors including both males and females. The females had a greater chance of survival than circumcised males so arguably there were about 3,500, or possibly 4,000 Jewish women and girls from Kraków who were still alive at the end of the Holocaust. This can only be a rough estimate since many survivors, men and women, hid their Jewish identities after the war.[450] However, it is important to remember that female survivors of the Holocaust in Kraków can be measured in the thousands. It is they who have shown outstanding resilience not only during the Holocaust itself but also in the decades which have followed and it is some of these thousands who have left testimonies which now form a very important part of Holocaust based literature.

Although Jewish females were less likely to be detected by German soldiers, or colluding Poles or Jewish collaborators, than Jewish circumcised males, they nevertheless had to use a wide range of qualities in addition to their bravery. These included Aryan looks, a perfect use of the Polish language, and a working knowledge of Roman Catholic practices. Additionally, they had to be able to think quickly on their feet in the light of circumstances and dangers which could change in an instant.[451]

---

[448] Edyta Gawron, 'Victims and Survivors. How many Cracovian Jews Survived the Holocaust? A Preliminary Survey of the Question'; Scripta Judaica Cracoviensia, vol 4, 2006, which is considered in the next chapter. See also, for example Joel Padowitz, 'Triumph and Tragedy; Journeying through 1,000 Years of Jewish Life in Poland'; JRoots, London, 6th Ed, 2019, page 132. Holocaust deniers offer a much higher survival rate. See for example, Julia Neuberger, 'Antisemitism; What it is. What it isn't. Why it Matters'; Weidenfeld & Nicolson, London, 2019, pages 90-99

[449] For example, Miriam Peleg-Mariańska and Mordecai Peleg, 'Witnesses; Life in Occupied Kraków'; Routledge, London, 1991, page xii

[450] Monika Rice, 'What! Still Alive?!; Jewish Survivors in Poland and Israel Remember Homecoming'; Syracuse University Press, Syracuse, NY, 2017, pages 20-22, where it is suggested that the survival rate was over ten per cent. See also Edyta Gawron, 'Victims and Survivors. How Many Cracovian Jews Survived the Holocaust?', Scripta Judaica Cracoviensia, vol 4, 2006, considered in the next chapter.

[451] See, for example, Joanna Sliwa, 'A Link Between the Inside and the Outside Worlds; Child Smugglers in the Kraków Ghetto' in Zeitschrift für Genozid Forschung, 2012, available on academia.edu

The information on the following pages is drawn from a wide range of sources but, at this stage, it may be useful to mention a few of the most important works which describe the role of women in Kraków during the Holocaust.

Martyna Grądzka-Rejak's detailed book 'Kobieta żydowska w okupowanym Krakowie (1939-1945)' (Jewish Women in Occupied Kraków) was published by Wysoki Zamek of Kraków, in conjunction with Instytut Pamięci Narodowej (The National Remembrance Institute) in 2016. The book is entirely in Polish but it includes an extensive bibliography and names index. The work covers aspects such as family life, occupations and roles undertaken by women, their religious life and their survival strategies. A review of the book in English can be found at www.academia.edu/72437477. The reviewer, Przemysław Sołga, notes that the purpose of the book is 'to analyse the lives of Jewish women in the occupied Cracow, and outline the changes occurring at that time and place in their family lives'. A short presentation about the book given by the author in Polish is available on YouTube.

Martyna Grądzka-Rejak's book follows on from her article, 'Jewish Women in the Kraków Ghetto: An Outline of Research Issues' which appears in volume 3 (2013), number 2 of 'The Person and the Challenges'.[452] One of the conclusions of the article is that 'apart from the changes of the traditional position and role of Jewish women during the occupation, as well as changes in the family structure, women took on new occupational roles ... They worked in various places irrespective of their background and education in order to survive and support or feed their families'.

The Historical Museum of Kraków published a book in 2011 which is devoted to the role of Jewish women in Kraków during the Holocaust. Entitled 'Is War Men's Business?' the book 'focuses on twelve Cracovians whose fates enable us to follow the history of a whole generation of women whose lives were permanently marked out by their wartime experience'. Anna Czocher, one author who contributed to the work introduces the term 'Heroines of Everyday Life' which 'aptly sums up the truth of the Cracovians' fate under the Nazi occupation; the fates marked by the desperate need to struggle with the daily reality which was a veritable battle for survival fought for themselves, their children and family'.

Reference can also be made to Felicja Karay's paper, 'The Women of the Ghetto, Kraków' which was published in Tel Aviv in 2001, and previously published in Hebrew in 'Yalkut Moreshet' volume 71.[453] Other works which describe the Holocaust in a chronological manner, rather than with specific reference to women, include Andrea Löw and Markus Roth, 'Juden in Krakau unter deutscher Besatzung, 1939-1945' (Jews in Kraków under German Occupation); Wallstein Verlag, Göttingen, 2011 and Katarzyna Zimmerer, 'Zamordowany świat; Losy Żydów w Krakowie, 1939-1945' (A Murdered World; The Fate of the Jews in Kraków); Wydawnictwo Literackie, Kraków, 2004.

---

[452] In this paper, the author notes that 860 memories of occupied Kraków are held in file number 31 at the Jewish Historical Institute in Warsaw and that further testimony is held by the Instytut Pamięci Narodowej (The Institute of National Remembrance) the website of which is at www.ipn.gov.pl/en
[453] Further information is on the website of the United States Holocaust Memorial Museum

A photograph of Jewish girls in the Kraków Ghetto in 1942 is available at

https://photos.yadvashem.org/photo-details.html?language=en&item_id=102580&ind=113

whilst a considerable number of photographs can be viewed on the website of Eilat Gordin Levitan at www.eilatgordinlevitan.com/krakow/krakow.html

Archives and museums

Over the years archives and museums have been established in many countries in order to preserve the memories of those who perished during the Holocaust. To a greater or lesser extent, they all hold collections of diaries and testimonials as well as other documents such as correspondence and official papers. Examples of their holdings are listed in the bibliographies of many books written about Kraków during the Holocaust period. The following institutions are worthy of particular mention, though the brief information which is given does not begin to illustrate the extent of the resources which are available.

The Jewish Historical Institute in Warsaw website at https://www.jhi.pl. A search in collections – online collections – Delet portal for 'Krakow kobiet' produces several images relating to women.

The National Archive in Kraków. Searches can be made at www.szukajwarchiwach.gov.pl and by choosing 'Archiwum Narodowe w Krakowie' in 'search the archive'. A search for 'Kobiet, 1939-1945' produces several items.

The POLIN Museum in Warsaw has its website at https://polin.pl. Whilst the Museum no doubt holds a lot of information about Kraków during the Holocaust period, a search for 'Kraków kobiet' shows only one result – a painting 'Portret kobiety' by Gela Seksztajn-Lichtenstein.

The United States Holocaust Memorial Museum website is at https://www.ushmm.org. A search for 'Kraków Women' produces over 1,000 matches, including over 650 images.

Yad Vashem in Jerusalem has its website at https://www.yadvashem.org and a search for 'Kraków Women' results in over 800 matches including large numbers of images and testimonies.

Brief reference is made in the next chapter to the KL Płaszów Memorial Museum in Kraków which arranges guided tours of the site of the former concentration camp.

Collaborators

Few authors have written about the difficult topic of the extent, if any, to which Jews collaborated with the Nazi authorities in Kraków in order to protect themselves and their families. Some material is available about the Ordnungdienst (OD), the Jewish Police Force, and the Judenrat (Jewish Council) but so far as is known neither the force nor the council in Kraków included any women. In any event, many commentators take the view that, with some notable exceptions, members of the OD and the Judenrat were not active collaborators but did what they could to minimise hardship despite the impossible situation in which they found themselves. This topic is revisited below in the subsection headed 'Absence of women in positions of formal authority'.

One author who has written extensively about Jewish collaborators in Kraków is Alicja Jarkowska-Natkaniec. She has written four papers on the subject. These are:

- 'On the So-Called Diamant Network; The Activities of Jewish Undercover Agents in Occupied Kraków in Relation to the Polish Underground',
- 'Collaborators, Informers and Agents in Occupied Kraków; A Contribution to Further Research', which appears in 'The City and History', vol 9, 2020,
- 'Selected Forms of Collaboration in the Płaszów Camp. Characteristics of the Phenomenon'. This appears in volume 38 of 'Krzystofory', published by Muzeum Historyczne Miasta Krakowa, and
- 'Donosicielstwo w Krakowie w latach 1939-1945; Zarys projektu badawczego i probleatyki' (Informers in Kraków in the Period 1939-1945; An Outline of a Research Project and its Problems). This article is included in Alicja Maślak-Maciejewska (Ed), 'Żydzi krakowscy; nowe kierunki badań' (Kraków Jews; New Directions of Research); Austeria, Kraków, 2021.

In these papers the author concludes that widespread Jewish collaboration was largely a myth and that the majority of Jewish collaborators were male. However, she does describe a group of about twenty Jewish collaborators led by Maurycy Diamant. This group included two women, Stefania Brandstätter (née Rottenberger) and Marta Puretz.

Stefania Brandstätter seems to have been particularly notorious, and for example she is the subject of an article on Salon24 dated 10 October, 2013.[454] She is also the subject of several comments by Martyna Grądzka-Rejak in her detailed book about Jewish women during the Nazi occupation.[455] The website of 'The Museum of Jewish Crimes' records that Brandstätter 'had a phone line in her apartment so that she could freely contact Gestapo office at Pomorska Street'. The site continues

'She wandered on the Aryan side of the city for Jewish children hidden there by Poles. When she found a toddler with a Semitic appearance she asked him about his parents, bribing him with sweets. The unexpected [unsuspecting] child revealed the address of the real parents. Brandstätter either handed them over to the Gestapo or blackmailed the victims.'[456]

The same website also refers to Marta Puretz. She was the daughter of a wealthy doctor from Dębniki, one of the districts of Kraków. Her career as a collaborator was

---

[454] www.salon24.pl 'Stefania B – Żydowska Agentka Gestapo
[455] Martyna Grądzka-Rejak, 'Kobieta żydowska w okuowanym Krakowie (1939-1945); Wysoki Zamek, Kraków, 2016, see the names index. See also Katarzyna Zimmerer, 'Zamordowany świat; losy Żydów w Krakowie, 1939-1945'; Wydawnictwo Literackie, Kraków. 2004, page 217 and Aleksander Bieberstein, 'Zagłada Żydów w Krakowie'; Wydawnictwo Literackie, Kraków, 1985, pages 173, 174
[456] www.museumofthejewishcrimes.org/en/ii-world-war/criminals/stefania-brandstatter/

remarkably similar to Stefania Brandstätter's. Beautiful with blue eyes, she was famous for finding her victims on trams or just on the street.[457]

Stefania Brandstätter and Marta Puretz also feature significantly in Witold Mędykowski's paper, 'Przeciw swoim; Wzorce kolaboracji żydowskiej w Krakowie i okolicy' (Against your own; Patterns of Jewish Collaboration in Kraków and the Surrounding Area'), which is available in an English translation on academia.edu. The author notes, for example, that Brandstätter was probably an informer from 1941, and that after the ghetto was established in Kraków, she stayed on the Aryan side, with Aryan papers, living at a house at ul Sławkowska, 6 with other informers including Maurycy Diamand. Witold Mędykowski also describes how Marta Puretz informed on an underground agent Elżbieta Jasińska, resulting in her arrest by the Gestapo and how she carried out a number of arrests following the attack on the 'Cyganeria' café in December, 1942.

Brandstätter survived the war and emigrated to New York where she is said to have lived into old age.[458] The fate of Marta Puretz is less certain. She was arrested in Hungary at the end of the war and according to Aleksandra Kasznik-Christian she was charged with collaboration, but acquitted by a People's Tribunal for lack of evidence. She later lived in France. According to Professor Kasznik-Christian, documents at the National Archive in Paris cast considerable doubt as to whether, or to what extent, Marta Puretz did in fact collaborate with the Nazis.[459]

In his account of life in the Kraków ghetto, Tadeusz Pankiewicz notes that Nazi informers included the OD leader Chilowicz 'and his wife'. On the other hand, testimony also relates how Mrs Chilowicz helped protect Jewish children.[460] Tadeusz Pankiewicz also names the Selingers as 'a very dangerous couple in the service of the Gestapo'. Mrs Selinger is described as 'petite, bleached blonde hair, a doll like beauty, who spoke poor Polish. They collaborated with Obersturmfuhrer Theodore Heinemayer who was counsellor of the Gestapo for political affairs. It is not clear whether or not Mrs Selinger survived the war.[461]

It is worth emphasising that the women who are noted here are mentioned in the interests of full disclosure, but that they appear to be exceptional in their conduct.

Diaries, memoirs and testimonies

Reference is made below, in the section headed 'Żydowska Organizacja Bojowa' to diaries maintained by members of the Jewish underground fighting forces such as

---

[457] www.museumofthejewishcrimes.org/en/ii-world-war/criminals/marta-puretz/
[458] www.hejto.pl/wpis/polacy-mordujacy-zydow-2-stefania-brandstatter
[459] Aleksandra Kasznik-Christian, 'Sprawa Marty Puretz, domniemanej agentki Gestapo z krakowskiego getta' (The Case of Marta Puretz, Alleged Gestapo Agent from the Kraków Ghetto' in Zagłada Żydów Studia i Materiały', 2020 available with an abstract in English at https://zagladazydow.pl/index.php/zz/article/view/668/849
[460] Tadeusz Pankiewicz, 'The Cracow Ghetto Pharmacy'; Holocaust Library, New York, NY, 1985, page 37, and Martyna Grądzka, 'A Broken Childhood'; Wydawnictwo Wysoki Zamek, Kraków, 2012, see names index
[461] Tadeusz Pankiewicz, 'The Cracow Ghetto Pharmacy', pages 37 and 38. For further references to Maria Chilowicz, see Ryszard Kotarba, 'Żydzi Krakowa w dobie zagłady (ZAL/KL Płaszów)'; Instytut Pamięci Narodowej, Kraków, 2022

Gusta Graenger-Dawidson. Her work was first published in Kraków as 'Pamiętnik Justyny' in 1946 and has since been translated into English as 'Justyna's Narrative'. It is essential reading for those who do not yet know about the bravery of Jewish women who fought a brutal enemy against impossible odds. On the other hand, important though they are, numerically, diaries written by members of the ŻOB represent only a very small proportion of the material which has been supplied by, or about, those who experienced the Holocaust in and around Kraków. Since girls and women had a higher survival rate than circumcised boys and men, it is reasonable to assume that the majority of diaries and other forms of testimony were written by females. Consistent with this view, in her paper, 'Jewish Women in the Kraków Ghetto; An Outline of Research Issues',[462] Martyna Grądzka notes that eleven of the sixteen diaries concerning Kraków held by the Jewish Historical Institute were produced by women or teenage girls.

Following the liberation of Kraków in January, 1945, many survivors returned to the city. The number of Jews who lived in Kraków before the war, and who survived it, is uncertain but has been considered by Edyta Gawron in her paper 'Victims and Survivors'.[463] It is estimated that by the beginning of 1946 the number of Jews in Kraków, whether natives of that city or not, had reached nearly 10,000. A number of institutions were established to meet the wide range of needs of those who returned, and one such institution was the Centralna Żydowska Komisja Hstoryczna w Polsce. (The CŻKH or The Central Jewish Historical Commission). From 1945 to 1947 the Commission produced many publications, including 'Pamiętnik Justyny', particularly accounts of those who had survived the Holocaust.

By 1950, the number of Jews in Kraków had fallen significantly. This is illustrated by the brief notes set out below, which relate to survivors who remained in the city for only a short period.

Referring to various forms of testimony, Martyna Grądzka notes 'Time is an extremely important factor whilst using this type of records. The earlier these reports, memoirs and statements were collected after the war, the more 'credible' they are. After all, time … is not an element beneficial to the memory processes.'[464]

In her book 'What! Still Alive?!' Monica Rice distinguishes between two types of testimony. The first is 'testimonies gathered in Poland immediately after the war by the CŻKH and currently stored in the archives of the Żydowski Instytut Historyczny, the Jewish Historical Institute, in Warsaw (collections 301 and 302)' whilst the second type is testimonies collected during the 1950's and 1960's by Yad Vashem. The author notes that the Kraków branch of the CŻKH collected more than

---

[462] Available on the website of the University of Pope John Paul II, Kraków, at
http://czasopisma.upjp2.edu.pl/the.personandthechallenges/article/view/498/425
[463] Edyta Gawron, 'Victims and Survivors. How many Cracovian Jews Survived the Holocaust? A Preliminary Survey of the Question'; Scripta Judaica Cracoviensia, vol 4, 2006
[464] Martyna Grądzka, 'A Broken Childhood'; Wydawnictwo Wysoki Zamek, Kraków, 2012, page 252

1,300 testimonies during the first three years of its activity because of its proximity to the liberated camps.[465]

An extensive list of testimonies of survivors from the Kraków area which are held by Yad Vashem is available on the JewishGen website at https://kehilalinks.jewishgen.org/krakow/kra_testimony.htm These testimonies are in addition to Yad Vashem's 'Pages of Testimony' which are documented memorials to those who did not survive the Holocaust.

In recent years an increasing amount of testimony relating to children has become available to the general public as a result of one researcher, Joanna Sliwa. She is based in New York City as a historian at the Conference on Jewish Material Claims against Germany. and her works include:

- 'Stopping the Spread of Moral Savagery; Child Relief Efforts in the Kraków Ghetto',
- 'Coping with Distorted Reality; Children in the Kraków Ghetto' (2010),
- 'Child Smugglers in the Kraków Ghetto' (2012),
- 'The Forced Relocation to the Kraków Ghetto as Remembered by Child Survivors' (2016),
- a book, 'Jewish Childhood in Kraków' (2021),[466]
- and 'Jewish Children Seeking Help from Catholic Institutions in Kraków during the Holocaust'.[467]

Joanna Sliwa's presentation, 'The Holocaust in Diaries and Memoirs of Child Holocaust Survivors' which was given on 20 November, 2023, is available on YouTube, whilst her article, 'Jewish Children in the Holocaust' appears in the March, 2024 issue of 'The Galitzianer' which is published by the genealogical group, Gesher Galicia.

Reference can also be made to a researcher with a similar surname, Wiktoria Śliwowska, who edited the first volume of 'The Last Eyewitnesses; Children of the Holocaust Speak'. A second volume, edited by Jakub Gutenbaum and Agnieszka Latała, was published in 2005. Both volumes include the testimonies of several children who survived in and around Kraków.[468] Three further volumes of 'Children of the Holocaust Speak' were published between 2019 and 2022 under the direction of Stowarzyszenie 'Dzieci Holocaustu' (The Association of Children of the Holocaust). Several of the testimonies which have been published can be found in English on the website https://zapispamieci.pl by using the tab for wspomnienia (memories).

---

465 Monika Rice, 'What! Still Alive?! Jewish Survivors in Poland and Israel Remember Homecoming', pages 7 and 61
466 Joanna Sliwa, 'Jewish Childhood in Kraków; A Microhistory of the Holocaust'; Rutgers University Press, New Brunswick, NJ, 2021
467 Included in 'Polin', vol 36, Littman, Liverpool, 2024
468 Wiktoria Śliwowska (Ed), 'The Last Eyewitnesses; Children of the Holocaust Speak'; Northwestern University Press, Evanston, IL, vol 1 1998 and vol 2, 2005

Additionally, reference is made below to material which is to be found in the book 'The Children Accuse'. This work was edited by Maria Hochberg-Mariańska and Noe Grüss, and published by Vallentine Mitchell in 1996.

In her PhD thesis, 'Writing in Captivity',[469] Cyndi Freiman examines seven Holocaust diaries written by young Jewish women in Nazi-occupied Poland. In her abstract she notes, 'The publication of diaries written during the Nazi occupation may be one of the most important tasks of post-Holocaust generations seeking to honour the memory of the Shoah ... Each diary serves as a witness to an experience that demands acknowledgement.' She continues, that the women's writing 'may be seen as an act of enormous courage and self preservation, given that many of the diarists did not physically survive the period they documented.'

Between them, archives such as Yad Vashem in Jerusalem, The Jewish Historical Institute in Warsaw and the United States Holocaust Museum in Washington, DC may well hold some thousands of diaries, memoirs and testimonies which relate in some way to Kraków. Some testimonies have been recorded orally rather than, or as well as, by way of the written word. Those of Celina Karp and Rena Finder are just two examples.[470] The paragraphs that follow, relating to some ninety individuals, therefore, refer to no more than a sample which were written or recorded by, or about, girls and women. The individuals are mentioned in alphabetic order of surname, partly to avoid the suggestion that the testimony of one survivor is more valuable than the testimony of any other. The lives of some of the survivors who returned to Kraków will be revisited in the next chapter.

One aspect of the diaries and testimonies is that in order to survive some girls and women had to move several times from village to village in order to avoid detection by suspicious residents. Janina Fischler-Martinho is just one example, as described below.

It must be emphasised that the following paragraphs should be read against the background of a very important warning. Testimonies have been written predominantly by survivors. The criticism could be made that the inclusion in this chapter of the testimonies of a large number of survivors serves to understate the fundamentally destructive, cruel and sadistic nature of the Holocaust and its perpetrators. Terms which are used below, such as 'she survived the ghetto, Płaszów, Auschwitz and Bergen Belsen' flow off the tongue all too easily and the expression does not begin to describe, even inadequately, the daily horrors of existence (the word 'life' is hardly appropriate) in these locations. Even if it is accepted that about ten percent of the Jewish population of Kraków survived, when we examine the testimonies of survivors, we must keep in mind the other ninety percent who perished under the most terrible circumstances. At the same time, though, it is

---

[469] Department of Hebrew, Biblical and Jewish Studies, School of Languages and Cultures, The University of Sydney, November, 2021

[470] See, for example, interviews 11133 and 21482 at the Visual History Archive, University of Southern California, Shoah Foundation, mentioned by Joanna Sliwa in her paper, 'The Forced Relocation to the Kraków Ghetto as Remembered by Child Survivors' which is included in Simone Gigliotti and Monica Tempian (Eds), 'The Young Victims of the Nazi Regime'; Bloomsbury, London, 2016

important to recognise and celebrate the strength of mind and body of those who did survive.

Sophia Aferiat (née Spiewak) was born in 1936 in Słomnicki, a village some 15 miles (24 km) to the north of Kraków. Her father sold milk. At the outbreak of the war Sophia and her mother took refuge in different farms before moving to the Kraków Ghetto. They survived the war. Whilst her mother remained in Poland, Sophia emigrated to Israel in the 1950's.[471]

Dora Agastein (later Dora Agastein-Dormont) wrote several works in the post war period. These include a chronology relating to the German occupation of Kraków which forms a chapter in 'W 3cia rocznicę zagłady ghetta w Krakowie' (On the Third Anniversary of the Destruction of the Ghetto in Kraków) published in Kraków in 1946. Her works also include a paper, 'Żydzi w Krakowie w okresie okupacji niemieckie' (Jews in Kraków during the Period of German Occupation).[472]

Miriam Akavia (née Matylda Weinfeld) was born in Kraków in 1927. Her financially successful father would walk every Friday to a synagogue in the Jewish quarter of Kazimierz from the centre of Kraków where the family lived. She has the dubious distinction of having survived the Kraków Ghetto, Płaszów, Auschwitz and Bergen-Belsen before emigrating to Palestine in 1946. Whilst in the ghetto she received some education, noting 'Before noon I used to go for clandestine education meetings'. Additionally she learned a trade – 'Besides the regular school program we were taught there also sewing, because everybody thought that one needs to have a solid profession'.[473] Her memoir, written as fiction but based on fact, was first published in Hebrew in 1975. An English translation. 'An End to Childhood' was published some twenty years later.[474] Miriam Akavia is also the author of several other works, including 'My Own Vineyard', a novel which tells the story of three generations of a Jewish family in Kraków.[475] Further information, including photographs, about Miriam Akavia's own extended family is set out in 'Jewish Families of Pre-War Cracow' which was published in 2015.[476]

Anna Allerhand survived the Kraków Ghetto, and when it was liquidated she came under the protection of Mirosława Gruszczyńska (née Przebindowska) and her

---

[471] The C Jewish Ledger, Connecticut, April, 24, 2017 and the website of the Holocaust Memorial Center, Farmington Hills, MI.

[472] Reproduced in 'Rocznika Krakowskiego', vol 31 and, in Hebrew, in Arieh Bauminger (Ed), 'Sefer Kraka; Ir v'Am b'Yisrael'; Rav Kuk Institute, Jerusalem, 1959, pages 381 to 407

[473] Joanna Sliwa, 'Coping with Distorted Reality; Children in the Kraków Ghetto', quoting Katarzyna Zimmerer, 'Zamordowany świat; Losy Żydów w Krakowie, 1939-1945'; Wydawnictwo Literackie, Kraków, 2004, page 87

[474] Miriam Akavia, 'An End to Childhood'; Library of Holocaust Testimonies, Vallentine Mitchell, London, 1995

[475] Miriam Akavia, 'My Own Vineyard; A Jewish Family in Kraków between the Wars'; Library of Holocaust Testimonies, Vallentine Mitchell, London, 2006 previously published as 'Karmi Sheli' (1984)

[476] Aleksander Skotnicki and Paulina Najbar, 'Rodziny Żydowskie przedwojennego Krakowa/Jewish Families of Pre-War Cracow'; Stradomska Centrum Dialogu w Krakowie, Kraków, 2015, pages 38-57 and Michał Galas and Antony Polonsky (Eds), 'Polin' vol 23; Littman, Oxford, 2011, page 386

family. Anna was given a Catholic identity with the name of Maria Malinowska, complete with a baptismal certificate. In May, 1945 Anna's father returned to Kraków from a prisoner of war camp. He was followed by Anna's brother, Aleksander, who had been protected by Oskar Schindler, and Anna's sister, Rozalia. The girls emigrated to Palestine shortly afterwards.[477] In July, 1951, Aleksander married Krystina, née Wohlfeiler, who had been born in Kraków in May, 1930. The two of them had met in Oskar Schindler's factory in 1945. After the war, Krystina had returned to Kraków, finished secondary school and studied at the Jagiellonian University. Aleksander and Krystina emigrated to Israel in 1957.[478]

Janet Applefield was born in Kraków as Gustawa Singer in June, 1935. Her parents surrendered her into the temporary care of a cousin's nursemaid before her father, who was in the Kraków Ghetto, obtained false papers for her in the name of Krystyna Antoszkiewicz. Subsequently, Gustawa was cared for by a Catholic family with whom she survived until the end of the war. In the face of continuing anti Semitism she and her father migrated to America in March, 1947.[479]

Hannah Bannett (née Marcus) was born in Kraków where she attended school and the University. She married in 1935 and left Kraków, but returned in 1942. She survived outside the ghetto living on Aryan papers, and working for a housekeeper of an influential Nazi sympathiser. In her testimony, Hannah Bannett notes that her employer often held parties which were attended by high ranking officers in the SS. She also describes how her son was temporarily sheltered 'in the home of a Polish teacher who demanded a lot of money'. She emigrated to Palestine in 1947.[480]

Rivka Bau (née Diamond), also known as Rebecca or Cyla, was born in 1897. She met her husband, Józef, a graphic artist, in Płaszów. As noted elsewhere in this chapter, the two went through a form of marriage ceremony in the camp. This ceremony was conducted by Józef's mother, as no Rabbi was available. It was only two years later that an official marriage could be arranged. A replica of Cyla's Kennkarte (identity document) is shown at the front of Józef's memoir, 'Dear God, Have You Ever Gone Hungry?' Józef and Cyla emigrated to Israel in 1950.[481]

Pearl Benisch (née Mandelker) was a teacher at Bais Ya'akov before the war. In March, 1941 she and her family left Kraków to take refuge in Słomniki, a village

[477] Monika Stępień (Ed),'Witnesses to Polish-Jewish History; The Stories of Holocaust Survivors, Former Prisoners of Nazi German Concentration Camps and Righteous Among the Nations'; Galicia Jewish Museum, Kraków, 2016, pages 36-39. See also entry for Mirosława Przebindowska on the website of The Jewish Foundation for the Righteous, West Orange, NJ
[478] Aleksander Skotnicki and Paulina Najbar, 'Jewish Families in Pre-War Cracow'; Stradomskie Centrum Dialogu w Krakowie, Kraków, 2015, pages 16, 17 and 24. See also https://collections.yadvashem.org/en/documents/11022305 and the names index in Ryszard Kotarba, 'Żydzi Krakowa w dobie zagłady (ZAL/KL Płaszów)'; Instytut Pamięci Narodowej, Kraków, 2022
[479] The Boston Globe and United States Holocaust Memorial Museum and interview on You Tube
[480] Brana Gurewitsch (Ed), 'Mothers, Sisters, Resisters; Oral Histories of Women who Survived the Holocaust'; University of Alabama Press, Tuscaloosa, 1998, pages 53-63
[481] www.holocaustresearchproject.org/othercamps/plaszow/bau/bau.html and Joseph Bau, 'Dear God, Have You Ever Gone Hungry?'; Arcade Publishing, New York, NY, 1990

about 15 miles (24 km) to the north of the city. She later spent time in the Kraków Ghetto, as well as Auschwitz and Bergen Belsen. After the war, Pearl Benisch wrote two books about the Bais Ya'akov movement. She died in 2017 at the age of 100.[482]

Rita Blattberg and her family lived a comfortable lifestyle in Kraków but as she notes in her appropriately titled memoir 'Like Leaves in the Wind' ('Blatt' being German for 'Leaf'), the last few weeks living in that city were comparable to 'dancing on the Titanic'. Rita was deported to the Soviet Union where she spent most of the war. She returned to Kraków but found it 'a hometown inhabited by ghosts' and she emigrated shortly afterwards.[483]

Maria Bojarkowa was a Catholic woman who lived in the town of Wieliczka, some 10 miles (15 km) to the south east of Kraków. Yad Vashem holds a copy of her diary in which she records her experiences of the Jews of Wieliczka and in the nearby Niepołomice Forest, and the destruction of the local Jewish communities during the Holocaust.[484]

Irena Bronner was born into an assimilated Jewish family and attended a state school in Kraków. However, following the German occupation of the city, she was forced to attend the Jewish Gymnazium until it was closed down. She survived two camps during the Holocaust, firstly at Skarżysko (Skarżysko-Kamienna in Kielce province) and then, from August 1944, at Częstochowa. She returned briefly to Kraków after the war.[485]

Natalia Bułat was not Jewish but is included in this section as an example of a Catholic political prisoner who was held at Płaszów. She was born in the village of Sosnowice, some 18 miles (30 km) south west of Kraków. in 1925 and was arrested in 1944. At Płaszów she worked in the kitchen before being sent to Ravensbrück and then Magdenburg. After the liberation, Natalia returned to Poland and settled in Skawina, some 12 miles (20 km) from Kraków.[486]

Laura Dientenfass spent time in the Kraków Ghetto, and when it was liquidated in March, 1943, she was sent to Płaszów. In her testimony she mentions detailed personal searches of Jewish women in the camp. She later spent time in Pionki in central Poland, and then Auschwitz-Birkenau, Ravensbrück and Malhoff.[487]

Ala Dychtwald arrived in Płaszów from Majdenek in 1943 She noted that at that time Jewish prisoners still wore their own clothes and the black market thrived. Her

---

[482] Pearl Benisch, 'To Vanquish the Dragon'; Feldheim, Jerusalem, 1991 and, for example, https://hamodia.com/2017/03/14/mrs-pearl-ila-perel-benisch-ah/

[483] Rita Blattberg, 'Like Leaves in the Wind'; Vallentine Mitchell, London, 2003

[484] https://collections.yadvashem.org/en/documents/3732491

[485] Irena Bronner, 'Okady nad Wisła i Jordanem'; Wydawnictwo Literackie, Kraków, 1991. An extract from the book is included in Maria Klańska (Ed), 'Jüdisches Städtebild Krakau'; Jüdischer Verlag, Frankfurt am Main, 1994, pages 213-227. See also the Jewish Virtual Library entry for Skarzysko-Kamienna

[486] www.ca.muzeumkrakowa.pl/wiezniowie/30403/natalia and https://plaszow.org/en/events/womens-perspective

[487] www.archiwumkobiet.pl/publikacja/relacja-laury-dientenfass See also the names index in Ryszard Kotarba, 'Żydzi Krakowa w dobie zagłady (ZAL/KL Płaszów); Instytut Pamięci Narodowej, Kraków, 2022

testimony includes her recollection of a 'selection' at Płaszów in May, 1944, when many children were taken away, never to be seen again.[488]

Pola (Priwa) Elbinger was born in 1932 in the village of Nowe Brzesko, about 20 miles (32 km) east of Kraków. A ghetto was established in the village but it was liquidated in 1942. Pola, together with various members of her family, were hidden by local Catholic farmers in Stregoborzyce and Wawrzenczyce until the liberation, though at considerable financial cost. After the war, Pola was cared for at the Jewish orphanage in Kraków. However, her younger sister did not survive.[489]

Ewa Feldman fled from the Kraków Ghetto with her mother and sister in 1942, when she was ten years old. Suffering from frostbite, Ewa came under the care of Żegota, a support group which is described in a separate section of this chapter. She was then transferred to Warsaw where she was protected and then adopted by a Catholic, Anna Sadowska. The two remained together until 1946 when Ewa moved to a Jewish orphanage. Anna Sadowska was recognised as Righteous Among the Nations in 1983.[490]

Maria Feldhorn was born in Kraków in 1934. Her father was Juliusz, a respected teacher at the Jewish Gymnazium and her mother, Stella, née Landy, was a Doctor of Philosophy, specialising in English. In 1939, Maria and her family fled to Lwów where they stayed until June 1941. They then hid in various villages, including Wiśnicz Nowy, near Bochnia, and Swoszowice and then Borek Fałęcki near Kraków. Her parents were transported to Wieliczka where they were shot but Maria survived the war, having spent some time in Łagiewniki, under the protection of the Trammer family, and then near Góra Kalwaria under the care of nuns. Fryda and Augusta Trammer were later recognised by Yad Vashem as Righteous Amongst the Nations.[491]

Bertha Ferderber-Salz was born in 1902 in the Galician town of Kolbuszowa, now in Ukraine. During the First World War she and her family moved to Austria but in 1918 they relocated to Kraków. Her first marriage took place in 1929. On the outbreak of the Second World War, Bertha hid with her children in the countryside before having to move into the Kraków Ghetto. She survived the labour and extermination camps at Płaszów, Auschwitz and Bergen-Belsen. After the liberation she regained custody of her two daughters who had been protected by a Catholic family, but her husband did not survive the Holocaust. Bertha emigrated to New

---

[488] Joanna Sliwa 'Jewish Childhood in Kraków'; Rutgers University Press, New Brunswick, NJ, 2021, pages 109 and 171 and see names index in Ryszard Kotarba,'Żydzi Krakowa w dobie zagłady (ZAL/KL Płaszów)'; Instytut Pamięci Narodowej, Kraków, 2022

[489] http://www.centropa.org/en/photo/pola-elbinger-childrens-home-cracow See also Wiktoria Śliwowska (Ed) 'The Last Eyewitnesses; Children of the Holocaust Speak' vol 1; Northwestern University Press, Evanston, IL, 1993, pages 30-36 (Emanuel Elbinger) and 37-41 (Pola Elbinger). Regarding the increasing cost of protection paid by the Elbinger family see Jan Grabowski, 'Rescue for Money; Paid Helpers in Poland, 1939-1945'; Yad Vashem, Jerusalem, 2008, page 31

[490] https://www.holocaustrescue.org/zegota-part-2 , the entry for Lubicz-Sadowska, Anna

[491] https://zapispamieci.pl/en/maria-feldhorn/ and Wiktoria Śliwowska (Ed), 'The Last Eyewitnesses', vol 1, Northwestern University Press, Evanston, IL, 1998, pages 42-44

York with her daughters and she married for a second time in 1948. Her memoirs are recorded in the book 'And the Sun Kept Smiling'.[492]

Rena Finder (née Ferber) was born in Kraków in 1929. She was a cousin of Roman Ferber, co-author of the book 'Journey of Ashes'.[493] Rena's testimony is held by the Visual History Archive at the University of Southern California and her memoir has been published as a book for children, 'My Survival; A Girl on Schindler's List'.[494] The inclusion of both Rena and Roman on Schindler's list, is described by Elinor J Brecher in her book 'Schindler's Legacy; True Stories of the List Survivors' published by Plume of New York in 1994. Rena married Mark Finder in a displaced persons camp in Austria in 1946 and later settled in America.[495]

Janina Fischler-Martinho was born in 1930 and orphaned by the age of eleven. She survived in the Kraków Ghetto which she describes in considerable detail in her book, 'Have You Seen my Little Sister?' Gradually, members of her family were taken away and by June, 1942 she was left alone, except for her brother, Jozef. She describes her accommodation as follows – 'All we could get was a basement room, more like a cellar or dungeon, with no sanitation, no running water. The walls were damp and slimy.'[496] Whilst the ghetto was being liquidated, she escaped through the sewers to the district of Zabłocie. Janina then lived 'on the Aryan side', working on various farms and smallholdings including one in the hamlet of Strychowa near Gdów, and another at Kujawy, an area which has since been incorporated into Nowa Huta, and also in a village called Olsza. She also spent time in the village of Mogiła under the care of the Kucharczyk family. She made her way back to Kraków in June, 1944. Alone, and in her desperation for information she went to a fortune teller who not only told her of the forthcoming Soviet victory, but also arranged for one of her friends to care for her in a village near Gdów, to the south east of Wieliczka. Her brother survived in various concentration camps and they were reunited in Kraków in August, 1945.[497]

Blanche Fixler (née Bronia (Brandel) Bruenner) was born in Kraków in May, 1936. Her parents were Bobover Chassidim, and friends of the Rebbe. Whilst her father and brothers fled to Lwów at the outbreak of war, Bronia and her mother sought refuge in the town of Bochnia. In 1942, Bronia was sent back to Kraków to live with her mother's sister in law, Róża Berger, and she attended the Tagesheim (Day Care Centre) in the ghetto. In 1943, at the age of seven, she was smuggled out

[492] Encyclopedia.com and Bertha Ferderber-Salz, 'And the Sun Kept Smiling' Holocaust Library, New York, NY, 1980, previously published as 'Un di Zun hot Geshaynt', 1965

[493] Anna Ray-Jones and Roman Ferber, 'Journey of Ashes; A Boyhood in the Holocaust'; Create Space Publishers, 2014

[494] Rena Finder and Joshua Greene, 'My Survival; A Girl on Schindler's List'; Scholastic Press, New York, NY, 2019

[495] See also Joanna Sliwa, 'The Forced Relocation to the Kraków Ghetto as Remembered by Child Survivors' in Simone Gigliotti and Monica Templan (Eds), 'The Young Victims of the Nazi Regime'; Bloomsbury, London, 2016, page 158

[496] Joanna Sliwa, 'Coping with Distorted Reality', quoting Kerry Blugass, 'Hidden from the Holocaust; Stories of Resilient Children who Survived and Thrived'; Praeger, Westport, CT, 2003

[497] Janina Fischler Martinho, 'Have You Seen my Little Sister?' The Library of Holocaust Testimonies, Valentine Mitchell, London, 1998. See also, Joanna Sliwa, 'Jewish Childhood in Kraków'; Rutgers University Press, New Brunswick, NJ, 2021

of Poland through a network run by Benzion Kalb to Czechoslovakia and then Hungary where she survived the remainder of the war. In 1946 she went to France before emigrating to America.[498] Her case is quoted by Joanna Sliwa as illustrating that, contrary to popular understanding, children from Chassidic backgrounds did participate in collective rescue missions.[499]

Alona Frankel was born in Kraków in 1937. She survived the Holocaust, largely in the Lwów Ghetto, but also under the protection of an uncaring and financially motivated Catholic woman. Living amongst farm animals, Alona taught herself to read and drew pictures on scraps of paper. Alona's 'protector' would send these drawings to Alona's parents as proof that the child was still alive, until the money ran out and Alona was returned to her parents. Her recollections of wartime events are recorded in her book, 'Girl; My Childhood and the Second World War'. In 1949 Alona left Poland for Israel where she became a successful author of children's books.[500]

Maria Freider is mentioned by Bruno Shatyn in his book, 'A Private War'. In August, 1942 she was saved by Count Potocki and his wife, Maria, from being deported from Skawina, near Kraków. For this and other acts the Count and Countess were recognised as Righteous amongst the Nations.[501]

Maryla Freiwald (1911-1962) was a very successful athlete in the 1920's and 1930's, breaking Polish records in hurdles and the relay race. During the war she cared for members of her family in Kraków and Lwów, taking great risk in travelling between the two cities, often in freezing weather. Maryla left Poland in 1946 and settled in Brazil.[502]

Felicia Friedman (1926-2020) was born in Kraków. She and her family were sent to Płaszów where she met her future husband. She later spent time in a displaced persons' camp in Germany. Her attempt to emigrate to Palestine was frustrated when she and her husband were turned back at the Italian border and they emigrated to the United States in 1947. Her testimony is held at The United States Holocaust Memorial Museum.[503]

Irena Fromowicz (later Fromowicz Pisek) was a member of an assimilated and well to do family in Kraków and she had a PhD in art. One of her sisters, Henryka (later Henryka Fromowicz Stillerowa) was an art historian and literary editor as mentioned in the chapter of this book relating to the interwar period. A third sister was called Maria. Following the outbreak of war, the family moved to Zamość in

---

[498] www.eilatgordinlevitan.com/krakow/krkw_pages/krkw_stories_bruenner.html and https://vinnews.com/2024/03/03/survivor-blanche-fixler-addresses-bais-yaakov-girls-about-holocaust/

[499] Joanna Sliwa, 'Jewish Childhood in Kraków', pages 88 and 136

[500] Wikipedia and 'Alona Frankel, 'Girl; My Childhood and the Second World War'; Indiana University Press, 2016

[501] Bruno Shatyn, 'A Private War; Surviving in Poland on False Papers, 1941-1945'; Wayne State University Press, Detroit, MI, 1985

[502] Ewa Dąbrowska and Anna Kielczewska (Eds), 'Residents of Jewish Kraków; Women'; Wydawca EMG, Kraków, 2021, pages 56-61

[503] See also press releases including The Jewish Telegraphic Agency and Forward dated 4 June, 2020

central Poland which was occupied by the Germans and then the Russians. They spent the winter of 1939-40 in Lwów, from where they were sent to Siberia – except for Henryka who had to stay behind as she was an invalid. She was killed in 1941. The family was allowed to leave Siberia for Persia (Iran) as part of the Anders Army. At the time Persia was under Soviet and British influence and there was a large Jewish community in the country. By 1942 the family had moved again and were living in Jerusalem.[504]

Maria Garber-Wierny was born in Kraków in 1929. Her father was an upholsterer and a member of the Polish Socialist Party. She had two brothers, and two sisters, Berta and Eleonora. The two brothers went to the USSR at the beginning of the war. Maria and the rest of the family managed to stay in Kraków, outside the ghetto, until 1941 because they were able to obtain Romanian nationality documents. They then escaped to Bieńczyce, then a village to the north east of Kraków, where they and several others were protected by several Catholic families. On a rare visit to the city centre, Maria and her father were captured by the Nazis and held within the ghetto – only to be released by way of a bribe. They returned to Bieńczyce until the liberation.[505]

Zuzanna Ginczanka (1917-1944) was born in Kiev but spent much of her early life in Warsaw and Lwów. In 1942 her janitor informed on her and she moved to Kraków, where she stayed with her husband, the art critic Michał Weinzieher. She lived on Aryan papers outside the ghetto until her arrest and imprisonment. Zuzanna was shot at the Montelupich prison or at Płaszów in 1944. Whist in Kraków she wrote poetry using the pen name Sara Ginzburg. Her piece, 'Non omnis moriar' (Not all of me will die) was published in the weekly 'Odrodzene' in 1946.[506]

Renata Goldberger (née Grünbaum) (1914, or 1916-1990) was in the city of Łódz, and heavily pregnant at the outbreak of the war. By February, 1940 she was staying at her mother's home in Kraków. Renata and her infant son then moved into the ghetto where she worked as a tailor in the 'Optima' factory. Her brother was a member of the Jewish police, the OD, and he enabled her to be with her son in Płaszów where she, but not her son, survived. After the war, Renata returned to Kraków where she was reunited with her husband, Józef, and where their daughter, Hava, was born in 1949. The family later settled in Holon, Israel.[507]

---

[504] Roland E Brown, 'From Krakow to Tehran to Jerusalem: One Jewish Family's Story' at https://iranwire.com/en/society/61783/

[505] Jakub Gutenbaum and Agnieszka Latała (Eds), 'The Last Eyewitnesses; Children of the Holocaust Speak'. Vol 2, Northwestern University Press, Evanston IL, 2005, pages 59-65

[506] Wikipedia and Rafael Scharf, 'From the Abyss' in 'Poland. What Have I to do with Thee.'; Vallentine Mitchell, London, 1998. Previously published as ''Co mnie i tobie Polsko … Eseje bez uprzedzeń'. See also W 3cia Rocznicę zagłady ghetta w Krakowie'; Centralny Komitet Żydów Polskich, Kraków, 1946, pages 83 and 84. Additionally, see Ewa Dąbrowska (Ed), 'Residents of Jewish Cracow; Art and Culture'; EMG Publishers, Kraków, 2020. Pages 120-125 and Ryszard Kotarba, 'Żydzi Krakowa w dobie zagłady (ZAL/KL Płaszów)'; Instytut Pamięci Narodowej, Kraków, 2022, pages 685-688 and https://ukrainianjewishencounter.org/en/zuzanna-ginczanka-1917-1945/

[507] Martyna Grądzka, 'A Broken Childhood'; Wydawnictwo Wysoki Zamek, 2012, pages 449 – 451, quoting the Jewish Historical Institute file 301/4215. See also the Geni

Helena Goldstein was 21 at the time of the Nazi invasion. The state school she had attended catered for Catholic and Jewish children. Helena then attended the Higher School of Economics in Kraków. She escaped from the city's ghetto with the help of a former school friend, Maria Nowak, and adopting a false identity as Maria Bożek, Helena managed to obtain work in Warsaw as a railway station announcer. This indicates that, like many if not most survivors, she had no trace of 'Jewishness' in her speech. Helena returned to Kraków after the war but emigrated to Australia in 1949. In recognition of her Holocaust education work, she was awarded the Order of Australia in 2014.[508]

In 1939, Malvina Graf was studying biology at Kraków's University. Her education was brought to an abrupt end. Malvina spent the early part of the Holocaust in Lwów but in 1941, against a background of deteriorating conditions there, she returned to Kraków. The following year she spent some time in the village of Wielka Wieś some 9 miles (13 km) north west of the city – only to be moved with thousands of others into the ghetto. Following the liquidation of the ghetto she spent two years at Płaszów. As the Russian advance approached the camp, she was forced marched, and after a week arrived at Auschwitz, and then Bergen Belsen. She survived the war and in 1989 her memoir was published as 'The Kraków Ghetto and the Płaszów Camp Remembered'.[509]

Natalie Grauer (née Natalia Rosenwald) was born in Kraków in 1929. Whilst some members of her family were protected by a local priest, Natalie and her brother survived for a short time in the countryside. However, following her capture she was sent to Mauthausen and then Ravensbruck concentration camps. She survived the war and was reunited with several members of her family. Natalie then travelled to America, via Germany, Cyprus, Palestine and Australia. She died in 2020.[510]

Luiza Grüner was born in Berlin in 1933. In June, 1939 she and her family moved to Poland. In October, 1942 she evaded capture by hiding in a sewer under the apartment building where she and her family lived. They stayed in the Kraków Ghetto until the liquidation in March, 1943. As Ausländers (foreigners), the family was allowed to remain in the area of the ghetto for a few weeks, following which they went to the district of Łagiewniki, some 5 miles (8 km) to the south of the city. They were then sent to Bergen-Belsen. Luiza Grüner's testimony is filed at the University of South Carolina.[511]

---

genealogical website, and the names index in Ryszard Kotarba, 'Żydzi Krakowa w dobie zagłady'

[508] Monika Stępień (Ed), 'Witnesses to Polish-Jewish History; The Stories of Holocaust Survivors, Former Prisoners of Nazi Concentration Camps and Righteous Among the Nations'; Galicia Jewish Museum, Kraków, 2016, pages 48-51 and The Daily Telegraph, Sydney, 10 June, 2014

[509] Malvina Graf, 'The Kraków Ghetto and the Płaszów Camp Remembered'; The Florida State University Press, Tallahassee, FL, 1989

[510] Jewish Press of Tampa, September 7. 2020

[511] Joanna Sliwa, 'The Forced Relocation to the Kraków Ghetto as Remembered by Child Survivors' in Simone Gigliotti and Monica Templan (Eds), 'The Young Victims of the Nazi Regime'; Bloomsbury, London, 2016, page 161 and the website of Archiwum Kobiet. See also Joanna Sliwa, 'Jewish Childhood in Kraków', for example, page 56

Franciszka Guter (née Grünes) was born in 1932 in Kraków. She and her sister, Halina lived in the ghetto which she describes in some detail in her testimony. At the end of October, 1942 Franciszka left the ghetto with the assistance of a Polish policeman and a Mr Skarawara, a Catholic acquaintance of her father's. They were taken out of the city into the care of Michalina Jaśko, and they were hidden in the village of Leńcze, some 20 miles (32 km) to the south west of Kraków. Franciszka and Halina survived the war in the village and returned to Kraków where they stayed until 1950, when they emigrated to Israel. In 2008, Yad Vashem recognised Michalina Jaśko as Righteous Among the Nations.[512]

Janina Heschele was almost twelve when she began writing her diary on the day the Germans took over her home town of Lwów. She and her mother were transported to the local concentration camp at Janowska. It was there, in 1943, that a group of prisoners, recognising Janina's literary skills, arranged for her to be taken to the Aryan side of Kraków, where she survived the war and lived to see her diary published as 'Oczma dwunastoletniej dziewczyny' (In the Eyes of a Twelve Year Old Girl), in 1943.[513]

Karolina Heuman was born in 1928 in Nowy Sącz. She survived the war in what is now Ukraine. In the winter of 1941-42 she and her family were deported to the ghetto at Drohobycz. However, they managed to escape after a few months and Karolina survived the war largely due to the Nuns of the Sisters of Charity in Czernonogród. After the war she settled in Kraków.[514]

Helena Hirsch was born in about 1915. She, along with Helena Sternlicht, worked as a housekeeper for Amon Göth, Commandant of Płaszów. She was saved by Oskar Schindler and after the war she gave evidence at Göth's trial, and settled in Israel. David Crowe notes that 'like most people who saw *Schindler's List*, I thought there was only one Jewish maid working for Göth' but he concludes that there were two. In order to differentiate between the two Helens, Göth renamed them Lena (Helen Hirsch) and Sussanna (Helen Sternlicht). Both worked for Göth for almost two years and suffered equally from his brutality.[515]

Maria (Marysia) Hochberg-Mariańska (1913-1996) was the editor of the children's supplement to the newspaper, Nowy Dziennik, in 1937. She was also active within the Polish Socialists' Party, the PPS. During the war she and her husband Mietek, survived on Aryan papers thanks to their Aryan appearance. Maria

---

[512] Yad Vashem website and Maria Hochberg-Mariańska and Noe Grüss, 'The Children Accuse'; The Library of Holocaust Testimonies, Vallentine Mitchell, London, 1996, pages 164-171

[513] Laurel Holliday, Children in the Holocaust and World War II; Their Secret Diaries'; Pocket Books, New York, NY, 1995, pages 67, 68. See also Azriel Eisenberg (Ed), 'The Lost Generation; Children in the Holocaust'; Pilgrim Press, 1982. See also the website of the Ghetto Fighters' House Archives

[514] Wiktoria Śliwowska (Ed), 'The Last Eyewitnesses; Children of the Holocaust Speak'; vol 1, pages 187-189

[515] David M Crowe, 'Oskar Schindler; The Untold Account of his Life, Wartime Activities and the True Story behind The List'; Westview Press, Cambridge, MA, 2004, page 259 and see names index. See also Elinor Brecher, 'Schindler's Legacy; True Stories of the List Survivors'; Plume/Penguin, New York, NY, page 53. See also names index in Ryszard Kotarba, 'Żydzi Krakowa w dobie zagłady'

was a member of the PPS underground, editing its paper 'Wolność' (Freedom). Her testimony is reflected in Joanna Sliwa's paper, 'Stopping the Spread of Moral Savagery; Child Relief Efforts in the Kraków Ghetto', and in other sources which are mentioned in the next chapter of this book. It appears that Maria Hochberg-Mariańska is the same person as Miriam Peleg-Mariańska who is listed below.

Berta Hollander lived in Kraków as did her three daughters, Klara Wimisner, Mania Nachtigal and Dola Stark. Between November 1939 and December 1941 mother and daughters wrote repeatedly to Berta's son, Joseph who had emigrated, illegally, to America. The correspondence was discovered in 1986 by Joseph's son, Richard and it has been published in a book, 'Every Day Lasts a Year'. On 5 November, 1940, after the Jewish residents had been forced out of the city, Dola Stark wrote, 'Kraków looks very different now. If you walked through the city, you would have the impression that you are somewhere else.' A review of the book by Shelley Baranowski highlights the resourcefulness and strength of the women in the family. However, Berta died of natural causes in 1942 and the daughters also died during the Holocaust.[516]

Mila Hornik was born in Kraków in 1924. Her testimony describes her time in the Kraków Ghetto and her daily departures to carry out labour at Płaszów. She escaped from the Kraków Ghetto through the sewers and spent some time in Bochnia before returning to Kraków. For a time, she worked at Wieliczka, a sub camp of Płaszów. Mila Hornik survived both Płaszów and Auschwitz.[517]

Niusia (Bronisława) Horowitz-Karakulska was born in Kraków in 1932. When she and her family were forced into the ghetto, they were 'spared the trauma of moving onto an apartment with strangers'. Instead, they moved in with Niusia's grandparents, Sara and Szachne Horowitz who had moved to ul. Limanowskiego, 20 several years earlier. Niusia describes how, before the ghetto was sealed, she would venture out to nearby hilly area of Krzemionki in order to escape her depressing surroundings. Nevertheless, she missed her toys which the family did not bring into the ghetto. She survived the ghetto and Płaszów due largely to the protection of Oskar Schindler. After the war she returned to Kraków, where she lived and qualified as a certified beautician. Niusia and her brother, Ryszard, are featured in Steven Spielberg's film, 'Schindler's List'.[518]

Ewa Janowska-Boisse (née Kleinberg) and her sister Anna Janowska-Ciońćka were born in 1931 and 1936 to a well established Kraków family. Their paternal grandfather, Wilhelm Kleinberg, was a well known photographer in the city. Before

---

[516] Richard Hollander (and others) (Eds), 'Every Day Lasts a Year; A Jewish Family's Correspondence from Poland'; Cambridge University Press, Revised edition 2007, reviewed at https://networks.h-net.org/node/3180/reviews/6331/baranowski-browning-and-hollander-and-tec-every-day-lasts-year-jewish and 'Polin', vol 23, page 392
[517] Testimony held at Yad Vashem. See also the names indexes in Ryszard Kotarba, 'Żydzi Krakowa w dobie zagłady' and in Martyna Grądzka-Rejak, 'Kobieta żydowska w okupowanym Krakowie'
[518] Joanna Sliwa, 'Coping with Distorted Reality', and Kararzyna Zimmerer, 'Zamordowany świat; Losy Żydów w Krakowie, 1939-1945'; Wydawnictwo Literackie, Kraków, 2004, page 62, and see other references in the names index. See also Wikipedia wolna encyklopedia entry for 'Bronisława Horowitz-Karakuska' and Elior J Brecher, 'Schindler's Legacy; True Stories of the List Survivors'; Plume Publishers, 1994, pages 39-52

the war, the sisters and their immediate family lived in the spa town of Rabka, to the south of Kraków. They were soon forced out of their comfortable home, into the town's newly created ghetto. Shortly afterwards the Nazi SS established a training college in Rabka, and the first of several 'Aktions' took place in May, 1942. Later that year, the two sisters, and their mother, were smuggled out of Rabka with the aid of a Catholic man, Marian Sikorski. He became recognised as a Righteous Amongst the Nations. The sisters and their mother survived the war in one village, and then another. After the war their mother married a Pole who had been connected with the partisans and who had protected the sisters and their mother.[519]

Judyta Joachimsmann was born in Wieliczka in 1928. Between 1940 and 1942 she hid on a farm near Gorlice to the south east of her home town. Her mother perished in the Holocaust, but Judyta and her father, Roman, survived. Her sister, Ruth, also survived the Holocaust but was killed in 1946 by antisemitic Poles. Judyta emigrated to Australia in 1954.[520]

Louise Joskowitz was born in 1925. She survived the Kraków Ghetto, living with her parents and her brother, Solomon, in a small apartment with almost a dozen others. When the ghetto was liquidated, she was sent Płaszów and in August, 1944 to Auschwitz where her mother, Pesla Stopincki was shot. Louise then went to a labour camp near Dresden. In 1949, Louise, her husband and their new born daughter emigrated to Houston, Texas.[521]

Irena Jung was born in Kraków, the daughter of Klara and her husband, a lawyer, Schilem who before September, 1939 'had lived a life of easy affluence in Kraków's prestigious main square with a maid and cook on staff'. Following the invasion, Irena and her family fled east and sheltered for a time in Lwów. Just before the Nazis reached that city, the family travelled to a remote logging camp in the USSR. In 1943, at the age of 22, Irena joined the Polish People's Army – a Polish army that would fight the Nazis alongside the Soviets. Her experiences in the army are preserved in her surprisingly detailed correspondence that survived the war. After May, 1945 Irena returned to Poland and she settled in Katowice with surviving members of her family. In 1950 she emigrated to Israel.[522]

Henia (Henryka) Karmel (1923-1984) and her sister, Ilona (1925-2000), were born in Kraków into a middle class family which included both non observant and Orthodox members. They wrote their testimonies in the form of poetry rather than

[519] Jakub Gutenbaum and Agnieszka Latała (Eds), 'The Last Eyewitnesses; Children of Holocaust Speak', vol 2; Northwestern Press, Evanston, IL, 2005 pages 97-106 and https://zapispamieci.pl , entry for 'Ewa i Anna Janowskie'. Testimony and other information is also included in Katarzyna Meloch and Halina Szostkiewicz (Eds) 'Children of the Holocaust Speak', vol 3; The Association of Children of the Holocaust in Poland, Warsaw, 2019 See also https://collections.ushmm.org/search/catalog/vha20512
[520] Australian Jewish News, 1 December, 2022
[521] www.chron.com/news/houston-texas/article/Holocaust-survivors-relive-agony-to-protect-living-1498137.php See also The Houston Review, vol 3, no 1
[522] Personal correspondence with Irena Jung's daughter, Shula Kopf, and Shula Kopf 'From Moscow to Berlin; An Exhibition focused on my Mother's Role in Polish History'; The Jerusalem Report, 8 April 2019. See also The Times of Israel, 2 May, 2019, https://www.timesofisrael.com/piece-by-piece-a-survivors-daughter-finds-a-trove-of-letters-inspires-art/

in diaries or as prose. They both spent time in the ghetto and at Płaszów. Ilona (Ila) wrote 'Ocznicza' (Anniversaries) in the ghetto during 1943. It starts, 'A w moim domu nie zalśnia żałobne gromnice' (In my house no mourning candles will ever glisten). The work was published three years later by the Centralny Komitet Żydów Polskich in its book, 'W 3cia rocznicę zagłady ghetta w Krakowie' (On the Third Anniversary of the Destruction of the Ghetto in Kraków). The poems of Henia and Ila survived and were published as 'Spiew za drutami' (Song behind the Wire) in 1947. They are now available in English as a book, 'A Wall of Two; Poems of Resistance and Suffering from Kraków to Buchenwald and Beyond'.[523] In 1948 both sisters went to the United States where Henia wrote a novel which was based on her experiences in Kraków, 'The Baders of Jacob Street',[524] and Ilona wrote a novel, 'An Estate of Memory'.[525]

Celina Karp was born in 1931 in Kraków. Both her parents worked as accountants. The family practised Judaism but lived outside the Jewish quarter. She was nine years old when she moved into the Kraków Ghetto with her family. They eventually came under the protection of Julius Madritsch, and then Oskar Schindler but Celina spent time at Płaszów and Auschwitz before she was liberated in May, 1945. After the war, the family returned to Kraków, but two years later, the family moved to Des Moines in America. Celina's testimony is held at the Visual History Archive, University of Southern California, Shoah Foundation. In 2016 she returned to Auschwitz through the USC Shoah Foundation and in her later life she has become increasingly engaged in Holocaust education. Her memoir 'Saved by Schindler; The Life of Celina Karp Biniaz' was published in 2022.[526]

Natalia Karpf (née Weissman) (1911-2007) was born in Kraków and began learning piano when she was only four. At the age of 13 she moved to Berlin, but returned to Kraków due to the death of her mother. In 1943, she was sent to Płaszów where she was forced to play for the camp commandant, Amon Göth, on his birthday. Göth was so impressed by the quality of her performance that he spared her life and that of her sister. Natalia and her sister were later sent to Auschwitz but they survived, and in 1947 Natalia claimed political asylum in London. Her biography is

[523] Henia Karmel and Ilona Karmel, 'Wall of Two; Poems of Resistance and Suffering from Kraków to Buchenwald and Beyond'; University of California Press, Berkeley, CA, 2007
[524] Henia Karmel Wolfe, 'The Baders of Jacob Street'; J B Lippincott, Philadelphia, PA, 1970
[525] Jewish Women's Archive entry for 'Ilona Karmel' at
https://jwa.org/encyclopedia/article/karmel-ilona
[526] Interview 11133 mentioned by Joanna Sliwa in her paper, 'The Forced Relocation to the Kraków Ghetto as Remembered by Child Survivors', which is included in Simone Gigliotti and Monica Tempian (Eds), 'The Young Victims of the Nazi Regime'; Bloomsbury, London, 2016. See also Elinor J Brecher, 'Schindler's Legacy; True Stories of the List Survivors'; Plume Publishers, New York, NY, 1994, pages 109- 122. See also Joanna Sliwa, 'Jewish Childhood in Kraków'; Rutgers University Press, New Brunswick, NJ, 2021 and The Los Angeles Daily News, 26 July, 2023 at
https://www.dailynews.com/2023/07/26/auschwitz-survivor-who-ended-up-on-schindlers-list-shares-harrowing-story-at-reagan-library-event/ Celina Karp's memoir has been published as William B Friedricks, 'Saved by Schindler; The Life of Celina Karp Biniaz'; Ice Cube Press, 2022

given in a book by one of her daughters, Anne, 'The War After; Living with the Holocaust'.[527]

As described in the previous chapter of this book, Laura Kaufman was a biologist and geneticist at the Jagiellonian University. From 1939 to 1942 she lived and worked in the town of Puławy in eastern Poland, where she served as secretary to the local commandant of the Home Army. She later spent time in and near Warsaw, and also in the village of Kraszewo near Słomniki, some 15 miles (24 km) north of Kraków. Laura Kaufman remained in Poland after the war, and she continued her work specialising in poultry science.[528]

Fryda Kiwetz worked in Oskar Schindler's enamelware factory from 1942. She records that he was a polite man who 'knew how to win people over'. She also notes that the workers in the factory were assigned 'relatively good Germans'. [529] However, Luise Danz appears to have been an exception. She is described in the following section headed 'Guards at Płaszów (Aufseherinnen)'.

Renia Knoll was born in 1927 and wrote her diary as a thirteen year old. It has since been published by the Jewish Historical Institute as 'Renia Knoll; Dziennik'.[530] As noted on the Institute's website, 'Renia's diary is by no means a chronicle of the fates of Cracow Jews during the occupation. It is a diary of a teenager who worries about anti Semitic repressions as much as about flirtation with her male friends, learning problems, or arguments with her parents.' Further information about Renia Knoll is given in the following section of this chapter headed 'Smugglers'.

Wiktoria Krell was born in Kraków in 1923. When the ghetto was being established, she and her family moved to Swoszowice, a village some 9 miles (14 km) to the south of the city. Eventually, she was transferred to the Kraków Ghetto and then to Płaszów where Wiktoria and her mother worked in the kitchens. In October, 1944, they were sent by train to Auschwitz where she survived until the end of the war. From Auschwitz she was transported to Stutthof concentration camp, east of Danzig, and then to Gross-Montan in East Prussia where she suffered hard labour on a farm. After that Wiktoria Krell was taken back to Stuthoff, and then to Lauenberg, some 185 miles (300 km) away. She received very little food, and on some days ate only snow. It was there that she contracted typhoid fever. Eventually, the Soviets came 'and found still [a] few living corpses'. Wiktoria Krell then returned to her home town of Kraków where she remained, living on ul. Brodzinski.[531]

---

[527] Wikipedia and Anne Karpf, 'The War After; Living with the Holocaust'; Heinemann, London, 1996

[528] Wiesław Kozub-Ciembroniewicz (Ed), Academics of Jewish Heritage in the Modern History of the Jagiellonian University'; Jagiellonian University Press, Kraków, 2014, pages 137-139

[529] www.archiwumkobiet.pl/publikacja/relacja-frydy-kiwetz See also the names index in Ryszard Kotarba, 'Żydzi Krakowa w dobie zagłady' and Martyna Grądzka-Rejak, 'Kobieta żydowska w okupowanym Krakowie', page 270

[530] Renia Knoll, 'Dziennik'; Żydowski Instytut Historyczny, Warsaw, 2nd Ed, 2014

[531] Website of Archiwum Kobiet, Institute of Literary Research, The Polish Academy of Sciences, and Arnon Rubin, 'The Rise and Fall of the Jewish Communities in Poland and their Relics Today, vol 3, District Kraków'; Tel Aviv University Press, Tel Aviv, 2009,

Irma Laksberger was born in Kraków in 1898. She was deported to the Prokocim Ghetto in August 1940 and stayed there until the liquidation of the ghetto in June 1942. She was then transferred to Wieliczka but escaped two weeks later. She later spent time in Biezanow, Prokocim and finally Skarzysko camp in Kielce province.[532]

Antonina Leser (née Bornstein) (1917-1999) was born in Kraków where she attended the Hebrew High School and began studies at the Jagiellonian University. A fervent Zionist, she was a member of Akiwa and Jutrzenka and promoted the use of the Hebrew language. In the ghetto she organised education for young children before being transferred to Płaszów, and then Auschwitz and Ravensbrück. Antonina returned to Kraków after the war, but emigrated to Palestine in 1945.[533]

Leah Lichtiger, who was born in September, 1930, is one of many child survivors who have been identified by Joanna Sliwa. Leah's testimony indicates that she had thought herself as unimportant, and so her life and daily routine seemed trivial.[534]

Rozalia Lieberfreund and her two children were amongst several Jews who, during the Holocaust, were sheltered by Serafina Fesenko in her home at Pychowice, an area of Kraków which now forms part of District VII, Dębniki.[535]

Roma Ligocka (née Liebling) was born on 13 November, 1938 in Kraków. In 1940 she and her mother were moved into the ghetto. In her memoir Roma writes about the pervasive cold, greyness and darkness of their surroundings. She and her mother managed to escape and throughout the rest of the war they were protected by a Catholic family. Following liberation, Roma studied painting and design in the Academy of Fine Ars in Kraków and she worked with considerable success in theatre, film and television. Her memoir, 'Dziewczynka w czerwonym płaszczyku' (The Girl in the Red Coat) was inspired by Steven Spielberg's film, 'Schindler's List' in which Roma Ligocka recognised herself as a Jewish child who wore a red coat.[536]

Anita Lobel (née Kempler) was born in Kraków in 1934. Following the Nazi invasion, she and her brother and their nanny hid in the surrounding countryside, and in a convent as well as spending time in the ghetto. In her testimony she notes that whilst in the ghetto, she, her brother and her mother slept in one bed in an

---

pages 377,378. See also Martyna Grądzka-Rejak, 'Kobieta Żydowska w okupowanym Krakowie, 1939-1945', page 192 quoting from AŻIH (Archive of the Jewish Historical Institute), Warsaw), file 301/3218

[532] Testimony at Yad Vashem. See also the names index in Ryszard Kotarba, 'Żydzi Krakowa w dobie zagłady'

[533] www.ca.muzeumkrakowa.pl/wiezniowie/28825/antonina_tonia_fani_jona

[534] Joanna Sliwa, 'Coping with Distorted Reality'

[535] Joanna Sliwa, 'Ma'am do you Know that a Jew Lives Here? The Betrayal of Jewish Women and the Jewish Children they Hid During the Holocaust. The Case of Cracow' in Denisa Nešťáková (Ed), 'If This is a Woman. Studies on Women and Gender in the Holocaust'; Academic Studies Press, Boston, MA, 2021

[536] Wikipedia entry for Roma Ligocka and Roma Ligocka, 'The Girl in the Red Coat'; Hodder and Stoughton, London, 2003, mentioned, for example in Joanna Sliwa, 'Coping with Distorted Reality' and in Monika Stępień, 'Housing Situation of Holocaust Survivors Returning to their Hometowns in Poland after the Second World War; Examples from Kraków and Łódź'; Scripta Judaica Cracoviensia, vol 16, 2018

apartment that they shared with three other family members. The children were always told to be quiet. For Anita and her brother, the existence in the ghetto made them feel as if they were trapped in a cage. She found greater comfort in Catholic medals that she had received from her nanny than in the Judaism which had placed her in the ghetto.[537] Later, Anita and her brother were sent to a concentration camp in Germany. They were rescued in 1945 by the Swedish Red Cross and reunited with their parents two years later. The family spent some time in Sweden before migrating to America, where Anita became an acclaimed illustrator of children's books. Her memoir was published as a book, 'No Pretty Pictures'.[538]

Feiga Maler (1919-1942) died in the Kraków Ghetto in 1942, along with her sister Chana. She is the subject of a poem 'Bone by Bone, She Remembered' written by her niece, Yerra Sugarman.[539]

Eugenia Manor (née Wohlfeiler) was 13 at the outbreak of war, the daughter of a chazan (cantor) at the Wysoka (High or Hoyche) Synagogue in Kraków. She survived the camp at Płaszów, largely as a result of being employed by Oskar Schindler as a metal worker in his enamel factory. Other members of the Wohlfeiler family were also saved by the intervention of Oskar Schindler. In August, 1944, Eugenia and other members of the family were taken from the factory back to the main camp at Płaszów and on to Auschwitz. Eugenia survived, along with her mother and brother. Eugenia returned to Kraków and emigrated to Israel in 1950.[540]

Jadwiga Maurer was born in Kielce in 1932. She and her family survived the Holocaust, mainly in Kazimierz, the pre war Jewish part of Kraków, on false papers, with the help of Żegota (The Council for Aid to Jews, which is described in a later section of this chapter). In 1944 she and her family were evacuated to Slovakia. After the war, Jadwiga Maurer emigrated to America where she eventually became a professor at the University of Kansas, and where she wrote extensively about her wartime experiences.[541]

Anna Mekler was born in 1932 in the village of Igołomia, some 14 miles (22 km) east of Kraków. For some two months, she hid with her family's former housekeeper in Kraków before returning to her family in the village of Wawrzyńczyce, some 18 miles (29 km) east of the city, near Nowe Brzesko.[542]

---

[537] Joanna Sliwa, 'Coping with Distorted Reality; Children of the Kraków Ghetto'
[538] Wikipedia and 'No Pretty Pictures: A Child of War'; Greenwillow Books, New York, NY, 1998. See also, www.remember.org/red-cross-white-bus-rescue/anita-kempler-lobel and Joanna Sliwa's YouTube presentation on 20 November, 2023, 'The Holocaust in Diaries and Memoirs of Child Holocaust Survivors'
[539] Colorado Review, March, 2020
[540] Michał Niezabitowski and others (Eds), 'Is War Men's Business? Fates of Women in Occupied Kraków in Twelve Scenes'; Muzeum Historyczne Miasta Krakowa, Kraków, 2011, pages 68-73.
[541] Katarzyna Zechenter, 'Interview with Professor Jadwiga Maurer' in 'Polin', vol 18' Jewish Women in Eastern Europe'; Littman, Oxford, 2005, pages 263-271. See also 'Polin', vol 23, pages 392, 393
[542] Website of Archiwum Kobiet. See also Joanna Michlic, 'Jewish Children in Nazi Occupied Poland'; Yad Vashem, Jerusalem, 2008, page 77, quoting file 301/807 at the

Sabina Mirowska (née Hochberger) was born in 1909 in Kraków and she married a doctor. In 1940 she was working in a local hospital. Later that year, she started to work at the Jewish orphanage which Sabina describes in her testimony. She also describes a major deportation from the ghetto in October, 1942, and how a number of children were saved, at least temporarily, by being moved into the Hospital for Infectious Diseases, where the Nazi soldiers were reluctant to search. Her testimony also includes a description of the liquidation of the ghetto in March, 1943. Later in 1943 she married in a ceremony officiated by Rabbi Sonnerschein. Sabina Mirowska survived both Płaszów and Auschwitz.[543]

Stella Müller Madej was born in 1930 in Kraków. She records that she celebrated her 12th birthday in the ghetto and received a gift from her grandmother. During her period in the ghetto, she largely rejected Jewish religious observance but made attempts to obtain some kind of secular education. She learned for a short time from older girls who gave her reading and writing assignments but, in the end 'nothing came out of reading and writing, nobody had the time nor the mind to take care of that'. She survived the ghetto and Płaszów and in 1944 she was shipped to Auschwitz. Her uncle managed to bring her under the protection of Oskar Schindler, and Stella was transferred to his factory in Czechoslovakia. Following the liberation, she returned to Kraków where she completed her education. Her book, 'Dziewczynka z listy Schindlera; Oczami dziecka' was published in 1991, and the work has since been expanded, and translated into English, as 'A Girl from Schindler's List'.[544]

Pola Neiger was born in Kraków in 1905. During the occupation, her husband, Ignac, joined the Ordnungdienst (Jewish police service) in the mistaken belief that this would enable him to protect the family's three children. Pola worked at the bath house and the kindersheim (children's home) in the ghetto. Together, Pola and her husband protected a number of children within the community and also transferred three children to the 'Aryan side'. Pola, but not her family, survived Płaszów.[545]

Halina Nelken (1924-2009) spent the early part of her life in Podgórze, across the river from Kazimierz. She describes Podgórze as 'democratic and progressive, proud of its gymnasium (secondary school) … and its beautiful park'. Halina wrote a diary relating to the period up to Spring, 1943 entitled 'Pamiętnik z getta w Krakowie' (A Diary from the Ghetto in Kraków). This now forms the basis of the

Jewish Historical Institute, Warsaw. Additionally see the Borwicz Collection at Yad Vashem
[543] Maria Hochberg-Mariańska and Noe Grüss, 'The Children Accuse'; The Library of Holocaust Testimonies, Vallentine Mitchell, London, 1996, pages 240-246. See also Joanna Sliwa, 'Jewish Childhood in Kraków' and Martyna Grądzka, 'A Broken Childhood'; The Fate of the Children from the Jewish Orphanage at 64 Dietla Street in Cracow during the German Occupation'; Wydawnictwo Wysoki Zamek, Kraków, 2012
[544] Website of the Kraków Jewish Community, https://gwzkrakow.pl/en/2022/02/05/stella-muller-madej-1930-2013-2/ and Stella Müller Madej, 'A Girl From Schindler's List'; Polish Cultural Foundation, London, 1997 and Wydawnictwo DjaF, Kraków, 2006. Also, Joanna Sliwa, 'Coping with Distorted Reality'
[545] Martyna Grądzka, 'A Broken Childhood', pages 444 and 445, quoting file 301/2401 at the Jewish Historical Institute

book, 'And Yet I am Here'.[546] The diary covers the periods which the author spent in the Ludwinów and Rakowice districts of Kraków, in the Ghetto, and at the Płaszów Camp, to the south of the city. It is one of seven Holocaust diaries written by young Jewish women in Poland which are considered by Cyndi Freiman in her PhD thesis. As the author states, Nelken's diary charts the destruction of their comfortable life as a prosperous assimilated family and their descent to a life of poverty and dispossession. The diary gives a unique account of the Nazi occupation juxtaposed with Nelken's youthful yearnings and romances.' [547] Halina Nelken's testimony is quoted by many other researchers, for example Martyna Grądzka-Rejak, Ryszard Kotarba, Joanna Sliwa and Katarzyna Zimmerer to mention just four.[548] Yad Vashem holds a copy of the diary, together with other papers, including poems, written by Halina Nelken. These include an account of a Luftwaffe storage facility in the Zabłocie district of Kraków. After the war, Halina Nelken became an authority on the history of Polish art, as described in the next chapter. Halina's mother, Regina, is mentioned below in the section relating to orphanages, both the one on Dietla Street and the one in the ghetto.

Ana Novac (1929-2010) was a teenager who, in 1944 wrote a diary which records a period of six months of her life in Auschwitz and Płaszów. After the war, Ana settled in Paris where her book, 'Les Beaux Jours de ma Jeunesse' was published in 1992. This has since been published in English as 'The Beautiful Days of my Youth'. Ana was a Hungarian and she reveals the contrast, and a degree of conflict, between her group of women in Płaszów who had come from Hungary and Romania with the majority who had come from Kraków and the surrounding area. She also describes the hierarchy of prisoners at the camp, their occupations and their means of survival.[549]

Miriam Peleg-Mariańska appears to be the same person as Maria Hochberg-Mariańska who is listed above. Both are described as being the editor of a children's supplement of a daily newspaper in Kraków and both were active with the Polish Socialists Party. Maria Hochberg-Mariańska is described above as being a member of the Socialist Party underground during the war, whilst in her book 'Witnesses' Miriam Peleg-Mariańska describes her and her future husband's activities in the Kraków branch of Żegota, The Council for Jewish Aid, which is the subject of a

---

[546] Halina Nelken, 'And Yet I am here'; University of Massachusetts Press, Amherst, MA, 1999. Extracts from the diary relating to 1940 are included in Fabian Schlang (Ed) ' … I pozostała tylko legenda'; Wydawnictwo Ekked, Tel Aviv, 1986. See also 'Rückkehr nach Krakau' in Maria Kłańska (Ed), 'Jüdisches Städtebild Krakau'; Jüdischer Verlag, Frankfurt am Main, 1994. Additionally, see references to Halina Nelken in Andrea Löw and Markus Roth, 'Juden in Krakau unter Deutscher Besatzung, 1939-1945'; Wallstein Verlag, Göttingen, 2011, and in Joanna Sliwa, 'Coping with Distorted Reality'
[547] Cyndi Freiman, 'Writing in Captivity: An Examination of Seven Holocaust Diaries Written by Young Jewish Women in Nazi-Occupied Poland'; Department of Hebrew, Biblical and Jewish Studies, The University of Sydney, 2021
[548] Martyna Grądzka-Rejak, 'Kobieta Żydowska w okupowanym Krakowie'; Ryszard Kotarba, 'Żydzi Krakowa w dobie zagłady'; Joanna Sliwa, 'Coping with Distorted Reality' and 'Jewish Childhood in Kraków' and Katarzyna Zimmerer, 'Zamordowany świat; Losy Żydów w Krakowie'.
[549] Ana Novac, 'The Beautiful Days of my Youth; My Six Months in Auschwitz and Płaszów'; Henry Holt & Co, New York, NY, 1997

separate section in this chapter. In the Polish version of the book, 'Wśród przyjaciół i wrogów' (Among Friends and Enemies) Miriam is called Marysia whilst her husband is named as Mietek. Miriam Peleg-Mariańska emigrated to Israel in 1949 and for twenty years worked for Yad Vashem.[550]

Maria Perlberger-Shmuel (1933-2019) was a teenager living in Wieliczka, some 10 miles (15 km) to the south east of Kraków, at the beginning of the Holocaust. Initially, her family did not suffer as much as many other Jewish families as her father had served in the Piulsudski Legion of the Polish Army. Maria was given false papers and was hidden in Warsaw before the liquidation of the Wieliczka Ghetto – and the death of her parents. She survived 'thanks to the 'lifeline' – a chain of actions of different people undertaken in many different places. This – in her own words – 'game of hide and seek with death' was a constant and continuous escape on a long route: Wieliczka – Kraków – Warsaw (two different places) – countryside close to Warsaw – Kraków (4 places). Maria Perlberger emigrated to Israel in 1948 and it was there that she married Ernst Shmuel, a Holocaust survivor from Berlin.[551]

Amalie Petranker-Salsitz was born in Munich in 1922. Before the war, she and her family moved to the town of Stanisław, Poland (now in Ukraine). She escaped from the ghetto there, to Kraków where she hid using Aryan papers. She worked as a chambermaid and then at a construction firm where she remained until January, 1945. She then travelled to Munich and Palestine before emigrating to the United States in 1947. Her testimony is held at the United States Holocaust Memorial Museum and it is also recorded in a book 'Against All Odds'.[552]

Lili Pohlmann (née Stern) was born in Lwów. She and her family moved to Kraków where her father worked as a bank manager, and her mother as a dress designer. On the outbreak of war, the family returned to Lwów. Only Lili and her mother survived and that was due to the protection of Irmgard Wieth and Andrej, Count Sheptytsky. The first of these was a German civil servant whilst the other was an Orthodox Archbishop who arranged for Lili and her mother to hide in a convent. In 1946, Lili was brought to London by Rabbi Schonfield. In 2007 she was awarded the Polonia Restituta medal for her work building bridges between her own and younger generations of Poles and Polish Jews.[553]

---

[550] Miriam Peleg-Mariańska and Mordecai Peleg, 'Witnesses; Life in Occupied Kraków'; Routledge, London, 1991 and M M Mariańscy, 'Wśród przyjaciół i wrogów; poza gettem w okupowanym Krakowie'; Wydawnictwo Literackie, Kraków, 1988. See also Monika Stępień, 'The Image of Post War-Kraków in Jewish Writing, 1945-1950' in 'Polin', vol 23, pages 361-363 and 369

[551] https://collections.ushmm.org/search/catalog/irn43558 and Wiesław Theiss, 'Help Care and Rescue of Children in Poland in the War and Occupation Period (1939-1945). An Outline' in 'Social Work in Poland', vol 2018 at www.academia.edu/42758361 See also Jakub Gutenbaum and Agnieszka Latała (Eds), 'The Last Eyewitnesses; Children of the Holocaust Speak'. Vol 2, 2005, Northwestern University Press, Evanston, IL, 2005, pages 165-195

[552] USHMM Oral History, Accession number 1990.389.1; RG no RG-50.030.0198 and Norman and Amalie Petranker-Salsitz, 'Against All Odds'; Holocaust Library, New York, NY, 1990

[553] https://www.ajrrefugeevoices.org.uk/RefugeeVoices/Lili-Pohlmann and 'Polin', vol 23, pages 404, 405

Anna Rabkin was born in 1935 in Kraków into a comfortable middle class family. In 1939, she and her family fled east to Lwów where they spent some time in the ghetto. Anna and her brother were smuggled out of the ghetto into the care of a Catholic family. After the war they made their way back to Kraków, and then to Berkeley, California via England.[554] Anna's testimony has been recorded on YouTube as part of the Oral History Project of the Berkeley Historical Society and Museum.

Dorota Rath and her brother, Władysław, spent their childhood in Kraków before being sent to the ghetto and Płaszów. Both of them worked at Oskar Schindler's enamel factories in Kraków and then at Brünnlitz in Czechoslovakia. Dorota was one of those who led Oskar Schindler to the American zone at the end of the war for fear that the Soviets might arrest him.[555]

Sara Rosen was born in Kraków into a prosperous family. She was fourteen when the Nazis invaded Poland. Her book, 'My Lost World; A Survivor's Tale' is a personal memoir in which she describes the religious life of her Chassidic family in the pre war city. The author then describes her survival in Tarnów, Bochnia, Hungary and Romania. In December, 1944, Sara left Bucharest, arriving in Haifa, Palestine the following month, She settled in Tel Aviv and then New York.[556]

Rita Ross was born in Vienna in 1936. Her mother was from Wieliczka, near Kraków, and had Aryan features. Rita's father was from Czechoslovakia and he managed to obtain a visa to travel to America before the outbreak of war, intending to arrange for his family to join him. This proved impossible, and the rest of the family fled Vienna and moved to Kraków. There, Rita and her brother aged three, took on Catholic identities, before their mother moved them into the ghetto. Rita, her mother and her brother spent some time in the notorious Montelupich prison, but due largely to papers received from America they became prisoners of war in an American-British civilian internment camp. The three of them arrived at Ellis Island in 1945. Rita's memoirs are set out in two books, 'Running from Home' and 'Journey to Happily Ever After'.[557]

Nella Rost (later Nella Rost-Hollander) was a daughter of the pre war Zionist and political leader Ozjasz Thon. She was a literary leader in her own right and, for example, contributed to the newspaper Głos Kobiety Żydowskiej (The Jewish Women's Voice). She also wrote about her father in the Jewish news weekly 'Nasza opinija' (Our Opinion) which was published in Lwów. In 1938 she stood as a candidate for the Kraków city council on behalf of the United Judaism party.

---

[554] The Jewish News of Northern California, April 8, 2019 and Anna Rabkin, 'From Kraków to Berkeley; Coming out of Hiding'; Afikomen Judaica, Berkeley, CA, 2018
[555] Newsletter of the Auschwitz-Birkenau Memorial and Museum, 18 May, 2017, 'Unique collection of historical documents collected by Władysław Rath at the Memorial Archives'. The book, 'Schindler's Ark' includes a reference to 'a nine year old daughter of one Phila Rath'; Thomas Keneally, 'Schindler's Ark'; Sceptre, London, 1986, page 347
[556] Sara Rosen, 'My Lost World; A Survivor's Tale'; The Library of Holocaust Testimonies, Vallentine Mitchell, London, 1993
[557] https://docslib.org/doc/8253823/holocaust-survivor-biography-rita-b-ross . See also 'Running from Home'; Hamilton Books, 2009 and 'Journey to Happily Ever After'; Create Space Independent Publishing, 2017

Immediately after the war she wrote for the Central Jewish Historical Commission (CŻKH) in Kraków. Her post war work includes 'Społeczeństwo Żydowskie w Krakowie w okresie okupacji', a description of Jewish society in the city during the period of the German occupation.[558] Between 1946 and 1951 Nella Rost was active with the Jewish Historical Commission in Stockholm.[559]

Jane Schein (née Janina Ast) is mentioned by Joanna Sliwa in at least two of her works. Her mother obtained a forged document falsifying her birth certificate so that her daughter's name could be entered on the official work register. In her testimony, Janina records that she found herself in a new place that did not resemble anything she had known before, and she soon realised that she was no longer allowed to be a child. She also observes that some children were overwhelmed by fear, and that they no longer even knew how to play.[560]

Rosalie (Rachel) Schiff (née Baum) (1922-2014) was born in Kraków and married in the city's ghetto. She and her husband, William, were forcibly separated in 1941. Rosalie survived Płaszów thanks to Oskar Schindler, and she became reunited with her husband after the war. The two of them, together with their young son emigrated to Dallas, TX, in 1949, whilst her and her husband's memoirs are recorded in their book, 'William and Rosalie'.[561]

Irena Schnitzer was born in 1938 in Kraków, the daughter of Roman and Rozalia. Following the Nazi invasion, she was sent to Warsaw where she was cared for by a Catholic lady. Later she was protected at a children's home which was run by nuns. However, Irena's 'Jewish looks' meant she had to leave the convent, and she was moved to Bełec, where she came under the protection of another non-Jewish lady. After the end of the war, this lady brought Irena back to Kraków.[562]

Brenda Schor was born in 1929. Before the war she lived in Kraków where her family ran a furniture store. The family had Turkish nationality and remained outside the ghetto for a time after it was established. However, they were arrested and placed in the ghetto in early 1943. Brenda and her brother, Yakov, were smuggled out of the ghetto into Hungary on false papers. In 1945 they moved to Palestine.[563]

Perel (Paula) Schulkind (née Stern) (1923-2022) was born in Kraków. During the Holocaust, she spent time in the village of Wisznicze (Lublin province) and in Bochnia before being captured and sent to Auschwitz. She survived that 'camp' (a word which in its modern sense gives a totally misleading impression of Nazi labour and concentration camps), and the ensuing Death March. After the war she returned

---

[558] Included in 'W 3cia rocznicę zagłady ghetta w Krakowie'; CŻKH, Kraków, 1946

[559] Sean Martin, 'Jewish Life in Cracow, 1918-1939' Vallentine Mitchell, London, 2004, page 46 and https://link.springer.com/chapter/10.1007/978-3-030-55532-0_2

[560] Joanna Sliwa, 'Coping wth Distorted Reality' and 'Jewish Childhood in Kraków', page 50. See also a reference to an interview in December, 1994 at https://search.libraries.emory.edu/catalog/9936812795402486

[561] William and Rosalie Schiff and Craig Hanley, 'William and Rosalie; A Holocaust Testimony'; University of North Texas Press, Denton, TX, 2007

[562] Maria Hochberg-Mariańska and Noe Grüss, 'The Children Accuse'; The Library of Holocaust Testimonies, Vallentine Mitchell, London, 1996, page 98

[563] Testimony held at Yad Vashem

briefly to Kraków before moving to the Williamsburg district of Brooklyn, New York.[564]

Leah Shinnar was born in Kraków and spent time in the ghetto, Płaszów, Auschwitz and Bergen Belsen. She was one of the few who survived so may concentration camps, and after the war she convalesced in Sweden, before arriving in Israel in the midst of the War of Independence. Her reminiscences are recorded in her book 'The Butterfly and the Flame'.[565]

In 1942, Halina Silber was 12 years old and living in Słomniki some 15 miles (24 km) north of Kraków. In advance of the liquidation of the ghetto there, Halina travelled to Płaszów where she obtained work at Oskar Schindler's factory. She became number 16 on Schindler's list. After the war, she returned to Kraków and was reunited with her brother and sister. All three went to the United States in 1951.[566]

Helena Sternlicht was born in Kraków in 1925. She survived the Kraków Ghetto before being taken to the camp at Płaszów. There she was forced to work as a housemaid for the notoriously sadistic camp commandant, Amon Göth, together with Helena Hirsch who is listed above. Both Helenas came under the protection of Oskar Schindler, as did Helena Sternlicht's sisters, Symonia and Bronia. Helena Sternlicht married in 1946 before emigrating to America.[567]

Gustawa Stending-Lundberg (1926-2008) was the daughter of a journalist and literary critic. Between 1941 and 1943, whilst in the Kraków Ghetto, Gustwa wrote a number of poems. After the war she became a pioneer in research on the use of magnesium in medicine and biology, carrying out research in Dublin, Stockholm and Tel Aviv. She wrote over 100 scientific publications and a similar number of poems. Her book 'History through my Eyes: Poems' was published by Sivan in 2003.[568]

Fryderyka Strenberg was the wife of the painter Abba Fenichel, and also a painter in her own right. She was killed during the Holocaust in Bronowice Małe, a village some 6 miles (10 km) to the north west of Kraków.[569]

---

[564] The Detroit Jewish News, 11 August, 2022

[565] Leah Shinnar, 'The Butterfly and the Flame and other Stories of Jewish Life – From Kraków to Israel'; Mazo Publishers, Jerusalem, 2004

[566] https://www.army.mil/article/78669/holocaust_survivor_recounts_being_on_schindlers_list and https://www.huffpost.com/entry/halina-silber-holocaust-survivor-oskar-schindler_n_3035400

[567] David M Crowe, 'Oskar Schindler' Westview Press, Cambridge MA, 2004, pages 259-264. See also Wikipedia and Aleksander Skotnicki, 'The Jewish Fellow Citizens of Cracow Rescued by Oskar Schindler'; The Stradom Centre for Dialogue, Kraków, 2014, and Elinor J Brecher, 'Schindler's Legacy; True Stories of List Survivors'; Plume/Penguin, New York, NY, 1994, pages 53-57

[568] Geni genealogical website and Amazon review of 'History through my Eyes'

[569] Ewa Dąbrowska (Ed), 'Residents of Jewish Cracow; Food and Culture'; EMG, Kraków, 2020, page 20

Gena Turgel (1923-2018) was born in Kraków into a large but financially comfortable family. She spent some time in Borek which she describes as 'a village about 30 kilometres outside Kraków' and then survived the Kraków Ghetto, Płaszów, Auschwitz and Belsen. When the British army liberated Belsen in April, 1945, Gena met Norman Turgel, a sergeant in the Intelligence Corps. They married in October and settled in London later in 1945. Gena's memoir was published as 'I Light a Candle'. Her mother also survived the war and settled in England, but her sister Miriam died at Płaszów.[570]

Janina Webber was born in 1932 in Lwów. She escaped from the ghetto there, and was hidden in the surrounding countryside before taking refuge in a convent in Kraków. Janina then worked as a maid for a local priest until the end of the war. She remained in Kraków for only a short time, and eventually settled in England where she became active in Holocaust education.[571]

Felicja Wohlfeiler was born in 1918 and lived in Kraków before the war. In March, 1943 she was in the Kraków Ghetto, along with her five month old son, and she worked at the Madtrisch factory. In her testimony she, like others, describes the separation of mothers from their children prior to the liquidation of the ghetto. Felicja notes that she did not have her son circumcised so as to be able to pass the baby to the Aryan side at the right moment, though in the end she did not give up the baby.[572] A JewishGen web page relating to Oskar Schindler does not refer to Felicja Wohlfeiler, but does mention that 'The three women of the Wohlfeiler family, numbered on the Madritsch list as Roza, 8022, Halina 8020 and Rena 8021, all worked for Julius Madritsch when Emalia closed.'[573]

Henia Wollerówna wrote a diary immediately after the war. This includes testimony relating to her time in Płaszów, and for example a separation of children from their parents on 7 May, 1944. She notes how, as the children were carted out, Goeth ordered the prisoners to sit with their backs to the road so as not to see the children, possibly because he feared acts of resistance as a result of the parents' desperation.[574]

Rose Zar (Zarnowiecki) (née Ruszka Guterman) was born in 1923 in Piotrkow. In 1942 she escaped from the ghetto there and hid, 'in plain sight' in Kraków on Aryan papers. In that city she obtained domestic employment with the local SS commander as a housemaid for his infant son. In 1983 her memoirs were published under the title 'In the Mouth of the Wolf'. As is stated on the back cover, 'Rose's iconic picture of Nazi domesticity and her genuine friendship with the colonel's wife

---

[570] Gena Turgel, 'I Light a Candle'; The Library of Holocaust Testimonies, Vallentine Mitchell, London, 1995, and various press reports, June, 2008

[571] Website of the Holocaust Educational Trust and, for example, the Mail on line; London, 22 January, 2023

[572] Martyna Grądzka, 'A Broken Childhood'; Wydawnictwo Wysoki Zamek, Kraków, 2012, pages 451-453, quoting Jewish Historical Institute file number 301/4532. The extract of the testimony which is given in the book does not make it clear whether Felicja's baby survived, but it appears not.

[573] https://www.jewishgen.org/Yizkor/Schindler/sch015.html and see also 'Post card from the Past'; Jerusalem Post, 4 May, 2008

[574] Joanna Sliwa, 'Jewish Childhood in Kraków', page 107. See also the names index in Martyna Grądzka-Rejak, 'Kobieta żydowska w okupowanym Krakowie'

make this a unique book from beginning to end.' Rose Zar and her fiancé Mayer married in 1945. They helped smuggle 135 Jewish children out of Soviet-occupied Poland before living in Germany in the American zone. They settled in America in 1951.[575]

Doctors and hospitals

An informative summary of the health service in Kraków during the Holocaust is given by Agnieszka Zajączkowska-Drożdż in her article 'The Jewish medical institutions in Kraków during the Holocaust and their activities: the Early Years in Occupied Kraków'.[576] Unfortunately, however, the author does not mention any female doctors or nurses by name.

As noted in the last chapter, volume 5 of the series 'Jewish Residents of Kraków' includes information about the city's Jewish Hospital and its staff in the interwar period,[577] and this work does refer specifically to the high number of medically qualified women who were employed at the hospital. Generally, for as long as circumstances permitted, these doctors continued to serve the community during the Holocaust.

Of the many books which describe medical services in the Kraków Ghetto and the Płaszów Camp, the following will be mentioned by way of example.

The classic work, 'The Cracow Ghetto Pharmacy' has been published in many languages. It is unique in that it was written by a non Jewish chemist, Tadeusz Pankiewicz, who was permitted to live within the Ghetto throughout its existence. Because the book was written by a chemist, it includes an account of many incidents concerning medical aid to those held within the ghetto walls. Female Jewish doctors mentioned in the book include Paulina Wasserberger and her sister Dora, Bertha Silverberg and Maria Pechner.[578]

Tadeusz Pankiewicz had three non Jewish female assistants, Irena Drozdziwowska, Aurelia Danek and Helena Krywaniuk. They acted as liaisons between Jews in the ghetto and those beyond it, smuggling information and food as well as medicines.[579]

A second book, 'The Kraków Ghetto and the Płaszów Camp Remembered', records the killing of Dr Silberberg by a stray bullet during one of the deportations

---

[575] Rose Zar and Eric Kimmel, 'In the Mouth of the Wolf'; The Jewish Publication Society, Philadelphia, PA, 1983

[576] Medical Review Auschwitz; Medicine Behind the Barbed Wire, Conference Proceedings, Kraków, 2022

[577] Ewa Dąbrowska (Ed), 'Residents of Jewish Kraków' vol 5, Places and People; EMG Publishers, Kraków, 2022, pages 116-129

[578] Tadeusz Pankiewicz, 'The Cracow Ghetto Pharmacy'; Holocaust Library, New York, NY, 1987, chapter V, page 121, originally published as 'Apteka w getcie Krakowskim'; Kraków, 1947

[579] https://www.lifebeyondtourism.org/institutions/the-eagle-pharmacy/ See also for example the names index in Ryszard Kotarba, 'Żydzi krakowa w dobie zagłady'; Instytut Pamęci Nardowej, Kraków, 2022 and Martyna Grądzka-Rejak, 'Kobieta żydowska w okupowanym Krakowie'; Wysoki Zamek, Kraków, 2016, page 178

from the Ghetto. However, it is not clear whether this refers to Dr Bertha Silberberg or her husband, Leon.[580]

Aleksander Bieberstein's book 'Zagłada Żydów w Krakowie' (The Destruction of the Jews in Kraków) includes a whole chapter devoted to the health service (Służba zdrowia),[581] reflecting the fact that the author was, himself, a doctor. The chapter includes references to many female health professionals, including those working at the Jewish Hospital at ul. Skawińska, 8 and at the Jewish Hospital for Infectious Diseases.

The fourth example is Martyna Grądzka-Rejak's book on Jewish Women during the Occupation of Kraków. Chapter 5 relates to the occupations of Jewish women, and includes specific reference to female doctors (kobiety lekarki), including Rozalia Blau, Klara Berger-Waltscher, Regina Fuchs-Katzowa, Amalia Goldmann, Fryderyka Ameisen and Bertę Silberberg.[582]

Ryszard Kotarba's extensive work on the destruction of Kraków Jewry will be mentioned as the fifth example. In his section on the Aktion of 28 October, 1942, the author refers to the hospital on Ul Józefińska and to various female doctors, including Fryderyka Amaisen-Diestler, Rachel Stieglitz-Sperlin, Amalia Goldmann, Regina Fuchs-Katz, Dr Rosenberg and Dr Róza Hof.[583]

Matilda Löw's testimony describes the functioning of one of the Jewish hospitals in the Kraków Ghetto, noting that it included a maternity ward. She also comments on the medical facility at the Płaszów camp which was housed in three barracks.[584]

Despite the increasingly harsh conditions at the Płaszów camp – and the sadistic nature of its commandant – some health care was available there. In a separate chapter concerning life at Płaszów, Ryszard Kotarba includes a section which describes 'służba zdrowja' – the health service. Here, also, the author refers to several female doctors, for example Helen Rozenzwajg, Maria Pechner and Anna Silberfeld. The author describes the health service in some detail. For example, he describes the outpatient department where patients were classified for possible hospital treatment, and notes that there were separate rooms for men and women.[585]

Additionally, Ryszard Kotarba describes the aid that was brought into the camp by Jewish and other relief groups. These include the Jüdische Unterstützungsstelle

---

[580] Malvina Graf, 'The Kraków Ghetto and the Płaszów Camp Remembered'; Florida State University Press, Tallahassee, FL, 1989, page 44
[581] Aleksander Bieberstein, 'Zagłada Żydów w Krakowie'; Wydawnictwo Literackie. Kraków, 1985, pages 175-207. For an article in English which draws information from Dr Bieberstein's book see Agnieszka Zajączkowska-Drożdż, 'The Jewish Medical Institutions in Kraków during the Holocaust and their Activities' in 'Medical Review Auschwitz; Medicine Behind the Barbed Wire, Conference Proceedings, Polish Institute for Evidence Based Medicine, 2022
[582] Martyna Grądzka-Rejak, 'Kobieta żydowska w okupowanym Krakowie (1939-1945), pages 300, 301
[583] Ryszard Kotarba, 'Żydzi Krakowa w dobie zagłady (ZAL/KL Płaszów)'; See also, by the same author, in English, 'A Historical Guide to the German Camp in Płaszów, 1942-1945'; Instytut Pamięci Narodowej, 2014
[584] https://www.archiwumkobiet.pl/publikacja/relacja-matyldy-low
[585] Ryszard Kotarba, 'Żydzi Krakowa w dobie zagłady'. pages 415-435

(Support Group) für das Generalgouvernement, which provided food and medical assistance, and the Zehnerschaft ('Community of Ten') which was a group of women that also supported those held in the camp.[586]

It might be mentioned that whilst Ryszard Kotarba, a historian, describes Płaszów's health facilities in detail, other authors, particularly survivors of the camp, are more dismissive. For example, Bernard Offen says of the camp infirmary, 'It was not a hospital in the true sense. Rather it served as a place for isolating diseases as well as a station for those who were to be killed during the next *Aktion*'.[587]

Joseph Bau is equally dismissive. He writes, 'Ladies and gentlemen, we are now entering the infirmary of Płaszów. We gave it the lofty title of 'hospital' which it certainly didn't deserve. The Germans kept the sick here in order to prevent epidemics, and in the event of an 'action' they didn't have to go looking for the 'idlers' in the barracks'.[588]

Other sources of information include Mariena Szewczyk's 2016 thesis, 'Opieka zdrowotna w Getcie Krakowskim' (Health Care in the Kraków Ghetto) which is filed at the Jagiellonian University, a bilingual booklet, 'Opieka medyczna w Getcie Krakowskim/ Medical Care in the Kraków Ghetto', which was published by Muzeum Historyczne Miasta Krakowa in 2012, and Jehuda Stein's 'Jüdische Ärzte und das jüdische Gesundheitswesen in Krakau' (Jewish Doctors and the Jewish Health Service in Kraków).[589]

Economic, social and administrative roles

Absence of women in positions of formal authority

Jewish women did not occupy positions of formal authority in the Kraków Ghetto, since it seems that the Nazi Powers were reluctant to give women such authority. Accordingly, no women appear to have been appointed to the Kraków Judenrat (Jewish Council). A photograph of the Council appears in Andrea Löw and Markus Roth, 'Juden in Krakau' and it shows that all seven members are male.[590] Having said that a woman, Bronisława Feld did work as an accountant to the Kraków Judenrat and her testimony was collected after the war.[591]

By contrast with Kraków, in the town of Wieliczka to the south east of Kraków, the first Judenrat which was appointed in November, 1939 comprised mainly women

[586] Ryszard Kotarba, 'Żydzi Krakowa w dobie zagłady', pages 435-450 and Wikipedia entry for 'Kraków-Płaszów concentration camp'

[587] Bernard Offen, 'My Hometown Concentration Camp'; Vallentine Mitchell, London, 2008, page 76

[588] Joseph Bau, 'Dear God, Have You Ever Gone Hungry'; Arcade Publishing, New York, NY, 1996, pages 148, 149

[589] Jehuda L Stein, 'Jüdische Ärtze und das jüdische Gesundheitswesen in Krakau'; Hartung-Gorre Verlag, Konstanz, Germany, 2006, pages 45-56

[590] Andrea Löw and Markus Roth, 'Juden in Krakau unter Deutscher Besatzung 1939-1945'; Wallstein Verlag, Göttingen, 2011, page 17

[591] https://sztetl.org.pl/pl/miejscowosci/k/512-krakow/104-teksty-i-wywiady/195739-likwidacja-getta-krakowskiego See also the names index to Ryszard Kotarba 'Żydzi Krakowa w dobie zagłady' and a reference in Martyna Grądzka-Rejak, 'Kobieta żydowska w okupowanym Krakowie' at page 190

'as hardly any men remained in the town'. Bronisława Friedmann was the leader with Berta Rakower as her deputy. One of their first tasks was to raise a substantial tax of 8,000 złoty which had to be paid over to the occupiers. When necessary, the Wieliczka Judenrat bribed German officials and in this way it succeeded in extracting from the Nazis a guarantee of safety for all men in hiding. When the men later returned to the town, women lost their majority on the Judenrat, but Bronisława Friedmann continued to serve on it.[592]

The role of the Jewish Police Force during the Holocaust is not altogether clear, but it is generally regarded unfavourably by commentators and survivors. Having said that, there is some argument to challenge 'the single story of the Jewish Police as sadistic oppressors, willing Nazi collaborators, or self hating Jews'.[593] The topic of the Jewish Police is discussed in Alicja Jarkowska-Natkaniec's paper, 'Jüdischer Ordnungdienst [The OD] in Occupied Kraków during the years 1940-1945'.[594] The author of this paper indicates that the Jewish police force in Kraków was entirely male. There is some evidence, though, of female OD members elsewhere, for example in Łódz.[595] In her book, 'The Butterfly and the Flame', Leah Shinnar describes how some women were imprisoned in Kraków by the OD.[596]

Education

Education for Jewish girls did not completely stop with the Nazi invasion, despite the early closure of Jewish schools.[597] Several Holocaust survivors and historical researchers describe how education went 'underground', and how, for example, older girls taught younger ones in private homes.[598] As Halina Nelken writes, 'I am attending clandestine courses held in different private houses, but it's

---

[592] Małgorzata Międzobrodzka, 'Żydzi w Wieliczce'; Wydawnictwo Żyznowski, Siercza, 2022, pages 381, 382, and Michael Zellner, 'Evidence' in the English section of Shmuel Meiri (Ed), 'Kehilat Wieliczka; Sefer Zikaron', Tel Aviv, 1980, available at https://www.jewishgen.org/Yizkor/Wieliczka/Wieliczka.html See also Arnon Rubin, 'The Rise and Fall of the Jewish Communities in Poland and their Relics Today'. Vol 3, District Kraków, page 346

[593] See Joanna Sliwa's review in English of Katarzyna Person's 'Policjanci: Wizerunek Żydowskiej służby porządkowej w Getcie Warszawskim' (Policemen: An Image of the Jewish Order Service in the Warsaw Ghetto); Jewish Historical Institute, Warsaw, 2018. The review does not mention any women serving in the Warsaw OD, and all officers illustrated on the front cover of the book are male

[594] Scripta Judaica Cracoviensia, vol 11 (2013), and https://www.academia.edu/6528819 See also an item in 'The Memorial Journal in Honor of the Jews of Cracow who Perished, 1939-1945'; The New Cracow Friendship Society, New York, NY (pages not numbered). A further source is Andrea Löw and Markus Roth, 'Juden in Krakau unter Deutscher Besatzung, 1939-1945'; Wallstein Verlag, Göttingen, 2011, pages 100 to 107. This section is headed 'Ordnungdienst und Jüdische Spitzel' (The OD and Jewish Spies)

[595] https://forum.axishistory.com/viewtopic.php?t=216412

[596] Leah Shinnar, 'The Butterfly and the Flame and other Stories of Jewish Life from Kraków to Israel'; Mazo Publishers, Jerusalem, 2004, chapter 5, 'In the Penitentiary'

[597] For a general summary of Jewish education during the Holocaust see www.academia.edu/33768075

[598] See, for example, Joanna Sliwa, 'Coping with Distorted Reality; Children in the Kraków Ghetto' in the section headed 'Secular Education'

not the same as school. There are about eight of us girls, two of them from my class.'[599]

According to Miriam Akavia, 'the one good kindergarten, still open when the Ghetto was established, was the well known school run by Mrs Mania; it was closed owing to the sudden death of that wonderful woman and many of the children were left neglected.[600] Other kindergartens were later established in the ghetto, for example as described by Joanna Sliwa in her book, 'Jewish Childhood in Kraków'.[601] Tadeusz Pankiewicz notes that a Kinderheim was opened in the ghetto by order of the Germans and that children there were taught sewing.[602] Similarly, Miriam Akavia notes, 'Besides the regular school program we were taught there also sewing, because everybody thought that one needs to have a solid profession'.[603]

It appears that religious as well as secular education was available to some girls and young women during the Holocaust period. Joanna Sliwa comments that 'no matter where the family was on the religious spectrum, introducing children to Judaism or Jewish studies enabled children to try to look for answers to their current predicament .... and to help them cope with ghetto life.' She adds, though, that 'not all children were comfortable with their Jewish identity'.[604]

A school timetable showing religious studies is to be found in a press report at www.ynetnews.com/articles/0,7340,L-4696654,00.html though it is not clear whether the school was attended by girls as well as boys. On the other hand, it seems inconceivable that students of Bais Ya'akov abandoned their studies, and Pearl Benisch notes that two teachers at the Kinderheim had received their teacher training at the Bais Ya'akov Seminary in Kraków.[605]

Further information relating to children in the Kraków Ghetto is set out in the following section headed 'Orphanages'.

Gallantry shown by women

Gallantry was shown not only by members of the Żydowska Organizacja Bojowa (The Jewish Underground Force), the Żegota support group, smugglers and others described in the following sections of this chapter, but also by another group of women – those who might have been able to save themselves but chose not to do so because that course of action would have required them to abandon friends or family members. Just one example is a young woman referred to only as 'Herta' who in 1942 was working on an agricultural estate at Borek Szlaczecki, and gave up an opportunity to be hidden in a convent because she would have had to leave her group

---

[599] Halina Nelken, 'And Yet I am Here'; University of Massachusetts Press, Amherst, MA, 1999, page 57

[600] Miriam Akavia, 'An End to Childhood'; Vallentine Mitchell, London,1995, page 43

[601] Joanna Sliwa, 'Jewish Childhood in Kraków', see index under 'Kinderheim', 'schools' and 'Tagesheim'

[602] Tadeusz Pankiewicz, 'The Cracow Ghetto Pharmacy'; Holocaust Library, New York, NY, 1985, page 103

[603] Joanna Sliwa, 'Coping with Distorted Reality; Children in the Kraków Ghetto'

[604] Joanna Sliwa, 'Coping with Distorted Reality' in the section headed 'Religion'

[605] Pearl Benisch, 'To Vanquish the Dragon'; Feldheim, Jerusalem, 1991, page 176

of workers. 'These girls are the only family I have', she said, 'and I must share their fate'.[606]

The reversal of women's and men's roles

Martyna Grądzka's paper, 'Jewish Women in the Kraków Ghetto; an Outline of Research Issues' describes in some detail the changes in family relationships and the professional and economic status of women during the period of the ghetto. These themes are considered in more detail in the same author in her book, 'Kobieta żydowska w okupowanym Krakowie (1939-1945)', (Jewish Women in Occupied Kraków) in chapters 3, 4 and 5. The author refers to the situation where women often turned out to be stronger and more resistant than men to the conditions of the time, so that they 'became heads of families, taking the place naturally assigned to men'. She added 'It was they [women] who had to worry about obtaining material resources, food and medicines. They were also responsible for making decisions regarding family life.' In support of this view, she uses information from the employment censuses that were conducted during the period of the ghetto. One of the examples she gives is that of Berta Müller, the mother of Stella. Berta was the main bread winner of the family, running the office of a button factory, thanks largely due to her proficiency in German and her 'dobrego wyglądu' – her good, i.e. Aryan, looks.[607]

As a further example, which illustrates the resourcefulness and strength of women, Lusia, a niece of Joseph Hollander, 'became an accomplished seamstress and could thus draw an income'.[608]

At the same time, many women continued to be engaged in routine household work, including the preparation of whatever food was available. A newspaper, Gazeta Żydowska, was published in the Kraków Ghetto from 1940 to 1942, about two or three times a week. The Gazeta included a section entitled 'Guide to Housewives' which contained recipes and other advice regarding the running of households. It must be remembered, however, that Gazeta Żydowska was under the control of the Generalgouvernment.[609]

As noted in the following section headed 'Smugglers', some females and children and teenagers were literally 'bread winners' as they smuggled food into the ghetto from the Aryan side. As Joanna Sliwa notes in her paper, 'Child Smugglers in the Kraków Ghetto', 'Parents faced losing control of their offspring, who were

---

[606] Bruno Shatyn, 'A Private War; Surviving in Poland on False Papers, 1941-1945'; Wayne State University Press, Detroit, MI, 1985, page 28
[607] Martyna Grądzka-Rejak, 'Kobieta żydowska w okupowanym Krakowie (1939-1945), page 294 and see also Stella Müller-Madej, 'A Girl from Schinder's List'; Polish Cultural Foundation, London, 1987
[608] Richard Hollander (and others) (Eds), 'Every Day Lasts a Year' reviewed at https://networks.h-net.org/node/3180/reviews/6331/baranowski-browning-and-hollander-and-tec-every-day-lasts-year-jewish
[609] Martyna Grądzka, 'Jewish Women in the Kraków Ghetto; An Outline of Research Issues'; The Person and the Challenges, vol 3 (2013), no 2, pages 123-141. See also Felicja Karay, 'The Women of Kraków Ghetto'; Tel Aviv, 2001, originally published in Hebrew in 'Yalkut Moreshet' 71, April, 2001

becoming more independent. The traditional role of the father as breadwinner and protector of the family became undermined.'

The topic of role reversal between the sexes has been discussed in other contexts, for example by Dobrochna Kałwa where she considers the effects of the First World War in her paper, 'Uneven Roads to Gender Equality: The Situation of Women in the Second Polish Republic'. The topic of women in the Second Polish Republic is also a theme which is explored by Anna Czocher in her work, 'Heroines of Everyday Life; Kraków Women of the German Occupation Period, 1939-1945'. Both of these papers are included in the book, 'Is War Men's Business?' which was published by the Muzeum Historyczne Miasta Krakowa in 2011. Unfortunately like several other authors, Dr Czocher, who works with the Institute of National Remembrance, distinguishes between 'Jewish' women and 'Polish' women, whereas the description of tasks and roles undertaken by both groups indicates that the Jewish women were also good Poles.

Social and romantic life and sexual violence

For a time, and to some extent, the Nazis were anxious to present an image of normality in the ghetto to the outside world, and to this end they allowed post (mail) to be sent to and from the ghetto. From time to time, items of correspondence are offered for sale on sites such as ebay and allegro.pl. For example, in December, 2023 the ebay site offered a post card, dated 1 April, 1942, from Berta Teitelbaum addressed to M Panzer in Bern, Switzerland. The card was sent from Limanowskiego 4/30 in Podgórze and is stamped 'Aufgeliefert durch den Judenrat' (delivered through the Jewish Council). It is apparent that Berta felt restricted in what she could say and the message on the card, written in German, is limited to the following:-

'Thank you very much for your lovely writing [letter]. I will [would] be very happy to receive a letter from you quite often. You are all greeted warmly by your loving ones, Berta'.

The wording is clearly more restrained than that used by Cyla Ferlier in October, 1941. She writes:-

'I feel imprisoned … you know that Kraków was cut into different sections … ours is extremely crowded … we [are] locked here as noodles in a pot … there is no hope for the future'.[610]

Several sources describe how women in the ghetto took steps to keep up a good appearance despite the reversal of some traditional roles. For example, there are accounts of women restyling old clothes in the absence of new ones. Some of the diaries written by younger women illustrate that, despite the death and destruction around them, they continued to be interested in young men. Having said that, some young women felt the need to maintain pre war standards of etiquette and courtesy, partly to avoid appearing as 'men chasers'.

---

[610] http://www.edwardvictor.com/Ghettos/krakow_main.htm More generally, see Henry F Kahn, 'The Third Reich; Concentration Camp and Ghetto Mail System under the Nazi Regime'; Judaica Historical Philatelic Society, 1966

As Leah Shinnar writes, 'Men chasers' was an appellation which contained so much contempt, that I did not have the courage to risk it. It is amazing to think today how deeply affected we had been by the *petit bourgeoisie* concepts of the time, how pedantic we were in our accepted norms of courtesy, to a degree of absurdity, even in those circumstances.[611]

There is some evidence that such self restraint was driven away by desperation and hunger following the liquidation of the ghetto. Bertha Ferderber-Saltz writes that 'The promiscuity at the Płaszów camp was disgraceful, and young women would sell their bodies for a slice of bread or a bowl of soup.'[612]

There are several recorded examples of couples being married during the Holocaust or shortly prior to it. Eda Dükler married Salek Künster in Kraków on 30 August, 1939, just two days before the German invasion of Poland. Eda became pregnant whilst she and her husband were in the ghetto and their daughter, Anita, was born in November, 1942. Anita was handed over to a Catholic family, the Senders, as the ghetto was being liquidated. Remarkably, both Eda and Anita survived the Holocaust and were reunited. Anita's story is recorded in her memoir, 'Miracle Child'.[613] For the sake of balance, however, it may be worth mentioning that the story of Anita's survival is described as a fake by Karl Radl, writing in The Purity Spiral on 25 July, 2019. The Purity Spiral has described itself as 'A National Socialist Community' whilst its website included a link to 'Judas Watch, documenting anti-White traitors, subversives, and highlighting Jewish influence'.

Gusta Dawidson ('Justyna') married Szymszon Draenger in early 1940.[614] Reizel Nechama Dym, a former pupil of Sarah Schenirer, also married in 1940. She and her husband, Chaim Schmuel Wohlhendler, survived the Holocaust and settled in New York,[615] whilst Rosalie Baum married William Schiff in the Ghetto. 'We didn't have any nice linen [with which to make a canopy or chupah] so strangers raised a rag up over our heads. The Rabbi said what he said. We said what we had to say. That was it – man and wife. Somebody found a half bottle of wine so I drank a toast and broke the glass. We were all wondering how we were going to stay alive'.[616]

The musician, Leo (Leopold or Poldek) Rosner married Helen (Hela) Haubenstock on 17 March, 1943, the day before he was sent to the camp at Płaszów.[617] Erna Kluger married Max Hilfstein in the Kraków Ghetto on 15 November, 1942. They survived the Holocaust and settled in the Bronx, New York.

---

[611] Leah Shinnar, 'The Butterfly and the Flame'; Mazo Publishers, Jerusalem, 2004, page 28

[612] Bertha Ferderber-Salz, 'And the Sun Kept Smiling'; Holocaust Library, New York, NY, 1980. Page 120

[613] Anita Epstein, 'Miracle Child; The Journey of a Young Holocaust Survivor'; Academic Studies Press, Boston, 2018. Anita Epstein died in 2019 at the age of 76 and her obituary is published in the Washington Post dated 9 July, 2019 and in the Boston Globe.

[614] 'Is War Men's Business?', page 50

[615] https://vinnews.com/2022/04/28/sara-schenirers-last-known-living-student-dies-at-104/

[616] William and Rosalie Schiff, 'William and Rosalie; A Holocaust Testimony'; University of North Texas Press, Denton, TX, 2007, page 31

[617] Anna Rosner Blay, 'Leo Rosner; A Man of Note' at www.hybridpublishers.com.au and then search for 'Rosner'. See also, for example, Elinor J Brecher, 'Schindler's Legacy'; Plume Publishers, 1994, pages 1 to 38 regarding the Rosner family

Erna became a teacher and professor.[618] Several members of the Kluger and Hilfstein families are commemorated in the Silver Anniversary Book of the New Cracow Friendship Society, published in New York in 1990.

Whilst in the camp at Płaszów, Jósef Bau went through a marriage ceremony with Rebecca. The groom traded four loaves of bread for a silver spoon, and in exchange for four more loaves the jeweller in the watchmakers' shop fashioned two rings from the spoon. In the absence of a Rabbi, Józef's mother officiated and gave the blessing. Józef and Rebecca were saved by Oskar Schindler, though Rebecca spent some time in Auschwitz. They found one another after the war and lived in Kraków until 1950 when they emigrated to Israel.[619]

Miriam Rosenthal (née Schwarc) married in Budapest in 1944. Within a few months she was deported to Auschwitz before spending a short time in Płaszów. At that camp she worked in a unit searching for valuables hidden in featherbeds and pillows which had been stolen from Jewish households. Later in that year she was transferred to a sub camp of Dachau in Bavaria where she joined a very small group of pregnant Jews who were allowed to keep their babies. Miriam died in Toronto in 2007 at the age of 95, survived by her son aged 72 and two other children.[620]

At the other end of the emotional spectrum, there are also accounts of 'gynaecological examinations' and systematic rapes. In her paper, 'And it was Something We did not Talk About; Rape of Jewish Women during the Holocaust',[621] Helene Sinnreich refers to evidence of a rape during an action in the Kraków Ghetto.[622] Some accounts record how women committed suicide in order to avoid becoming enforced prostitutes. The most widely known of these is a document relating to students at the Beis Ya'akov School in Kraków. However, Naomi Seidman and other researchers now consider this account to be a myth.[623]

Lieba Tiefenbrun gives an account of sexual violence in the Płaszów camp, evoking 'the obscene and vulgar language of male and female prisoners'. This

---

[618] www.poles.org quoting 'Who's Who in Polish America, 1996-7'.
[619] Katarzyna Pabis, 'Józef Bau; A History of Life; A History of Remembrance', available on www.researchgate.net and Joseph Bau, 'Dear God, Have You Ever Gone Hungry?' Arcade Publishing, New York, NY, 1990, pages 135. See also the 'Jews Rescuing Jews' website at www.en.jrj.co.il/BRPortal/br/P102.jsp?arc=2512054
[620] Google search 'Miriam Rosenthal Holocaust'. See also Brana Gurewitsch (Ed), 'Mothers, Sisters, Resisters'; Oral Histories of Women who Survived the Holocaust'; University of Alabama Press, Tuscaloosa, 1998, pages 187-203, quoted in Martyna Grądzka-Rejak, 'Kobieta Żydowska w okupowanym Krakowie (1939-1945)', pages 191,197, 198 and 311
[621] Holocaust Studies, Vallentine Michell, 2008, available at https://www.academia.edu/1545832 , quoting the testimony of Jan Rozanski held at the United States Holocaust Memorial Museum
[622] For an account of a maternity unit at Bergen Belsen which was necessary largely as a result of rape, see Bertha Ferderber-Salz, 'And the Sun Kept Shining'; Holocaust Library, New York, NY, 1980, pages 158-161, 'Confinements in the Camp'
[623] Naomi Seidman, 'Beautiful Martyrs; The Ninety Three Bais Ya'akov Girls' at https://www.academia.edu/13843997 For further information about the Beis Ya'akov movement see, for example, a book by the same author 'Sarah Schenirer and the Bais Ya'akov Movement; A Revolution in the Name of Tradition': Littman, Liverpool, 2017

suggests that some violence occurred between the prisoners themselves, and was not limited to acts perpetrated by the camp guards.[624]

Work at the Płaszów Labour Camp

The Kraków Ghetto was liquidated in March, 1943 when the remaining survivors were transferred to the labour camp to the south of the city at Płaszów. A commemorative book of the New Cracow Friendship Society states,

'Several women were asked (sic) to sit down in carriages which were brought and the Germans were taking pictures to publicize the humane way of treating the Jews'.

'[The] first women were taken into the camp in June, 1942, when small Jewish communities near Cracow had been wiped out. They did their hard work in the kitchen, cooking for prisoners. They also had to serve as cleaning women in the SS and camp-guard barracks. They were very decent and tried to help the starving prisoners.'[625]

Work undertaken by women at Płaszów is described by Martyna Grądzka-Rejak in her book about Jewish women in Kraków during the Nazi occupation.[626] Groups of women worked in various locations, and the example has already been given of Miriam Rosenthal who worked in a unit searching for valuables hidden in featherbeds and pillows. The best known locations are Oskar Schindler's enamel works and his 'armaments' factory which is said to have produced goods which, in modern parlance, were not 'fit for purpose'. Other women worked in the Madritsch brush and clothing factories and in other workshops both on camp and off site.[627] In her book 'And the Sun Kept Shining', Bertha Ferderber-Salz briefly describes working in the camp's sewing workshop where she sewed trousers (pants) on an assembly line,[628] whilst in his testimony, Wilhelm Kranz describes the role of women, including Gitla Katz, in caring for children in the prison at Płaszów. He

---

[624] Justyna Kowalska-Leder, 'Camp sexual violence and obscenity in Lieby Tiefenbrun's account of her experiences in the Płaszów camp at
https://www.ejournals.eu/Konteksty_Kultury/2017/Tom-14-zeszyt-4/art/11342 For further references to Lieba Tiefenbrun see the names index to Ryszard Kotarba, 'Żydzi Krakowa w dobie zagłady' and also in Martyna Grądzka-Rejak, 'Kobieta żydowska w okupowanym Krakowie'
[625] Memorial Journal in Honor of Jews from Cracow [who] Perished, 1939-1945'; The New Cracow Friendship Society, New York, NY, 1967 (pages not numbered)
[626] Martyna Grądzka-Rejak, 'Kobieta żydowska w okupowanym Krakowie (!939-1945)' starting at page 308
[627] Amongst the wide range of books which describe Płaszów, see Bernard Offen, 'My Hometown Concentration Camp'; The Library of Holocaust Testimonies, Vallentine Mitchell, London, 2008 and Joseph Bau, 'Dear God, Have You Ever Gone Hungry?'; Arcade Publishing New York, NY, 1996. Other sources include Arnon Rubin, 'The Rise and Fall of the Jewish Communities in Poland and their Relics Today', vol 3, District Kraków and Mario Wenzel, 'Arbeitszwang und Judenmord; Die Arbeitslager für Juden im Distrikt Krakau des Generalgouvernements, 1939-1944'; Metropol Verlag, Berlin, 2017, particularly pages 160-182
[628] Bertha Ferderber-Salz, 'And the Sun Kept Shining'; Holocaust Library, New York, NY, 1980, pages 118, 119.

notes that 'the children learned Hebrew from a prayer book that Gitla had brought to the prison with her'.[629]

Working in a unit searching for hidden valuables, or in a sewing shop or looking after children may sound like relatively comfortable occupations – under the circumstances of war – but survivors emphasise that they were in constant fear of harsh treatment by the Nazi guards and their agents. Furthermore, some women were engaged in work that in no way can be described as 'comfortable'. The Jewish Virtual Library shows a photo of 'Jewish women at forced labor pulling hopper cars of quarried stones along 'industry street' in Płaszów concentration camp, 1944'.[630]

Guards at Płaszów (Aufseherinnen)

Two of the following sections, which relate to Righteous Amongst the Nations and Żegota, describe how some non Jewish women put themselves and their families at serious risk in order to project Jews. On the other hand, there were also a few women who were exceptionally brutal and sadistic. Amongst these were the female guards at Płaszów and the other Nazi camps. These guards were known as Aufseherinnen. It is estimated that out of a total of 55,000 guards at Nazi labour and extermination camps, some 3,700 were women. The testimony of survivors records that the Aufseherinnen treated prisoners very badly. For example, Rena Ferber notes that 'when we were loaded on the train in Płaszów, an SS woman hit me hard on the head. They were so vicious and brutal, more so than men'.[631]

In her testimony given in 1947, Anna Lermer describes the conduct of Luise Danz (born in Walldorf, Thuringia, Germany in 1917). She was an Aufseherin who was assigned to Oskar Schindler's factory in Zabłocie in 1944. Danz treated the factory workers very badly. For example, the testimony includes an account of punishment she imposed on the workers after they had made alterations to their prisoners' striped and bulky clothing.[632] Elsewhere, Danz is described as 'a specialist in punching jaws with her fist and at the same time bringing her knee up to the stomach'.

Elsa Ehrich was born in Bredereiche, Germany and before the war she worked in a slaughter house. In August, 1940 she volunteered for service at Ravensbrück as an SS guard. Having then served in Majdanek, in 1944 she was transferred to Płaszów where she was promoted to the rank of Oberaufseherin, or supervisor.

---

[629] Maria Hochberg-Mariańska and Noe Grüss, 'The Children Accuse', The Library of Holocaust Testimonies, Vallentine Mitchel, London, 1996, pages 252, 253. See also, Ryszard Kotarba, 'Żydzi Krakowa w dobie zagłady (ZAL/KL Płaszów)', the section headed Dzieci w obozie' pages 486-496. For example, see references to Amalia Mandelbaum-Hofstätter on pages 489-493

[630] https://www.jewishvirtuallibrary.org/women-at-forced-labor-in-plaszow

[631] Elinor J Brecher (Ed), 'Schindler's Legacy; True Stories of the List Survivors'; Plume Publishers, 1991, page 151 and Wikipedia entries for 'Kraków-Płaszów Concentration Camp' and 'Female Guards in Nazi Concentration Camps'

[632] The Chronicles of Terror website at https://www.zapisyterroru.pl entry for Anna Lermer. See also www.archiwumkobiet.pl/publikacja/relacja-anny-lermer and the names index entries for Luise Danz, Fryda Kiwetz and Anna Lermer in Ryszard Kotarba, 'Żydzi Krakowa w dobie zagłady' and the entries for Luisa Dans (Danz) in Martyna Grądzka-Rejak, 'Kobieta żydowska w okupowanym Krakowie'

Female guards who worked with Elsa Ehrich included not only Luise Danz but also Alice Orlowski (born in Berlin in 1903), Gertrud Heise (Berlin, 1921) and Hildegard Lächert (Germany, 1920). Alice Orlowski was in charge of a work detail on Lager Strasse in Płaszów where she was known for her viciousness. Her conduct is described by Róża Nass who notes that she beat Jews and Catholics, men and women.[633] Joanna Ringel is another survivor who describes the harsh treatment meted out by Orlowski, including an attack on a female doctor, Dr Freund.[634]

In her memoir, Halina Nelken has special memories of the Aufseherinnen whom she describes as 'our plague, starting with their boss, Else Ehrich'. She then continues, 'We all knew Alice Orlowska, a thickset enormous bitch .... She operated on the main street of the camp where as a boss, she shouted, beat and drank vodka .... and whipped women so mercilessly that they lost consciousness'.[635]

It is sometimes remarked that the most brutal guards in Nazi concentration camps were Poles, Ukrainians and Lithuanians. No doubt some guards of these nationalities were extremely brutal but the female guards who have been mentioned were German.

Literature

Most of the literature written by women during or about the Holocaust is in the nature of diaries, memoirs and testimonies. These are the subject of a separate section in this chapter. However, between 1940 and 1942 a newspaper, Gazeta Żydowska was published two or three times a week under the control of the Generalgouvernement. The paper included articles written, sometimes anonymously, by Jewish journalists on matters relating to Jewish cultural and every day life.[636] The Gazeta included a section entitled 'Guide for Housewives' which contained recipes and other advice regarding the running of households.[637] Marta

---

[633] Chronicles of Terror website at https://zapisyterroru.pl For further references to Róża Nass, see the names index in Ryszard Kotarba, 'Żydzi Krakowa w dobie zagłady' and in Martyna Grądzka-Rejak, 'Kobieta żydowska w okupowanym Krakowie'.

[634] Chronicles of Terror website and for further references to Joanna Ringel, see the names index in Ryszard Kotarba, 'Żydzi Krakowa w dobie zagłady'

[635] Wikipedia and Mario Wenzel, 'Arbeitszwang und Judenmord; Die Arbeitslager für Juden im Distrikt Krakau des Generalgouvernments 1939-1944'; Metropol Verlag, Berlin, 2017, page 314, and Halina Nelken, 'And Yet I am Here'; University of Massachusetts Press, Amherst, MA, 1986, pages 216 and 217. For wider reading see, for example, Susannah Heschel, 'Does Atrocity Have a Gender? Women in the SS' in Jeffry M Dietendorf (Ed), 'Lessons and Legacies', Northwestern University Press, Evanston, IL, 2004, pages 300-324. For a study based on two female guards at Majdanek, see Ellissa Mailänder, 'The Violence of Female Guards in Nazi Concentration Camps (1939-1945); Reflections on the Dynamics and Logics of Power' See also Alette Smeulers, 'Female Perpetrators: Ordinary or Extra-ordinary Women?' Universities of Groningen and Tilburg, 2014

[636] Galicia Jewish Museum, 'Fighting for Dignity; Jewish Resistance in Kraków'; Kraków, 2008, page 25

[637] Martyna Grądzka, 'Jewish Women in the Kraków Ghetto: An Outline of Research Issues'; The Person and the Challenges, vol 3 (2013), no 2, pages 123-141, available at http://czasopisma.upjp2.edu.pl/thepersonandthechallenges/article/view/498/425

See also Martyna Grądzka, 'A Broken Childhood: The Fate of the Children from the Jewish Orphanage at 64 Dietla Street in Cracow during the German Occupation'; Wydawnicwo

Hirschprung has been identified as one of the Jewish journalists who contributed to Gazeta Żydowska, particularly to its children's supplements.[638]

During part of 1943 Justyna Draenger, a leading member of the underground fighting movement, Żydowska Organacja Bojowa, produced a weekly ten page news sheet 'Hechalutz Ha'Lochem' (Fighting Pioneer) together with her husband Shimshon (Simek). Issues 29 to 38 have survived and they are held at the Ghetto Fighters' House (Beit Lochamei ha'Geta'ot) in Israel. An extract from the issue dated 27 August, 1943, which has been translated into English, can be found on the web at http://www.jewishgen.org/yizkor/schindler/sch015.html. In 1984 Ghetto Fighters' House published a book, 'Hechalutz Ha'Lochem: Organ of the Chalutz Underground Movement in Occupied Cracow, August – October, 1943'. A list of names in the book, including the names of many women, is available at https://kehilalinks.jewishgen.org/krakow/hechalut.htm.[639]

The Żegota Council for Jewish Aid also produced a newsletter, 'Wolność' (Liberty). Miriam Peleg-Mariańska was on the editorial staff. She recalls that it appeared three times a week, and included information obtained by radio broadcasts from London. The newsletter was distributed from a 'letter box' in a shop on Karmelicka Street. The operation was largely directed by three women, Mrs Fischer, the owner of the shop, Danuta, her daughter, and 'Madame Zofia'.[640]

Orphanages

It has been noted in previous chapters that the Jewish orphanage in Kazimierz was managed predominantly by women. It is true that following the death of Róza Rock in 1926, the leadership was taken over by two men, Dr Rafał Landau and Dawid Kurzmann, but during the Holocaust the orphanage returned to leadership by three women, Anna Feuerstein, Regina Nelken, and Sabina Mirowska.

Anna Feuerstein was the director of the Jewish orphanage from the latter part of 1939, and continued to act in this capacity after the orphanage was transferred to Józefińska Street in the Ghetto. In October, 1942 the Nazis liquidated the orphanage. Although Anna Feuerstein was given the opportunity to remain in the Ghetto, she together with her colleague Dawid Kurzmann went with the children to Belżec, where they died together.[641]

Wysoki Zamek, Kraków, 2012, page 325. Additionally, see Martyna Grądzka-Rejak, 'Kobieta Żydowska w okuowanym Krakowie (1939-1945)'

[638] Monika Szabłowska-Zarmeba, 'Marta Hirschprung: A Forgotten Journalist and Author from Cracow'; Rocznik Historii Prasy Polskiej, vol XXII (2019)

[639] See also, for example, Arieh Bauminger, 'The Fighters of the Cracow Ghetto'; Keter Press, Jerusalem, 1986, pages 60 and 61 and 102-107, and Judy Batalion, 'The Light of Days; Women Fighters of the Jewish Resistance'; Virago, London, 2020, page 140, and note on page 485

[640] Miriam Peleg-Mariańska and Mordecai Peleg, 'Witnesses; Life in Occupied Kraków', pages 6 and 7

[641] Sean Martin, 'Future Generations; Associations for Jewish Children in Kraków' in 'Polin', vol 23, Littman, Oxford, 2011, pages 311 and 317. See also several refences to Anna Feuerstein in Martyna Grądzka, 'A Broken Childhood; The Fate of the Children from the Jewish Orphanage at 64 Dietla Street in Cracow during the German Occupation' and in

Regina Nelken was the mother of Halina who wrote a diary relating to the period up to the spring of 1943 entitled 'Pamiętnik z getta Krakowie' (Memories from the Kraków Ghetto). Regina's testimony describes events at the orphanages on Dietla Street and in the Ghetto, as well as at Płaszów.[642] As a teacher she writes, 'The children in the Tagesheim [the day care in Ghetto A] played strange games. They did not laugh but they shouted, did not play but fought each other, gave orders, evacuated, hanged or robbed each other; almost always these games ended with an adult having to intervene'.[643]

Pearl (Ita Perel) Benisch (née Mandelker) (1917-2017) was also deeply involved in the education and care of children – before and during the Holocaust as well as afterwards. She was a member of the orthodox community and active within the Bais Ya'akov movement. She and her family lived on the same street as the movement's founder Sarah Schenirer and Pearl became one of her students. During the Holocaust she became a teacher in the Kinderheim in Ghetto B. She is quoted as noting, 'On the last festival of Purim in the ghetto, Ruchla organised the children to put on a play. She let them choose their own roles. Strangely they wanted to play OD or SS men… In their acting, the little observers displayed all the cruelty the OD had inflicted on their siblings'.[644]

As previously noted, Sabina Mirowska (née Hochberger) started to work at the Jewish orphanage in 1940. In her testimony, she describes the orphanage and also a major deportation from the Ghetto in October, 1942, and the liquidation of the Ghetto in March, 1943.[645]

Matylda Schenker ran the orphanage's dormitory at 53 Krakowska Street during the interwar years. She was later in charge of the Craftsmen's dormitory for boys of 14 years or older in the Ghetto at 29 Józefińska Street.[646]

---

the same author's book, 'Kobieta żydowska w okupowanym Krakowie'. Additionally, see Aleksander Bieberstein, 'Żagłada Żydow w Krakowie'. page 215 and Katarzyna Zimmerer, 'Zamordowany świat; losy Żydów w Krakowie,1939-1945'; Wydawnictwo Literackie, Kraków, 2004, pages 90 and 154. For further references, see Andrea Löw and Markus Roth, 'Juden in Krakau unter deutscher Besatzung, 1939-1945';Wallstein Verlag, Göttingen, 2011, page 162, and Joanna Sliwa, 'Jewish Childhood in Kraków', pages 72 and 86
[642] Martyna Grądzka, 'A Broken Childhood', pages 440-444, quoting Jewish Historical Institute file 301/2047. See also Maria Hochberg-Marianska and Noe Gruss, 'The Children Accuse'; The Library of Holocaust Testimonies, Vallentine Mitchell, London, 1996, pages 246 to 251, and several references in Joanna Sliwa, 'Jewish Childhood in Kraków.
[643] Joanna Sliwa, 'Coping with Distorted Reality' quoting the testimony of Regina Nelken
[644] Joanna Sliwa, 'Coping with Distorted Reality' quoting Pearl Benisch, 'To Vanquish the Dragon'; Feldheim, Jerusalem and New York, 1991 page 177 and
https://hamodia.com/2017/03/14/mrs-pearl-ita-perel-benisch-ah/
[645] Maria Hochberg-Mariańska and Noe Grüss, 'The Children Accuse', pages 240-246, and Joanna Sliwa, 'Jewish Childhood in Kraków. See also Andrea Löw and Markus Roth, 'Juden in Krakau unter deutscher Besatzung', particularly page 163
[646] Martyna Grądzka, 'A Broken Childhood', pages 287 and 440, and the testimony of Sabina Mirowska in Maria Hochberg-Mariańska and Noe Grüss, 'The Children Accuse'. See also Katarzyna Zimmerer, 'Zamordowany świat', page 90 and Sean Martin in 'Polin' vol 23, page 307

Other women who took important roles in the care of children during the Holocaust included Rachela Mahler (an inspector in charge of the Department for the Care of Children and Teenagers), Dr Gizela Thon, and Maria Biliżanka (Billig-Kleinberg).[647] Mention can also be made of Ewa Aleksandrowicz who, in 1940, at the age of 17, volunteered to work at an orphanage run by the 'Centos' charity on Agnieszki Street, and of Dr Pola Wasserberg who was supervisor of the Kinderheim.[648]

Joanna Sliwa's works describing the lives of Jewish children in Kraków have been listed in the earlier section headed 'Diaries, memoirs and testimonies'. These works, and works by other authors, particularly Martyna Grądzka in her book, 'A Broken Childhood', refer not only to the main orphanage on Józefińska, but also institutions such as:

- CENTOS (Centralna Opieki nad Dziećmi i Sierotami) – The Association for the Care of Children and Orphans
- The Vocational Hostel for Jewish Orphaned Boys
- The Kinderheim, a children's home in Getto A, and
- The Tagesheim, a care centre in Ghetto B

Recognition should be given to the work of the Żydowska Samopomoc Społczna, or ŻSS. This was a Jewish social self help group tasked with caring for the most vulnerable members of the ghetto society, including children. In his book, 'Zagłada Żydów w Krakowie' (The Destruction of the Jews in Kraków), Aleksander Bieberstein describes the work of the ŻSS, and mentions the pharmacist, Helena Anisfeld. She was active in the distribution of medicines which were acquired mainly through the Red Cross and from the pharmacy of Tadeusz Pankiewicz.[649] Arieh Bauminger writes 'During the darkness of the German occupation, the Ż.S.S. (Żydowska Samopomoc Socjalna), the Jewish Social Aid Organization, provided a ray of light.'[650]

It should also be recognised that a number of Jewish children spent some time in non Jewish orphanages during and immediately after the war. For example, Bronisława Wajngarten, who was born in Drohobycz spent time in the large orphanage in Kochanów, which is about 11 miles (17 km) north west of Kraków. Bronisława did not admit to being Jewish, adding in her testimony, 'At the end of

---

[647] Joanna Sliwa, draft paper, 'Stopping the Spread of Moral Savagery – Child Relief Efforts in the Kraków Ghetto' and, by the same author 'Jewish Childhood in Kraków'. See also Martyna Grądzka-Rejak, 'Kobieta żydowska' and Aleksander Bieberstein, 'Zagłada Żydów'

[648] George J Alexander, 'Generations'; Congress for Jewish Culture, New York, NY, page 279

[649] Aleksander Bieberstein, 'Zagłada Żydów w Krakowie', page 161. See also Martyna Grądzka-Rejak, 'Kobieta Żydowska w okuowanym Krakowie', page 228, note 110, Arnon Rubin, 'The Rise and Fall of the Jewish Communities in Poland and their Relics Today, vol 3, District Kraków', page 386, and the Geni genealogical website

[650] Arieh Bauminger, 'The Fighters of the Cracow Ghetto'; Keter Press, Jerusalem, 1986, page 33

the war, many of them [the other children] found their parents and families. I, however, did not.'[651]

Radę Główną Opiekuńczą – The Main Guardianship Council

As noted elsewhere in this chapter, a number of Catholics put themselves and their families at great risk by coming to the aid of Jews during the Holocaust. The aid group, Żegota, is mentioned towards the end of the chapter. However, this was not the only group which should be mentioned. The group, Radę Główną Opiekuńczą was active in Kraków as is described in some detail by Ryszard Kotarba. The group included women such as Maria Zazulowa.[652]

Maria Zazulowa was born in 1880. She received a rounded education and spoke German fluently. She became a devout Catholic following the death of her husband in 1926. On the outbreak of war, and at the age of 59, Maria amongst other ladies from Kraków worked with the Polish Red Cross to support prisoners, including those at the notorious Montelupich prison. She, and others, continued this function even after the Nazis banned the Polish Red Cross from carrying out this type of work.[653]

Righteous amongst the Nations

This book is almost entirely an account about Jewish women in the Jewish community of Kraków. Yet, such an account would not serve its purpose if it were not also to describe, however inadequately, the heroism and bravery of non Jewish women who came to the aid of Jews in severe distress. It is for this reason that the work includes this section concerning the Righteous amongst the Nations and also a later one, relating to the support group Żegota.

Put another way, in assessing the role of women during the Holocaust, it is important to refer to non-Jewish women who put themselves and their families at extreme risk whilst protecting, or attempting to protect, Jewish citizens. The various elements of risk are described by Joanna Sliwa in her article, 'Ma'am, do you know that a Jew lives here? The Betrayal of Polish Women and the Jewish Children they Hid during the Holocaust – the Case of Cracow'. In this work the author describes by way of example the actions of a Polish policeman, Adam Juny, against Serafina Fesenko who was protecting several Jews, including Rozalia Lieberfreund and her two children.[654] Rozalia is mentioned in the previous section of this chapter which is headed 'Diaries, memoirs and testimonies'.

On its website, Yad Vashem in Jerusalem describes itself as 'The world Holocaust Remembrance Center' and 'the ultimate source for Holocaust education, documentation and research'. In these roles it has recognised both men and women

---

[651] Jakub Gutenbaum and Agnieszka Latała (Eds), 'The Last Eyewitnesses; Children of the Holocaust Speak', vol 2, page 330. The orphanage is also mentioned in passing by Joanna Sliwa in her book, 'Jewish Childhood in Kraków', at page 131
[652] Ryszard Kotarba, 'Żydzi Krakowa w dobie zagłady', pages 520-528
[653] https://ipn.gov.pl/pl/historia-z-ipn/144433,Anna-Czocher-Ciotka-opiekunka-wiezniow.html
[654] A chapter in Denisa Nešťáková (Ed) (and others), 'If this is a Woman. Studies of Women and Gender in the Holocaust'; Academic Studies Press, 2021

as 'Righteous Amongst the Nations'. Of over 6,350 Polish rescuers recognised in this way, most are female.[655]

In his book, 'The Rise and Fall of the Jewish Communities in Poland and their Relics Today'[656] Arnon Rubin states that there are 196 files, each including one or more Polish people, who were awarded the title and which refer to the Kraków district. He then sets out brief information relating to more than a hundred of these individuals, generally with surnames beginning with letters A to J. The women he lists include

Ludwika Bachul, Janina Siwiec-Bachul, Maria Rzeszutka-Bachul, Anna Radon-Bachul, Helena Bereska, Anna Bereta, Anna Blasiak-Bereta, Klara Bradlo, Francziszka Koziol-Bradlo, Rozalia Bruzda, Sabina Buczek, Julia Bugajska, Stanislawa Cebulak, Anna Kociel-Kowalczyk, Justyna Celuch, Magdalena Chajec, Franciszka Czajowska, Jozefa Dadak, Anna Dobrowolska-Michalska, Stefania Dobrowolska, Zofia Drewniak, Janina Druzkowiecka, Zofia Duszczynska, Franciszka Dynowska, Ludwika Dynowska, Edwarda Dzielska, Eligia Dzielska, Joanna Fialkowska, Anna Fedorowicz, Katarzyna Filipek, Jaina Filozof-Walega, Maria Flondra, Bronislawa Gawelczyk, Antonina Gebel, Anita Gere, Otylia Emiia Trnka, Jozefa Gibes, Maria Glas, Anna Godawa, Maria Godawa, Janina Cicha-Godawa, Zofia Krzeszowiak-Gorecka, Leonia Gregorowicz, Anna Kaczmarczyk-Heleniak, Jozefa Herteli, Milica Horbacka, Ludmila Waluszewska-Horbacka, Czeslawa Jaksz, Marta Kowalczyk-Jaksz, Zofia Jamiol, Walera Jamro, Maria Augustyn-Jamro, Genowefa Janczarska, Irena Grzybowska, Bronislawa Janton, and Agata Janusz.

A catalogue published in Polish by Muzeum Historyczne Miasta Krakowa in 2013 under the title 'Krakowscy sprawiedliwi' (The Righteous of Kraków) gives information about the following women from Kraków who saved or protected Jews during the Holocaust:

Teresa Dietrich, Stefania Filo-Wilkosz, Mirosława Gruszczyńska, Maria Habiniak, Maria Kot, Maria Nowak, Maria Rudzka, Janina Strychalska, Augusta Szemelowska, and Zofia Włodarczyk.[657]

As mentioned in a following section, several female members of the Żegota support group were also awarded the status of Righteous amongst the Nations. These include

Maria Bobrowska, Bogna Domanska, Emila Hizowa, Wanda Janowska, Janina Wasowiczowa-Raabe, Józefa Rysińska and Wanda Wojcikowa.[658]

---

[655] Joanna Michlic, 'Gender Perspectives on the Rescue of Jews in Poland; Preliminary Observations' in 'Polin' vol 30, Littman, Liverpool, 2018
[656] Eng Arnon Rubin, 'The Rise and Fall of the Jewish Communities in Poland and their Relics Today, vol 3, District Kraków', pages 436-453
[657] http://sprawiedliwi.mhk.pl/o-projekcie
[658] See, for example, references to some of these women at www.eilatgordinlevitan.com/krakow/krkw_pages/krkw_right.html

Others from Kraków or the surrounding area who have been named Righteous include Franciszka Ziemiańska,[659] Rosalia Nataniec,[660] and Zofia Tomaszewska[661] as well as Mirosława Gruszczyńska (née Przebindowska), Michalina Jaśko,[662] Maria Nowak[663] and Aniela Tosza who lived in the village of Radziszów, some 15 miles (24 km) to the south of Kraków.[664]

Additionally, Emilie Schindler was named Righteous in her own right, and not merely as the wife of Oskar. Her memoir was published in English by W W Norton & Co as 'Where Light and Shadow Meet' in 1997.[665] Reference can also be made to Mimi Reinhard, who as Oskar Schindler's secretary drew up lists of workers that helped save hundreds of Jews. Ms Reinard was born in Austria and worked for Oskar Schindler until 1945. After the war she moved to New York, and then to Israel where she died in 2022 at the grand age of 107.[666]

The profiles of several female rescuers in Kraków, including Mirosława Przebindowska and Teresa Bobrowska are recorded on the website of The Jewish Foundation for the Righteous which is based in West Orange, NJ.

The Bachul family provide a good example of the bravery and humanity shown by those who took enormous risk in order to save Jewish lives. The Bachuls were a poor working class family who lived in a village not far from Kraków. Miriam Sztern stayed in the village in the 1930's when she sold fabric to Ludwika Bachul. Miriam gave birth to a daughter, Sara, during the Holocaust. The baby was smuggled out of the Ghetto and was cared for by Ludwika, and her daughters. Miriam survived the war and was reunited with her four your old daughter. The Bachuls received nothing in return for giving the child a home, and their motives in saving her were purely humanitarian. Yad Vashem recognised the Bachul family as Righteous in September, 1990.[667]

---

[659] Joanna Sliwa, 'Jewish Childhood in Kraków', page 120

[660] Eugeniusz Duda, 'The Jews of Cracow'; Wydawnictwo Hagada, Kraków, 1999, page 72

[661] Michał Niezabitowski and others (Eds), 'Is War Men's Business? Fates of Women in Occupied Kraków in Twelve Scenes'; Muzeum Historyczne Miasta Krakowa, Kraków, 2011, pages 92-95

[662] See above re Franciszka Guter in the section headed 'Diaries, memoirs and testimonies'

[663] Monika Stępień (Ed), 'Witnesses to Polish-Jewish History: The Stories of Holocaust Survivors, Former Prisoners of Nazi German Concentration Camps and Righteous Among the Nations'; Galicia Jewish Museum, Kraków, 2016, pages 36-39 and 48-51. See also Rabbi Avi Baumol, In my Grandfather's Footsteps'; A Rabbi's Notes from the Frontlines of Poland's Jewish Revival'; Austeria, Kraków, page 39.

[664] http://sprawiedliwi.org.pl/en/

[665] See also, for example, Brana Gurewitsch (Ed), 'Mothers, Sisters and Resisters; Oral Histories of Women who Survived the Holocaust'; University of Alabama Press, Tuscaloosa, AL, 1998, pages 237-241, and Rena Finder, 'My Survival; A Girl on Schindler's List'; Scholastic Press, New York, NY, pages 74-79 as well as references in a wide range of other books about Oskar Schindler

[666] Various newspaper reports, April, 2022

[667] Arnon Rubin, 'The Rise and Fall of the Jewish Communities in Poland and their Relics Today, vol 3 District Kraków', page 436. The Bachul family are not to be confused with Stefania and Jan Buchala who saved Roman Polanski and were awarded Righteous Among the Nations Status in 2020

By way of a further example, the courage of Karolina Sapetowa is typical of that shown by the Righteous Amongst the Nations. Karolina was a nanny to Sala (Salomena) and Solomon Hochheiser who were born in 1932 and 1933. She continued to be their nanny in the Kraków Ghetto, and she smuggled the children out during the liquidation of the ghetto in 1943. She looked after the children in her home village of Witanowice, some 29 miles (46 km) south west of Kraków, where she withstood the threats from her neighbours to denounce her and the children.[668] After the war she became the children's sole guardian. She stated that she did not wish to marry a non Jewish Pole because she believed he would treat the children badly. She even offered to emigrate to Palestine if that would be beneficial to the children.[669]

Another Karolina, Karolina Maciag, is a third example. She was also a nanny, in this case to Mordechaj Przeworski. At about the time the Kraków Ghetto was being reduced in size, Mordechaj went to live with Karolina, and adopted the identity of one of her sons who was being raised elsewhere in Poland. He survived the war and emigrated to Israel. Karolina died in 1979 but was recognised as Righteous Amongst the Nations in 2011. At the time, three other Krakowian women were similarly honoured. These are Franciszka Zajac, and sisters Eleonora Haslinger and Wanda Oesterreicher.[670]

Several of the Righteous are mentioned with gratitude in survivors' testimonies. For example, Maria Feldhorn, the daughter of Juliusz, describes how she was sheltered in Łagiewniki by Augusta Trammer and her mother in a house which served as a meeting place of the partisans of the Home Army. Maria notes that her 'bad looks' attracted the attention of neighbours, who began to blackmail the women who were sheltering her. In March, 1944, she was therefore 'transported by some strangers to Czersk, near Góra Kalwaria, to an orphanage managed by the Sister Servants of the Most Holy Virgin Mary'.[671]

Maria and Danuta Gelles are further examples of Gentiles who have been recognised as Righteous Amongst the Nations. They protected Irene and Henry Haber, and their son Richard, after they escaped from the Kraków Ghetto in March, 1943.[672] Mention can also be made of Zygmunta Królikowski and her husband

---

[668] Regarding the attitude and reaction of many villagers see Joanna Michlic, 'The Stigmatization of Dedicated Polish Women Rescuers during the Second World War and its Aftermath'; East European Memory Studies, no 13, March, 2013. See also, for example, Joanna Michlic, 'Gender Perspectives on the Rescue of Jews in Poland; Preliminary Observations' in 'Polin' vol 30, Littman, Liverpool, 2018

[669] Joanna Michlic,'Rebuilding Shattered Lives; Some Vignettes of Jewish Children's Lives in Early Postwar Poland', pages 63 and 64, available on academia.edu and also, by the same author, 'Jewish Children in Nazi Occupied Poland; Survival and Polish-Jewish Relations during the Holocaust as Reflected in Early Postwar Recollections'; Yad Vashem, Jerusalem, 2008, pages 89-91.

[670] International Fellowship of Christians and Jews, 'With Open Arms' or Google, 'Five Women Honoured as Righteous Gentiles' on the Radio Poland website.

[671] Wiktoria Śliwowska, 'The Last Eyewitnesses; Children of the Holocaust Speak', vol 1, pages 43 and 44, and see also, for example, the website of the 'Polin' Museum in Warsaw.

[672] https://www.australianjewishnews.com/remarkable-story-of-bravery-and-hope/

Franciszek who protected members of the Mosberg family,[673] and to Zofia Włodarczyk and her husband Marian who protected, amongst others, Dr Mosze Bejski, who in due course became a judge in the Israeli Supreme Court.[674]

Whilst most of the Righteous were from middle class or poor families, special mention should be made of Countess Maria Potocki, and her husband Count Jerzy. They owned significant estates in and around Kraków, including one at Borek Szlachecki near Skawina. They protected several Jews whom they employed as agricultural workers, including Bruno Shatyn, author of 'A Private War'.[675]

Although many rescuers were highly righteous, and were recognised as such, some rescuers did not act well. Maria Staucher who was born in 1938 was interviewed at the Kraków Jewish orphanage in 1947. According to her testimony, her rescuers treated her like a servant, requiring her to carry out heavy tasks and treating her with physical and mental abuse.[676] As Jan Grabowski notes, other rescuers acted only out of financial greed, and some denounced 'their Jews' to the Nazis once they could no longer extract money or goods from them.[677]

Bertha Ferderber-Saltz, in describing her saviour Sigmund Szeliga, contrasts him with those 'who were interested only in our money and did not keep their promise to help us' and others who 'tried to keep their promises but the moment they felt danger approaching abandoned the victims to their bitter fate.'[678]

The role of the Roman Catholic Church

The view is often expressed that the Roman Catholic Church did little to protect Jews during the Holocaust and that, at best, it was a bystander. It may well be that individual Catholics were active anti-Semitic collaborators. For example, there is testimony that when in February, 1945, Holocaust survivors returned to Sosnowiec, some 40 miles (64 km) north of Kraków, 'Catholic nuns attacked schoolgirls for their Jewishness'.[679] As a further example, Emanuel Elbinger recounts how in Nowe Brzesko, some 18 miles (30 km) to the east of Kraków, nuns told villagers that they shouldn't help Jews in hiding as the Jews murdered Christ.[680] Even in current times there are reports of priests in Poland giving antisemitic sermons.

---

[673] Aleksander Skotnicki and Paulina Najbar, 'Jewish Families of Pre-War Cracow'; Stradomskie Centrum Dialogu w Krakowie, 2015, page 94

[674] Aleksander Skotnicki and Władysław Klimczak, 'Jewish Society in Poland: Many Faces of Cracovian Jewry'; Wydawnictwo AA, Kraków, 2009, pages 200, 201

[675] www.savingjews.org/righteous/pv.htm and Bruno Shatyn, 'A Private War; Surviving in Poland on False Papers, 1941-1945'; Wayne State University Press, Detroit, MI, 1985

[676] Joanna Michlic, 'Rebuilding Shattered Lives'

[677] Jan Grabowski, 'Rescue for Money; Paid Helpers in Poland, 1939-1945'; Yad Vashem, Jerusalem, 2008. See also 'Nechama Tec, 'When Light Pierced the Darkness'; Christian Rescue of Jews in Nazi-Occupied Poland'; Oxford University Press, 1986, part II, 'Paid and Anti Semitic Helpers'

[678] Bertha Ferderber-Salz, 'And the Sun Kept Shining'; Holocaust Library, New York, NY, 1980, pages 64 and 65

[679] Monika Rice, 'What! Still Alive?!; Jewish Survivors in Poland and Israel Remember Homecoming': Syracuse University Press, Syracuse, NY, 2017, page 5

[680] http://www.centropa.org/en/biography/emanuel-elbinger

Having said that, many priests were murdered by the occupying forces during the Holocaust. Monica Rice, quoting Eugeniusz Duraczyński, notes that during the Holocaust Poland lost more than 18% of its clergy, so for that and other reasons the Church itself was a victim.[681] Whatever the role of the Bishops and the Vatican, it is clear that many individual priests and nuns did take steps to protect Jewish children. This topic is explored in some detail in at least two publications. The first is Ryszard Tyndorf's comprehensive work, 'Wartime Rescue of Jews by the Polish Catholic Clergy; The Testimony of Survivors and Rescuers'. This was published in 2023 by The John Paul II Catholic University of Lublin and Wydawnictwo KUL. The second source is Ewa Kurek's book, 'Your Life is Worth Mine'.[682] This book includes transcripts of interviews with several nuns and with some children who were saved. For example, Sister Magdalena Kaczmarczyk describes the work which was carried out in a shelter at 47 Krakowski Street and at an orphanage at 10 Keletek Street, both in Kraków.[683]

It is possible to criticise both of these works, like some others, using the argument that the authors have close links with the Catholic church and therefore have had predetermined agendas. Ewa Kurek has been described as 'maybe the only legitimate Holocaust scholar to have become an alleged Holocaust revisionist or distorter during the later phase of her career'.[684] Her work has been criticised on the grounds that it 'contains a rather biased perspective colored by anti-Jewish prejudices rooted in the belief system of the early post war period'.[685] It might also be possible to identify cases where the Catholic authorities sought to convert Jewish children against the wishes of parents who survived the war. Nevertheless, both of the works do illustrate many examples of the Catholic clergy putting themselves and their communities at serious risk whilst protecting the lives of Jewish children.

Whether or not it is justifiable to question the religious independence of Ryszard Tyndorf and/or Ewa Kurek, there would seem to be no grounds to raise the same concern regarding Joanna Sliwa, who has written a book and several articles about

---

[681] Monica Rice, 'What! Still Alive?!', pages 17 and 18. Two of the very many sources which describe the position of the Polish Church during the Holocaust are Dariusz Libionka, 'The Catholic Church in Poland and the Holocaust, 1939-1945' which is available on the Yad Vashem website, and the Wikipedia article, 'Nazi Persecution of the Catholic Church in Poland'.

[682] Ewa Kurek, 'Your Life is Worth Mine; How Polish Nuns Saved Hundreds of Jewish Children in German- Occupied Poland, 1939-1945'; Hippocrene Books, New York, NY, 1997. The book was originally published as 'Gdy klasztor znaczył zycie'; Wydawnictwo Znak, Kraków, 1992. An extract from the book is included in Aleksander B Skotnicki and Władysław Klimczak, 'Jewish Society in Poland; Many Faces of Cracovian Jewry'; Wydawnictwo AA, Kraków, 2009, pages 206-213

[683] See also Fr Pawel Rytel-Andrianik, 'Priests and the Jewish People at the Time of the Holocaust; Reflections in the Light of the Newest Research'; Cincinnati, OH, 2014 available on academia.edu

[684] David Silberklang, editor in chief of Yad Vashem Studies, quoted in the Wikipedia article on 'Ewa Kurek'. See also Barabara Finkelstein, 'Why was Historian who Blames Jews for Complicity with Nazis Considered for Humanitarian Prize?' Forward, New York, NY, 16 April, 2018.

[685] Joanna Michlic, 'Jewish Children in Nazi-Occupied Poland; Survival and Polish-Jewish Relations during the Holocaust as Reflected in Early Postwar Recollections'; Yad Vashem, Jerusalem, 2008, page 12

the fate of Jewish children in Kraków during the Holocaust. She currently works at the Claims Conference at Clark University in New York. This is an organisation which negotiates with the German government for compensation for Jewish Holocaust survivors. One of her works is entitled, 'Jewish Children Seeking Help from Catholic Institutions in Kraków during the Holocaust'. In this article, the author notes that Catholic institutions provided some of the few refuges available to Jews seeking to survive on the 'Aryan' side.[686]

Zenobia Krzyżanowska describes how during the period of the Nazi occupation her father worked as a carpenter in the Benedictine Cloister in Staniątki near Kraków. Her mother was a seamstress, and in return for her parents' work the cloister rented an apartment and extended protection to the entire family. Zenobia continued to live in Staniątki after the war.[687]

'Nina E' was another Jewish girl who was saved by nuns in Staniątki, but by Felician sisters rather than those of the Benedictine Order. Previously, Nina had been protected by a Catholic family in Wieliczka. In her testimony she states that when she moved to Staniątki in 1944 the nuns were looking after a total of six Jewish girls.[688]

Bronisława Wajngarten was born in 1933. She spent her childhood in Drohobycz and spent the early years of the Holocaust in that town's ghetto. She was then handed over to a Catholic family who gave her protection, and who then sent her to Kraków. It was there, armed with a false baptism certificate, that she was placed with the Sisters of the Presentation, who ran an elementary school and a high school on St John Street. Bronisława remembers attending Mass and pumping the organ bellows in the organ loft. However, the convent required the payment of subsidies and she had to leave when these came to an end.[689]

Cecylia Roszak was a nun who joined the Dominican Monastery of Gródek in Kraków in 1938. Shortly afterwards, she moved with other Dominican sisters to Kolonia Wileńska near to Vilna with the aim of establishing a new congregation there. Following the Nazi invasion, she hid around a dozen Jews including several members of the partisans. After the war Sister Cecylia returned to Kraków, and in 1984 Yad Vashem honoured her and the other sisters of the Kolonia Wileńska as

[686] Joanna Sliwa, 'Jewish Children Seeking Help from Catholic Institutions in Kraków during the Holocaust' in 'Polin', vol 36, Liverpool, 2024. See https://muse.jhu.edu/pub/105/article/917641/summary
[687] Wiktoria Śliwowska, 'The Last Eyewitnesses; Children of the Holocaust Speak', vol 1, Nothwestern University Press, Evanston, IL, 1993, page 284. See also, for example, Mary Fraser Kirsh, 'Remembering the Pain of Belonging; Jewish Children Hidden as Catholics in Second World War France' in Simone Gigliotti (Ed), 'The Young Victims of the Nazi Regime'; Bloomsbury, London, 2016 during the Holocaust'. See https://muse.jhu.edu/pub/105/article/917641/summary
[688] Ewa Kurek, 'Your Life is Worth Mine'; Hippocene Books, New York, NY, 1996, pages 179-185
[689] Jakub Gutenbaum and Agnieszka Latała (Eds), 'The Lat Eyewitnesses; Children of the Holocaust Speak', vol 2 Northwestern University Press, Evanston, IL, 2005, pages 329, 330

Righteous Amongst the Nations. Sister Roszak remained in Kraków until her death in 2018 at the age of 110, having been recognised as the oldest nun in the world.[690]

Smugglers

The various roles of women during the Holocaust are described in an exhibition catalogue, 'Fighting for Dignity; Jewish Resistance in Kraków', published by the Galicia Jewish Museum in 2008. Particular reference is made to the role of travelling as messengers between occupied cities and towns, smuggling 'letters and other correspondence, orders between fighting organisations, underground newspapers, and very often guns and grenades or other explosives'.[691] Such female messengers are sometimes described as 'couriers', but it has been noted that 'the word courier does not do these women justice'. Partly for this reason they are also known as 'kashariyot' from the Hebrew word for 'connection'. This description reflects the fact that the women were often the only connection between ghetto dwellers and the outside world.[692]

The work of kashariyot is described by Sheryl Silver Ochayon on the website of Yad Vashem at https://www.yadvashem.org/articles/general/couriers.html, and by Braden Thompson in his excellent YouTube presentation at https://youtu.be/QnQwZICJogU entitled 'Female Couriers; Unsung Heroes of the Holocaust'.

One such kashariyah was Hela Rufeisen-Schüpper (Schipper/Szyper) who was born into a Chassidic Kraków family in 1921. Despite some resistance from her family, Hela joined the Akiva youth movement. During the war she acted as a courier of weapons between Warsaw and Kraków, and also between Kraków and other branches of Akiva. For example, she 'brought the first five revolvers from Warsaw'. Her activities are described by Yael Margolin Peled on the website of the Jewish Women's Archive at https://jwa.org/encyclopedia/article/schupper-hella-rufeisen as well as in Judy Batalion's book, 'The Light of Days'.[693] In her later life Hela Rufeisen-Schüpper wrote a book. The first edition was published in Hebrew in 1990 as 'Peridah mi-mila 18; Sipurah shel kasharit'. Later editions were in Polish, 'Pozegnanie milej 18', and in English, 'Farewell to Mila 18; A Courier's Story'. As

---

[690] https://sprawiedliwi.org.pl/en/stories-of-the-rescue/the-story-of-sister-cecylia-maria-roszak

[691] Tomek Strug (Ed), 'Fighting for Dignity: Jewish Resistance in Kraków/Walka o godność; Żydowski ruch oporu w Krakowie'; Galicia Jewish Museum, Kraków, 2008, page 91. See also Diane Plotkin, 'Smuggling in the Ghettos; Survivor Accounts from the Warsaw, Łódz and Kraków Ghettos' in Eric J Sterling (Ed), 'Life in the Ghettos during the Holocaust'; Syracuse University Press, Syracuse, NY, 2005

[692] Sheryl Ochayon, 'The Female Couriers during the Holocaust' at https://www.yadvashem.org/articles/general/couriers.html See also 'Kashariyot' on the website of the Jewish Women's Archive, and J Weitzman, 'Women of Courage; The Kashariyot (Couriers) in the Jewish Resistance during the Holocaust' in Jeffry Diefendorf (Ed), 'Lessons and Legacies'; Northwestern University Press, Evanston, IL, 2004

[693] Judy Batalion, 'The Light of Days; Women Fighters of the Jewish Resistance'; Virago, London, 2020, see the index. See also Arieh Bauminger, 'The Fighters of the Cracow Ghetto'; Keter Press, Jerusalem, 1986, page 43, quoting Justyna's Diary

noted below, Hela was not only a kashariyah; she was also a member of the underground fighting force, the ŻOB.

Chavka Folman-Raban was born in Kielce in 1924. She was a member, not of Akiva, but of the Labour Zionist youth movement, Dror. She acted as a courier throughout the Generalgouvernement, and whilst in Kraków she worked with Yitzchak Zuckerman on the day of the attack on the Cyganeria Café.[694] After the war, Chavka Folman-Raban became a founding member of Kibbutz Lohamei He'ghetaot.[695] Her death in 2014 was widely reported in the press, and her testimony is available on YouTube.

It was not only papers, arms and information that were smuggled. In her diary written during 1940 and 1941, the 14 year old Renia Knoll describes how her father brought food to her family in Kraków. The diary has been published by the Jewish Historical Institute, in Polish, as 'Renia Knoll; Dziennik'.[696] As noted on the Institute's website, 'Renia's diary is by no means a chronicle of the fates of Cracow Jews during the occupation. It is a diary of a teenager who worries about anti Semitic repressions as much as about flirtation with her male friends, learning problems, or arguments with her parents.' Extracts from the diary concerning the smuggling of food are to be found in Andrea Löw's and Markus Roth's book 'Juden in Krakau unter deutscher Besatzung' (Jews in Kraków under the German Occupation).[697]

Whilst some parents would use their children as decoys to enable them to smuggle food into the ghetto, smuggling activity was by no means restricted to adults. Children and young teenagers were also actively engaged in bringing food into the Kraków ghetto, and smuggling young children out of it. As Joanna Sliwa explains in her article 'Child Smugglers in the Kraków Ghetto',[698] young children attracted less suspicion outside the Ghetto than adults, and for a time their exemption from a number of regulations enabled them to move about with some degree of freedom. Dr Sliwa explores this topic, too, in her book, 'Jewish Childhood in Kraków'. As an example, she writes, 'Janina Fischler learned the meaning of smuggling at an early age …. She capitalised on her less stereotypically Jewish

---

[694] See the names index in Katarzyna Zimmerer, 'Zomordowany świat; losy Żydów w Krakowie, 1939-1945', and Arieh Bauminger, The Fighters of the Cracow Ghetto'; Keter Press, Jerusalem, 1986, pages 71-73 as well as
https://he.wikipedia.org/wiki/file:Chavka_Folman_Raban_1940.jpg
[695] www.eilatgordinlevitan.com/krakow/krkw_pages/krkw_stories_cyganeria.html
[696] Renia Knoll, 'Dziennik'; Żydowski Instytut Historyczny, Warsaw. See also the names index in Martyna Grądzka-Rejak, 'Kobieta żydowska w okupowanym Krakowie (1939-1945)'
[697] Andrea Löw and Markus Roth, 'Juden in Krakau unter deutscher Besatzung, 1939-1945', pages 84 and 85. A set of food coupons (lebensmittelkarte) for October, 1941 is illustrated on page 85. See also Katarzyna Zimmerer, 'Zamorodowany świat; losy Żydów' page 84
[698] Zeitschrift für Genozid Forschung, 13 Jahrgang 2012, heft 1-2; Wilhelm Fink Verlag. Other works by Joanna Sliwa include 'Clandestine Activities and Concealed Presence; A Case Study of Children in the Kraków Ghetto', 'The Forced Relocation to the Kraków Ghetto as Remembered by Child Survivors' and 'Coping with Distorted Reality; Children in the Kraków Ghetto'

features and moved freely in the city, bringing the food that her family spared for her relatives in the ghetto'.[699]

Joanna Sliwa makes it clear that whilst some children carried out smuggling, others were the subject of smuggling. For example, she describes how Salo and Eda Kunstler arranged for Mr Sendler (first name not known), a Pole who worked as a driver for the Polish authorities to take their daughter Anita out of the ghetto for safe keeping.[700]

Janina Fischler, one of the female smugglers identified by Joanna Sliwa, published her memoir 'Have You Seen my Little Sister?'.[701] Janina had the required Aryan looks, a perfect use of the Polish language, and a degree of self assuredness which she mixed with pure chutzpah. Sometimes she slipped in and out of a Ghetto gate with the connivance of a friendly policeman who turned a blind eye; at other times she would use the sewers or a small gap in the perimeter wall.

The qualities which were required to pass as a Christian Polish child are considered by Joanna Michlic in her paper, 'Jewish Children in Nazi Occupied Poland'. The author lists these as 'the right physical appearance, possessing a 'good look' (dobry wygląd), i.e. a look not easily recognizable as Jewish, the ability to speak Polish fluently without traces of a Jewish accent or Yiddish words: familiarity with Polish culture or the ability to learn it quickly and individual assertiveness'. The author notes that red hair gave a particularly bad appearance – to such an extent that one rescuer in Kraków preferred to hide a circumcised boy rather than a red haired girl.[702]

Janka Warszawska began smuggling in the Kraków Ghetto when she was only eleven years old. In her testimony she describes how she developed confidence and expertise, at first bringing food into the Ghetto but latterly also smuggling out children to the Aryan side. In advance of the October, 1942 aktion, she smuggled out two children of the Neuman family. The timing made the task particularly dangerous and, in her testimony, Janka Warszawska criticises the children's father, noting. 'He didn't give them [his two children] to me when it was quiet, but rather kept them until the last minute'.[703]

Ester Friedman, née Spagatner, was about ten years old at the beginning of the Holocaust. However, like most Jewish youngsters at the time, she matured beyond her years and, for example took care of her three year old sister, Lusia. She also

[699] Joanna Sliwa, 'Jewish Childhood in Kraków; A Microhistory of the Holocaust'; Rutgers University Press, New Brunswick, 2021, pages 59 and 60.
[700] Joanna Sliwa, 'Jewish Childhood in Kraków'. Page 65. See also general index for 'smuggling'
[701] Janina Fischler-Martinho, 'Have You Seen my Little Sister?'; Library of Holocaust Testimonies, Vallentine Mitchell, London, 1998. See also, for example, Andrea Löw and Markus Roth, 'Juden in Krakau unter Deutscher Besatzung, 1939-1945', page 83
[702] Joanna Michlic, 'Jewish Children in Nazi Occupied Poland; Survival and Polish-Jewish Relations during the Holocaust as Reflected in Early Postwar Recollections'; Yad Vashem, Jerusalem, 2008, pages 48-53
[703] Joanna Sliwa, 'Jewish Childhood in Kraków', pages 64 and 66. See also, for example, Martyna Grądzka-Rejak, 'Kobieta żydowska w okupowanym Krakowie (1939-1945), page 188

bought goods from supportive shop keepers. She not only smuggled those goods into the Kraków Ghetto but she also travelled by train to Brzesko, some 30 miles (48 km) to the east in order to deposit valuables with a gentile friend of her family.[704] In her later years Ester published her memoir, 'Daleka droga do domu' (A Long Way Home) which was translated into Hebrew.[705]

Janina Stefaniak was born in Proszowice, about 18 miles (28 km) to the north east of Kraków. However, she spent much of her youth in Kraków. As a Catholic Pole aged about eleven, she lived at 30 Lwowska Street right outside the ghetto. Her testimony relates how she frequently saw children smuggling food and other goods into the ghetto.[706] Her testimony, including an oral interview is held at the United States Holocaust Memorial Museum and her book, 'The Ghetto in Kraków as Seen by a Child' was published in 2004.

Żegota – The Council for Jewish Aid

Several Jewish women fought in the Jewish underground as is described in the following section headed 'Żydowska Organizacja Bojowa (ŻOB) and in other fighting forces. Others fought in combat units or with the support group Żegota. For example, Maria Hochberg-Mariańska (1913-1996) was a Jewish member of the underground attached to the Polish Socialists' Party, editing its paper, 'Wolność' (Freedom).[707] Together with her husband, Mordecai Peleg, Ms Hochberg-Mariańska went on to become a leading figure in The Council for Jewish Aid, known as Żegota. In 1942 and 1943 they were registered under Aryan papers in the suburb of Dębniki and they also spent some time in the village of Mogilany, some 12 miles (20 km) to the south of Kraków. The memoirs of Maria (Miriam) and her husband are recorded in their book, 'Witness; Life in Occupied Kraków'.[708]

Żegota was established in 1942 by the Polish underground in Kraków and Warsaw for the specific purpose of helping Jews 'on the Aryan side'. Many, if not most, of its agents were Catholics. The topic of smugglers has been considered in a separate section of this chapter, but it can be noted here that Żegota agents were active in supplying false papers, money and food to their 'charges', Jewish fugitives in hiding.[709]

---

[704] Joanna Sliva, 'Child Smugglers in the Kraków Ghetto' and 'Jewish Childhood in Kraków', pages 16 and 33

[705] JewishGen discussion group posting by Jacob Rosen, 'Brzesko-Krakow-Auschwitz- A Book', 21 September, 2004

[706] Joanna Sliwa, 'Jewish Childhood in Kraków', page 61

[707] Archive of the Victims of the Nazi and Communist Terror in Kraków, 1939-1956 at www.krakowianie1939-56.mhk.pl/ and 'Is War Men's Business? The Fates of Women in Occupied Kraków', pages 54-57

[708] Miriam Peleg-Mariańska and Mordecai Peleg, 'Witnesses; Life in Occupied Kraków'; Routledge, London, 1991, previously published as 'Wśród przyjaciół i wrogów' and 'Mi'huts l'homot ha'geto'. Pages xvii, 7 and 14 of the English version refer to the publication 'Wolność'

[709] For a general description see for example Yisrael Gutman and Shmuel Krakowski, 'Unequal Victims; Poles and Jews during World War II'; Holocaust Library, New York, NY, 1986, chapter 7, 'Żegota: The Council for Aiding Jews'. See also Władysław

As is stated on the website of the Polin Museum in Warsaw, in an article 'Żegota in Kraków Established 75 years ago' (March 2018), 'This [Żegota] was the first organisation in which the Zionists, Bundists, Catholics, Polish Democrats, Polish Socialists, peasants – Jews and Poles – all sat together at the same table and were active, secretly, against the Germans.'

The Kraków committee included not only Maria Hochberg-Mariańska but also another Jewish woman, Anna Dobrowolska ('Michalska') who served as Treasurer and represented the Democratic Movement.[710]

Arieh Bauminger refers to Żegota as the R.P.Ż. (Rada Pomocy Żydom). He notes, 'The wife of one of the PPR (Communist Party) leaders, Janusz Szczalski, Niunja, was the director of an orphanage in Cracow and saved there many Jewish children'. He then continues, 'A special 'workshop' for the fabrication of forged documents was set up in the home of Wanda, the sister in law of the noted Polish writer Leon Kruczkowski. She ran a beauty parlor in her home where the two professions intertwined: facial cosmetics and document cosmetics'. The author also mentions Maria Harikowa, a clerk in the Arbeitsamt (employment exchange) who stamped forged documents, and Teresa Lasocka (Tal) who kept up letter contact with activists in Auschwitz.[711]

The following females are recognised by Yad Vashem as being members of the Kraków branch of Żegota:

Bogna Domanska, Emila Hizowa, Janina Wasowiczowa-Raabe and Wanda Wojcikowa,[712] whilst Józefa Rysińska and Wanda Nelken were also members.

Józefa ('Ziutka') Rysińska was a Catholic member of the Kraków branch of Żegota. One of her feats was to smuggle a group of Jewish prisoners from the Janowska Street labour camp in Lwów to Kraków. The group included the author and underground member Max Boruchowicz, who was later known as Michał Borwicz. Józefa Rysińska was awarded Righteous amongst the Nations in 1981.[713]

Wanda Nelken (1913-2015) was born into an assimilated Jewish family in Kraków and educated in a Catholic environment. Prior to the war she was a member of the Polish Socialist Party. She was active in the Kraków group of Żegota until

---

Bartoszewski and Zofia Lewin (Eds), 'Righteous Among Nations'; Earlscourt Publications, London, 1969, pages 94-98

[710] https://sprawiedliwi.org.pl/pl/hisorie-pomocy/historia-pomocy-dobrowolska-annahttps://sprawiedliwi.org.pl/pl/historie-pomocy/historia-pomocy/ and then enter 'Maria Hochberg-Mariańska' or 'Anna Dobrowolska' in the search box. See also Arnon Rubin, 'The Rise and Fall of the Jewish Communities in Poland and their Relics Today, vol 3, District Kraków', page 441. See also Arieh Bauminger, 'The Fighters of the Cracow Ghetto', pages 34-36

[711] Arieh Bauminger, 'The Fighters of the Cracow Ghetto', pages 34-36

[712] www.eilatgordinlevitan.com/krakow/krkw_pages/krkw_right.html

[713] https://righteous.yadvashem.org/?searchType=righteous_only&language=en&itemid=4017296&ind=NaN . See also Miriam Peleg-Mariańska and Mordecai Peleg, 'Witnesses; Life in Occupied Kraków'

April, 1941 when she fled to Warsaw. She survived the war and lived to the age of 101.[714]

Other female members identified in Miriam Peleg-Mariańska's and Mordecai Peleg's book include

Maria Bobrowski, Mituska Hochberg, Maria Hrabykowa, Wanda Janowska, Teresa Lasocka, Jadwiga Rysiewicz, and Helena Szlapak.

The home of Maria Bobrowski and her husband Mieczysław, in Wieliczka, has been described as an 'address for Jewish refugees seeking help in Kraków and the environs' and as serving as a meeting place for their fellow activists'. Both Maria and Mieczysław were awarded 'Righteous Among the Nations'. Other Żegota agents working from Wieliczka included Józef Jedynak's daughters, Wanda and Józefa.[715]

Additionally, Zofia Posmysz (1923-2022) was a Catholic who served in the Polish resistance in the Kraków area until her arrest in 1942. She survived both Auschwitz and Ravensbrück, and after the war she became a journalist and novelist. Her autobiographical account of the Holocaust, 'Pasażerka z kabiny 45' (Passenger from Cabin 45) was published in 1959.[716]

The 'Holocaust Rescue' website is a further source of information. The pages which can be found at https://www.holocaustrescue.org/zegota-part-1 and https://www.holocaustrescue.org/zegota-part-2 list, and give information about, the following female members of Żegota who operated in the Kraków area.

Zofia Batko-Molenda, Weronika Blicharz, Maria Bobrowska, Stanisława Cebulakowa, Anna Dobrowolska, Stefania Dobrowolski, Wanda Dymek-Jedynak, Maria Hochberg (Miriam Peleg), Maria Hrabyk-Dziurzyńska, Zofia Jamioł, Maria Jekielek-Kluska, Janina Jetkiewicz, Józefa Kaliczyńska, Łucia Kobylińska, Anna Kociel-Kowalczyk, Lucylla Kowalska-Chmura, Wadysława Kuźma, Maria Łopuszańska-Jetkiewicz, Helena Mazur, Aleksandra Mianowska, Józefa Panuszko-Jedynak, Zofia Przetaczek, Ewa Rybicka, Józefa Rysińska, Helena Wójcik, and Wanda Wójcik.

Żydowska Organizacja Bojowa (ŻOB) and other fighting forces

An overview

A popular perception of the Holocaust is that, except during the Warsaw Uprising, there was little Jewish resistance to the increasingly harsh regime that was suffered by a passive and accepting Jewish population. It follows that too little recognition has been given by the Jewish public, let alone the non Jewish public, to

---

[714] Search for 'Wanda Nelken' on https://sprawiedliwi.org.pl/pl/historia-pomocy/historie-pomocy/ See also Miriam Peleg-Mariańska and Mordecai Peleg, 'Witnesses; Life in Occupied Kraków', page 4

[715] Yad Vshem database – https://righteous.yadvashem.org/?searchType=righteous_only&language=en&itemid=4034403&ind=NaN

[716] Wikipedia and The Times of Israel, 11 August, 2022

the gallantry of men and women in the Jewish Fighting Forces, particularly the Żydowska Organizacja Bojowa, but also other combat units.[717]

Although Zivia Lebetkin (code name Celina) was based in Warsaw, and was one of the few who survived the Warsaw Uprising, she should be noted here as the only woman on the national governing body – the High Command on the ŻOB.[718]

Even Martyna Grądzka-Rejak devotes only half a page to the ŻOB in her paper, 'Jewish Women in the Kraków Ghetto: An Outline of Research Issues' which runs to a total of nearly twenty pages. However, the same author does deal with the topic a little more fully in her important book, 'Kobieta Żydowska w okupowanym Krakowie (1939-1945)' (Jewish Women in Occupied Kraków)[719] which was published three years after her paper 'Jewish Women in the Kraków Ghetto'. The book has been described as the first monograph showing the dynamics of Jewish women during World War II in the context of one city. It includes chapters relating to a wide range of topics but in the context of the ŻOB, reference should be made to the first part of chapter 7 which is entitled 'At the Crossroads; Survival Strategies of Jewish Women'. Having said that, one reviewer, Przemysław Sołga, observes that the book 'overwhelmingly deals with orthodox women'.[720] If this is true, then arguably the activities of secular socialist and communist women in the fighting forces are not fully recognised in the book.

A further authoritative source is Aleksander Bieberstein's book, 'Zagłada Żydów w Krakowie' (The Destruction of the Jews in Kraków) which was published by Wydawnictwo Literackie during the Communist era, in 1985. This book was reviewed by Rafael Scharf who notes, 'This is a document of singular importance. It is a comprehensive and faithful record by an eye-witness of the systematic process of destruction'.[721] Whilst the work relates primarily to life in, and the destruction of, the Ghetto, it includes a full chapter about the Żydowska Organizacja Bojowa. The chapter not only describes the ŻOB in general terms but, for example, describes the resistance movement in the Płaszów Camp and includes a list of the members of the force in the Kraków district. Membership of the ŻOB was by no means limited to men, and the names of the following female members are listed:-

Hanka Blassman (Blas), Marysia Brenner-Minka, Gustawa Deutscher, Gusta (Justyna) Dränger-Dawidsohn, Czarna Ceśka Dränger-Szchora, Regina (Rena) Feuerstein, Anka Fischer, Chawa (Ewa) Follman, Czesia Frimat, Fryda Marta Fuchs-Towa, Pola Goldwasser, Irka, Ewa Jolles, Klara, Rajza Klingberg, Miriam (Mira) Liebeskind, Ewa Liebeskind-Spinner, Elza Łapa, Maciusia, Gola (Lidia) Mirer,

---

[717] See, for example, Shmuel Krakowski, 'The War of the Doomed; Jewish Armed Resistance in Poland, 1942-1944'; Holmes & Meier Publishers, New York, NY, 1984, chapter 7, 'The District of Cracow'

[718] Wikipedia

[719] Published by Instytut Pamięci Narodowej and Wydawnictwo Wysoki Zamek, Kraków, 2016

[720] www.academia.edu/72437477

[721] 'Polin', volume 2, 'Jews and the Emerging Polish State', Liverpool University Press, pages 458-460. More recent reviews of the book are available on https://www.jewsandpolesdatabase.org and https://justiceforpolishvictims.org These reviews indicate that the books justifies conclusions such as The Germans – not the Poles – forced Jews into the Ghettos and Polish denouncers of fugitive Jews were uncommon.

Róża Otter-Goldwasser, Hela (Halina) Rubinek, Hela Schipper (Szyper), Helena Schneider, Hanka Spritzer, Tóska Stark, Stasia, Helena Sternlicht, Gizela Stockhammer, Pesia Warszawska and Gena Wortsman.

A list of fighters can also be seen at
http://kehilalinks.jewishgen.org/krakow/hechalut.htm.

This list shows 133 mainly Jewish names which appear in the book 'Hechalutz ha'Lochem'.[722] It includes the names of the following women who are not mentioned in Aleksander Bieberstein's book:-

Hella Artman, Hanka (Tamar) Ballsem, Ruth Bauik, Kuba Berkowitz, Margot Drenger, Lea Drenger-Stern, Toschka Fridman, Toschka Fukss, Franka Goldberger-Shomron, Erna Goldfuss, Irene Hararand, Marya (Reiza) Kalina, Rivka (Waschka) Kupper/Schpiner-Libskind), Kuba Libreich, Stephania Libskind, Zviya Lubetkin, Ogenia Meltzer-Scheinberg, Esthuschya Michaelowitz, Dresze Michaelowitz, Miriam Perlberg-Reich, Rivka Perlis, Dora Rubinstein, Sala (Stasya) Schemyuk, Giza Schloss, Luzka Schpritzer, Rozya Schreibtapel, Mania Weintraub, Sabina Wulkan, Irena Yohanss and Danka Zelemeister.

Other sources refer to Gena Goldfluss.[723]

Members of the ŻOB were largely recruited from the ranks of the Akiva (Agudat ha'No'ar ha'Ivri Akiva) and Hashomer ha'Tzair youth movements. Information about the force can be found in various sources, including Arieh Bauminger's work, 'The Fighters of the Cracow Ghetto'.[724] That work describes the attack on the Cyganeria Café in December, 1942 and gives information about two leading female members of the Kraków unit of the ŻOB. These are Justyna Draenger (listed by Aleksander Bieberstein as Gusta (Justyna) Dränger-Dawidsohn) and Gola Mire (Gola (Lidia) Mirer). The activities of both of these heroines are described below.[725]

[722] 'Hechalutz ha'Lochem'; Organ of the Chalutz Underground Movement in Occupied Cracow, August-October, 1943'; Ghetto Fighters' House, Israel, 1984
[723] For example, see Katarzyna Zimmerer, 'Zamordowany świat; Losy Żydów w Krakowie, 1939-1945', pages 131. 132
[724] Arieh L Bauminger, 'The Fighters of the Cracow Ghetto'; Keter Press, Jerusalem, 1986, previously published in 1967 as 'Lochmi Gito Krakuv'; ha'Menorah Publishers, Tel Aviv. See also a chapter in Arieh Bauminger (Ed), 'Sefer Kroke; Ir v'Am b'Yisrael'; Rav Kuk Publishers, Jerusalem, 1959
[725] Additional information is set out in two books published by The New Cracow Friendship Society in New York. These are 'Memorial Journal in Honor of Jews from Cracow [who] Perished, 1939-1945' which was published in 1967, and the Silver Anniversary Book, 1990. See also Shmuel Krakowski, 'The War of the Doomed; Jewish Armed Resistance in Poland, 1942-1944'; Holmes & Meier, New York, NY, 1984 and Yael Peled (Margolin), 'Krokuv ha'Yehudim. 1939-1945'; Ghetto Fighters' House, Israel, 1993. Additionally, see 'Z ruchu oporu' (With Resistance) in 'W 3cia Rocznicę Zagłady Ghetta w Krakowie'; Centralny Komitet Żydów Polskich, Kraków, 1946 and Katarzyna Zimmerer, 'Zamordowany świat; Losy Żydów w Krakowie, 1939-1945', pages 129-144. See also Andrea Löw and Markus Roth, 'Juden in Krakau unter Deutscher Besatzung, 1939-1945'; Wallstein Verlag, Göttingen, 2011, pages 182-195, 'Bewaffneter Kampf' (Armed Fight). An article on the Yad Vashem site is available at https://www.yadvashem.org/articles/general/armed-resistance-in-krakow-and-bialystock.html

Arieh Bauminger also describes the escape of women prisoners from their gaol on ul Helzlow on 29 April, 1943. On 19 March of that year twenty female fighters who had been captured by the Nazis were taken from their cell, but thirty remained. These included Gusta Dränger, Gola Mire, Wuszka Jules and Genia Melzer. Before Passover, 5703 (1943) the thirty young women were transferred to a cell in the cellar of the prison.... The next day they were led out to be loaded on to trucks and taken to Płaszów where they were to be executed. Suddenly, a signal was given and the women started to run in different directions. Wuszka Jules and Gola Mire were shot and died on the spot, but ten others including Gusta Dränger and Genia Melzer managed to escape.[726]

Additionally, Shmuel Krakowski describes the Jewish Fighting Organization in the Kraków area, and in the Płaszów Camp in his book, 'The War of the Doomed', whilst Martyna Grądzka-Rejak, Andrea Löw, Markus Roth and Katarzyna Zimmerer are amongst other authors who cover this topic.[727]

The web page at
https://kehilalinks.jewishgen.org/Krakow/kra_ghettofighters_bauminger.htm
shows a list of names mentioned in Arieh Bauminger's book. This has been extracted by Lili Haber of the Association of Cracovians in Israel.

As would be expected, information relating to the ŻOB and to the Jewish fighting forces generally is available on the website of the Ghetto Fighters' House in Western Galilee, Israel at www.gfh.org.il/eng/. A search of the site for 'Kraków women' produces several results including a photograph, 'Five young women from the Akiva movement in Kraków'. The five include Minka Liebeskind and Hanka Landwirt. The Ghetto Fighters' House publishes a newsletter and operates an extensive library.

In 1993, The Ghetto Fighters' House published a book by Yael Peled (Margolin). The book is in Hebrew but its title, translated to English, is 'Jewish Cracow, 1939-1943; Resistance, Underground, Struggle'. The book includes two lists of the names of individual fighters, and the groups to which they belonged.[728] The book also includes as chapter 15 an account of the underground fighting force in Kraków, 'Irguni ha'Machtrut Yehudit ha'Polin b'Krokuv, 1942'.

An address in the 1960's by Rivka Liebeskind-Kupper describing the Jewish underground in Kraków is included in a publication, 'Dapeh Hantzacha' (Memorial Pages) which was published by Municipal Secondary School number 5 of Tel Aviv in 1969. Rivka, née Spiner, was born in Rzeszów in 1920 and graduated from the Hebrew Gymnasium in Kraków in 1938. In the meantime, she had joined the Akiva movement at the age of 14. In 1939, she married Dolek Liebeskind, the leader of the Akiva movement in Poland, following which she served in Warsaw and other

---

[726] Arieh Bauminger, 'The Fighters of the Cracow Ghetto', pages 97-99
[727] Shmuel Krakowski, 'The War of the Doomed; Jewish Armed Resistance in Poland, 1942-1944'; Holmes & Meier, New York, NY, 1984, pages 223-228 and 249-252.Martyna Grądzka-Rejak, 'Kobieta Żydowska w Okupowanym Krakowie', pages 380-388, Andrea Löw and Markus Roth, 'Juden in Krakau unter Deutscher Besatzung', pages 182-195 'Bewaffnetter Kampf' (Armed fight), and Katarzyna Zimmerer, 'Zamorodowany Świat; Losy Żydów w Krakowie', pages 129-144
[728] Yael Peled (Margolin), 'Krakuv Yehudit, 1939-1943'; Ghetto Fighters' House, Israel, 1993 pages 279-282

locations. After her arrest in 1942, Rivka Liebeskind was sent to Birkenau and Auschwitz. She emigrated to Palestine in 1948.[729]

Despite the bravery of the ŻOB members, they did not have support from all sections of the Jewish community. As Leah Shinnar states, 'The people in the ghetto disapprove of those in the underground, and see them as irresponsible madmen, who endanger all the Kraków Ghetto Jews'.[730]

Diaries – Gusta Graenger-Dawidson

Diaries form a particularly important type of literature relating to the Holocaust generally, and some relate more specifically to the Jewish fighting forces. In her paper, 'Jewish Women in the Kraków Ghetto'[731] as noted in a previous section of this chapter, Martyna Grądzka notes that a collection of diaries is held at the Jewish Historical Institute in Warsaw under file group 302, 'Pamiętniki'. She states that eleven out of sixteen diaries concerning occupied Kraków in the collection were produced by women or teenage girls. Some of the authors, for example Pola (Pesia) Warszawska have filed their testimonies at Yad Vashem.

An extensive list of testimonies and diaries which are held at the Jewish Historical Institute is shown on page 237 and 238 in Andrea Löw and Markus Roth, 'Juden in Krakau unter Deutscher Besatzung, 1939-1945' published by Wallstein Verlag of Göttingen in 2011. The following female authors are listed:

File group 301 Relacje (reports)

Luiza Grüner, Matylda Löw, Laura Duntenfass, Ester Fefer, Stefannie Rosenberg, Berta Majerhof, Zofia Irena Müller, Regina Nelken, Sabina Mirowska, Anna Lermer, Hermina Wisniowska, Julia Hoffman, Szyfra Westreich, Dr Laura Eichorn, Franciska Guter, Wanda Lewka, and Zuzanna Kwasnicka.

File group 302 Pamiętniki (diaries)

Cesia Frymer, Pola Warszawska, Renia Knoll and Irena Glück.

Other female authors of diaries mentioned by name by Martyna Grądzka are

Maria Steczko, Fela Schechter, Henai Karmel-Wolf, Berta Liebermann and Janina Hescheles.

Whilst some of these authors were not active in the ŻOB or other fighting forces, they were all engaged in the wider resistance movement in that they employed survival techniques and passive resistance against the Nazi occupiers.

[729] Article by Yael Margolin Peled at https://jwa.org/encyclopedia/article/liebeskind-rivka-kuper
[730] Leah Shinnar, 'The Butterfly and the Flame and other Stories of Jewish Life from Kraków to Israel'; Mazo Publishers, Jerusalem, 2004, page 38
[731] Martyna Grądzka, 'Jewish Women in the Kraków Ghetto; An Outline of Research Issues'; The Person and the Challenges, vol3 (2013), no 2, pages 123-141, available at http://czasopisma.upjp2.edu.pl/thepersonandthechallenges/article/view/498/425 See also Felicia Karay, 'The Women of the Kraków Ghetto'; Tel Aviv, 2001, originally published in Hebrew in 'Yalkut Moreshet', April, 2001

In the context of the ŻOB, probably the best known wartime diary of a female Jewish author is 'Pamiętnik Justyny', which was first published in Kraków in 1946. The work has been translated into English as 'Justina's Narrative' and into Hebrew as 'Yomna shel Yustina'.[732] This is essential reading for those who do not yet know about the Kraków unit of the ŻOB. The diary was written by Gusta Draenger-Dawidson (Dränger-Dawidsohn) (1917-1943) in a cell in the women's prison attached to the notorious Montelupich Gaol between February and April 1943. In his work that has already been mentioned, Arieh Bauminger describes how the diary was written on scraps of toilet paper which were smuggled out of the prison.[733] The original handwritten diary is held at the Ghetto Fighters' House Museum (Bet Lohemei) in Ramat ha'Sharon, Western Galilee, Israel with a catalogue reference, 1708.

A list of the names appearing in Gusta Draenger-Dawidson's work can be found under 'Books' at www.kehilalinks.jewishgen.org/krakow/site_index.asp.

The activities of Gusta Draenger-Dawidson are described in 'Three Lines in History – A Krakówian Christmas Surprise' which is a chapter in Judy Batalion's book on women fighters of the Jewish resistance.[734] The 'Christmas surprise' mentioned in the title is the attack in December, 1942 on the Cyganeria (Bohemia) café in Kraków in which several Nazi officers were killed. By way of background, the author states that Gusta had grown up in an extremely religious family and was a leading member of the religious Akiva Zionist group rather than a secular leftist group. As might be expected, the chapter includes extensive extracts from the English version of the diary 'Justyna's Narrative'. Judy Batalion also describes the 'office' which was established in Rabka which was often attended by Hanka Blas, courier to Gusta's husband, Shimshon (Simek). Reference is also made to Akiva's leading courier, Hela Schüpper (Schipper, Szyper) who often operated between Warsaw and Kraków and whose actions are described in the previous section of this chapter headed 'smugglers'.

During the second half of 1943, the Chalutz Underground movement published a news sheet in Polish, which was known by its Hebrew name 'Hechalutz ha'Lochem'. Gusta/Justina worked on its publication along with her husband. Further information about the publication is given above in the section headed 'Literature'.

Further information about Gusta Graenger-Dawidson is available on the Jewish Women's Archive site at https://jwa.org/encyclopedia/article/draenger-gusta-dawidson and in a book, 'Is War Men's Business?' which has been mentioned in the introduction to this chapter. Her activities in the area of Nowy Wiśnicz, some 30

---

[732] Gusta Draenger, 'Pamiętnik Justyny'; Centralna Żydowska Komisja Historyczna przy C K Żydów Polskich, Kraków, 1946. The English version is Justyna's Narrative'; University of Massachusetts Press, Amherst, MA, 1996.

[733] Arieh L Bauminger, 'The Fighters of the Cracow Ghetto', pages 94, 95

[734] Judy Batalion, 'The Light of Days; Women Fighters of the Jewish Resistance; Virago, London, 2020, pages 134-147, and concerning Justina's imprisonment in the women's section of Montelupich, pages 370-372 and 513

miles (48 km) to the south east of Kraków, in the second half of 1943 are analysed by Eran Zohar.[735]

Reizia Cohen Klingberg

Reizia Cohen Klingberg returned to Kraków in 1942 when she joined the underground movement. Despite being betrayed, arrested and deported, she survived to be liberated by American soldiers at Auschwitz, and subsequently moved to Palestine.[736]

Rivka Kuper Liebeskind

Rivka Kuper Liebeskind joined Akiva as a teenager. When the movement transitioned to resistance activities in 1942, she helped young people leaving the Kraków Ghetto. She survived her deportation to Birkenau, and after the war moved to Israel where she gave evidence at the trial of Adolf Eichmann.[737]

Gola Mire

Gola Mire (1911-1943), previously listed as Gola (Lidia) Mirer, was another prominent female member of the ŻOB in Kraków. Information about her is available on the website of the Jewish Women's Archive at http://jwa.org/encyclopedia/article/gola-mire as well as in the books by Martyna Grądzka-Rejak, Andrea Löw and Markus Roth, Judy Batalion and Katarzyna Zimmerer which have already been mentioned.

Gola worked closely with Justina Draenger-Dawidson. Although she had been born into a Chassidic family, before the war she became active in the Communist party in Przemysl and then in Lwów. Because of her links with the party she arranged for Dolek Liebeskind and Shimshon Draenger to meet with representatives of the Polish Workers Communist Party in the spring of 1942. Her activities in the ŻOB included the publication of a newspaper and pamphlets, and whilst in the Kraków Ghetto she wrote a number of poems in Yiddish and Hebrew. Some were dedicated to her husband and dead child. Others were revolutionary and included 'Instead of Progress' which was written whilst she was held in the women's gaol adjoining Montepulich prison.[738]

Hela Schüpper

Hela Schüpper (Schipper, Szyper, Rufeisen Schüpper) was born into a traditional Jewish family, in Podgórze. Before the war she grew up in two cultures, Polish and Jewish.[739] She is mentioned as a leading member of the ŻOB by a wide range of

---

[735] Eran Zohar, 'Jewish resistance group in the Nowy Wiśnicz area; a new approach'; Holocaust Studies, Routledge, published on line 20 May, 2023
[736] https://jwa.org/encyclopedia/author/peled-yael
[737] https://jwa.org/encyclopedia/article/liebeskind-rivka-kuper and Arieh L Bauminger, 'The Fighters of the Cracow Ghetto'; Keter Press, Jerusalem, 1986, pages 28 and 75
[738] Arieh L Bauminger, 'The Fighters of the Cracow Ghetto', pages 91-93
[739] Katarzyna Zechenter, 'Kraków in Jewish Literature Since 1945', in 'Polin', vol 23, pages 388 and 397

researchers. She was Akva's leading courier who often operated between Warsaw and Kraków as described in the earlier section of this chapter headed 'Smugglers'.

THE COMMUNIST PERIOD
Return and exile – the final chapter?

Introduction

During the 1970's and 1980's a number of writers and photographers visited what was then Communist Poland in order to interview members of the ageing Jewish population, and to record the steady but inevitable decline of the Jewish community as it passed in to history. In 1977, one such writer gave a descriptive title to his book, 'Polish Jews; The Final Chapter'. Several pages are devoted to Kraków, in which the author refers mainly to ageing and decaying buildings and men – but not to women.[740]

In 1984, the very knowledgeable former Krakovian, Rafael Scharf, said the following, as recorded in his book, 'Poland, What Have I to do with Thee ...'. 'The fabric of Polish Jewish cohabitation on Polish soil has been irreversibly destroyed. No one is under any illusion that the few thousand Jews remaining in Poland, who openly consider themselves as such and who, as it were, apologise for being alive, are not physically and spiritually a community in terminal decline. They have no schools, no synagogues, no rabbis, no contact with Israel, no leadership, no future. ...From the Jewish point of view, we are talking not about current affairs but exclusively about history.'[741]

1986 saw the publication of 'Remnants: The Last Jews of Poland'. The author notes that about five thousand Jews remained in the country. 'They are mostly old, lonely, ill people' with an average age of 70, adding, they all share the consciousness that something is irrevocably coming to an end'. Chapter five is devoted to Kraków, and is perhaps a little less pessimistic than the other chapters in that it is entitled 'The Community' and Kraków is stated to have the largest congregation in Poland. Particular mention is made of Róża Jakubowicz who is described as 'the mother of the community'. It is she who makes the Passover seder meal an annual special event. 'Seventy, in poor health, she never holds anything back and is always ready to work for the community, to help those who need her.'[742]

Based on studies in Kraków between September 1988 and April 1990, Beata Kowalska writes, 'The book we might entitle 'Jewish History on Polish Soil' is closing. In a couple of years, communities such as the one in Cracow will not exist'. Her research showed that the Orthodox Jewish community in Kraków consisted of

---

[740] Earl Vinecour, 'Polish Jews: The Final Chapter'; McGraw Hill, 1977.

[741] In Rafael Scharf, 'Poland, What have I to do with Thee? Essays without Prejudice'; Vallentine Mitchell, London, 1996, page 71 reproducing the text of a lecture given in Oxford in 1984. For further references to the testimony of Rafael Scharf see, for example, the names index in Bogusław Krasnowolski, 'Krakowski Kazimierz; Historia i kultura'; Biblioteka Krakowska, nr 168 Towarzystwo Miłośików Historii i Zabytków Krakowa'; Kraków, 2022

[742] Małgorzata Niezabitowska and (photographer) Tomasz Tomaszewski, 'Remnants; The Last Jews of Poland'; Friendly Press, New York, NY, 1986

about 190 members, the majority of whom were women.[743] The individuals she interviewed were not identified by name, but one 65 year old woman observed that it was important to attend synagogue on Yom Kippur (The Day of Atonement) in order to remember the dead. Another woman, aged 85, remained in Kraków even though her son and grandchildren lived in Israel.[744]

The fall of the Iron Curtain could not reasonably have been forecast when Rafael Scharf spoke in 1984. The impact of the impending political earthquake could not have been forecast with any degree of confidence even at the time Beata Kowalska was conducting her research. Yet we now know that the predictions proved to be too pessimistic, and this chapter about the Communist period is not 'The Final Chapter' of this book.

Edyta Gawron has posed the question 'How Many Cracovian Jews Survived the Holocaust?'[745] She notes that the usual answers to this question indicate between 4,000 and 6,000, representing fewer than 10% of the total. However, she then highlights a number of problems in reaching a reliable estimate. These include the fact that there were significant movements in the Jewish population of the Kraków area during the 1930's, making it difficult to establish just how large the Jewish population was just before the Nazi invasion. Furthermore, not all Jews who came to Kraków in 1945 had originally come from the Kraków area, and not all chose to identify themselves as Jews. She then notes that 'the number of Jews in Cracow in the first years after the end of Second World War varies from 500 (February 1945) to over 20,000 in the second half of the 1940s'. Her article includes a table entitled 'Jewish population in Cracow 1946 according to the last 'place of stay' during the Holocaust' which shows a total of 6,637 people. She then notes that most of the Jews who decided to stay in Kraków were not originally from that city. This is illustrated by a census in 1947 provided by the Centralny Komitet Żydowski which shows that only some 2,200 former residents of Kraków still lived in the city. However, that clearly does not include former Cracovians who had survived and returned to the city, but left it prior to the 1947 census. Taking all these matters into account, the author's best estimate is that 6,000 to 7,000 Jewish Cracovians survived the Holocaust, representing about 10% of the pre war population. As noted in a previous chapter, females had a greater chance of survival than circumcised males so arguably about 3,500 or even 4,000, Jewish women and girls who had lived in Kraków before the Holocaust were still alive at the end of it.

The remnants of the Jewish community that returned to Kraków and other cities were met with a range of reactions, including incredulity and hostility. The incredulity of some members of the non Jewish population is captured by the title of a book, 'What! Still Alive?!',[746] whilst some anti Semitic violence and policies are

---

[743] Likewise, in 'Remnants; The Last Jews of Poland' at page 167, Małgorzata Niezabitowska states ,' Among the two hundred members of the congregation, women predominate, because it was easier for them to survive the war.'

[744] Beata Kowalska, 'A Receding World: The Religious Community in Cracow Today' in Andrzej Paluch (Ed), 'The Jews in Poland'; Jagiellonian University Press, Kraków, 1992

[745] Edyta Gawron, 'How Many Cracovian Jews Survived the Holocaust? A Preliminary Survey of the Question'; Scripta Judaica Cracoviensia, vol 4, 2006

[746] Monica Rice, 'What! Still Alive?!; Jewish Survivors in Poland and Israel Remember Homecoming'; Syracuse University Press, Syracuse, NY, 2017.

described in the next section of this chapter. The brief biographies of survivors which are set out in the previous chapter, which relates primarily to the Holocaust, show that very many of the women who came to Kraków immediately after the war emigrated from Poland during the second half of the 1940's. However, a few remained and this is a topic considered by Filip Mazurczak in his paper, 'Why We Stayed'. As part of his research, the author interviewed two female Krakowians, Zofia Radzikowska and Fryda Zawada.[747]

The immediate post war experiences of women is described by Barbara Klich-Kluczewska in her article, 'Women in Post War Poland; Paradoxes of the Communist Reality.' This is included in a book 'Is War Men's Business?' published by the Krakow City Historical Museum in 2011.[748] The author refers to the sense of isolation and loneliness which was suffered by Jewish men and women on returning to Kraków in the hope of discovering family and friends. She also refers to equal opportunities legislation as being one of the mainstays of socialist modernisation; however, it is clear that Jewish women had other priorities, not least of which were those brought about by the anti Semitic attacks in Kraków in 1945, and the pogrom in Kielce the following year.

'The Cultural Life of Kraków Jews after 1945' is the title of a paper by Monika Stępień in another book which was published by the Kraków City Historical Museum, called 'We Were; We Are: We Will Be'.[749] In the paper, the author describes a number of institutions which were established to support remnants of the Kraków Jewish community, and other Jews who had lived elsewhere before the war but had sought refuge in that city during the Communist period. Under the Communist regime, these institutions tended to be cultural rather than religious. They included the Wojewódzka Żydowska Komisia Historyczna w Krakowa, a branch of the Central Jewish Historical Commission which was responsible for gathering and publishing a wide range of testimony from survivors.[750] As the years went by, the community's pre-war interest in books was rekindled and several Holocaust related books were published in Kraków.[751] Maria Seiden opened a bookshop on ul Szpitalna with her cousin Szaja Taffett, whilst several women had book collections which they took with them when they emigrated. Some, for example the collection of Eda Kupfer, formed the basis of new libraries in Israel.[752]

The Jewish Aid Society was established at ul. Długa, 38 and its premises served as a centre for Holocaust refugees. Most of the communal institutions were run

---

[747] Filip Mazurczak, 'Why we stayed; Polish Jews' reasons for remaining in Poland during two waves of postwar emigration'; Wrocławski rocznik historii mówionej, vol 13 (2013). See https://orcid.org/0000-0003-1014-1723

[748] Anna Biedrzyczka (Ed), 'Is War Men's Business? Fates of Women in Occupied Kraków in Twelve Scenes'; Muzeum Historyczne Miasta Krakowa, Kraków, 2011, pages 96-103

[749] Barbara Cisowa, (Ed), 'We Were; We Are; We Will Be'; Muzeum Historyczne Miasta Krakowa, Kraków, 2015, pages 16-53

[750] For the work of the Central Jewish Historical Commission, see Monika Rice, 'What! Still Alive?! Jewish Survivors in Poland and Israel Remember Homecoming' Syracuse University Press, Syracuse, NY, 2017

[751] See, for example, 'Jewish Literature in Kraków, 1918-1948' available on academia.edu

[752] Mare Sroka, 'Migrating Volumes; Jewish Immigrants from Kraków and their Personal Book Collections, 1949-1950'; University of Illinois, based on a paper presented in 2017

predominantly by men, but several catered for the needs of girls and women. For example, the paper by Monika Stępień which has already been mentioned, includes a photograph of a girls' choir at the Kraków club of the Socio-Cultural Association of Jews in Poland during the 1960's. Having said that, in 1954 the Association's membership included only 118 women, and a 'women's commission' had only 22 members at its peak.

Anti Semitic violence and policies

As previously noted, Jews who returned to Kraków or came to Kraków, having lived elsewhere before the Holocaust, were met with a range of reactions including verbal and physical hostility. This reached a peak with an attack on the city's Jewish community in August, 1945. Róża Berger was born in 1889. Having escaped from the Kraków Ghetto she was caught, with her daughter and granddaughter, in August 1944 and deported to Auschwitz. After the liberation she returned to Kraków, only to be shot and killed by the security forces in her home, whilst standing behind closed doors, during the attack on 11 August, 1945.[753]

The violence in Kraków, and the circumstances surrounding those events, are considered by Marcin Zaremba in his paper, 'The Myth of Ritual Murder in Post-War Poland; Pathology and Hypotheses'. He refers to the numerous rumours circulating in Kraków regarding alleged murders of Catholic children by Jews. For example, in July 1945 a Jewish woman was arrested by the militia because it was (incorrectly) suspected that she had kidnapped a Catholic child. In fact, the child's mother had merely left her child in the care of the woman.[754]

Lena Kuchler-Silberman describes an event 'one Sunday morning when most Cracow residents were returning home from church services and scores of Jews milled about outside our building on Deluga Street.... A mob of several hundred people was shouting 'Kill the Jews! They've taken a Catholic girl to kill for their matzos'. The crowd dispersed only when they thought the Jews were armed with bombs.[755]

Yet even in 1945 not all of the Jews in Kraków were equally affected by the violence. For example, Zofia Radzikowska recalls that she did not feel threatened, since the violence was limited to the Jewish quarter, and 'it was not as if it had all flooded the entire city'. Indeed, her testimony and that of some other survivors is that Kraków was generally more tolerant of its Jewish population than other Polish cities. On the other hand, Fryda Zawada, who is mentioned below, records that she

---

[753] Wikipedia, 'Krakow Pogrom' and several other sites for 'Roza Berger'
[754] Marcin Zaremba,'The Myth of Ritual Murder in Post-War Poland' in Michał Galas and Antony Polonsky (Eds), 'Polin', vol 23; Littman, Oxford, 2011 page 474, quoting Anna Cichopek, 'Pogrom Żydów w Krakowie'. See more generally, pages 474-482 regarding the Kraków pogrom. See also, for example, Joanna Tokarska-Bakir, 'Cries of the Mob in Pogroms in Rzezów (June 1945), Cracow (August 1945) and Kielce (July 1946) as a Source for the State of Mind of the Participants'; East European Politics and Societies, 2011. See also Anna Cichopek-Gajraj, 'Pogroms in Kraków in 1918 and 1945; Historical Analysis'
[755] Lena Kuchler-Silberman, 'One Hundred Children'; Doubleday & Co, New York, NY, 1961 pages 145 and 146. In the following pages the author explains that the events leading up to the threats of violence involved a Jewish father taking his daughter from a convent

experienced significant and 'terrible' anti Semitism in post war Kraków, though she also observes that most of her girlfriends were Catholics who treated her well.[756]

The following year saw a pogrom in Kielce, some 75 miles (120 km) to the north east of Kraków. On 4 July, 1946, violence by Polish soldiers, police officers and civilians resulted in the death of 42 Jews and the injury of 40 more. The dead included women and children, one of the women being a Jewish nurse, Estera Proszowska.[757] A memorial to the pogrom is located in the Kraków's Jewish cemetery on ul. Miodowa.

Sabina Cyns (née Goldstein) (1907-1947) lived in Kraków and survived the Ghetto and Płaszów. In 1947, she and her family took a vacation in the resort of Rabka, to the south of the city. Whilst there, she was fatally shot by members of the Ogień, a right wing nationalist extremist group.[758]

Whereas the antisemitism immediately after the end of the war was largely physical, some twenty years later anti Semitism took the form of discriminatory policies by the Communist government. The trigger for these policies was the Six Day War between Israel and its neighbouring states in 1967. As Filip Mazurczak puts it in his paper, 'Why We Stayed', 'Whereas the antisemitism right after the war lead to hundreds of Jewish deaths and was popular rather than official, in 1967-1968 it was non violent and came from the top.' Yet, again the level of anti Semitism is noted to have been lower in Kraków than in other Polish cities. For example, although discrimination was directed largely at the Jewish intelligentsia in other parts of Poland, Zofia Radzikowska 'worked at the Jagiellonian University which was largely untouched by state antisemitism'. Fryda Zawada notes that Władysław Gomułka, who was effectively the head of the Polish government, was concerned with 'kicking out all the Jewish lawyers, engineers, and doctors' whilst Filip Mazurczak states that many working class Jews like Fryda who worked as a nurse were less targeted by the state persecutions.[759]

Anti Semitism in its various forms resulted in different waves of emigration during the several decades of Communist rule. This topic is considered in some detail by Edyta Gawron in her paper, 'Post-War Emigration of Jews from Poland: The Case of Kraków'. Much of the material considered by the author relates to the period up to the early 1950's, but the author also writes the following concerning a

---

[756] Filip Mazurczak, 'Why We Stayed'. The author suggests that the experiences of Holocaust survivors depended partly on their religious and social background, and factors such as education and where they lived in the city.
[757] Wikipedia, 'Kielce pogrom'
[758] Wiktoria Śliwowska, 'The Last Eyewitnesses; Children of the Holocaust Speak' vol 1; Northwestern University Press, Evanston, IL, 1993, page 269 and the Holocaust Survivors' Database at the United States Holocaust Memorial Museum. For a discussion regarding the murder of Jews in Poland following the end of the Second World War, see Monica Rica, 'What! Still Alive?!'; Syracuse University Press, Syracuse, NY, 2017, pages 29-38, where the author refers to the mass murder near Krościenko, in the Tatra Mountains, on 2 May, 1946 by the 'anti-Communist partisan division commanded by Józef Kuraś, who was also known as 'Ogień' (Fire)'. See also pages 69-73 and 119-120
[759] Filip Mazurczak, 'Why We Stayed'

period which coincided with the Suez Crisis in the Middle East, and major political changes within Poland.

'A rise in antisemitic feeling, the deteriorating economic situation, and finally the introduction of Catholic instruction in schools in December, 1956 contributed to increased emigration. Between July 1956 and April 1957, a particularly large number of Jews registered to immigrate to Israel'. Indeed, the total of emigration of Jews from Poland as a whole was significantly higher in 1957 than in the period following the Six Day War ten years later.[760]

Filip Mazurczak notes that the high level of emigration in the mid 1950's coincided with the thaw under Władysław Gomułka in post Stalinist Poland which led to a liberalisation in emigration policies.[761]

An extensive list of Jews from Kraków and the surrounding area who emigrated to Israel, before or after the Holocaust, is available at https://kehilalinks.jewishgen.org/krakow/kra_pioneers.htm

Art

As suggested in the previous chapter, most of the pre-war Jewish artists in Kraków were male. Of the females, very few continued their work in Krakow after the Holocaust. For example, Dorota Berlinerblau-Seydenmann was shot by the Nazis in 1942, whilst Henryka Fromowicz-Stiller died in Lwów in the same year. Berta (Blima) Grünberg and Henryka Kerner emigrated from Kraków to Paris in 1937 and 1939 respectively, whilst Alicja Halicka had also moved there well before the war. Helena Grabschrift and Maria Fromowicz both survived the Holocaust. The first and emigrated to Israel, and the second moved to Milan. The photographer, Margaret Michaelis managed to leave Poland for Australia as late as September, 1939.[762]

Erna Rosenstein (1913-2004) was one of the very few female Jewish artists who were active in Kraków during the period immediately following the Holocaust. She returned to the city after the war, and co-founded the Second Kraków Group. A surrealist painter and poet, she was at the forefront of the Kraków avant-garde movement and she was involved in the first post war Exhibition of Modern Art in Kraków in 1948. Like others, she perceived Kraków as a place of death, a cemetery. In 1949, Erna Rosenstein left Kraków for Warsaw where she died at the age of 91.[763]

---

[760] In Feliks Tych and Minika Adamczyk-Garbowska (Eds), 'Jewish Presence in Absence; The Aftermath of the Holocaust in Poland, 1944-2010'; Yad Vashem, Jerusalem, 2014, particularly pages 492 and 499
[761] Filip Mazurczak, ''Why We Stayed'
[762] Various entries in Wikipedia. See also Ewa Dąbrowska and Anna Kielczewska (Eds), 'Residents of Jewish Kraków, vol 4, Women', EMG Publishers, Kraków, 2021, page 24
[763] Wikipedia and https://culture.pl/en/artist/erna-rosenstein. Also ', Katarzyna Zechenter, 'Kraków in Jewish Literature since 1945' in Polin', vol 23; Littman, Oxford, 2011, pages 398. 399 and ''Holocaust Survivors, Jonah Stern, Erna Rosenstein and Artur Nacht-Samborski' published by the Muzeum Historyczne Miasta Krakowa. See also Monika Stępień 'The Cultural Life of Kraków Jews after 1945' in 'We Were, We Are, We Will Be'; Muzeum Historyczne Miasta Krakowa,, 2015 page 48

Roma Ligocka (née Liebling) was born in Kraków in November, 1938 and, as noted in the previous chapter, she and her mother were protected during the Holocaust by a Catholic family. Following the liberation, Roma studied painting and scenic design in the Academy of Fine Arts in Kraków. She then worked with considerable success as a set designer in theatre, film and television. She and her husband left Poland and moved to Munich in 1965, but she has run a studio in Kraków since the fall of Communism.[764]

Ewa Kuryluk is a Polish painter, photographer and author. She was born in May, 1946 in Kraków. Her mother, Miriam, née Kohany, (1917-2001) was a poet, writer and translator. In 1947, the Kuryluk family moved to Warsaw.[765]

Book trade

Krakow's thriving interwar book trade was largely driven by Jewish merchants and collectors, as described in an earlier chapter. Some collections survived the Holocaust in whole or in part and during the Communist period, among the items that emigrating Jews took with them were books from their private libraries. Most of the book shops in and around Szpitalna Street did not re-open, but by way exception, Maria Seiden opened an antiquarian bookstore with her cousin, Szaja Taffet. This last Jewish antiquarian bookstore in postwar Kraków operated until 1969 when Szaja Taffet emigrated to Israel.[766]

Diaries, memoirs and testimonies

The passing years have seen the publication of an increasing number of testimonies which describe life in Kraków during the communist period. The following notes describe the post war activities of several survivors whose diaries, memoirs and testimonies have been mentioned in the previous chapter of this book which relates to the Holocaust. The notes also refer to a few other individuals, some of whom were born in Kraków after the war. As in the previous chapter, the individuals are mentioned in alphabetical order of surname.

Whilst many of the individuals who are mentioned left Poland in the 1940's, others remained, and worked within the Communist system. In her book 'Kraków i jego mieszkańcy w latach 1945-1947' (Kraków and its Residents in the years 1945-1947) Agnieszka Chłosta-Sikorska writes, 'Some inhabitants of Kraków believed that Jews are supporters of the new political system and act to the detriment of Poland ... Those statements are false'. In a review of the book, Przemysław Sołga writes, 'The Stereotype related to the phenomenon of the so called 'Judeo-Communism' is for sure unfair to many Jews, however, it does not mean that many Jews did not support the new political system in post-war Poland'.[767]

---

[764] Wikipedia, and 'We Were, We Are, We Will Be', page 47
[765] Wikipedia
[766] Marek Sroka, 'Migrating Volumes; Jewish Immigrants from Kraków and their Personal Book Collections, 1949-1950'. Female collectors mentioned by the author include Maria Lejman, Rozalia Weinberger and Róza Lustbader
[767] Przemysław Sołga, review of Agnieszka Chłosta-Sikorska, 'Kraków i jego mieszkańcy w latach 1945-1947'; Wydawnictwo Libron-Filip Lohner. Kraków, 2016

Dora Agastein was one of the survivors who returned to Kraków. Her post war works included a chronology relating to the Nazi occupation which was included in 'W 3cia rocznicę zagłady ghetta w Krakowie' (On the Third Anniversary of the Destruction of the Ghetto in Kraków) in 1946, and a paper, 'Jews in Kraków during the Nazi Occupation'.[768]

After the Holocaust, Irena Bronner returned to her home town, Kraków – but not initially to a friendly welcome. She records that when she arrived at the railway station a woman remarked, 'They were supposed to have been killed and look how many of them have come back'. It was only after she found her brother in law that she received support. Nevertheless, Irena found she could not remain in Kraków, 'the city that was the cemetery of her family' and she moved to Silesia. In 1945 she attended a nursing college at Wałbrzych and she then worked as a nurse until she emigrated to Israel in 1957. Her memoir, Okady nad Wisła i Jordanem' (Between the Vistula and the Jordan) was published in 1991.[769]

Pola Elbinger was born in Nowe Brzesko in 1932, and survived the Holocaust with her brother. However, her mother and sister did not. After liberation, Pola and her brother were placed in the children's home in Kraków and she remained in the city throughout the Communist era.[770]

At the end of the war, Janina Fischler-Martinho was near Gdów, some 9.5 miles (15 km) south east of Wieliczka. She was 'amongst people who were total strangers and who knew nothing of the joy and despair' which the liberation brought. After a few days she made her way back to Kraków, passing the corpses of German soldiers lying by the side of the icy and snow bound road. In exchange for working as a domestic servant, Janina was given accommodation on Dietla Street by a couple she had known before the war. She chose not to stay at the orphanage which was established by the newly formed Jewish Council but was able to attend a local school. In August 1945, Janina was re-united with her brother, Joseph who had survived various concentration camps. A year later they arrived in Edinburgh, Scotland before Janina settled in London.[771]

Maria Gaber-Wierny survived much of the Holocaust in the village of Bieńczyce, to the north east of Kraków, and now a district of that city. After the war, Maria enrolled in the Workers' University Association, an organisation affiliated with the Polish Socialist Party. However, her education was cut short by the need to earn a living, and care for her mother. At the age of 27 she was introduced to a prospective

---

[768] In Aryeh Bauminger (Ed), 'Sefer Kraka; Ir v'Em b'Yisrael'; Rav Kuk Institute, Jerusalem, 1959

[769] Irena Bronner, ''Okady nad Wisła i Jordanem'; Wydawnictwo Literackie, Kraków, 1991. An extract from the book is included in Maria Klańska (Ed), 'Jüdisches Städtebild Krakau'; Jüdischer Verlag, Frankfurt am Main, 1994, pages 213-227. See also Monika Stępień, 'The Image of Post-War Kraków in Jewish Writing, 1945-1950' in Michał Galas and Antony Polonsky, (Eds), 'Polin', vol 23; Littman, Oxford, 2011, pages 363, 365 and 367

[770] Wiktoria Śliwowska, 'The Last Eyewitnesses; Children of the Holocaust Speak' vol 1; Northwestern University Press, Evanston, IL, 1993, pages 37-41 and https://zapispamieci.pl/en/pola-elbinger and https://www.centropa.org/en/photo/pola-elbinger-childrens-home-cracow

[771] Janina Fischler-Martinho, 'Have You Seen My Little Sister?'; Vallentine Mitchell, London, 1998, pages 264-277

husband by a 'shadchan' (Jewish matchmaker) and shortly afterwards the marriage took place in accordance with Orthodox ritual, including a visit to the mikveh (religious bath house). The marriage did not succeed, though it produced a son. The couple divorced in 1969 and Maria suffered several bouts of clinical depression. Maria eventually recovered, due largely to the support of her son and more recently her grandson. She joined the Jewish association, 'Children of the Holocaust'.[772]

Eleonora Gajzler came from an educated well to do and assimilated family who was unfamiliar with Orthodox Judaism and she rarely visited Kazimierz before the war. Her diary, 'Tamten Kraków, tamta Kyrnica' (That Kraków, that Krynica [the name of a spa town]), was first published in 1972.[773]

Malvina Graf, having survived Płaszów, Auschwitz and Bergen Belsen, was sent after the liberation to a displaced persons' camp at Feldafing, a short distance from Munich. It was there that, after a year, she was reunited with her brother, and that she spent two years as a teacher. She left Feldafing at the end of 1947 and emigrated to America.[774]

Lili (Lidia, Lea) Haber (née Leser) was born in Kraków in September, 1947. She and her family left Poland when she was still a small child, emigrating to Israel where she studied at the Hebrew University in Jerusalem. Lili, who now lives in Herzliya, has for many years been the President of, and the leading force behind, the Association of Cracovians in Israel. She is editor of the Association's newsletter, 'Nowiny Krakowskie'.[775]

Karolina Heuman, born in 1928, who is mentioned in the previous chapter, came to Kraków after the war and it was there that she attended school. She then studied law at the Jagiellonian University, before taking apprenticeships with a judge and an attorney. Having married in 1955, she worked as a legal counsel for the Leather Workers' Co-operative, for the Society of the Blind, and in the Bureau of Projects. Karolina Heuman retired in 1990, but continued to live in Kraków.[776]

Maria Hochberg, who was a journalist before the war, collected testimonies from children and teenagers during 1945 and 1946. These form the basis of 'The Children Accuse' which includes several references to Kraków.[777] The author's work, 'Dzieci' (Children), was published in 'W 3cia rocznicę' in 1946.

---

[772] Jakub Gutenbaum and Agnieszka Latała (Eds), 'The Last Eyewitnesses; Children of the Holocaust Speak', vol 2; Northwestern University Press, Evanston, IL, 2005, pages 65-69
[773] Katarzyna Zechenter,'Kraków in Jewish Literature since 1945' in 'Polin' vol 23, pages 394, 395
[774] Malvina Graf, 'The Kraków Ghetto and the Płaszów Camp Remembered'; The Florida State University Press, Tallahassee, FL, 1989, chapter 7
[775] https://sztetl.org.pl entry for Lili Haber. The activities of the Association of Cracovians in Israel are described in Barbara Cisowska (Ed), 'We Were; We Are; We Will Be'; The Jewish Community of Kraków after 1945'; Muzeum Historyczne Miasta Krakowa, Kraków, 2015
[776] Wiktoria Śliwowska, 'The Last Eyewitnesses; Children of the Holocaust Speak', vol 1, Northwestern University Press, Evanston, IL, 1993, page 189
[777] Library of Holocaust Testimonies, Vallentine Mitchell, London, 1996

Eva Hoffman (née Ewa Wydra) was born in Kraków in 1945. Her parents had survived the Holocaust by hiding in a forest bunker, and then by being hidden by Polish and Ukrainian neighbours. Ewa describes her childhood experiences in her book, 'Lost in Translation'. Having returned to Kraków, due largely to her father's activities in smuggling and dealing in foreign currency, Ewa and her family lived a middle class life in the fashionable district of Nowa Wieś, 'situated on the periphery of the city, in an area where urban houses give way to small rural cottages'. In her book, the author speaks of the need to live off one's wits, a skill which both men and women developed in order to increase their chances of survival both during and after the Holocaust. Ewa stayed in Kraków until she and her family emigrated to Vancouver in 1959.[778]

Natalia Karpf (1911-2007) was a pianist. After the Holocaust, she returned to her home town of Kraków. She soon acquired a piano and started to give music lessons. In March, 1946 she gave her first post war public performance - a Tchaikowsky Piano Concerto with the Kraków Philharmonic Orchestra. That marked the recommencement of her international career. Having moved to London, she continued to give performances into her nineties.[779]

Janina Katz (1939-2013) who was born in Kraków, was protected during the Holocaust by a Catholic family in Dobczyce, to the south of Wieliczka. Returning to her home town after the liberation, she lived with her mother who had survived imprisonment in various concentration camps. During the late 1940's her mother applied unsuccessfully to emigrate to Israel. Janina went on to study sociology and literature at the Jagiellonian University, and she then worked as a literary critic during the 1960's. She supported both Communism and Catholicism. However, following the middle east war of 1967, Janina emigrated to Denmark where she became a well known author. Her memoir, 'Moje życie barbarzyńcy' (my Life as a Barbarian) was published in Warsaw in 2006.[780]

Zenobia Krzyżanowska (née Adamowski) was born in 1939 in Kraków into a Jewish working class family. She and her family survived the Holocaust under the protection of the Benedictine Monastery at Staniątki, some 15 miles (24 km) to the east of the city. After the war, Zenobia continued to live in Staniątki, attending school there, and also attending the Lyceum in the nearby village of Niepołomice. Following the failure of her marriage, she brought up her daughter alone, whilst working in a municipal co-operative.[781]

---

[778] Wikipedia and Eva Hoffman, 'Lost in Translation'; Vintage Books, London, 1998, particularly pages 13-17

[779] Anne Karpf, 'The War After'; Heinemann, London, 1996. See, for example, page 119

[780] Wikipedia and Alicja Ososińska, 'The Undiscovered History of a Kraków Writer. Biographical and Outline of Artistic Activity of Janina Katz (1939-2013) in 'Krzysztofory', nr 35, Muzeum Historyczne Miasta Krakowa, 2017. See also Ewa Dąbrowska and Anna Kielczewska (Eds), 'Residents of Jewish Kraków; Women'; Wydawca EMG, Kraków, 2021, page 152 and Monika Stępień, 'The Image of Post-War Kraków in Jewish Writing, 1945-1950' in 'Polin', vol 23. pages 373 and 378

[781] Wiktoria Śliwowska, 'The Last Eyewitnesses; Children of the Holocaust Speak' vol 1; Northwestern University Press, Evanston, IL, 1993, page 284

Emilia Leibel (1910-2008) spent her early years in the Kraków district of Łagiewniki, and nearly all of the remainder of her long life within the city limits. She recalls how, before the war, her mother was excluded from Rabbi Skawiński's Synagogue in Podgórze because she did not wear a sheitel, a wig worn by orthodox married Jewish women. Emilia survived the Holocaust spending much of her time in the town of Koz'modem'yansk in the Soviet Union. She returned to Kraków and worked in the Jewish orphanage there. However, in about 1951 the Communist authorities fired her on the pretext that she was involved in the smuggling of children to Israel. Emilia Leibel then worked for the Towarzystwo Przyciol Dzieci (Friends of Children Society) as an inspector of children's homes. Following that she was engaged in vocational training, joining the Polish Teaching Union. She retired when she was nearly 70 years old and remined in Kraków until the end of her life.[782]

Roma Ligocka has been mentioned previously in this chapter in the section relating to art. Whilst watching Steven Spielberg's film 'Schindler's List', she recognised herself as a Jewish child wearing a red coat and this inspired her to write an account of her experiences during the Holocaust. The account was published as 'Dziewczynka w czerwonym płaszczyku' (The Girl in the Red Coat).

She describes how, in 1945, her father was arrested by the Communist regime on the grounds that he had collaborated with the Nazis as a member of the Jewish police at Płaszów, and how he was held and ill treated at the Montelupich prison. He died in November 1946.[783]

The testimony of Roma Ligocka is also reflected in Monika Stępień's article, 'Housing Situation of Holocaust Survivors'. Ms Ligocka is quoted as saying, 'Suddenly Kraków is full of people. That's because so many bombs fell on Warsaw that hardly any homes are left standing there. Almost none of the little Jewish towns still exist. Finding an apartment in Kraków is now very difficult.'[784]

In addition to 'The Girl in the Red Coat', Roma Ligocka wrote a further autobiography, 'Kobieta w podróży' (A Travelling Woman) which was published by Wydawnictwo Akademicka, Kraków, in 2002.

Hanna Mesz was born in 1927 in Warsaw, where her mother, Klara Ratner-Masz, was a gynaecologist. Hanna and her mother survived the Warsaw Ghetto and in the autumn of 1945 they moved to Kraków. Hannah completed her medical studies there, gaining her doctorate in 1968. Her mother worked as a physician in the city.[785]

Stella Müller (1920-2013) was born in Kraków to a middle class family. She survived the Kraków Ghetto, Płaszów and Auschwitz together with her parents and brothers, like others as a result of their strength and good luck – and also thanks to Oskar Schindler. The family returned to Kraków in 1945 and she describes how the

---

[782] https://www.centropa.org/en/biography/emilia-leibel
[783] Monika Stępień, 'The Image of Post-War Kraków in Jewish Writing, 1945-1950' in 'Polin', vol 23, page 371. See also the index for further references
[784] Monika Stępień, 'Housing Situation of Holocaust Survivors Returning to their Hometowns in Poland after the Second World War; Examples from Kraków and Łódz'; Scripta Judaica Cracoviensia, vol 16, 2018, page 110
[785] Wiktora Śliwowska (Ed), 'The Last Eyewitnesses; Children of the Holocaust Speak' vol 1, page 123

Communist authorities tried unsuccessfully to persuade her father to change his name to something less Jewish and less German than Müller. She graduated from the Junior High School in 1952. She emigrated to America in 1959, but returned to her home town three years later. In 1991 she published her memoir, 'Oczami dziecka' (A Child's Eyes). The English version was published as 'A Girl from Schindler's List'. She continued to live in Kraków until her death in 2013, and is buried in the city's Rakowicki Cemetery.[786]

Halina Nelken (1924-2009), who has been mentioned in the previous chapter, returned to Kraków. In her memoir she describes her search for her mother, Regina, with whom she was reunited in July, 1945. In the first poem she wrote after the war she describes the dire situation of Jewish Holocaust survivors, some of whom arrived in Kraków dressed only in their camp 'striped pyjamas', sleeping on park benches in the Planty, a local park.[787] Despite these circumstances, Halina Nelken gained a degree in the History of Art and Philosophy at the Jagiellonian University. She then worked as a curator at the National Museum in Kraków and delivered lectures at meetings of the Social-Cultural Association of Jews in Poland. She also wrote a book devoted to the Polish playwright, painter and poet, Stanisław Wyspiański. Halina Nelken left Poland in 1958, before working initially at the Academy of Fine Arts in Vienna.[788]

Joanna Olczak-Roniker was born in 1934 in Warsaw, into a literary family. After the war she settled in Kraków where, working with Piotr Skrzynecki, she founded the legendary cabaret 'Piwnica pod Baranami' loosely translated as 'The Cellar'. This comprised authors, musicians, graphic artists and actors, and soon became one of the most popular art groups in Poland. It was a favourite venue for Jewish artists and contributors to culture. In 1994 Joanna Olczak-Roniker wrote about the cabaret and Piotr Skrzynecki. She has received several literary awards, including one for her

---

[786] Website of the Kraków Jewish Community, https://gwzkrakow.pl/en/2022/02/05/stella-muller-madej-1930-2013-2/ and Stella Müller-Madej, 'A Girl from Schindler's List'; Polish Cultural Foundation, London, 1997 and Wydawnicwo DjaF, Kraków, 2006. Additionally see Aleksander Skotnicki, 'The Fellow Jewish Citizens of Cracow Rescued by Oskar Schindler'; The Stradom Centre for Dialogue, Kraków, pages 16-19. See also references in Joanna Sliwa, 'The Forced Relocation to the Kraków Ghetto as Remembered by Child Survivors' in Simone Gigliotti and Monica Tempian (Eds), 'The Young Victims of the Nazi Regime'; Bloomsbury, London 2016, page 159. Additionally, see 'Mit den Augen des Kindes' in Maria Kłańska (Ed), 'Jüdisches Städtebild Krakau'; Jüdischer Verlag, Frankfurt am Main, 1994 and references in Andrea Löw and Markus Roth, 'Juden in Krakau unter Deutscher Besatzung, 1939-1945'; Wallstein Verlag, Göttingen, 2011, and 'Polin', vol 23, page 371, and see names index for other references
[787] Monika Stepień, 'The Image of Post-war Kraków in Jewish Writing, 1945-1950' in 'Polin', vol 23, pages 367, 368 and see generally in the index, and Halina Nelken, 'And Yet I am Here'; University of Massachusetts Press, Amherst, MA, 1986, chapter 4, 'Return to Kraków'
[788] Notes from Halina Nelken, 'Images of a Lost World; Jewish Motifs in Polish Painting'; I B Taurus & Co, London, 1991. See also Halina Nelken, 'And Yet I am Here', originally published in 1987 as 'Pamiętnik z getta Krakowie'. See also Monika Stępień, 'The Cultural Life of Jews after 1945' in Barbara Cisowska (Ed), 'We Were; We Are; We Will Be', Kraków, 2015, page 33

memoir about her family's history, 'W ogrodzie pamięci' (In the Garden of Memory).[789]

Maria Straucher was born in Bosnia in May, 1938. Although she survived the war her rescuer treated her very badly and Maria was forced to carry out may household chores despite being only a young child. After the war she was interviewed at the Jewish orphanage in Kraków, having been reunited with her mother's sister, who found her in her rescuer's home.[790]

Anna-Teresa Tymieniecka (1923-2014) was born into a well established Jewish family in Mazovia in northern Poland. After the Holocaust, she studied philosophy at the Jagiellonian University and, at the same time, she studied at the Kraków Academy of Fine Arts. Her first husband was the Kraków artist, Leszek Dutka. Following her studies, Anna-Teresa Tymieniecka moved to Switzerland, and then America, where she became an influential philosopher.[791]

Ela Waśniewska was born in 1930 and she spent her early years in Warsaw. During the Holocaust she was transported to Skawina, near Kraków, and after the liberation she was sent to an emergency shelter in Kraków. She records that many of the children there had mange, a skin disease. Ela was then transferred to an orphanage and, whilst there, she completed her studies in middle and secondary school, before taking a teaching course. Ela Waśniewska then studied education and culture at the Jagiellonian University.[792]

Fryda Zawada (née Aronowicz) (1936-2022) was born into a working class family. Her father was a tailor whilst her mother worked in a shop. They did not practice Judaism. During the Holocaust, Fryda and her parents were deported to Siberia and her parents died there. At the end of the war Fryda was repatriated to Kraków where she was placed in an orphanage.[793]

Education

A summary of the educational facilities available to Jewish children during the communist period is included in an article, 'A History of Jewish Education in Kraków', which can be found at www.academia.edu/33768075 . Reference is made there to the testimony of Roma Ligocka who writes:

'A small Jewish school has reopened in Kraków. It is located in a shabby dark building with tiny rooms. I am put into the second form because I already know how to read and write and because I'm almost seven years old.

---

[789] Wikipedia and Monika Stepień, 'The Cultural Life of Kraków Jews after 1945' in Barbara Cisowska (Ed), 'We Were; We Are; We Will Be', pages 48-51

[790] Joanna Michlic, 'The War Began for me After the War; Jewish Children in Poland, 1945-49'. See also by the same author, 'The Aftermath and After; Memories of Child Survivors of the Holocaust'

[791] Wikipedia

[792] Katarzyna Meloch and Halina Szostkiewicz (Eds), 'Children of the Holocaust Speak', vol 3; The Association of Children of the Holocaust in Poland, Warsaw, 2019, pages 77-93 and www.zapispamieci.pl/en/ela-wasniewska/

[793] www.gwzkrakow.pl/en/2022/02/15/fryda-zawada-born-aronowicz-1936-2022/ and Filip Mazurczak, 'Why We Stayed'

I had looked forward to school, but now it leaves me speechless. The atmosphere in the classroom is so tense. Hardly a minute passes when someone doesn't break down in tears..... All that's needed is for someone to raise his voice, and the teacher, a woman who was also in one of the camps, flinches and begins to sob.'[794]

Not all Jewish girls attended the Jewish school in Kraków. For example, and as noted below, Maria Orwid attended the Urszulanka Secondary School, whilst Eva Hoffman also attended a State school until 1957 when 'prayers and religion classes begin to be instituted in Polish schools'.[795]

Jagiellonian University

Despite the general level of anti Semitism in Communist era Poland, there does seem to have been a degree of acceptance of Jews at the Jagiellonian University in Kraków. References have already been made to a number of young Jewish women who studied at the university in the period following the end of the Holocaust. This topic is considered in a book edited by Wiesław Kozub-Ciembroniewicz, 'Academics of Jewish Heritage in the Modern History of the Jagiellonian University' which was published by the Jagiellonian University Press in 2014. One of the contributors, Janusz Sondel, notes 'During the years of the Polish People's Republic and particularly in 1968 despite the anti Jewish demonstrations within the country, the Jagiellonian University as a whole witnessed no serious excesses or persecutions of Jewish members of staff. He further notes that an interfaculty unit for the history and culture of Jews was opened in 1986.[796]

The book ''Academics of Jewish Heritage' and other sources include biographies of some of the following women who pursued successful academic careers at the University. The biographies do not generally highlight membership or support of the Communist party but it may be assumed that such membership or support might have been a requirement of the university.

Zofia Ameisen (1897-1967) studied and worked at the University in Kraków in the 1920's. She wrote extensively on the subject of illuminated manuscripts. Unlike most of her family, she survived the Holocaust and returned to the University. She became an associate professor in 1995, and was promoted to a full professor four years later. Her post war work included the cataloguing of documents and books which were held in the Jagiellonian Library. Her last book, published in the year of her death, was a study of four illuminated manuscripts of the sixteenth century which were held in foreign collections. Zofia Ameisen died on 25 December, 1967 in Nowa Huta, and is buried in the Jewish cemetery in Kraków on ul. Miodowa.[797]

---

[794] Roma Ligocka, 'The Girl in the Red Coat'; Sceptre, London, 2003, page 135
[795] Eva Hoffman, 'Lost in Translation'; Vintage Books, London, 1998, page 54
[796] Wiesław Kozub-Ciembroniewicz (Ed), 'Academics of Jewish Heritage' page 24 see also the chapter by Michał Zajda, 'The Events of March, 1968 at the Jagiellonian University'
[797] Wiesław Kozub-Ciembroniewicz (Ed), 'Academics of Jewish Heritage', pages 69-76. See also Agnieszka Kutylak (Ed), 'Krakowianie; Wybitni Żydzi Krakowscy XIV-XX w'; Muzeum Historyczne Miasta Krakowa, Kraków, 2006, pages 133-135 and Ewa Dąbrowska (Ed), 'Residents of Jewish Cracow; Art and Culture'; Wydawca EMG , Kraków, 2020, pages 100-107

As noted in a previous chapter, Maria Einhorn-Susułowska (1915-1998) graduated from the Jagiellonian University, and then obtained her teaching diploma in 1938. Having survived the Holocaust, largely in Lwów, she returned to Kraków and spent the whole of her academic life there, specialising as a clinical psychologist. During the 1950's she worked closely with the Psychiatric Clinic of the Medical Academy, and carried out research into the experiences of concentration camp survivors. Despite the anti Semitic atmosphere of the time, she became a professor in 1969. She supervised hundreds of masters' and doctoral theses, and became known as 'the creator of Polish clinical psychology'.[798]

Daniela Gromska (née Tenner) (1889-1973) was born into a Jewish family in Lwów. She and her family survived the Holocaust in Warsaw and then moved to Kraków. Between 1957 and 1960, Daniela taught history of ancient philosophy at the Jagiellonian University and in 1959 she became a full professor there. She was remembered not only as an unusual scholar and translator but also as a language feminist who demanded that Polish feminine noun forms should be used.[799]

Danuta Hawel was born in 1940 in Zawiercie, some 44 miles (70 km) north west of Kraków. In 1956 she was accepted at university and she later graduated from the Medical Academy in Kraków. She specialised in neurology and continued to practice well into the post Communist period.[800]

Maria Orwid (née Pfeffer) (1930-2009) was born in Przemyśl. She survived part of the war in that city's ghetto, and then on Aryan papers in Lwów. After the war she moved with her mother and step father to Kraków where she attended the Urszulanka (Ursuline) Secondary School. She became attracted to Marxist-Leninist ideology and whilst at the Jagiellonian University she joined the Association of Polish University Students which supported that cause. Between 1959 and 1964 Maria Orwid conducted research on the psychological effects of the experiences of former Jewish and Roma prisoners of concentration camps. She became a leading researcher of psychiatric issues affecting children and adolescents and wrote several works on the subject. Maria Orwid continued her work following the fall of Communism, and from 2000 she headed the postgraduate training programme at the Department of Psychiatry in Kraków.[801]

---

[798] Wiesław Kozub-Ciembroniewicz (Ed), 'Academics of Jewish Heritage', pages 103-108, and Ewa Dąbrowska and Anna Kiełczewska (Eds), 'Residents of Jewish Kraków; Women' Wydawca EMG, Kraków, 2021, page 160
[799] Ewa Dąbrowska (Ed), 'Residents of Jewish Kraków; Places and People'; Wydawca EMG, 2022, page 144
[800] Katarzyna Meloch and Haina Szostkiewicz (Eds), 'Children of the Holocaust Speak', vol 3, page 292 and www.zapispamieci.pl/en/danuta-hawel/ See also www.znanylekarz.pl/danuta-hawel/neurolog/zawiercie
[801] Wikipedia and Wiesław Kozub-Ciembroniewicz (Ed), 'Academics of Jewish Heritage' pages, 179-186. See also Monika Stępień, 'The Image of Post War Kraków in Jewish Writing, 1945-1950' in Michał Galas and Antony Polomsky (Eds), 'Polin', vol 23,. See also Dr Katarzyna Prot-Klinger and others, 'Psychotherapy of Holocaust Survivors – Integration of Traumatic Experiences?' in The Israel Journal of Psychiatry, vol 56, no 1, 2019, and A Szymusik, 'The Medical Examination of Concentration Camp Survivors in the Kraków Psychiatric Clinic'; Medical Review – Auschwitz, 2020, Additionally see an article by Edyta Gawron, 'Maria Orwid (1930-2009)' written in 2014 and available on academia.edu.

Zofia (Zosia) Radzikowska (née Melzer) was born in 1935 into a middle class Jewish family, which had strong links to the Jewish culture and religion. Her father was a furrier who owned a shop in the centre of Kraków. He died during a transport to a death camp. However, she and her mother survived the Holocaust, spending some time in villages, including Łeg and Borek Fałęcki, near to Kraków. She returned to the city and attended the newly opened Jewish school, which was Zionist, before studying law at the Jagiellonian University. For more than thirty years Zofia Radzikowska taught criminal law at the University, and she became a professor there. In the 1980's she joined Solidarność and worked as the editor of an anti-Communist newspaper.[802] She has been interviewed by several researchers, including Katarzyna Meloch[803] and Filip Mazurczak.[804]

Literature

As previously noted, most of the material written by Jewish authors in the Communist period was in the form of diaries, memoirs and testimonies. However, a few authors were engaged in other forms of writing. For example, again as previously noted, Janina Katz was a literary critic during the 1960's.

Wisława Szymborska (1923-2012) lived in Kraków from 1931 until the end of her life. She was of Jewish birth and a prolific poet and essayist. At the outbreak of the war, she continued her education in underground classes and from 1943 she worked on the railways. In 1945, Wisława started studying at the Jagiellonian University and in the same year she published her first poem. Her first book was to be published in 1949 but it did not pass censorship as it 'did not meet socialist requirements'.

Nevertheless, Wisława became an active Socialist and a member of the ruling Polish United Workers' Party. In due course, she was to grow estranged from socialist ideology and she renounced her earlier political work. During the 1990's she was awarded several prestigious literary prizes, including the Nobel Prize in Literature. In the year before her death, Wisława Szymborska was awarded the Order of the White Eagle.[805]

Orphanages

Once survivors of the Holocaust began to make their way back to Kraków in search of friends and relatives there was a need for a new orphanage to be established. One of the papers which has been written on this topic is Lucjan

---

Finally see Jakub Gutenbaum and Agnieszka Latała (Eds), 'The Last Eyewitnesses; Children of the Holocaust Speak', vol 2, Northwestern University Press, Evanston, IL, 2005, pages 147-150

[802] Rabbi Avi Baumol, 'In my Grandfather's Footsteps'; Austeria, Kraków, 2019, pages 216-221. See also pages 96 and 175

[803] www.zapispamieci.pl/en/zofia-radzikowska See also Joanna Sliwa, 'Jewish Childhood in Kraków'; Rutgers University Press, 2021, page 125, quoting record 301/3277 at the Jewish Historical Institute

[804] Filip Mazurczak, 'Why we stayed' see https://orcid.org/0000-0003-1014-1723

[805] Wikipedia and, for example, the Jerusalem Post, 22 February, 2019. See also Joanna Gromek-Illg's book, 'Szymborska, znaki szczególne; biografa wewnętrzna'; Wydawnictwo Znak, Kraków, 2024

Dobroszycki's work, 'Children Living in the Orphanage in Cracow Shortly after Liberation'.[806] A further paper of relevance is Boaz Cohen's work, 'The Rehabilitation of Jewish Child Holocaust Survivors, Poland, 1944-1947'. This is included as a chapter in volume 36 of 'Polin', which is devoted to Jewish Childhood in Eastern Europe.

A more detailed work is Noemi Bażanowska's book, 'To był mój dom' (This was my Home), which describes the Children's Home in Kraków in the period from 1945 to 1957.[807] Several extracts from the book are quoted by Helena Datner in her article 'Children in the Polish Jewish Community from 1944 to 1968'.[808] One of the girls who is named in the book is Dora Zoberman. She had survived by working for a wealthy farmer in the pretence to him that she was planning to convert to Christianity.[809] Dora is shown in a photograph, taken in 1950, together with other female survivors, Musia Liberman, Hela and Regina Bojm, Ala Kleiman, Marisia Strauch, Pola Zoberman and Zosia Horn.[810]

Maria Hochberg-Mariańska (1913-1996) has been mentioned in the last chapter concerning the Holocaust. In 1945 and 1946 she collected testimonies from children and teenagers who had come out of hiding. These testimonies form the basis of a book, 'The Children Accuse'.[811] Maria Hochberg's work, 'Dzieci' (Children) was included in the 1946 work, 'W 3cia rocznicę zagłady ghetta w Krakowie' which was published by the Centralny Komitet Żydów Polskich in Kraków. After the war she continued to be involved in the Jewish orphanage and her testimony is reflected in the works of Noemi Bażanowska, particularly her book, 'To był mój dom', and in the works of Joanna Sliwa. Maria Hochberg-Mariańska notes that children from small towns or villages were most likely to survive on their own (as cowherds, household help or child carers). They were more resilient physically and psychologically and spoke the local dialect.[812]

The experience of Jewish child survivors following the liberation of Kraków in January, 1945 is described by Joanna Sliwa in the epilogue to her book, 'Jewish Childhood in Kraków'.[813] The author describes how the Voivodship Jewish

---

[806] Lucjan Dobroszycki, 'Children Living in the Orphanage in Cracow Shortly after Liberation who Survived in Hiding, Disguised as Christians, or in Camps' in 'Survivors of the Holocaust in Poland: A Portrait based on Jewish Community Records, 1944-1947'; M E Sharpe, Armonk, NY, 1994

[807] Noemi Bażanowska, 'To był mój dom; Żydowski Dom Dziecka Krakowie w latch 1945-1957'; Księgarnia Akademicka, Kraków, 2011

[808] In Feliks Tych and Monika Adamczyk- Garbowska (Eds), 'Jewish Presence in Absence; The Aftermath of the Holocaust in Poland, 1944-2010'; Yad Vashem, Jerusalem, 2014

[809] Joanna Michlic, 'What Does a Child Remember? Recollections of the War and the early Post War Period among Child Survivors from Poland

[810] https://www.infocenters.co.il/gfh/notebook_ext.asp?book=13372&lang=eng&site=gfh

[811] Maria Hochberg-Mariańska and Noe Grüss, 'The Children Accuse'; The Library of Holocaust Testimonies, Vallentine Mitchell, London, 1996, originally published as 'Dzieci okarżają' by the Jewish Historical Commission, Kraków, 1947

[812] Helena Datner, 'Children in the Polish-Jewish Community from 1944 to 1968' in 'Jewish Presence in Absence', page 286

[813] Joanna Sliwa, 'Jewish Childhood in Kraków; A Microhistory of the Holocaust'; Rutgers University Press, New Brunswick, NJ, 2021, pages 138-143

Committee operated from 38 Długa Street and that its institutions included an orphanage and schools.

Lena Kuchler (Kichler) Silberman (1910-1987) is mentioned by both Noemi Bażanowska and Joanna Sliwa. Lena was born in Wieliczka about 10 miles (16 km) to the south east of Kraków. She attended the Hebrew Gimnazjum (secondary school) in Kraków and then the Jagiellonian University, where she studied child psychology and education, before working as a teacher. Much of her time during the Holocaust was spent in Lwów and Warsaw, but in 1945 she was one of those who returned to Kraków in search of relatives and friends. A cousin, Frania, found her. She had become a high ranking communist and was known as Lt. Col Franciska Eliaszowna Honig of the Polish army. With her help Lena was restored to health.

Lena experienced the poor working conditions in the Jewish Community Centre at ul Długa, 38, and this led a large number of children to be transferred to the southern hill spa town of Rabka and to the mountain resort of Zakopane, in order to improve the children's health and in an (unsuccessful) attempt to protect them from anti Semitism. The hostility of the local populations, together with inadequate funding, resulted in Lena taking the children to Palestine in 1946. Information about the home in Zakopane is available on the website of the Ghetto Fighters House Archives.[814]

Lena Kuchler Silberman published her memoirs, 'Me'ah Yeladim Sheli' in 1959. Her work has been translated from Hebrew into many languages and the English version is 'One Hundred Children'.[815] The memoirs were presented as a film in 1987. Unfortunately, from the point of view of researchers, the book does not include a names index and, in any event, the names of the children and most of the other individuals mentioned in the book are fictional, presumably to protect their true identity. It is believed, however, that one of the children was Edith (Edyta) Zierer (1932-2014) who at the end of the war was aided by a young priest, Karol Wojtyla – later Pope John Paul II.

After Lena took her children out of Poland, the orphanage in Kraków continued to operate for more than a further ten years – as is described by Noemi Bażanowska in her book.

The children's homes in Kraków, Rabka and Zakopane are described by Emanuel Elbinger who notes that Maria, the wife of Professor Julian Aleksandrowicz, gave gymnastic lessons at the homes. Mr Elbinger and his sister Pola stayed at the homes

---

[814] www.infocenters.co.il/gfh/notebook_ext.asp?book=124826&lang=eng and, for example, Boaz Cohen, 'Survivor Caregivers and Child Survivors: Rebuilding Lives and the Home in the Postwar Period'; Holocaust and Genocide Studies, 2, no 1 (Spring 2018), pages 49-65.
[815] Lena Kuchler Silberman, 'One Hundred Children'; Doubleday, Garden City, NY, 1961. Some of the background information about the author has been taken from Wikipedia. Further information about the author and her work is available by searching 'my 100 children' on YouTube. See also Boaz Cohen, 'Survivor Caregivers and Child Survivors; Rebuilding Lives and the Home in the Post War Period'; Holocaust and Genocide Studies, 32 (2018), and Sarah Silberstein Swartz, 'A Surrogate Mother to Many' in 'The Galitianer'; Gesher Galicia, March, 2024, pages 28-34

in the period following the liberation.[816] He also notes that, as mentioned previously in this chapter, Emilia Leibel was one of the carers.

Ela Waśniewska describes how she was moved to an orphanage in Kraków after the liberation. The building had previously been used as a blood transfusion centre. 'When you entered, you could see sinks filled with blood. It was gruesome. There was nothing to sleep on. They brought a lot of straw … We'd stuff this into straw mattresses and would sleep on them.'[817]

Róża Jakubowicz

Róża Jakubowicz (née Pistol) (1918-2007) has already been mentioned in the introductory section of this chapter, but her importance to the Kraków Jewish community in the Communist period justifies a separate section devoted to her. She has been described as 'mother to the community'. Her husband, Meir, also known as Maciej Meir (1911-1979) led the Orthodox community, the gmina, for nearly thirty years. Meir was succeeded in 1979 by his nephew, Czesław who, in turn, was succeeded by Róża's son, Tadeusz in 1997. Tadeusz continued to be President of the gmina until his daughter, Helena, took over in 2022.

Rosa, sometimes known as Maria Róża, was born in Dobczyce into a wealthy family. Her father had a large tannery that supplied the army. Before the war she graduated from the Kraków School of Economics and Trade in order to help her father as an accountant. Her son, Tadeusz, was born in 1939 in Kraków. Although most of Róża's family were murdered in the Holocaust, she and her son survived the Kraków Ghetto and Płaszów before spending three years hiding on Aryan papers in a shelter, more accurately a pit, in the forest.

She arrived in Kraków in June, 1945, and began working with the Regional Jewish Committee at Długa, 38. She was primarily engaged in the care of children and, together with her husband, is credited with helping arrange several children to emigrate to Israel.

Róża worked throughout her remaining life with the Jewish gmina, the Kongregacji Wyznania Mojżeszowego, and served the community in very many ways, from organising large scale Passover meals to baking challah and embroidering Torah mantles.

Róża Jakubowicz is buried in the main alley of the 'new' Jewish cemetery on ul. Miodowa. One of several obituaries published in Dziennik Polski read, 'A noble person with a huge heart and an open mind who devoted her life to others; an irreplaceable guardian of those in need.'[818]

---

[816] https://www.centropa.org/en/biography/emanuel-elbinger Regarding Maria Aleksandrowicz, see the website of the Polin Museum, 'Story of Rescue – Zurowski, Ludwik'

[817] Katarzyna Meloch and Halina Szostkiewicz (Eds), 'Children of the Holocaust Speak', vol 3, page 89 and www.zapispamieci.pl/en/ela-wasniewska/

[818] Małgorzata Niezabitowska, and Tomasz Tomaszewski, 'Remnants; The Last Jews of Poland'; Friendly Press, New York, NY, 1986, pages 159-163 and https://gwzkrakow.pl/en/2022/05/01/maria-roza-jakubowicz-1918-2007-2/ . See also Helen

de Borchgrave, 'Silent Memories'; The Jewish Chronicle Supplement, London, 19 September, 1986 and Minika Stępień (Ed), 'Witness to Polish-Jewish History; The Stories of Holocaust Survivors, Former Prisoners of Nazi German Concentration Camps and Righteous Among the Nations'; Galicia Jewish Museum, Kraków, 2016, pages 40-43. For further references to the Jakubowicz family, see for example, Bogusław Krasnowolski, 'Krakowski Kazimierz; Historia i Kultura'; Biblioteka Krakowska nr 168; Towarzystwo Miłośnikow Historii i Zabytków Krakowa, Kraków, pages 427, 428.

THE POST COMMUNIST PERIOD
Resurrecting the Jew

Introduction

With the benefit of hindsight, we now know that the predictions of the late 1980's were too pessimistic, and that the Communist period was not the final chapter in what is the ongoing story of the Jews of Kraków. The post Communist period has been described as one of rebirth or renewal, but perhaps the most striking description is a period of 'Resurrecting the Jew'. This is the title of a book by professor of sociology, Geneviève Zubrzycki.[819] In her work the author describes how the revival of an interest in Jewish matters has been driven largely by non Jews, many of whom want to break the association between Polishness and Catholicism, promote the idea of a multicultural Poland, and resist the policies of the right wing government. She highlights the development of museums and memorials and a growth in the number and scope of Jewish Cultural Festivals. In the context of Kraków she describes in detail how non Jewish volunteers are active at the Jewish Cultural Centre. To this aspect can be added the numerous academic research programmes which document the history of the Jews in Poland, and particularly in Kraków.

Females make up a particularly high proportion of the non Jewish Poles who have taken a close interest in Jewish matters. Geneviève Zubrzycki adopts the term 'philosemitism' to denote a wide spectrum of practices guided by a curiosity and desire to learn about Judaism, Jewishness and Jewish history, and she notes that some researchers have suggested that many philosemites have adopted 'virtual Jewishness' or 'vicarious Jewishness'.[820]

In another work, Geneviève Zubrzycki refers to 'de-assimilation', which she defines as 'the complex process of individual discovery and communal recovery of Jewish identity'. The same term is used by Stanisław Krajewski in his article 'The Concept of De-assimilation: The Example of Jews in Poland'.[821]

Katarzyna Czerwonogóra is another researcher into the role of Jewish women in Kraków during the post Communist period. Her MA thesis at the Jagiellonian University in 2009 was entitled 'Tożamość i rola kobiety Żydowskiej w Polsce na przykładzie Krakowa; Persektywa feministyczna' (The Identity and Role of the

---

[819] Geneviève Zubrzycki, 'Resurrecting the Jew; Nationalism, Philosemitism and Poland's Jewish Revival'; Princeton University Press, NJ, 2022. See also, for example, Stanisław Krajewski, 'The Concept of De-assimilation; The Example of Jews in Poland' at https://link.springer.com/article/10.1007/s12397-023-09532-8 For an overview of recent research which includes several references to Kraków, see Joanna Cukras-Stelągowska, 'Research on the Jewish Community in Polish Social Sciences: Achievements, Perspectives and Scientific Challenges over the Last Two Decades'; Acta Universitatis Nicolai Copernici, Pedagogika XXXV/1/2018

[820] Geneviève Zubrzycki, 'Resurrecting the Jew', pages 9, 10

[821] Geneviève Zubrzycki, 'The Social Context of De-assimilation and its Challenges'; Contemporary Jewry, 2023 – see https://link.springer.com/article/10.1007/s12397-023-09529-3 and for the article by Stanisław Krajewski, https://link.springer.com/article/10.1007/s12397-023-09532-8

Jewish Woman in Poland as Exemplified by Kraków; A Feminist Perspective),[822] and this was followed by her paper 'Były Żydówki, są Zydówki – kobiety żydowskie w Polsce na przykładzie Krakowa' (There were Jews, there are Jews – Jewish Women in Poland in the Example of Kraków). In that second paper, the author describes herself as 'a representative of the third generation, a Pole of Jewish origin', and she refers to feminist sociology. Like other researchers, she bases her work on interviews with 'women who actively co-create the Jewish community in Kraków'.

Reference should also be made to the Krakowski Szlak Kobiet (Kraków Women's Trail) which has been established by the tourist group, Magiczny Kraków (Magic Kraków). The group's website at www.krakow.pl has an alphabetic search facility which gives information relating to a large number of Jewish women. Two publications can be mentioned regarding the Kraków Women's Trail. These are a five volume work edited by Ewa Furgal, and a tourist guide book, 'Kraków kobiet; Przewodnik turystyczny'.[823]

The following paragraphs describe how a number of young women have discovered their Jewish roots and have adopted some form of Jewish identity. Yet another group of women should be mentioned – those who have hidden their roots and have revealed them only in their final days.

One such example is Halina Opałko who, a few days before she died in 1999, told her son, Mariusz, that she was a Jewish Holocaust survivor. She told her son that his father had also been Jewish, and a kohen, and that their real last name had been Lederman. In advice to her son she added, 'I'm Jewish and so are you. If you want to be Jewish, be Jewish. If you don't, then don't. Being a Jew in Poland is very difficult'.[824]

Rabbi Avi Baumol gives another example. He tells how a young woman aged 19, named only as Magda Z, was invited by her grandmother 'for a chat'. The grandmother revealed that she, and her mother, and her mother's mother were Jewish. The grandmother passed away a week later.[825]

Academic and other researchers

This book would not be complete without a tribute to the many academics and other researchers who have devoted their time and effort to the recording of the history of the Jewish community in Kraków. Indeed, this book could not have been written without those people, and their ability to search out and translate source material from a wide range of languages. In common with trends in other areas of

---

[822] Noted by Marta Duch-Dyngosz in 'The Revival of Jewish Life in Kraków' in 'We Were, We Are, We Will Be', Muzeum Historyczne Miasta Krakowa, Kraków, 2015, page 155.

[823] Ewa Furgal (Ed), 'Krakowski szlak kobiet; Przewodniczki po Krakowie emancypantek'; Fundacja Przestrzeń Kobiet, Kraków, 2009-2013 and Agata Dutkowska and Wojciech Szymański (Eds), 'Kraków kobiet; Przewodnik turystyczny'; Korporacja Halart, Kraków, 2011

[824] Cnaan Lipshshitz, 'When Elders Reveal They Are Jewish on their Deathbeds, Their Children Often Return to Judaism' at https://www.jta.org/2019/06/27/global/when-elders-reveal-they-are-jewish-on-their-deathbeds-their-children-often-return-to-judaism

[825] Rabbi Avi Baumol, 'A Polish Deathbed Confession and a Lost Challah Recipe' in 'In My Grandfather's Footsteps'; Austeria, 2019, pages 126-129

endeavour, the proportion of academics and other researchers who are female is much greater now than in previous decades. Accordingly, the following appendix sets out the names of some of the female researchers who, since the downfall of Communism in Poland, have written about topics relating to Jewish Kraków, together with brief descriptions of their specialist topics. The list is not exhaustive and, for example, does not include Holocaust survivors, whose testimony is described elsewhere in this book. No criticism is intended of those authors whose names have been omitted.

Book publishers

Many of the large number of academic researchers who have written about Jewish subjects have been supported by a small but significant number of publishers. These include Księgarnia Akademicka which was established in Kraków in 1992, and the University's publishing house, Wydawnictwo Uniwersytetu Jagiellońskiego. As noted below, some museums have also published works.

Malgosia (Małgorzata) Ornat, a native of Kielce, discovered her Jewish roots following the fall of Communism. She, together with her husband, Wojtek, founded the Ariel Café and the Klezmer Hois Hotel, both of which are located in the Kazimierz district of Kraków. Additionally, in 2003, they formed the 'Austeria' publishing house which has produced a large number of books of Jewish interest. These have included prayer books as well as academic works, which have enabled a significant development of Jewish education in Poland by bringing a wide range of works to a varied audience. Just two examples are Anna Jakimyszyn's book about The Jews of Kraków at the time of the Kraków Republic which was published in 2008, and Rabbi Avi Baumol's book, 'In My Grandfather's Footsteps', published in 2019. Female editors working for Austeria include not only Małgorzata Ornat but also Elżbieta Jogałła, Bella Szwarcman-Czarnota, Justyna Rochacewicz, Márta Eles, Natalia Ślazyk and Sabina Wojtasiak.[826]

To give an indication of the high quality of this editorial team reference can be made to Bella Szwarcman-Czarnota. Her experience includes editorship of Państwowy Wydawnictwo Naukowe (The National Scientific Publishing House), and of the Midrasz magazine, and being the editorial secretary of the Bulletin of the Jewish Historical Institute.[827]

Urszula Żyznowski is co-owner, with her husband, Wiesław, of the Żyznowski publishing company which is based at Siercza, near Wieliczka. She is also its editor in chief. In 2022, the company published the award winning book by Małgorzata Międzobrodzka, 'Żydzi w Wieliczce; Opowieść dokumentalna'. (Jews in Wieliczka; A Documentary Story). Urszula Żyznowski completed an MBA course at the Kraków School of Business, and has a number of commercial interests.[828]

---

[826] 'Jewish Renaissance', London, January, 2014, page 18 and https://austeria.pl/en/o-sklepie

[827] Wikipedia

[828] www.zyznowski.pl/wydarzenia/nagroda-im-ks-stanislawa and www.zyznowski.pl/wydawca

According to her LinkedIn profile, Iwona Tokarska has been the owner of the publishing house Wysoki Zamek Iwona Tokarska since 2010. Books which have been published by that company include two works by Barbara Zbroja on the subject of architects and builders of Jewish origin in Kraków. Iwona graduated with a master's degree in history from the Jagiellonian University.

Connie Webber is another publisher who works and lives in Kraków. English by birth, she is married to Jonathan Webber, an academic who was instrumental in the development of the Galicia Jewish Museum. Connie has for very many years been involved in the field of Polish-Jewish relations and her roles have included being managing editor of the Littman Library of Jewish civilisation. In 1998 the Polish government awarded her a Silver Cross of Merit.[829]

Czulent Association

The Czulent Asociation was established in 2005 to cater for young adults in the Jewish community. Anna Makówka-Kwapisiewicz was one of its founders. According to her LinkedIn profile, Anna is a historian, journalist, social activist and educator.[830] One of the many achievements of the Czulent Association has been the publication of award winning books for children, with illustrations by Urzula Palusińska.

The association currently operates in Kraków as an advocacy organisation from premises in ul. Sebastiana. Whilst its chairman is male, the two other members of the management board are female. These are Anna Zielińska and Aleksandra Jach. Anna serves as Secretary to the board. She is a lawyer and specialises in counteracting anti Semitism. Aleksandra, a social activist, serves as treasurer.[831]

In her article about the revival of Jewish life in Kraków, Marta Duch-Dyngosz refers to the BA thesis of A Skuza – whose first name is not given – 'Proces odradzania się kultury żydowskiej w Polsce. Tożamość żydowska 'trzeciego pokolenia' na przykladzie członków krakowskiego Żydowskiego Stowarzyszenia Czulent' (The Process of the Rebirth of Jewish Culture in Poland. The Jewish Identity of the 'third generation' as exemplified by members of the Czulent Jewish Association of Kraków').[832]

Dzieci Holocaustu (Children's Holocaust Association)

Dzieci Holocaustu has its main centre in Warsaw but operates branches in various cities, including Kraków. Its main objectives are to support the ageing members who were children during the Nazi occupation, and to bring Holocaust

---

[829] Limmud Johannesburg, 2019. Jonathan Webber is a professor at the Institute of European Studies at the Jagiellonian University. See Rabbi Avi Baumol, 'In My Grandfather's Footsteps'; Asteria, Kraków 2019, page 47

[830] An interview with Anna Makowa-Kwapisiewicz is featured in a newspaper article by Cnaan Lipshitz, 'Polish Jews Celebrate Community's Revival Amid Increasing Xenophobia'. In April, 2018 this appeared in several publications, including the Times of Israel, the Jewish Telegraphic Agency and the Manchester (UK) Jewish Telegraph.

[831] https://czulent.pl/zarzad-stowarzyszenia

[832] In 'We Were, We Are, We Will Be'; Muzeum Historyczne Miasta Krakowa, 2015, page 155, note 5

education to later generations. For example, the Association publishes survivors' testimonies in a series of works, 'Children of the Holocaust Speak'. Its active members include Zofia Radzikowska who is mentioned below in the section relating to the Jewish Community Centre.

Anna Grygiel-Huryn was the chair of Dzieci Holocaustu in Kraków, even though she lived some two hours away in Nowy Sącz. She passed away in February, 2024 at the age of 82.[833]

Hevre

Hevre is the name of a restaurant and educational centre in the premises of the former Hevre Tehillim Synagogue on ul Meisela in Kazimierz. Izabela Chyłek is the manager there. Izabela graduated from the Jagiellonian University and has a career in tourism and culture. Hevre 'is a famous cultural and religious place for the Polish and Jewish communities' and 'is the cradle of unconventional and expansive events'.[834]

Jewish Community Centre

The Jewish Community Centre, which opened in 2008, is situated in a modern building on ul Miodowa in Kraków, close to the Progressive Temple. It is largely secular in nature, and with over 850 members, it offers a very wide programme of activities to the local Jewish population and to philosemites. These include, 'programming for Jewish holidays, weekly Shabbat dinners, education for all ages, targeted welfare services, arts and cultural programs and numerous social activities.'[835] In recent times the Centre has also been a haven for those, mainly women and children, who have come to Kraków as a result of the Russian invasion of Ukraine.

During the course of her research, Geneviève Zubrzycki interviewed twenty non Jewish volunteers at the Centre. 'All the interviewees were young women (the median age was twenty three). This profile was representative of all the volunteers; very few are over thirty, and even fewer are men..... All were Catholic; half of them observant, the others not'. Different influences led to these young women volunteering but one third of the interviewees attended the Cultural Centre 'because they were enrolled in a Jewish studies program and wanted contact with Jewish life'.[836]

Daniel Barrio Ferro, of the University of Groningen in the Netherlands is another researcher who has considered the renewal of Jewishness in Poland, and in particular the Jewish Community Centre in Kraków. His paper 'Young Jews from the Old Continent; Europe as a catalyst for identity reconciliation amongst Polish-Jewish

---

[833] https://blogs.timesofisrael.com/the-last-jew-of-nowy-sacz/
[834] www.wszib.edu.pl/urbantalk/prelegenci/izabela-chylek
[835] www.friendsofjcckrakow.org/what-we-do See also, for example, Geneviève Zubrzycki, 'Resurrecting the Jew', pages 164-166
[836] Geneviève Zubrzycki, 'Resurrecting the Jew' pages 144-150. See also the Jewish Chronicle, London at a Google search for 'At Krakow's Jewish Community Centre 90 percent of the volunteers are Catholic' and Rabbi Avi Baumol, 'In My Grandfather's Footsteps', pages 130-136, 'Non-Jewish Volunteers in Kraków's Jewish Community'

youth' was published in 2012. The author examines the complex identification process of young people who have recently discovered their Jewish origins. The paper is based partly on interviews with eight young people who were members of the Community Centre's youth group. Most of these identified primarily as Polish above Jewish. However, one interviewee, Maria had become religiously observant, and regretted the lack of orthodox facilities in the Kazimierz district.

Kasia Ornstein, née Leonardi, is a volunteer of a somewhat different nature. She and her sister, Marta, were raised in a mainly atheist household in Kraków. Kasia was 21 when she discovered that her grandparents on both sides were Jewish. Marta brought Kasia to the Jewish Community Centre and introduced her to the Centre's director, Jonathan Ornstein. In 2017, Kasia and Jonathan were married in a traditional Jewish ceremony in Kazimierz. Kasia is currently the kosher caterer at the Centre.[837]

Agnieszka Kocur-Smoleń is the Director of Programming at the Cultural Centre. A graduate of the Jagiellonian University, she has also worked at the Auschwitz-Birkenau Museum. Previously, Anna Gulińska was the Director of Programming.[838]

The Hillel Gimel Jewish Students' Club is one of the various groups which operates from the premises of the Jewish Cultural Centre, and it caters for people aged 18 to 30 who have some Jewish descent. This criterion is similar to those adopted by several communal institutions in Kraków and elsewhere and is deliberately sufficiently wide to admit into membership individuals who have some Jewish ancestry but who are not necessarily Jewish according to orthodox tradition. To illustrate this point, the current director of Hillel Kraków is Mariia Hershova who came from Dnipro, Ukraine to Kraków in 2015. Mariia's father is Jewish but her mother is not.[839] The varied activities of Gimmel include taking part in the annual bicycle ride from Auschwitz to Kraków.[840]

Marcjanna Kubala was interviewed in 2020 when she was programme director of Hillel Gimel. She was 13 when she discovered her Jewish origins. As she said, 'it can be a lot to take in when you make the initial discovery'.[841]

The Frajda (Joy) kindergarten and nursery have been operating from the Community Centre since 2017, under the direction of Młgorzata Pustuł.[842]

Olga Adamowska is the education co-ordinator at the Cultural Centre. As part of her work, she works with a group of people who visit schools to teach their pupils

---

[837] www.theworld.org/stories/2020-02-05/young-people-poland-are-rediscovering-their-jewish-roots and Rabbi Avi Baumol, 'In My Grandfather's Footsteps', pages 199-206

[838] Facebook and for an interview with Agnieszka Kocur-Smoleń see https://jguideeurope.org/en/region/poland/galicia/krakow/ . See also Rabbi Avi Baumol, 'In My Grandfather's Footsteps'; Austeria, page 15

[839] Pittsburgh Jewish Chronicle, 10 August, 2022 and the Times of Israel, 10 August, 2022, and LinkedIn

[840] Rabbi Avi Baumol, In My Grandfather's Footsteps', page 261. See also page 122

[841] www.theworld.org/stories/2020-02-05/young-people-poland-are-rediscovering-their-jewish-roots

[842] See, for example, www.timesofisrael.com/krakow-jccs-new-preschool-signals-hope-for-a-communitys-rebirth/

about Jewish life. She is also President of the Mifgash Foundation which is mentioned below.[843]

The following individuals attend, or have attended, the Community Centre on a regular basis.

Maria Goldman was born in the Ukraine in the 1990's. She was brought up Jewish but was told not to display her religious identity. She came to Kraków in 2011 to study at the university but for nearly four years she made no contact with the local Jewish community. In 2015 Maria enrolled as a volunteer with the Jewish Culture Festival and this led her to the Jewish Community Centre, where she became an active member.[844]

Monika Goldwasser was born on 1941 in Myślenice, to the south of Kraków, to professional well educated parents. They handed Monika into the care of local farmers, and then to Ursuline nuns in Kraków. At the age of three, Monika was adopted by non Jews who in due course were awarded 'Righteous Among the Nations'. Monika Goldwasser discovered her Jewish roots at the age of 22, shortly before the death of her adoptive mother. Shortly afterwards she met the sister of her biological mother who came to Poland from Israel. This led to her actively re-establishing her Jewish identity. Monika continues to live in Kraków where she attends the Jewish Community Centre and events organised by the Galicia Jewish Museum.[845]

Born in 2005, twins Dasza and Mesia Makosz are members of the Jewish community together with their mother, Perl. The twins celebrated their bat mitzvah at the Tempel Synagogue in a service attended by Rabbi Baumol and the Chabad (Lubavitch) Rabbi Gurary.[846]

Lidia Maksymowicz (née Ludmila Boczarowa) was born in 1941 in Belarus. In December, 1943 she and her family were transported to Auschwitz where Ludmila was the subject of medical 'experiments' by Dr Mengele. She survived the Holocaust and was raised by a Catholic family. Lidia now lives in Kraków where she is an active Holocaust educator and an opponent of extremism and populism. Her life has been the subject of a documentary, and more recently the subject of two books. In 2022, Lidia Maksymowicz was awarded the Honoris Gratia badge by the city of Kraków.[847]

---

[843] 'In the Shadow of the Holocaust; A Jewish Community Begins to Take Root'; Wall Street Journal, 13 November, 2021, available on subscription at www.wsj.com/articles/in-the-shadow-of-the-holocaust-a-jewish-community-begins-to-take-root-11636822801 and the website of the Galicia Jewish Museum concerning a talk by Olga Adamowska on 28 June 2023

[844] Rabbi Avi Baumol 'In My Grandfather's Footsteps', pages 146, 147

[845] Monika Stępień (Ed), 'Witnesses to Polish-Jewish History; The Stories of Holocaust Survivors, Former Prisoners of Nazi German Concentration Camps and Righteous Among the Nations'; Galicia Jewish Museum, Kraków, 2016, pages 32-35, available on line and for example, an interview at www.sztetl.org.pl/en/oral-history/182507-monika-goldwasser

[846] Rabbi Avi Baumol, 'In My Grandfather's Footsteps', pages 177-181

[847] Wikipedia and various press reports, May 2021. See also, for example www.dailymail.co.uk/home/books/article-11814221/How-two-mothers-saved-death-

Zofia (Zosia) Radzikowska has been mentioned in the chapter regarding the Communist period, in relation to both the post war anti Semitism in Kraków, and her academic career at the Jagiellonian University. Following the fall of Communism, she was active in local politics and she served on the Kraków City Council between 1994 and 2002. Additionally, Zofia Radzikowska was active on the board of Kraków's Jewish Religious Community, the gmina, the city's branch of the Association of Children of the Holocaust, and B'nei B'rith Polska, which was re-activated in 2007.[848] Zofia celebrated her batmitzvah at the age of 12 plus 70 in 2017.[849] In 2021, she was mentioned in an article about the Kraków Jewish community.[850] More recently, along with other members of the Centre, she has become a strong supporter of Ukraine, and Ukrainians in Kraków, following the Russian invasion.[851]

Monika Wszołek is an active member of the Cultural Centre, who discovered her Jewish roots as a result of DNA testing. Her story is told in the September/October, 2021 issue of the Centre's newsletter 'Jesteśmy' (We are here).[852]

Małgorzata Zajda was born in 1948 and has lived in the same second floor apartment in Kraków all her life. She is 'one of the motors behind the Jewish Cultural Centre' Her father served in the Polish army during the war. Małgorzata has clear memories of anti Semitism in the post war period and is cautious about the future, saying 'You must always keep in mind that history repeats itself'.[853]

Alfreda Zawada was born in 1937 not far from Warsaw. During the war she and her family were deported to Siberia, where her parents died. After the liberation Alfreda arrived in Kraków where she lived in an orphanage. With the fall of Communism, she was one of those who re-established their Jewish identity and she became active in the Jewish Community Centre. Fryda passed away in 2022.[854]

camp.html and
www.krakow.pl/aktualnosci/266447,29,komunikat,lidia_maksymoicz_uhonorowana_przez_prezydenta.html
[848] Wikipedia and Filip Mazurczak, 'Why We Stayed; Poland's Remaining Jews' Experiences, Identities and Reasons for not Emigrating 1939-2018'; Columbia University, 2018, available on academia.edu
[849] Rabbi Avi Baumol 'In My Grandfather's Footsteps', pages 216-221. See also pages 96 and 175
[850] 'In the Shadow of the Holocaust; A Jewish Community Begins to Take Root'; Wall Street Journal, 13 November, 2021
[851] Ukrainianjewishencounter.org/en/ posting 5 June, 2023
[852] 'In the Shadow of the Holocaust' Wall Street Journal, 13 November, 2021 and a JCC Facebook posting dated 8 November, 2021. See note 25
[853] Joe-Lize Brugge, 'How Kraków's Jews Overcame Communism'; CNE News, 14 September, 2022
[854] Philip Mazurczak, 'Why We Stayed; Poland's Remaining Jews' Experiences, Identities and Reasons for not Emigrating, 1939-2018'; Columbia University Press, 2018, available on academia.edu and, by the same author, 'Why We Stayed; Polish Jews' Reasons for Remaining in Poland during Two Waves of Postwar Emigration', 2023 at
http://orcid.org/0000-0003-1014-1723

In summary, then, although the director of the Jewish Community Centre, Jonathan Ornstein, is male, most of the Centre's day to day activities seem to be led by women.

Jewish Culture Festival

Kraków's Jewish Culture Festival started in 1988 as a two day local event consisting primarily of films and lectures with a limited public appeal. It has developed year by year in duration, scope and stature so that it is now an important international event under the patronage of the President of the Republic of Poland. Furthermore, the Kraków Festival has led to the development of many similar but smaller events which are held around the country. As such, the Festival features prominently in Geneviève Zubrzycki's book 'Resurrecting the Jew' where she describes the production, performance and consumption of Jewish culture in post Communist Poland. The author notes that the event now lasts for ten days and is attended by some thirty thousand people from Poland and abroad. Local guides arrange a number of tours during the period of the Festival, one such tour being titled 'Jewish Women's Kraków'.[855]

The Festival has attracted large numbers of Jewish and non Jewish volunteers and performers. These include Aleksandra Makuch, the daughter of Janusz who is primarily to be credited with establishing and developing the festival. Aleksandra studied at the Jagiellonian University, and she co-ordinated volunteers at the Festival between 2007 and 2013. In 2015 she joined the staff of the Taube Centre for the Renewal of Jewish Life in Poland Foundation, which is based in Warsaw.[856]

The singer of Yiddish songs, Shura Lipovsky, sang at the third Festival in 1992.[857] Other examples include Marzena Dudziuch-Koluch, founder and leader of the Kachol Israeli Dance Group, and the artist Anna Kolek who discovered her maternal grandfather was Jewish. They also include the Makosz sisters who sing Yiddish songs, and the actress, Hanna Kossowska. She appeared in the film 'Schindler's List' and has also led at least one Jewish cooking workshop.[858]

Monika Krajewska was awarded the Lifetime Achievement Award of the Taube Foundation at the 23rd Jewish Culture Festival. Monika is a Polish-Jewish artist, writer, photographer and educator, based in Warsaw. Her photographs showing Jewish cemeteries and tombstone art in Poland, 'Czas kamieni' (Time in Stone) was published in 1982.[859]

Kachol Israeli Dance Group

The Kachol Israeli Dance Group (Zespól tanća Kachol) has been operating for some twenty years. It holds its classes and performances at various locations in Kraków, but is based at a youth cultural centre, the Staromiejskie Centrum Kultury

---

[855] Geneviève Zubrzycki, 'Resurrecting the Jew', pages 118-130

[856] Website of the Taube Centre. See also Rabbi Avi Baumol, 'In My Grandfather's Footsteps', pages 133, 134. See also pages 196-200 regarding Tad Taube

[857] Janusz Makuch, 'The Origins of the Jewish Culture Festival in Kraków, 1988-1992' in 'We Were, We Are, We Will Be', page 108

[858] Geneviève Zubrzycki, 'Resurrecting the Jew', pages 65, 66 and 122

[859] Wikipedia and The Galicia Jewish Museum, 4 November, 2020

Młodziezy, on ul J Dietla. Most of its members appear to be women, and the group is led by its founder Marzena Dudziuch-Koluch.[860]

March of the Living

The March of the living is an annual event lasting several days which provides Holocaust education to young people from around the world. The event takes in several cities in Poland, including Kraków.

Carolyn Slutsky was 18 when she took part in the March in 1996. A few years later she moved to Kraków. In an interview she commented that the March no longer conveys 'the internal and external opposition of Poland and Israel, where Poland is the bad country [and] Israel is the opposite'. Whilst in Kraków, Carolyn was a reporter for the Jewish Telegraphic Agency. Her article 'Kraków Jews mark 700 years' was published in December, 2004.[861]

Mifgash Foundation

Mifgash (a Hebrew word for 'meeting') was set up in 2009 when a group of young passionate students from Kraków began meeting with Israeli youth in Poland. The group has since expanded the range of its activities to include workshops about Judaism and has produced a programme 'Between Kraków and Jerusalem'. This has been enjoyed by schools throughout the Kraków region for several years.

As mentioned above, Olga Adamowska is an activist with Mifgash, as well as with the Jewish Cultural Centre. The mifgash website at www.mifgash.org.pl/en/ describes her as the Director of Programming. The site also shows that Małgorzata Kucharska co-ordinates 'Between Kraków and Jerusalem' as well as running anti discrimination workshops. Małgorzata is a graduate of the Pontifical University of John Paul II in Kraków and is an educator. Her work includes leading tours round the Kazimierz district.

The page at www.mifgash.org.pl/team/ gives brief details of the management, the revision committee and the programme board of the Foundation. Substantially all the individuals who are shown on that page are female.

Museums

The Historical Museum of the City of Kraków (Muzeum Historyczne Miasta Krakowa) has several branches which relate to the city's Jewish community. The oldest of these branches is located in the former Old Synagogue at the southern end of ul Szeroka in Kazimierz. Other branches include those at the former pharmacy of Tadeusz Pankiewicz, and in Oskar Schindler's former factory. The Museum has published a number of books concerning Jewish women including the 2011 work, 'Is War Men's Business? Fates of Women in Occupied Kraków in Twelve Scenes'.

---

[860] Geneviève Zubrzycki, 'Resurrecting the Jew', page 151 and www.sckm.krakow.pl/zespol-tanca-kachol
[861] Katarzyna Zechenter, 'Kraków in Jewish Literature since 1945' in 'Polin' vol 23, page 406, and https://www.jta.org/2004/12/16/lifestyle/krakow-jews-mark-700-years

The Galicia Jewish Museum was established in 2004 by its founding director Chris Schwarz. Over the last twenty years, the museum has staged many exhibitions and events, some of which relate to the role of women. For example, its catalogue 'Fighting for Dignity; Jewish Resistance in Kraków' which was published in 2008 featured several young women who fought in the Jewish Underground, whilst in July, 2013 the museum arranged a discussion on 'Jewish Women in Polish History' which included Professor Edyta Gawron as one of the speakers.

In May, 2022, the Museum gave a themed guided tour of Kazimierz under the title 'Jewish Women of Kraków'. The purpose of this was to highlight 'doctors, company owners, thinkers, lawyers, psychologists and teachers who co-created the history of the Jewish communities of Kraków and Kazimierz'.[862]

In March, 2024 the Galicia Jewish Museum announced the passing of one of its supporters and speakers, Anita Panek. Anita (née Haubenstock) was born in Kraków in September, 1930. At the outbreak of the Second World War, she and her family were on holiday in France and in the early 1940's they emigrated to Brazil. It was in that country that Anita Panek became an eminent biochemist, supervising many doctoral students, and writing some 170 scientific papers. In 2017 she returned to Kraków where she was active in Holocaust education.[863]

The KL Płaszów Memorial Museum arranges guided tours around the site of the former concentration camp. In August, 2022 the museum arranged a tour with a 'Women's Perspective', featuring the educator Sarah Schenirer, the Zionist Antonina Leser, the Catholic political prisoner Natalia Bułat and the Jewish architect Diana Reiter.[864]

The question as to whether Kraków needs a Women's Museum has been discussed, for example by a panel in November, 2011.[865] In the absence of such a museum mention can be made of the website at http://www.herstorie.pl which refers to the Fundacja Przestrzeń Kobiet (The Women's Space Foundation) and the Archiwum Historii Kobiet (Women's History Archive) in Kraków.

Polish Union of Jewish Students

According to the Polin Virtual Shtetl site, The Polska Unia Studentów Żydowskich was founded in 1992 to cater for Jewish youth from 16 to 35 years old. In 2004, Aleksandra (Ola) Wilczura was head of the Kraków branch. At that time, she was sceptical about the future of Jewish life in Poland, noting that most Krakovian Jews went to Israel or the US. Ola did in fact leave Krakow for Oxford and then Jerusalem but whilst in Poland, she graduated from the Jagiellonian University and served as President of the Cukunft Jewish Association and the Hasmonea Jewish Sports Club, both in Wrocław. Additionally, in 2005 she co-

---

[862] www.galiciajewishmuseum.org/en/themed-guided-tour-jewish-women-of-krakow
[863] Wikipedia and newsletter of the Galicia Jewish Museum, March, 2024
[864] https://plaszow.org/en/events/womens-perspective
[865] https://en.mocak.pl/does-krakow-need-a-women-s-museum

founded the Czulent Association, which is mentioned in a separate section of this chapter.[866]

Religious organisations and life

The Jewish residents of Kraków, however they define their Jewishness, have a choice of religious customs and organisations. These include the official orthodox congregation, known as the gmina, the Lubavitch congregation, and the Progressive (Reform) community.

Following the tradition of the city's Progressive community prior to the Holocaust, it is the Progressives who give the greatest role to women. This is exemplified by the community's Rabbi (or Rabba in the feminine form), Tanya Segal, the first female Rabbi in the history of Poland. The Rabbi was born in Russia, made Aliya in 1990, and was ordained in 2007 at the Hebrew Union College, Jerusalem. At the end of that year, she became the second Rabbi at Beit Warszawa before moving to Kraków in 2009. Together with a few young Jewish activists she founded the first Progressive community in the area following the 70 year long vacuum created by the war and the Communist regime.

Tanya Segal is also the director of the Midrash Theatre, a professional Jewish theatre in Kraków which works to inspire the creation of modern Jewish art, and undertake educational projects. Since 2019, Tanya Segal has also been the Rabbi of the Jewish community of Ostrava in the Czech Republic.[867]

The Progressive community in Kraków, known as Beit Kraków, offers a wide and inclusive range of activities as shown by its website at www.beitkrakow.org. The site shows that its Board is entirely female, its members being Magda Rubenfeld Koralewska, Aneta Kuberska and Marta Kalamar.

Magda Rubenfeld Koralewska is the longest standing of the board members of the Progressive community. Originally, she did not have any Jewish connection, but she found herself being drawn to Judaism. She moved to Warsaw in about 2004 and started to attend events organised by the Reform community there. She converted to Judaism and eventually became President of the Warsaw community before returning to Kraków and taking on a similar role there.[868] She currently works as Limmud's Regional Co-ordinator for Central and Eastern Europe. She is also co-director of FestivalALT, a Jewish arts collective which is based in Kraków. In 2021, Magda was active in discussions concerning, and had some reservations about, the establishment of a new museum on the site of the Płaszów concentration camp.[869] Magda is also active beyond the Jewish community, being a strong supporter of a political movement called 'Inicjatywa Polska' (Initiative Poland).

Aneta Kuberska is co-owner of the Galeria Szalom which was established in 1994. The gallery is located on ul Józefa in Kazimierz. As well as exhibiting works

[866] https://www.jta.org/2004/12/16/lifestyle/krakow-jews-mark-700-years and https://humanityinaction.org/person/aleksandra-wilczura
[867] The Jewish Women's Archive at https://jwa.org/rabbis/narrators/segal-tanya and Wikipedia
[868] 'Jewish Renaissance', London, January, 2014, page 21
[869] The Times of Israel, November 24, 2021

of art, Aneta organises concerts and takes an active part in the annual Jewish Culture Festival.[870] The third member of the board, Marta Kalamar, is the owner of a business developing computer software, and is a keen mountaineer.[871]

Aga (Agata) Pinkosz was born in 1987 in Częstochowa and is a graduate of the Academy of Fine Arts in Kraków. She designs sets for the theatre, films and advertising and is very active in the Midrash Theatre. She was one of the co-founders of the Beit Kraków community.[872]

It is clear from these paragraphs that the Beit Kraków Progressive community has a strong policy offering equality of opportunity to women. A further illustration of this is that the community has adopted the practice of including an orange on the Pesach Seder Plate (the Passover ceremonial dish). This practice is said by some to relate back to a traditional and sarcastic Rabbinic opinion that 'a woman belongs on a bimah (a place of authority in a synagogue) as much an orange belongs on a seder plate'.

The Gmina Wyznaniowa Żydowska, orthodox congregation, is the one that is officially recognised by the State. The congregation's website at https://gwzkrakow.pl shows that since 2022, the congregation has been led by Helena Jakubowicz. She is the daughter of the previous President, Tadeusz, and a member of the family which has provided leadership for decades. Even prior to her appointment as President, Helena managed the community's real estate, which is substantial following the restoration of several properties which were seized from the community during the Holocaust. In that capacity, in 2019 Helena became involved in a serious dispute between the gmina and the Lubavitch group. This resulted in the Lubavitchers being temporarily excluded from the Izaak Synagogue which they had used for many years.[873]

Helena Jakubowicz is not the only female member of the Gmina board. Magdalena Jenner is also on the board, as well as being active at the Jewish Community Centre, whilst in the past Mina Gottlieb has acted as treasurer and Monika Górecka as board member.

Miriam Synger lives with her husband and five children in Kraków. She is a sociologist, involved in education about Jewish culture, religion and history. She describes herself as a progressive Orthodox Jew and she has spoken to audiences at venues which include the Jewish Community Centre and the Galicia Jewish Museum. Her book 'Jestem Żydówką; Pamiętnik religijnej feministki patrioki wieldzietnej matki Polki' (I am a Jew; A Diary of a Religious Feminist, a Patriot, a Polish Mother with many Children) was published in 2023.[874]

---

[870] Facebook and Wikipedia
[871] Facebook and LinkedIn
[872] https://www.beitkrakow.org/aga-pinkosz and correspondence with Tanya Segal
[873] See, for example, Jewishpress.com, 7 July, 2019, 'Lubavitch; Barring Jews from Historic Kraków Synagogue Unforgivable', and the Jewish Chronicle, London, 12 July, 2019. For a reference to an earlier strained relationship with the Gmina, see Rabbi Avi Baumol, 'In My Grandfather's Footsteps'; Austeria, Kraków, 2019, page 11
[874] https://www.cricoteka.pl/pl/powroty-miriam-synger/

Lubavitch have for many years had a presence in Kraków in the person of Rabbi Eliezer Gurary and his wife Esty. More recently they have been joined by Rabbi Refael Popack and his wife, Dini.

Righteous Amongst the Nations

Mention has been made in the chapter relating to the Holocaust to Catholic men and women who put themselves and their families at great risk whilst protecting Jews against the Nazis. In the Communist and post Communist periods, many of these brave individuals have been honoured by Yad Vashem as 'Righteous Amongst the Nations'. Some were awarded the honour posthumously, but several honourees continue to live in Kraków or the surrounding area.

Janina Rościszewska is a person whose life spans many decades. Shortly before the outbreak of the Second World War, she and her family moved from Kraków to Dolina Będkowska (The Będkowska Valley), about 14 miles (22 km) to the north west. From 1940 onwards the family sheltered a number of Catholics and Jews from the Nazis, including the Jewish Bierzyński family who survived the Holocaust. In 1990, Yad Vashem honoured Janina, her husband and children as Righteous Amongst the Nations.[875]

In 2024, at the time of the Israel-Gaza War, a group of Righteous of the Nations, and their families, sent a message to Gaza residents, urging them to act to save the lives of Israeli hostages held by Hamas. At the time Janina Rościszewska lived in Kraków. 'On behalf of the Righteous Amongst the Nations, I ask the people holding the hostages to release them', she said, adding 'They have done nothing wrong. They bear no guilt for having been born Jewish, just as I bear no guilt for having been born Polish'.[876]

Tour guides

Reference has already been made to the Krakowski Szlak Kobiet (Kraków Women's Trail) and at least one guided tour arranged by the Galicia Jewish Museum, which are examples of a wider group of events designed to show visitors the physical remnants of Jewish Kraków. Other groups such as the Community Centre and the Mifgash Foundation also offer tours around Kazimierz.

Agnieska Legutko is an example of a young woman who began to guide tours around Kraków whilst, or shortly after, studying at the Jagiellonian University. She remembers that when she was a child her mother took her to a concert at the Tempel synagogue and to a Jewish cemetery on one of the smaller towns near Kraków. Having discovered Jewish roots on her mother's side, she received her MA from the Jagiellonian University in 2002, and she wrote 'Krakow's Kazimierz; Town of Partings and Returns', a historical guidebook which was published in Polish in 2004, and then in English in 2009. Agnieszka Legutko is currently a senior lecturer in Yiddish at the Columbia University in the City of New York.[877]

---

[875] www.sprawiedliwi.org.pl/en/stories-of-rescue/story-rosciszewski-family
[876] https://www.israelnationalnews.com/news/384242
[877] 'Jewish Renaissance', London, January, 2014, page 19 and
https://germanic.columbia.edu/content/agnieszka-legutko

Eliza Mrozińska is a tour guide with Kraków Private Jewish Tours. She was born in the Podgórze district of the city in 1975 and is a graduate in Tourism. She spent four years in America, returning to Kraków in 2006. Eliza has attended several courses about Judaism and has been a volunteer at the Jewish Community Centre in Kraków. She works with her colleague Agnieszka Misina who was born in Kraków in 1980.[878]

Marta Weigel is one of several other tour guides operating in Kazimierz,[879] as are Janina Naskalska-Babik, who gives guided tours in French as well as Polish and English,[880] and Maria Baryła who is a guide for 'my Jewish Learning'.

---

[878] www.krakowjewishtours.pl
[879] www.jpost.com/j-spot/article-784046
[880] www.fsp.krakow.pl/en/przewodnik/janina-naskalska-babik-2/

APPENDIX
Female researchers of the post Communist period

Name	Specialist subjects
Natalia Aleksiun	education and female Jewish university students
Aleksandra Bańkowska	Jewish social welfare institutions during the Holocaust
Adina Bar-el	Jewish Children's periodicals between the wars
Noemi Bażanowska	the Jewish orphanage in Kraków between 1945 and 1957
Ewa Bąkowska	the Jewish press
Judy Batalion	women fighters of the Jewish resistance
Anna Bednarek	19th century photographers
Pearl Benisch	Sarah Schenirer and the Bais Ya'akov movement
Janina Bieniarzówna	Jewish trade in the 17th and 18th centuries
Monika Biesaga	the Ezra Jewish library
Iris Brown	Sarah Schenirer and the Bais Ya'akov movement
Mirosława Bułat	Yiddish theatre
Marie Buňatová	commercial relations between the Jews of Prague and Kraków
Fay Bussgang	genealogical sources
Anna Cichopek-Gajraj	pogroms in 1918 and 1945
Katarzyna Czerwonogóra	Jewish women and feminism in the post Communist period
Anna Czocher	women during the holocaust
Ewa Dąbrowska	joint editor of 'Residents of Jewish Kraków; Women'
Elżbieta Długosz	Kraków Rabbis, 16th century to 1939, Gusta Draenger
Marta Duch-Dyngosz	the revival of Jewish life
Magdalena Duda-Seifert	Jewish heritage tourism
Agata Dutkowska	visual signs and symbols of Jewishness in Kazimierz
Iris Fishof	Torah Ark doors at the Israel Museum, Jerusalem
Kamila Follprecht	deputy director at the national museum, Kraków, compiler of data relating to the 1790-1792 census of the Kraków region
Cyndi Freiman	women's Holocaust diaries
Ewa Furgal	Krakowski szlak kobiet (the Kraków Women's Trail)
Ewa Gaczoł	photographs in the Kraków Historical Museum
Bina Garncarska-Kadary	legal and economic status of Jews in the 19th century
Katarzyna Gawel	Yiddish theatre
Edyta Gawron	author or editor of books and articles covering a wide range of topics concerning the contemporary history of Polish Jews, and Kraków Jews, including

	the Holocaust and Holocaust survivors, the post Holocaust period and emigration
Joanna Gellner	photographs in the Kraków Historical Museum
Martyna Grądzka-Rejak	the orphanage, and the role of women during the Holocaust
Judith Grunfeld Rosenbaum	Sarah Schenirer and the Bais Ya'akov movement
Lili Haber	the interwar period, the holocaust and post holocaust periods
Anna Halambiec	football
Anna Jakimyszyn-Gadocha	the Jewish Statute of Kraków, 1595, the mikveh (ritual bath), the Jewish community and education during the 19th century
Aleksandra Jakubczak	prostitution
Sylwia Jakubczyk-Śleczka	music within the Jewish community
Agnieszka Janczyk	the Fromowicz family
Alicja Jarkowska-Natkaniec	the Ordnungdienst (Jewish police) and collaborators during the Holocaust
Anna Jodłowiec-Dziedzic	Jewish life between the world wars and during the Holocaust, places of interest in Kazimierz
Judith Kalik	the Catholic church and the Jews in the pre-partition period
Anna Kargol	the B'nei B'rith Lodge in Kraków
Iwona Kawalla-Lulewicz	trading corporations between the world wars
Aniela Kielbicka	the liquidation of Jewish associations during the Nazi occupation
Anna Kielczewska	joint editor of 'Residents of Jewish Kraków; Women'
Maria Klańska	editor of 'Jüdisches Städtebild Krakau'
Zipora Kleinman	Klasno, near Wieliczka
Barbara Klich-Kluczewska	women during the Communist period
Żanna Komar	architecture in German occupied Kraków
Beata Kowalska	the post Communist period
Hanna Kozińska-Witt	progressive Judaism in the 19th century, Jewish self government and participation in local government, industrialists in Kraków and Podgórze and the interwar period
Justyna Kozioł-Marzec	teachers at the Hebrew Secondary School
Ewa Kurek	how Polish nuns saved Jewish children during the Holocaust
Justyna Kutrzeba	Jewish converts to Christianity
Agnieszka Kutylak	editor of a book concerning famous Jews, 14th to 20th centuries
Anna Kwiatek	photographs in the Kraków Historical Museum
Sabina Kwiecień	the Jewish press in the 20th century
Andrea Löw	Kraków during the Holocaust

Beata Łabno	the role of women during the Holocaust
Anna Lebet-Minakowska	Judaica in the Czartoryski Museum, 19th century birth and marriage registrations
Agnieszka Legutko-Ołownia	Kazimierz history and walking tours
Galina Lochekhina	Jewish heritage in Kraków
Rachel Manekin	orthodox Judaism and conversion of Jewish women to Christianity at the turn of the 19th and 20th centuries, marriage legislation, the Galician Jewish vote, 1873
Alicja Maślak-Maciejewska	the Progressive Jewish community in Kraków, St. Anne Secondary School, 19th century, industrialists
Ewa Mermer	St Anne Secondary School
Joanna Michlic	Jewish children in the Holocaust and post Holocaust period
Małgorzata Międzobrodzka	the Jews of Wieliczka
Sonia Misak	Jewish identity and tourism
Monika Murzyn-Kupisz	Jewish heritage in Kazimierz
Jadwiga Muszyńska	18th century censuses and poll tax records
Paulina Najbar	Jewish families of pre war Kraków
Maria Obrębska	Jewish revival and heritage in Kazimierz
Agnieszka Oleszak	Sarah Schenirer and the Bais Ya'akov movement
Alicja Ososińska	the writer, Janina Katz
Agata Paluch	Kabbala
Monika Paś	Bezalel School exhibition in the National Museum, Kraków
Yael Peled (Margolin)	resistance and the underground during the Holocaust
Heidemarie Petersen	Jewish communal organisation in the 16th century
Anna Piskorz	Judaica in the Jagiellonian University Museum
Viktoria Pollmann	the Jewish question in the Catholic press
Eugenia Prokop-Janiec	literature. Yiddish theatre and 'mapping modern Jewish Kraków'
Katarin Regaira	the Kraków Ghetto Pharmacy
Monika Rice	the Holocaust and the post Holocaust period
Shoshana Ronen	Ozjasz Yehoshua Thon
Agnieszka Sabor	Art and the memory of Kazimierz
Krystyna Samsonowska	education within the Jewish community
Caroline Scharfer	Sarah Schenirer and the Bais Ya'akov movement
Naomi Seidman	Sarah Schenirer and the Bais Ya'akov movement
Sheryl Silver-Ochayon	female couriers during the Holocaust
Joanna Sliwa	children in Kraków during the Holocaust
Marta Smagacz	Social changes in Kazimierz in the post Communist period
Elżbieta Szlufik	Jewish trade in the 16th and 17th centuries
Marta Smagacz-Poziemska	revitalisation of urban space in Kazimierz

Krystyna Samsonowska	the Hebrew Secondary School
Anna Smywińska-Pohl	St Anne Secondary School and the Jagiellonian University
Rachel Steindel-Burdin	the linguistic landscape of Kazimierz
Monika Stępień	the Jewish community, particularly in the post war period
Maria Stinia	teaching staff at Jewish schools
Natasza Styrna	Jewish artists in Kraków
Izabela Suchojad	the memory of Kazimierz in Polish-Jewish literature
Monika Szabłowska-Zaremba	journalists of the interwar Jewish press
Małgorzata Śliż-Marciniec	Dawid Rosenman and St Anne Secondary School
Magda Teter	early Hebrew printing
Joanna Tokarska-Bakir	post war pogroms
Melania Turak	Podgórze
Anat Vaturi	relationships between Catholics and Jews in the pre-partition period, new born care in early modern Poland
Kamila Wasilewska-Prędki	Judaica in the Seweryn Udziela Museum, St. Anne Secondary School
Chava Weissler	Yiddish prayers for women
Kinga Węgrzyn	the Hebrew Secondary School
Bogna Wilczyńska	football
Alexandra Wössner	memorial sites in Kazimierz
Bożena Wyrozumska	Jews and trade in the mediaeval period
Agnieszka Yass-Alston	Jewish art collectors
Agnieszka Zajączkowska-Drożdż	Jewish medical institutions during the Holocaust
Hanna Zaremska	the Jewish community in the middle ages
Barbara Zbroja	Jewish architects in Kraków and the Jewish community in Podgórze
Kararzyna Zechenter	Kraków and Jewish literature since 1945
Katarzyna Zimmerer	the Nazi occupation of Kraków
Geniève Żubrzycki	'resurrecting the Jew' in the post Communist period
Leah Esther Zussman	Sarah Schenirer and the Bais Ya'akov movement
Lidia Zyblikiewicz	19th century censuses
Renata Żurkowa	the book trade in the 17th century

NAME INDEX

Note: Some individuals are listed more than once to reflect the fact that their names are spelt differently in different sources of information. Others are listed more than once, for example, to reflect their maiden and married names.

A

Adamowska, Olga, 207, 211
Adler, Shosana, 87
Aferiat, Sophia, 125
Agastein, Dora, 125, 189
Agnon, S Y, 19
Ajzenstein, Sara, 6
Ajzenstejn, Sara, 40
Akavia family, 111
Akavia, Miriam, 86, 125, 151
Albert, John, 39
Aleksandrowicz family, 77, 109
Aleksandrowicz, Ewa, 161
Aleksandrowicz, Julian, 199
Aleksandrowicz, Luśka, 100
Aleksandrowicz, Regina, 109
Aleksandrowicz, Róża, 109
Aleksiun, Natalia, 90, 217
Alexander, George, 39, 40, 69, 95
Allerhand family, 111
Allerhand, Aleksander, 126
Allerhand, Anna, 125
Allerhand, Rozalia, 126
Altschul, Moshe, 28, 35
Altszul, Aszer, 38
Altszul, Chawa, 38
Amaisen-Diestler, Fryderyka, 148
Ameisen, Fryderyka, 148
Ameisen, Zofia, 53, 88, 195
Anisfeld family, 111
Anisfeld, Helena, 161
Anschel, Rabbi, of Kraków, 27
Ansky, S, 108
Antolabnet, Jozef, 38
Antolabnet, Maita, 38
Antoszkiewicz, Krystyna, 126
Appenszlak, Paulina, 91
Applefield, Janet, 126
Apte, Maria, 112, 113

Araten, Michalina, 51, 64, 65
Armer, Anna, 72
Arnold, Róża, 97
Arnold-Herstein, Roza, 97
Arnold-Hersztajn, Róża, 97
Artman, Hella, 176
Ashkenazi, Hannah, 41
Ast, Janina, 144
Aszkenaze, Eliezer, 38
Aszkenaze, Rachela, 38
Attermann, Jetta, 72
Auerbach, Gitel, 38
Auerbach, Mojzesz, 38
Auerbach, Ryfka, 67
Augustyn-Jamro, Maria, 163

B

Bachul family, 164
Bachul, Ludwika, 163, 164
Bacon, Gershon, 6, 9, 94, 112
Bąkowska, Ewa, 217
Bałaban, Majer, 6, 15, 29, 37, 40
Balinska, Maria, 20, 21
Ballsem, Hanka/Tamar, 176
Balsiger, Maria, 99
Bałucki, Michał, 8
Banasik, Kinga, 67
Bańkowska, Aleksandra, 217
Bannet, Olga, 104
Bannett, Hannah, 126
Baranowski, Shelley, 134
Bar-el, Adina, 217
Baron, Ryfka, 111
Bartal, Israel, 56
Baruch family, 48
Baryła, Maria, 216
Baskin, Judith, 36
Batalion, Judy, 169, 179, 180, 217
Batko-Molenda, Zofia, 174

Bau, Jósef, 155
Bau, Joseph, 149
Bau, Józef, 126
Bau, Rivka, 126
Bauer, Helene, 52
Bauik, Ruth, 176
Baum, Rosalie, 154
Baumgarten, Jean, 29, 31
Bauminger, Arieh, 161, 173, 176, 177,
    179
Bauminger, Arye, 82
Bauminger, Rena, 113
Baumol, Avi, 86, 203, 204
Bażanowska, Noemi, 198, 199, 217
Bednarek, Anna, 217
Beigel, Rywka, 111
Bejski, Mosze, 166
Belsky, Yisroel ha'Levi, 23
Benisch, Pearl, 82, 126, 127, 151, 160,
    217
Bereska, Helena, 163
Bereta, Anna, 163
Berger, Róża, 129
Berger, Róża, 185
Berger-Waltscher, Klara, 148
Berggrün, Helena, 56
Berglas, B Bilha, 113
Bergmann, Fanny, 72
Bergmann, Malka, 72
Berkelhammer, Sara, 78
Berkowitz, Kuba, 176
Berlinerblau, Dorota, 111
Berlinerblau-Seydenmann, Dorota, 74,
    187
Bertig, Irena, 101, 102
Bester, Salomea, 54
Bieberstein, Aleksander, 148, 175, 176
Bieberstein, Helena, 161
Bieniarzówna, Janina, 217
Bierzyński family, 215
Biesaga, Monika, 217
Biliżanka, Maria, 161
Birenbaum, Devorah, 80
Birenbaum, Hinda, 80
Birnbach, Dora, 112
Birnbaum, Golde, 67
Blamkstein, Felicja, 102
Blas, Hanka, 179

Blasiak-Bereta, Anna, 163
Blassman, Hanka, 175
Blatt, Irena, 100
Blattberg, Rita, 127
Blau, Rozalia, 102, 148
Blicharz, Weronika, 174
Bloss, Hanka, 113
Blumenstock family, 65
Blumenstock, Dora, 113
Bobrowska, Maria, 163, 174
Bobrowska, Teresa, 164
Bobrowska-Bendziszewska, Anna, 48
Bobrowski, Maria, 174
Bojarkowa, Maria, 127
Bojm, Hela, 198
Bojm, Regina, 198
Boruchowicz, Max, 173
Borwicz, Michał, 173
Bożek, Maria, 132
Bradlo, Klara, 163
Brandsdorfer, Rega, 113
Brandstätter, Stefania, 120, 121
Brauman, Hanna/Halina, 104
Brecher, Elinor J, 129
Brechsler, Perla, 59
Brenner, Channe Jentel, 72
Brenner, Mina, 113
Brenner-Minka, Marysia, 175
Bronner, Irena, 86, 127, 189
Bross, Anna, 83
Brown, Iris, 82, 217
Broza, Czesław, 77
Bruch-Mezler, Anna, 68
Brünn, Helena, 96
Bruzda, Rozalia, 163
Brzoza, Czesław, 77
Brzoza, Czesław, 107
Buchweitz, Paulina, 78
Buczek, Sabina, 163
Bugajska, Julia, 163
Bułat, Mirosława, 108, 217
Bułat, Natalia, 127, 212
Buňatová, Marie, 217
Bünen, Chana, 60
Burman, Rickie, 8
Bussgang, Fay, 217

C

Carter, F W, 42
Cebulak, Stanislawa, 163
Cebulakowa, Stanisława, 174
Celuch, Justyna, 163
Chajec, Magdalena, 163
Chalpnisa, Leib, 38
Chamberlain, Maria, 50
Chilowicz, Mr and Mrs, 121
Chłosta-Sikorska, Agnieszka, 188
Chyłek, Izabela, 206
Cicha-Godawa, Janina, 163
Cichopek-Gajraj, Anna, 217
Ciechanowska, Helena, 65
Cohen, Boaz, 198
Cohn, 66
Conforte, David, 5
Crowe, David, 133
Cygielman, Shmuel, 16, 17, 22
Cyns, Sabina, 186
Czaecka, Bogusław, 78
Czajowska, Franciszka, 163
Czapnicka, Helena, 102
Czerwonogóra, Katarzyna, 202, 217
Czocher, Anna, 118, 153, 217

D

Dąbrowska, Ewa, 217
Dadak, Jozefa, 163
Dallet, Cecylia, 104
Danek, Aurelia, 147
Dankowicz, Rabbi, 47
Danz, Luise, 137, 157, 158
Darshan, David, 17, 19, 24, 28, 33
Datner, Helena, 198
Dattelbaum, Salomea, 65
Dawidson, Gusta, 154
Dembitzer, Lea, 72
Deutscher, Gustawa, 175
Deutschlander, Leo, 82
Diamand, Maurycy, 121
Diamant, Maurycy, 120
Dientenfass, Laura, 127
Dietrich, Teresa, 163
Distler, Fryderyka, 102
Długosz, Elżbieta, 217

Dobroszycki, Lucjan, 198
Dobrowolska, Anna, 173, 174
Dobrowolska, Stefania, 163
Dobrowolska-Michalska, Anna, 163
Dobrowolski, Stefania, 174
Domanska, Bogna, 163, 173
Donhajser, Helena, 49
Dortheimer, Stella, 96
Drach, Anna, 104
Draenger, Justyna, 159, 176
Draenger, Shimshon, 180
Draenger, Szymszon, 154
Draenger-Dawidson, Gusta, 179
Draenger-Dawidson, Justina, 180
Dränger, Gusta, 177
Dranger, Gustawa, 113
Dranger, Szelona, 113
Dränger-Dawidsohn, Gusta/Justyna,
     175, 176
Dränger-Szchora, Czarna Ceśka, 175
Dreizner, Anna, 67
Dreizner, Rebeka, 67
Drenger, Margot, 176
Drenger-Stern, Lea, 176
Drewniak, Zofia, 163
Drobner, Anna, 111
Drozdziwowska, Irena, 147
Druzkowiecka, Janina, 163
Duch-Dyngosz, Agata, 217
Duch-Dyngosz, Marta, 205
Duda, Eugeniusz, 37, 84
Duda-Seifert, Magdalena, 217
Dudziuch-Koluch, Marzena, 210, 211
Dükler, Eda, 154
Duntenfass, Laura, 178
Duraczyński, Eugeniusz, 167
Duszczynska, Zofia, 163
Dutka, Leszek, 194
Dutkowska, Agata, 217
Dychtwald, Ala, 127
Dym, Ester, 97
Dym, Reizel Nechama, 80, 154
Dym, Yehuda, 80
Dymek-Jedynak, Wanda, 174
Dynowska, Franciszka, 163
Dynowska, Ludwika, 163
Dzielska, Edwarda, 163
Dzielska, Eligia, 163

E

Eckstein, Zvi, 20
Ehrich, Elsa, 157
Eibenschütz, 66
Eibenschütz, Erna, 105
Eibenschutz, Salomea, 77
Eichmann, Adolf, 180
Eichorn, Laura, 178
Einhorn-Susułowska, Maria, 89, 196
Eker, Anda, 91
Elbinger, Emanuel, 166, 199
Elbinger, Pola, 189
Elbinger, Pola/Priwa, 128
Eles, Márta, 204
Elster, Adel, 59
Epstein, 66
Epstein, Anita, 154
Esterka, 24, 40

F

Faierstein, Morris, 34
Fajer, Rywka, 114
Fallman, Regina, 83
Falter, Jadwiga, 56
Fater, Issachar, 97
Fater, Issacher, 95
Fedorowicz, Anna, 163
Fefer, Ester, 178
Feintuch family, 64, 65
Feld, Bronisława, 149
Feldhorn, Julius, 93
Feldhorn, Juliusz, 128
Feldhorn, Maria, 128, 165
Feldhorn, Stella, 93, 128
Feldman, Ewa, 128
Feldman, Maria, 54
Feldman-Sternberg, Fryderyka, 83
Fenich, Fryda, 77
Fenichel, Abba, 145
Fenichel, Zygmunt, 105
Ferber, Rena, 157
Ferber, Roman, 129
Ferderber-Saltz, Bertha, 154, 166
Ferderber-Salz, Bertha, 128, 156
Ferlier, Cyla, 153
Ferro, Daniel Barrio, 206

Fesenko, Serafina, 138, 162
Feuerstein, Anna, 159
Feuerstein, Regina/Rena, 175
Fialkowska, Joanna, 163
Filipek, Katarzyna, 163
Filo-Wilkosz, Stefania, 163
Filozof-Walega, Jaina, 163
Finder, Mark, 129
Finder, Rena, 124, 129
Fink, Maria, 78
Fischer, Anka, 175
Fischler, Janina, 171
Fischler-Martinho, Janina, 124, 129,
    189
Fishof, Iris, 217
Fiszel, Raśka/Rachel, 25, 39, 40, 41, 43
Fiszel, Stefan, 39
Fixler, Blanche, 129
Flaster, Juta, 97
Flaster, Jutta, 96
Fleischman, Hanna, 102
Flinter, Amalia, 60
Flondra, Maria, 163
Fogelstrauch, Karolina, 65, 67
Folkman, Irena, 104
Follman, Chawa/Ewa, 175
Follprecht, Kamila, 217
Folman-Raban, Chavka, 170
Fortheimer, Helena, 116
Fraenkel, Maria, 99
Fraenkel/Fränkel, Eliza, 56
Fram, Edward, 5, 17, 18, 22, 25, 27, 30,
    31, 32, 34, 36, 43
Frank, Chaja, 72
Fränkel family, 84
Frankel, Alona, 130
Fränkel, Debora/Dora, 56
Fränkel, Eliza, 84
Freider, Maria, 130
Freiman, Cecylia, 113
Freiman, Cyndi, 124, 141, 217
Freiman, Izabella, 96
Freiman-Sosnowska, Isabella, 97
Freiwald, Maryla, 106, 130
Freund, Dr, 158
Fridman, Toschka, 176
Friedberg, Bernhard, 6, 15, 37
Friedman, Ester, 171

Friedman, Felicia, 130
Friedmann, Bronisława, 150
Frimat, Czesia, 175
Fromowicz, Irena, 130
Fromowicz, Maria, 76, 113, 130, 187
Fromowicz-Nassau/Fromowicz-Simeoni,
    Maria, 93
Fromowicz-Pisek, Irena, 93
Fromowicz-Stiller, Henryka, 76, 77, 187
Fromowicz-Stillerowa, Henryka, 53, 92,
    93
Frromowicz, Henryka, 130
Frydman, Tosia, 114
Frymer, Cesia, 178
Fuchs, Rena, 114
Fuchs-Katz, Regina, 148
Fuchs-Katzowa, Regina, 148
Fuchs-Towa, Fryda Marta, 175
Fukss, Toschka, 176
Furgal, Ewa, 203, 217

G

Gaber-Wierny, Maria, 189
Gaczoł, Ewa, 217
Gajzler, Eleonora, 190
Galas, Michał, 66
Galster, Celina, 113
Garber-Wierny, Maria, 131
Garfeinowa-Garska, Malwina, 54
Garncarska-Kadary, Bina, 217
Gąsiorowski, Stefan, 21, 40
Gawel, Katarzyna, 217
Gawelczyk, Bronislawa, 163
Gawron, Edyta, 66, 122, 183, 186, 212,
    217
Gebel, Antonina, 163
Geisler, Teresa, 67
Gelles, Danuta, 165
Gelles, Maria, 165
Gellner, Joanna, 218
Gere, Anita, 163
Gernreichowa, Baza, 60
Gibes, Jozefa, 163
Ginczanka, Zuzanna, 91, 131
Ginzburg, Sara, 131
Glaser, Moniek, 100
Glasner, Julia, 50, 52

Glassheit, Franciszka, 54
Glassscheib, Scheindl, 72
Glück, Irena, 178
Glückstein, Salomea, 113
Godawa, Anna, 163
Godawa, Maria, 163
Goldberg, Jacob, 23
Goldberger, Hava, 131
Goldberger, Józef, 131
Goldberger, Loria, 72
Goldberger, Renata, 131
Goldberger-Shomron, Franka, 176
Goldblum, 65
Goldblum, Gittel, 60
Goldfluss, Gena, 176
Goldfuss, Erna, 176
Goldgart, Cerka, 56
Goldgürtel, Ester, 59, 60
Goldlust, Hana, 72
Goldman, Amalia, 102
Goldman, Franciszka, 7
Goldman, Maria, 208
Goldmann, Amalia, 148
Goldschmidt, Blima, 72
Goldschmidt, Feitsche, 72
Goldstein, Helena, 132
Goldstoff, Ester, 80
Goldwasser, Monika, 208
Goldwasser, Pola, 175
Goldwasser, Rachel, 83
Gomułka, Władysław, 186, 187
Górecka, Monika, 214
Göth, Amon, 96, 133, 136, 145
Gottlieb, Henryka, 103
Gottlieb, Maria, 104
Gottlieb, Mina, 214
Grabowski, Jan, 166
Grąbowski, Klemens, 22
Grabschrift, Helena, 187
Grabschrift-Taffet, Helena, 75
Grądzka, Martyna, 56, 122, 152, 161,
    178
Grądzka-Rejak, Martyna, 11, 118, 120,
    141, 148, 156, 175, 177, 180, 218
Graenger-Dawidson, Gusta, 122, 178
Graf, Malvina, 90, 132, 190
Granite, Lauren, 80
Grauer, Natalie, 132

Gregorowicz, Leonia, 163
Gromska, Daniela, 196
Gross, Adolf, 58
Gross, Dora, 78
Gross, Jakób, 110
Gross, Sara, 110
Grossbart-Perlmutter, Sara, 112
Grossfeld, Chana, 80
Grossman, Reisla, 72
Grossmann, Frimet, 72
Grozmark, Josef bar Mordechai, 29
Grübner, Gusta, 72
Grün, Regina, 113
Grünberg, Berta/Blima, 75, 76, 187
Grüner, Luiza, 132, 178
Grunfeld, Judith, 82
Grüss, Noe, 124
Gruszczyńska, Mirosława, 125, 163, 164
Grygiel-Huryn, Anna, 206
Grzybowska, Irena, 163
Gulińska, Anna, 207
Gumplowicz, Ludwik, 7
Gumplwicz, Felix, 52
Gurary, Eliezer, 215
Gurfein, Riwka/Regina, 91
Gutenbaum, Jakub, 123
Guter, Franciska, 178
Guter, Franciszka, 133
Guter, Halina, 133
Guterman, Ruszka, 146
Gutmann, Gizela, 49
Güttel, Sara, 72
Guttman, Gizella, 102

H

Haber, Dora, 102
Haber, Henry, 165
Haber, Irene, 165
Haber, Lili, 177, 218
Haber, Lili/Lidia/Lea, 190
Haber, Richard, 165
Haber, Rifka, 83
Habiniak, Maria, 163
Halambiec, Anna, 218
Halberstam, Chaya Fradel, 79
Halicka, Alicja, 75, 76, 187

Halicz brothers, 27, 33
Halkowski, Henryk, 82
Hararand, Irene, 176
Harikowa, Maria, 173
Haslinger, Eleonora, 165
Haubenstock, Helen/Hela, 154
Hausman-Juer, Regina, 83
Hawel, Danuta, 196
Healey, Maureen, 57
Hecht, Ada Nadel, 83
Hecker, Helena, 54
Heinemayer, Theodore, 121
Heise, Gertrud, 158
Heksel, Bartosz, 104, 105
Heller, Daniel Kupfert, 100
Henry, Sondra, 8, 29
Herbstów, Frania, 49
Herschberger, Baila, 72
Hershova, Mariia, 207
Herszlowiczowa, Chaja, 60
Herteli, Jozefa, 163
Heschele, Janina, 133
Hescheles, Janina, 178
Heskel, Bartosz, 58
Heuman, Karolina, 133, 190
Hilfstein family, 155
Hilfstein, Max, 154
Himmelblau, family, 109
Hirch, Weronika Koplowitz, 110
Hirsch, Fryda Margules, 110
Hirsch, Helena, 133, 145
Hirschberg, Dan, 55
Hirschowa, Gitle, 110
Hirschprung, Marta, 93, 159
Hirschtal, Maria, 102
Hizowa, Emila, 163, 173
Hochberg, Maria, 174, 190, 198
Hochberg, Mituska, 174
Hochberg-Mariańska, Maria, 124, 141, 172, 173, 198
Hochberg-Mariańska, Maria/Marysia, 133
Hochberżanka/Hochberg-Mariańska, Maria, 91
Hochheiser, Sala, 165
Hochheiser, Solomon, 165
Hochman, Stephania, 103
Hochstein, Ludwika, 67

Hof, Róza, 148
Hoffman, Dola, 97
Hoffman, Eva, 191, 195
Hoffman, Julia, 178
Hoffman, Lawrence, 19
Hofstatter, Anna, 116
Holcer, Rachel, 107
Holcer/Holzer,
    Rachela/Róża/Rejzl/Rokhl, 107
Hollander, Berta, 134
Hollander, Erna, 102
Hollander, Joseph, 152
Hollander, Sara, 53
Hońdo, Leszek, 37
Honig, Franciska Eliaszowna, 199
Hönig, Rozalia, 111
Horbacka, Milica, 163
Horn, Etla, 83
Horn, Maurycy, 20, 27, 40
Horn, Zosia, 198
Hornik, Mila, 134
Horowicz, Benjamin Zev Wolf Sirkes,
    38
Horowitz, Bronisława, 104
Horowitz, Leah, 30, 41
Horowitz, Maria, 49
Horowitz, Rachel, 67
Horowitz, Sara, 134
Horowitz, Szachne, 134
Horowitz-Karakulska,
    Niusia/Bronisława, 134
Hrabyk-Dziurzyńska, Maria, 174
Hrabykowa, Maria, 174
Hubler, Julius, 96
Hundert, Gershon, 21, 44, 63, 69, 70,
    115

I

Ickowa, 60
Immerglück, Dora, 49
Immergluck, Helena, 96, 97
Infeld, Bronia, 84
Infeld-Stendig, Felicja, 92
Isserles, Drezel, 38
Isserles, Malka, 38
Isserles, Miriam Bella, 38
Isserles, Mojzes, 38

Isserles, Mojzesz, 38
Isserles, Moshe, 15, 17, 19, 20, 25, 26,
    31, 34, 36, 37, 42
Izaak, Chaja, 38
Izaak, Mojzesz, 38

J

Jach, Aleksandra, 205
Jagiellon, Alexander, 39
Jagiellon, Casimir, 39
Jakimyszyn, Anna, 35, 48, 51, 66, 204
Jakimyszyn-Gadocha, Anna, 49, 52, 218
Jaksz, Czeslawa, 163
Jakubczak, Aleksandra, 60, 61, 218
Jakubczyk-Ślęczka, Sylwia, 96, 218
Jakubowicz, Braindel, 38
Jakubowicz, Helena, 214
Jakubowicz, Izaak, 38
Jakubowicz, Mojzesz, 38
Jakubowicz, Róża, 12, 38, 182, 200
Jamiol, Zofia, 163
Jamioł, Zofia, 174
Jamro, Walera, 163
Janczarska, Genowefa, 163
Janczyk, Agnieszka, 218
Janowska, Wanda, 163, 174
Janowska-Boisse, Ewa, 134
Janowska-Ciońćka, Anna, 134
Janton, Bronislawa, 163
Janusz, Agata, 163
Jarkowska-Natkaniec, Alicja, 120, 150,
    218
Jarosz, Mrs, 87
Jasińska, Elżbieta, 121
Jasińska-Filipowska, Zofia, 107
Jaśko, Michalina, 133, 164
Jedynak, Józef, 174
Jenner, Magdalena, 214
Jetkiewicz, Janina, 174
Joachimsmann, Judyta, 135
Jodłowiec-Dziedzic, Anna, 57, 58, 218
Joffe, Gusta, 100
Joffe, Gustawa, 102
Jogałła, Elżbieta, 204
Johannes, Gustawa, 83
John Paul II, Pope, 199
Jolles, Ewa, 175

Joskowitz, Louise, 135
Jospa, Joseph, 62
Judkiewicz, R, 65
Judt, Józefina, 99
Jules, Wuszka, 177
Jung, Irena, 135
Juny, Adam, 162
Jurkowicz, Amalia, 103
Jurowicz, Czesława, 102

K

Kaczmarczyk, Magdalena, 167
Kaczmarczyk-Heleniak, Anna, 163
Kalamar, Marta, 213, 214
Kalb, Benzion, 130
Kaliczyńska, Józefa, 174
Kalik, Judith, 33, 218
Kalina, Marya/Reiza, 176
Kallas, Aniela, 54
Kallas/Korngut, Aniela, 107
Kałwa, Dobrochna, 56, 74, 153
Kamińska, Ida, 108
Kanfer, Irma/Irena, 90
Kanfer, Mojżesz, 107
Karay, Felicja, 118
Kargol, Anna, 218
Karmel, Henia/Henryka, 135
Karmel, Ilona/Ila, 135
Karmel, Matylda, 113
Karmel-Wolf, Henai, 178
Karp (Karpf), Natalia, 96
Karp, Celina, 124, 136
Karpf, Anne, 96, 137
Karpf, Natalia, 136, 191
Kasuzek, Szymon, 42
Kasznik-Christian, Aleksandra, 121
Katz, Gitla, 156
Katz, Janina, 191, 197
Kaufman, Laura, 53, 88, 137
Kawalla-Lulewicz, Iwona, 109, 110,
    218
Kazimierczyk, Adam, 33
Kazimierz the Great, 24, 40, 66
Keneally, Thomas, 116
Kerner, Henryka, 76, 187
Kielbicka, Aniela, 78, 98, 218
Kielczewska, Anna, 218

Kiesler, Betti, 61
Kiwetz, Fryda, 137
Klańska, Maria, 218
Kleiman, Ala, 198
Kleinberg, Wilhelm, 134
Kleinberger family, 95
Kleinberżank, Malwina, 78, 83
Kleinman, Zipora, 218
Klibaner-Schill, Elie, 81
Klich-Kluczewska, Barbara, 184, 218
Klimczak, Władysław, 58
Klingberg, Rajza, 175
Klingberg, Reizia Cohen, 180
Klinghofer family, 95
Kluger family, 155
Kluger, Anna, 51, 52, 53, 54
Kluger, Erna, 154
Kluger, Regina, 113
Kneller, Rachela, 104
Knobloch, Deborah, 72
Knoll, Renia, 137, 170, 178
Kobylińska, Łucia, 174
Kociel-Kowalczyk, Anna, 163, 174
Kocur- Smoleń, Agnieszka, 207
Kolberg, F, 65
Kolek, Anna, 210
Kolländer, Sara, 60
Komar, Żanna, 218
Königsberger, Blima, 72
Koralewska, Magda Rubenfeld, 213
Korngold, Irena, 59
Korngut, Aniel, 66
Korngut, Aniela, 54
Kornitzer, Breindel Blanka, 78
Kossowska, Hanna, 210
Kot, Maria, 163
Kotarba, Ryszard, 141, 148, 149, 162
Kowalczyk-Jaksz, Marta, 163
Kowalska, Beata, 182, 183, 218
Kowalska-Chmura, Lucylla, 174
Kozińska-Witt, Hanna, 47, 48, 58, 83,
    218
Koziol-Bradlo, Francziszka, 163
Kozioł-Marzec, Justyna, 218
Kozub-Ciembroniewicz, Wiesław, 195
Kożuchowska, Gitl, 40
Kragen, Wanda, 93
Krajewska, Monika, 210

Krajewski, Stanisław, 202
Krakowski, Shmuel, 177
Kranikowa, Resel, 60
Kranz, Wilhelm, 156
Krell, Wiktoria, 137
Krieger, Amalia, 110
Krieger, Ignacy, 110
Krieger, Nathan, 110
Kriwaczek, Paul, 22
Królikowski, Franciszek, 166
Królikowski, Zygmunta, 165
Kruczkowski, Leon, 173
Krywaniuk, Helena, 147
Krzeszowiak-Gorecka, Zofia, 163
Krzyżanowska, Zenobia, 168, 191
Kubala, Marcjanna, 207
Kuberska, Aneta, 213
Kucharczyk family, 129
Kucharska, Małgorzata, 211
Kuchler-Silberman, Lena, 185
Kuklo, Cezary, 45
Kulczykowski, Marius, 52
Künster, Salek, 154
Kunstler, Eda, 171
Kunstler, Salo, 171
Kupfer, Eda, 184
Kupper (Schpiner-Libskind,
    Rivka/Waschka, 176
Kurek, Ewa, 167, 218
Kuryluk family, 188
Kuryluk, Ewa, 188
Kuryluk, Miriam, 188
Kurzmann, Dawid, 159
Kutrzeba, Justyna, 64, 218
Kutylak, Agnieszka, 82, 218
Kuźma, Wadysława, 174
Kwalwasser, Beila, 72
Kwalwasser, Hinda, 72
Kwasnicka, Zuzanna, 178
Kwiatek, Anna, 218
Kwiecień, Sabina, 218
Kwiek, Julian, 89

L

Lächert, Hildegard, 158
Lachs, Wanda, 103
Ladau, Eda, 114

Laksberger, Irma, 138
Lamensdorf, Emilia, 104
Landau, Helena, 96, 97
Landau, Rafał, 159
Landau/Landau-Eiger, Hanka, 108
Landsberger, Maria, 71
Landwirt, Hanka, 177
Landwirth, Hanka, 113
Lasocka, Teresa, 173, 174
Latała, Agnieszka, 123
Lauer, Helena, 77
Lauterbach family, 95, 111
Lazer, Deborah, 102
Lazer, Dora, 103
Lebetkin, Zivia, 175
Lebet-Minakowska, Anna, 55, 70, 219
Ledicerowa, Chana, 60
Legutko, Agnieska, 215
Legutko-Ołownia, Agnieszka, 219
Leibel, Emilia, 87, 192, 200
Leinkram, Marja, 103
Leinkram, Róża, 104
Leinkram, Zofia, 83
Leissner, Omi Morgenstern, 20
Lermer, Anna, 157, 178
Leser, Antonina, 138, 212
Levin, Bracha, 80
Levitan, Eilat Gordin, 119
Lew, Myer S, 43, 44
Lewinger, Gruna Spira, 102
Lewita, Debora, 111
Lewka, Wanda, 178
Lewkower, Bluma, 60
Lewkowicz, Deborah, 64, 72
Lewkowicz, Hanka, 108
Liban, Julia, 67
Liberman, Musia, 198
Libreich, Kuba, 176
Libskind, Stephania, 176
Licht family, 95
Licht, Lea, 72
Lichtiger, Leah, 138
Lichtingowa, Petra, 60
Lieberfreund, Rozalia, 138, 162
Liebermann, Berta, 178
Liebeskind, Dolek, 177, 180
Liebeskind, Mina, 113
Liebeskind, Minka, 177

Liebeskind, Miriam/Mira, 175
Liebeskind, Rivka, 178
Liebeskind, Rivka Kuper, 180
Liebeskind-Kupper, Rivka, 177
Liebeskind-Spinner, Ewa, 175
Ligocka, Roma, 138, 188, 192, 194
Lillienthal, Flora, 104
Lindenbaum, Golda/Gusta, 78
Lindenbaum, Gustawa, 56
Lindenbaum-Kohn, Gusta, 108
Lipovsky, Shura, 210
Lobel, Anita, 138
Lochekhina, Galina, 219
Löw, Andrea, 118, 149, 170, 177, 178, 180, 218
Löw, Matilda, 148
Löw, Matylda, 178
Löw, Ryszard, 109, 110
Lubetkin, Zviya, 176
Lustgarten-Ogrodzka, Helena, 77
Lux, Róża, 114

Łabno, Beata, 219
Łapa, Elza, 175
Łopuszańska-Jetkiewicz, Maria, 174

M

Maciag, Karolina, 165
Madej, Stella Müller, 140
Madritsch, Julius, 136
Magerowa, Szaba, 60
Maharal, 5
Mahler, Rachela, 161
Mahler, Raphael, 6
Mahler, Teofila, 89, 93
Maimonides, 28
Majerhof, Berta, 178
Makosz, Dasza, 208
Makosz, Mesia, 208
Makówka-Kwapisiewicz, Anna, 205
Maksymowicz, Lidia, 208
Makuch, Aleksandra, 210
Małecki, Jan M, 42
Maler, Feiga, 139

Malinowska, Maria, 126
Mandelbaum, Amalia, 89
Mandelbaum, Kalman, 106
Mandelbaum, Mala, 89
Manekin, Rachel, 7, 51, 52, 53, 55, 64, 65, 72, 79, 80, 88, 219
Mania, Mrs, 151
Manne, Tauba, 72
Manor, Eugenia, 139
Margulies, Stella, 97
Maria Jekielek-Kluska, Maria, 174
Mariańska, Maria Hochberg, 92
Markowski, Stanisław, 71
Markusfeld family, 65
Markusfeld, Scheindla, 59
Markusfeld, Szachna, 59
Martin, Sean, 77, 84, 85, 87, 106, 107, 113
Maślak-Maciejewska, Alicja, 47, 49, 50, 52, 65, 219
Maurer, Jadwiga, 139
Mazur, Helena, 174
Mazurczak, Filip, 184, 186, 187, 197
Mędykowski, Witold, 121
Meisels, Symche, 38
Meisels, Tsherna/Czerna, 41
Mekler, Anna, 139
Meloch, Katarzyna, 197
Meltzer-Scheinberg, Ogenia, 176
Melzer, Emanuel, 113
Melzer, Genia, 177
Mengele, Dr, 208
Mermer, Ewa, 219
Mesz, Hanna, 192
Metzger, Anna, 113
Metzger, Rozalia, 113
Mianowska, Aleksandra, 174
Michaelis, Margaret, 187
Michaelis-Sachs, Margaret, 77
Michaelowitz, Dresze, 176
Michaelowitz, Esthuschya, 176
Michlic, Joanna, 171, 219
Międzobrodzka, Małgorzata, 71, 72, 88, 111, 114, 204, 219
Migowa, Jadwiga, 93
Minakowski, Marek, 55, 60
Minakowski, Marek Jerzy, 70
Mire, Gola, 177, 180

Mire, Mirer, Gola/Lidia, 176
Mirer, Gola/Lidia, 175
Mirowska, Eugenia, 102
Mirowska, Sabina, 140, 159, 160, 178
Misak, Sonia, 219
Misina, Agnieszka, 216
Monderer, Julia, 107
Mosberg family, 111, 166
Moszkowska, Dora, 62
Mrozińska, Eliza, 216
Müller, Berta, 152
Müller, Stella, 192
Müller, Zofia Irena, 178
Murzyn-Kupisz, Monika, 219
Muszyńska, Jadwiga, 219

N

Nachtigal, Mania, 134
Nadel-Hecht, Ada, 83
Nadler, Moniek, 100
Najbar, Paulina, 83, 219
Naskalska-Babik, Janina, 216
Nass, Róża, 158
Nataniec, Rosalia, 164
Natel, Ela, 102
Neiger, Pola, 140
Nelken, Halina, 85, 86, 140, 141, 150,
    158, 160, 193
Nelken, Regina, 159, 160, 178
Nelken, Wanda, 173
Neuman family, 171
Niedzielska, Maria, 75
Novac, Ana, 141
Nowak, Maria, 132, 163, 164
Nowotarska, Róża, 109

O

Obrębska, Maria, 219
Ochayon, Sheryl Silver, 169
Oesterreicher, Wanda, 165
Ofer, Yehoshua, 114
Offen, Bernard, 149
Olczak-Roniker, Joanna, 193
Oleszak, Agnieszka, 82, 219
Opałko, Halina, 203
Oppenheim, Ryfka, 113

Orleska, Miriam, 108
Orlowski, Alice, 158
Ornat, Małgorzata, 204
Ornat, Malgosia/Małgorzata, 204
Ornstein, Jonathan, 207, 210
Ornstein, Kasia, 207
Orwid, Maria, 195, 196
Ososińska, Alicja, 219
Osterwa, Julisz, 107
Ostry, Moniek, 100
Otter-Goldwasser, Róża, 176

P

Paliborska, Beila, 111
Paluch, Agata, 219
Palusińska, Urzula, 205
Panek, Anita, 212
Pankiewicz, Tadeusz, 121, 147, 151,
    161
Panuszko-Jedynak, Józefa, 174
Panzer, M, 153
Pappenheim, Bertha, 83
Parush, Iris, 16
Paś, Monika, 219
Pastuszka, Sławomir, 66
Pechner, Maria, 83, 102, 147, 148
Peled, Yael Margolin, 169
Peled/Margolin, Yael, 177, 219
Peleg, Miriam, 174
Peleg, Mordecai, 172, 174
Peleg-Mariańska, Miriam, 92, 134, 141,
    159, 174
Perlberger family, 95
Perlberger, Golda, 72
Perlberger, Maria, 142
Perlberger-Shmuel, Maria, 142
Perlberg-Reich, Miriam, 176
Perlberg-Schinaglow, Ilza, 83
Perlis, Rivka, 176
Perlmutter, Sara, 83
Petersen, Heidemarie, 219
Petranker-Salsitz, Amalie, 142
Pfefferberg, Mina, 110
Piłsudski, Józef, 86
Pinkosz, Aga/Agata, 214
Piskorz, Anna, 219
Pleszowska, Ela, 104

Pniowerówna, Regina, 54
Pohlmann, Lili, 142
Polak, Jacob, 39
Pollak, Jakob, 25
Poller, Hanka, 114
Pollmann, Viktoria, 219
Pomeranc, Bronia, 100
Pomeranc, Róża, 100
Pomeranc-Melcer, Róża, 92
Pomianowski, Piotr Zbigniew, 55
Poniatowski, August, 34
Popack, Refael, 215
Posmysz, Zofia, 174
Potocki, Count, 130
Potocki, Jerzy, 166
Potocki, Maria, 166
Praetzel, Gustawa, 102
Prager, Moshe, 82
Prokop-Janiec, Eugenia, 50, 51, 53, 54,
    85, 89, 90, 93, 107, 219
Propper, 66
Prostitz, Yitshak, 5
Proszowska, Estera, 186
Przebindowska, Mirosława, 164
Przetaczek, Zofia, 174
Przeworski, Mordechaj, 165
Purchla, Jacek, 64, 65
Puretz, Marta, 120, 121
Pustuł, Młgorzata, 207

R

Rabkin, Anna, 143
Radl, Karl, 154
Radon-Bachul, Anna, 163
Radzikowska, Zofia, 184, 185, 186, 206
Radmilowska, Zofia/Zosiu, 107, 200
Radzillowski, Krzystof, 21
Rakovsky, Puah, 7, 113
Rakower family, 111
Rakower, Berta, 150
Rakower, Reizli/Rozy, 110
Ramos-Gonzáles, Alicia, 41
Ramos-González, Alicia, 27
Rapaport, A, 65
Rapaport, Karolina, 65
Rapaport, Rachel, 60
Rapaport-Albert, Ada, 63

Rath, Dorota, 143
Rath, Władysław, 143
Ratner-Masz, Klara, 192
Regaira, Katarin, 219
Rehefeld, Gertha, 51
Reicher-Thon, Gizela, 89, 93
Reid, Edward, 115
Reinhard, Mimi, 164
Reiter, Diana, 101, 212
Reitman/Próchnik, Runa, 91
Reyzl bas Yosef ha'Levi, 41
Reyzl reb Fishls, 41
Rice, Monica, 122, 167
Rice, Monika, 219
Richter, Hannes, 57
Ringel, Joanna, 158
Rivkah bat Meir, 42
Robinson, Marilyn, 50
Rochacewicz, Justyna, 204
Rock, Róża, 98, 159
Rohden, Frauke von, 29
Romowicz, Julia, 107
Ronen, Shoshana, 219
Rościszewska, Janina, 215
Rosen, Sara, 63, 94, 105, 143
Rosenbaum, Judith Grunfeld, 218
Rosenberg, Dr, 148
Rosenberg, Stefannie, 178
Rosenblatt, Marya, 72
Rosenstein, Erna, 76, 187
Rosenthal, Miriam, 155, 156
Rosenzweig, Gittel, 50
Rosenzweig, Józefa, 65
Rosenzweig-Hecker, Helena, 49
Rosin, Freidle, 59
Rosman, Moshe, 8, 9, 15, 26, 30, 36,
    40, 43, 44
Rosner family, 97
Rosner, Leo/Leopold, 154
Rosner, Marysia, 97
Rosner, Mela, 97
Ross, Rita, 143
Rossenberg, 66
Rost, Nella, 78, 83, 91, 112, 143, 144
Roszak, Cecylia, 168
Roth, Markus, 118, 149, 170, 177, 178,
    180
Rozenzwajg, Helen, 148

Rozenzweig-Hecker, Helena, 83
Rubenstein, Dora, 102
Rubenstein, Gittel, 66
Rubenstein, Helena, 66
Rubenstein, Hirsch & Co, 110
Rubenstein, Naftali Hirsz, 66
Rubin, Arnon, 68, 163
Rubinek, Hela/Halina, 176
Rubinstein, Dora, 176
Rudzka, Maria, 163
Rufeisen-Schüpper, Hela, 169
Rybicka, Ewa, 174
Rybińska, Agata, 54
Rympl, Laura, 83
Rysiewicz, Jadwiga, 174
Rysińska, Józefa, 163, 173, 174
Rzeszutka-Bachul, Maria, 163

S

Sabor, Agnieszka, 219
Sadowska, Anna, 128
Salz-Zimmerman, Maria, 97
Salz-Zimmerman, Marie, 96
Samsonowska, Krystyna, 48, 219, 220
Sapetowa, Karolina, 165
Sarah bas Tovim, 37
Sare, Celina, 76
Sare, Elza, 76
Sare, Józef, 76
Saulson, Rozalia, 35, 54
Scharf, Rafael, 94, 110, 175, 182, 183
Scharfer, Caroline, 82, 219
Schechter, Fela, 178
Scheidlinger, Ewa, 104
Schein, Jane, 144
Schemyuk, Sala/Stasya, 176
Schenirer family, 111
Schenirer, Bezalel, 106
Schenirer, Helena, 106
Schenirer, Lea, 106
Schenirer, Matylda/Mania, 106
Schenirer, Róża, 106
Schenirer, Sarah, 61, 62, 68, 79, 81, 82,
    83, 105, 106, 111, 154, 160, 212
Schenkel, Bronisława, 102
Schenker, Matylda, 98, 160
Schiff, Rosalie/Rachel, 144

Schiff, William, 144, 154
Schiffmann, Franciszka, 53
Schiller, Rivka Chaya, 29
Schindler, Emilie, 164
Schindler, Oskar, 97, 110, 116, 126,
    133, 134, 136, 137, 139, 140, 143,
    144, 145, 146, 155, 156, 157, 164,
    192
Schipper (Szyper), Hela, 176
Schleichkorn, Stéphane, 96
Schloss, Giza, 176
Schmarcek, Mala, 77
Schmeidler, Rela, 101
Schmerlowitz, Erna, 113
Schmerlowitz, Fryda, 113
Schneide, Helena, 113
Schneider, Fela, 113
Schneider, Helena, 176
Schnitzer, Irena, 144
Schnitzer, Roman, 144
Schnitzer, Rozalia, 144
Schonberg, Marja, 103
Schonfeld, Helena, 114
Schönfeld, Helena, 106
Schonfield, Rabbi, 142
Schor, Brenda, 144
Schorr, Irena, 95
Schorr, Nitta, 95
Schpritzer, Luzka, 176
Schreiber, Maria, 56
Schreiber, Olga, 106
Schreiber, Rebbetzin, 47
Schreiber, Simon, 56
Schreibtapel, Rozya, 176
Schulkind, Perel/Paula, 144
Schüpper, Hela, 179, 180
Schwartzbart, Berta, 99
Schwartzbart, Ignacy, 99
Schwartzbart, Isaac, 112
Schwartzfeld, Flora, 113
Schwarz, Chris, 212
Segal, Tanya, 108, 213
Seiden family, 109
Seiden, Dina, 109
Seiden, Maria, 109, 184, 188
Seiden, Paulina, 109
Seidenfrau, Sara, 72
Seidman, Naomi, 81, 82, 108, 155, 219

Seksztajn-Lichtenstein, Gela, 119
Selinger, Mr and Mrs, 121
Sender family, 154
Shacter, Jacob, 31
Shatyn, Bruno, 130, 166
Sheptytsky, Count Andrej, 142
Shinnar, Leah, 145, 150, 154, 178
Shmuel, Ernst, 142
Sieradzka, Anna, 48
Sikorski, Marian, 135
Silber, Halina, 145
Silberberg, Berta, 102
Silberberg, Bertę, 148
Silberberg, Bertha, 148
Silberberg, Leon, 148
Silberberg, Stefania, 102
Silberfeld, Anna, 148
Silberfeld, Antonina, 54
Silberman, Lena Kuchler, 99, 199
Silberman, Lena Kuchler/Kichler, 199
Silberman, Minka, 91
Silberstein, Elza, 113
Silberstein, Mania, 100
Silver, Yitzchock, 24
Silverberg, Bertha, 147
Silver-Ochayon, Sheryl, 219
Singer, Gustawa, 126
Singer, Isaac Bashevis, 19
Singer, Perel, 103
Sinnreich, Helene, 155
Sirkis, Joel, 22, 36
Siwiec-Bachul, Janina, 163
Skarawara, Mr, 133
Skotnicki, Aleksander, 58, 83
Skrzynecki, Piotr, 193
Skuza, A, 205
Śládek, Paweł, 5
Sliwa, Joanna, 61, 123, 130, 134, 138,
    141, 144, 151, 152, 161, 162, 167,
    170, 171, 198, 199, 219
Slonik, Benjamin, 28, 29, 31, 35
Słowacki, Juliusz, 89
Slutsky, Carolyn, 211
Smagacz, Marta, 219
Smagacz-Poziemska, Marta, 219
Smywińska-Pohl, Anna, 220
Sołga, Przemysław, 118, 175, 188
Sondel, Janusz, 195

Sonnerschein, Rabbi, 140
Sperling-Cetic, Jadwiga, 75
Spielberg, Steven, 138, 192
Spilling, Helena, 100
Spira family, 111
Spira, Chavaleh Frieda, 38
Spira, Debora, 38
Spira, Natan, 38
Spira, Nathan Nata, 38
Spira, Paulina, 104
Spritzer, Hanka, 113, 176
Sroka, Łukasz, 22, 47
Stampfer, Shaul, 16
Stark, Dola, 134
Stark, Tóska, 176
Staucher, Maria, 166
Steczko, Maria, 178
Stefaniak, Janina, 172
Stein, Jehuda, 149
Steinberg, Aniela, 104
Steinberg, Emil, 104
Steinberger, Hudes, 83
Steindel-Burdin, Rachel, 220
Steinhaus, Halina, 100
Stendal, Moshe, 41
Stending-Lundberg, Gustawa, 145
Stępień, Monika, 184, 185, 192, 220
Sternlicht, Bronia, 145
Sternlicht, Helena, 133, 145, 176
Sternlicht, Symonia, 145
Stieglitz-Sperlin, Rachel, 148
Stiel, Helena, 113
Stiller, Henryka, 113
Stiller, Henryka Fromowicz, 85
Stinia, Maria, 220
Stockhammer, Gizela, 176
Stoplnckl, Pesla, 135
Strauch, Marisia, 198
Straucher, Maria, 194
Strenberg, Fryderyka, 145
Strychalska, Janina, 163
Styrna, Natasza, 74, 75, 76, 220
Suchmiel, Jadwiga, 89
Suchojad, Izabela, 220
Sugarman, Yerra, 139
Süsskind, Mala, 78
Swierzowna, Miss, 87
Synger, Miriam, 214

Syrkin-Binstejn, Zofia, 103
Szablowska-Zaremba, Monika, 93
Szabłowska-Zaremba, Monika, 220
Szachny, Golda, 38
Szachny, Szalom, 38
Szczalski, Janusz, 173
Szeliga, Sigmund, 166
Szemelowska, Augusta, 163
Szewczyk, Mariena, 149
Szlapak, Helena, 174
Szlufik, Elżbieta, 219
Szmulewicz family, 95
Szmulewicz, Nina, 78
Sznajder, Pauline, 96
Sztern, Miriam, 164
Szwarcman-Czarnota, Bella, 204
Szymborska, Wisława, 197

Ślazyk, Natalia, 204
Śliwowska, Wiktoria, 123
Śliż-Marciniec, Małgorzata, 220

Tisch, Rozalia, 111
Todros, David, 40
Tokarska, Iwona, 205
Tokarska-Bakir, Joanna, 115, 220
Tollet, Daniel, 18, 29
Tomaszewska, Zofia, 164
Tosza, Aniela, 164
Tramer, H, 65
Trammer family, 128
Trammer, Augusta, 128, 165
Trammer, Fryda, 128
Tribitscher, Yakov Lezer, 38
Trnka, Otylia Emiia, 163
Tschapek, Ludmila, 51
Turak, Melania, 220
Turczynowicz, Father, 33
Turgel, Gena, 146
Turgel, Norman, 146
Turniansky, Chava, 27, 28
Twardowska, Kamila, 101
Tymieniecka, Anna-Teresa, 194
Tyndorf, Ryszard, 167

T

Taffet, Etta, 83
Taffet, Szaja, 188
Taffett family, 109, 110
Taffett, Szaja, 184
Taitz, Emily, 8, 29
Tarnowska, Mrs, 87
Ta-Shma, Israel, 20
Taube family, 111
Taube, Lola, 95
Teitelbaum, Berta, 153
Templer, Sala, 72
Tenger, Laura, 99
Teter, Magda, 27, 220
Thon, Gizela, 161
Thon, Maria, 113
Thon, Nella, 85
Thon, Ojasz, 99
Thon, Ozjasz, 91, 143
Thur, Regina, 102
Tiefenbrun, Lieba, 155
Tigner, Laura, 78
Tiktiner, Rivka bat Meir, 29
Tiktiner, Rivkah bat Meir, 29

U

Ulrich, Laurel Thatcher, 9

V

Vaturi, Anat, 20, 40, 220
Vogel, Róża, 83

W

Wachs, Bracia, 78
Wachsman, Ryeka, 72
Wachtel, S, 65
Wajngarten, Bronisława, 161, 168
Wajsman, Ela, 50
Waluszewska-Horbacka, Ludmila, 163
Wandstein, Lila, 102
Warszawska, Janka, 171
Warszawska, Pesia, 176
Warszawska, Pola, 178
Warszawska, Pola/Pesia, 178
Wasilewska-Prędki, Kamila, 220
Waśniewska, Ela, 194, 200
Wasowiczowa-Raabe, Janina, 163, 173

Wasserberg, Dora, 103
Wasserberg, Dorota/Dora, 103
Wasserberg, Paulina, 103
Wasserberg, Pola, 161
Wasserberg, Pola/Paulina, 100
Wasserberger, Amalia/Małka, 98
Wasserberger, Paulina, 147
Wasserheardt, Feigel, 72
Wasssserberger, Amelia/Malka, 78
Webber, Connie, 205
Webber, Janina, 146
Webber, Jonathan, 205
Węgrzyn, Kinga, 220
Weigel, Marta, 216
Weinberger, David, 31
Weinberger, Dowra, 111
Weinberger, Jentl, 72
Weinberger, Joehebet, 72
Weinberger, Lewsza, 72
Weinberger, Marian, 72
Weindling, Lola, 104
Weinryb, Bernard, 8, 44
Weintraub, Mania, 176
Weinzieher, Michał, 131
Weiskerz family, 69
Weiskerz, Benjamin, 70
Weiskerz, Dawid, 70
Weiskerz, Dwojra, 70
Weiskerz, Dwora, 69
Weiskerz, Ester, 69
Weiskerz, Izaak, 69, 70
Weiskerz, Rachel, 70
Weiskerz, Szmul, 69
Weiss family, 95
Weiss, Julia, 50
Weiss, Rachel, 72
Weiss, Wojciech, 70
Weissbardt, Bella, 114
Weissler, Chava, 16, 18, 27, 28, 31, 32, 220
Weisslitz, 65
Weissman, Deborah, 80, 81
Weissman, Natalia, 96
Weissman-Hubler, Natalia, 96, 97
Wellner, Runa, 107
Westreich, Szyfra, 178
Wetstein, Feivel Hirsch, 6, 15, 25, 37, 38

Wieth, Irmgard, 142
Wilczura, Aleksandra/Ola, 212
Wilczyńska, Bogna, 220
Wimisner, Klara, 134
Wimmer family, 95
Wimmer, Chaja, 111
Wischnitzer, Mark, 38, 39
Wisniowska, Hermina, 178
Włodarczyk, Marian, 166
Włodarczyk, Zofia, 163, 166
Wodzinski, Marcin, 62
Wohlfeiler family, 139
Wohlfeiler, Felicja, 146
Wohlfeiler, Krystina, 126
Wohlhendler, Chaim Shmuel, 80, 154
Wójcik, Helena, 174
Wójcik, Wanda, 174
Wojcikowa, Wanda, 163, 173
Wojtasiak, Sabina, 204
Wojtyla, Karol, 199
Wolf, Lea, 72
Wolfgang, Cyla, 100
Wollerówna, Henia, 146
Wortsman, Gena, 176
Wössner, Alexandra, 220
Wszołek, Monika, 209
Wulkan, Sabina, 176
Wydra, Ewa, 191
Wyrozumska, Bożena, 42, 220
Wyspiański, Stanisław, 193
Wyżga, Mateusz, 44

Y

Yahrblum, Moshe, 88
Yass-Alston, Agnieszka, 220
Yohanss, Irena, 176

Z

Zahorska, Stefania, 53
Zajac, Franciszka, 165
Zajączkowska-Drożdż, Agnieszka, 147, 220
Zajda, Małgorzata, 209
Zaks, Wanda, 102
Zaremba, Marcin, 185
Zaremba, Monika Szabłowska, 91

Zaremska, Hanna, 39, 40, 220
Zarnowiecki/Zar, Rose, 146
Zarubin, Przemysław, 33, 44
Zarzycki, Zdzisław, 55, 95
Zastocka, Wacława, 83
Zawada, Alfreda, 209
Zawada, Fryda, 184, 185, 194
Zazulowa, Maria, 162
Zbroja, Barbara, 101, 205, 220
Zechariah Mendel ben Arieh Loeb, 32
Zechenter, Kararzyna, 220
Zeif, Adela, 114
Zelemeister, Danka, 176
Zentara, Maria, 76
Zielińska, Anna, 205
Ziemiańska, Franciszka, 164
Zierer, Edith/Edyta, 199
Zimmerer, Katarzyna, 118, 141, 177, 180, 220
Zimmerman, Hannah, 97
Zimmerman, Maria, 96

Zimmermann, Regina, 78
Zoberman, Dora, 198
Zoberman, Pola, 198
Zohar, Eran, 180
Zollmanówna, Erna, 76
Zonnenfeldowa, Hanna, 60
Zubrzycki, Geneviève, 202, 206, 210
Zubrzycki, Geniève, 220
Zucker, Manesse, 102
Zuckerman, Yitzchak, 170
Zuckermann, Anna, 111
Zuckermann, Helena, 111
Zussman, Leah, 68
Zussman, Leah Esther, 82, 220
Zyblikiewicz, Lidia, 45, 46, 59, 220

Żurkowa, Renata, 41, 220
Żyznowski, Urszula, 204

Printed in the USA
CPSIA information can be obtained
at www.ICGtesting.com
CBHW050622201124
17649CB00038B/438